ROOSEVELT TO REAGAN

Roosevelt to Reagan

The Development of the Modern Presidency

JOHN HART
RICHARD HODDER-WILLIAMS
JOHN D. LEES
DAVID MERVIN
MALCOLM SHAW (*editor*)
PHIL WILLIAMS
ROBERT WILLIAMS

C. HURST & COMPANY, LONDON

First published in the United Kingdom by
C. Hurst & Co. (Publishers) Ltd.,
38 King Street, London WC2E 8JT
© C. Hurst & Co. (Publishers) Ltd., 1987
Printed in England on long-life paper

ISBNs
Cased: 0-905838-85-8
Paper: 0-905838-86-6

To the memory of
John D. Lees

PREFACE

In this book the authors seek to examine the American presidency from a distinctive perspective. They explore what has happened to the office over time. In particular, they assess the validity of the proposition that something fundamental happened when Franklin Roosevelt entered the White House in 1933. They examine whether his incumbency and what followed brought changes which made all the post-1933 or 'modern' presidencies basically different from the pre-1933 or 'traditional' presidencies.

Except for the editor, the contributors to this book are British. While the editor is an American, he too has strong British connections in that he has lived in England for the past twenty-five years. The authors have not sought to bring a 'British' focus to bear on their contributions nor is the study in any sense 'comparative', but their common non-American backgrounds cannot be an insignificant circumstance. The seven chapter-writers became aware of their common interest in the United States through their shared participation in the annual conferences of the American Politics Group, an affiliate of the Political Studies Association of the United Kingdom.

Various people provided useful advice as the project developed, particularly in the early stages. An acknowledgement of their assistance, and thanks for it, are due to David Morgan, Philip Norton, Nelson Polsby, Michael Turner and Maurice Vile. I would also like to thank the Research Fund Committee of the University of Exeter for financial assistance. Helen Liggat provided admirable secretarial support.

Finally, I must sadly record that one of the contributors – John Lees – has died since he wrote his chapter. For many years Dr Lees was in the forefront of endeavours in Britain to bring an understanding of the complexities of American government to British students, and it is to him that we dedicate this book.

After the book was already in proof, events relating to arms sales to Iran by the Reagan administration seemed sufficiently important to justify the addition of a 'postscript' on this development at the end of the concluding chapter. The rest of the book deals with the position as it was before 'Irangate'.

Exeter
June 1987

MALCOLM SHAW

CONTENTS

KEY TO ABBREVIATIONS

ABM	Anti-Ballistic Missile (Treaty)
AWACS	Airborne Warning and Control System (Aircraft)
BOB	Bureau of the Budget
EOP	Executive Office of the President
ERA	Equal Rights Amendment
FCC	Federal Communications Commission
HEW	Dept. of Health, Education and Welfare
NATO	North Atlantic Treaty Organisation
NSC	National Security Council
OCB	Operations Coordinating Board
OEO	Office of Economic Opportunity
OMB	Office of Management and Budget
OWM	Office of War Mobilization
SALT	Strategic Arms Limitation Treaty
SDI	Strategic Defence Initiative ('Star Wars')
SES	Senior Executive Service
START	Strategic Arms Reductions Talks

NOTES ON THE CO-AUTHORS

JOHN HART is Senior Lecturer in Political Science at the Australian National University at Canberra. He is the author of *The Presidential Branch* and articles in *Political Studies, Public Administration, Presidential Studies Quarterly* and other journals. Formerly he was Lecturer in Politics at the University of Wales at Swansea.

RICHARD HODDER-WILLIAMS is Reader in Politics at the University of Bristol, England. He has had works published on several aspects of politics and is the author of *The Politics of the United States Supreme Court* and co-editor of *Politics in Britain and the United States: Comparative Perspectives*. He has been a visiting professor at the University of California, Berkeley, and chairman of the American Politics Group.

The late JOHN LEES was Reader in American Studies at the University of Keele, Staffordshire, England, and chairman of the American Politics Group. He was the author of *The Political System of the United States, The Committee System of the United States Congress* and *The President and the Supreme Court*, co-author of *American Politics Today* and co-editor of *Committees in Legislatures: A Comparative Analysis* and *Political Parties in Modern Britain*. He died in 1986.

DAVID MERVIN is Senior Lecturer in Politics at the University of Warwick, England, and Director of the University of Warwick Summer School. His articles have appeared in *Political Studies, Presidential Studies Quarterly* and the *Journal of American Studies*.

MALCOLM SHAW is Senior Lecturer in Anglo-American Comparative Studies at the University of Exeter, England, and was Head of the Department of Politics at Exeter in 1980–5. He is the author of *Anglo-American Democracy*, co-editor of *Committees in Legislatures: A Comparative Analysis* and *The House of Commons: Services and Facilities*, and the author of articles on American, British and comparative government.

PHIL WILLIAMS is Lecturer in International Relations at the University of Southampton, England. He is the author of *Crisis Management* and *The Senate and U.S. Troops in Europe*, co-author of *Contemporary Strategy*, and co-editor of *The Carter Years*. In 1984–6 he was a Research Fellow at the Royal Institute of International Affairs, London, where he directed a major research project on superpower *détente*.

xi

ROBERT WILLIAMS is Lecturer in Politics and Deputy Dean of the Faculty of Social Sciences at the University of Durham, England, and a former chairman of the American Politics Group, and has lectured at universities in the United States, Canada and Australia. He is the author of articles on the presidency, government regulation and political corruption. He is currently writing a book on public policy-making in the United States.

INTRODUCTION

Malcolm Shaw

Franklin D. Roosevelt took his first oath of office as President on March 4, 1933. Rather more than half a century has elapsed since his New Deal began. The contributors to this book examine the period since 1933. In doing so, they seek to explore the nature of the presidency as it has evolved during this period. Their purpose is to determine what is meant by the concept of the modern presidency.

The period under examination is not brief in the context of the history of political institutions. Many, perhaps most, of the world's national political institutions have lasted for less than half a century. The years under examination are of course only part of the lifetime of the American presidency. The span of time since George Washington was President is matched by even fewer of the world's political institutions. The presidency will be 200 years old — as will the United States — in 1989, and thus the President who is elected in 1988 will be America's bicentennial President.

We are therefore dealing with an old, if not ancient, office and, in particular, with the most recent quarter of its existence. It needs to be acknowledged that there is always an element of arbitrariness in carving out an historical epoch. The years since 1933 are far from a self-contained period in the history of the presidency. Franklin Roosevelt was neither the first President to have staff aides nor the first to broadcast to the people. Yet 1933 is more than a convenient landmark. It is widely considered to mark a significant break with the past for the presidency and therefore for the American political system. It marks the beginning of the modern presidency.

As Norman Thomas has said: 'It is taken for granted among students of American politics that the modern presidency began under Franklin D. Roosevelt.'[1] Fred Greenstein distinguishes between the pre-1933 'traditional presidencies' and the post-1933 'modern presidency', adding that under FDR 'the presidency began to undergo not a shift but rather a metamorphosis'.[2] As Richard Rose puts it,

---

1. Norman C. Thomas, 'Reforming the Presidency', in Thomas E. Cronin and Rexford G. Tugwell (eds), *The Presidency Reappraised*, 2nd edn, New York, 1977, p. 322.
2. Anthony King (ed.), *The New American Political System*, Washington, DC, 1978, p. 45.

1

'the entry of Franklin D. Roosevelt to the White House brought an end to the nondirective presidency'.[3] 'The modern presidency really dates from the administration of Franklin Roosevelt,' according to William Mullen, 'and no chief executive since has been able to operate a totally passive presidency.'[4] It is clear that, like the realigning election of 1932, the new order that began in the White House in 1933 was to change the character of American political life for decades to come. It was not a one-time development.

Purpose and Methods

While the importance and permanence of this development is often mentioned in discussions of the presidency, there has been little extended analysis of the substance and significance of the changes that have taken place. The intention in this book is to explore the nature of this development by examining the evolution of the presidency over time. Accordingly, a group of political scientists have addressed themselves to various aspects of presidential development since 1933. Thus, Richard Hodder-Williams considers the development of constitutional doctrine since 1933 as it relates to the presidency. John Lees examines relations between President and party. David Mervin examines presidential-congressional relations. Robert Williams looks at the President and the executive; and John Hart discusses the President and his staff. Phil Williams examines the President's involvement in world affairs since 1933. Finally, in the concluding chapter, I endeavour to weave together the themes which have emerged and explore some strands which were not within the concerns of the authors of the specialised chapters.

This project incorporates a reasonable degree of coordination. Four of the seven authors were involved, first, in a conference panel on what turned out to be the subject of the book. There were two subsequent conferences of contributors during which the methodology and substance of the project were discussed. As editor, I produced a research plan which dealt with the general content of the chapters, matters of common concern to all contributors and possible explanations concerning the significance of the post-1933 period for the presidency. This plan, which was distributed at the outset, was not intended to be unreasonably constricting and did

---

3. Richard Rose, *Managing Presidential Objectives* London, New York, 1977, p. 39.
4. William F. Mullen, *Presidential Power and Politics,* New York, 1976, p. 27.

not turn out to be, as a reading of the chapters makes clear. At the same time, the evolutionary focus provided a strong common theme.

While each contributor had his specialised task, all contributors were asked to consider the following questions: What has been the nature of the change that has occurred in relation to their aspect of presidential activities? Was change modest or rapid? Was it linear or oscillatory? Was there a watershed during the period in question after which things were different? How did each of the nine Presidents who served during the period contribute to such change as occurred? What was it about Franklin Roosevelt's incumbency that made it the beginning of a new order and not just a 'strong' interlude like Lincoln's or Theodore Roosevelt's?

This kind of project involves boundary problems. For example, what is the 'presidency'? Is it the man in the Oval Office? Is it the President and the White House Office? Is it the President and the Executive Office of the President? Is it the President and the executive branch? The presidency is of course intertwined with institutions outside the executive branch, and it can obviously be misleading to extract a part from the whole. When does change occur in a 'windowless' White House, and when does it reflect changes in society? Not only is the presidency different from what it was before 1933, but so, too, is the United States.

Our focus on change may be seen from two perspectives. We are concerned first with the changes in the presidency that differentiate the period after 1933 from what existed before 1933, and secondly with the changes that have occurred during the era of the modern presidency. In the former context it is hoped that a distinctive general configuration of the modern presidency will emerge. In the latter context it is hoped that the specific ways in which the institution has evolved during its most recent half-century will become clear.

In analyses of political systems, political scientists are not usually self-consciously concerned with evolutionary considerations. Case-studies notwithstanding, their approach tends to be analytical rather than chronological. Nevertheless, discussions of the American presidency often seem to fall naturally into a chronological description of the practices of successive Presidents. This use of chronology may be associated with the fact that the presidency is generally perceived as a one-man institution, in spite of the boundary considerations mentioned earlier. Explanations concerning individuals lend themselves to evolutionary treatment more easily than explanations concerning, say, the American Congress. One is not told that the 81st Congress dealt with foreign policy in one way while the 85th Congress did it in another, but one may be advised that Truman and Eisenhower used their White House staffs in particular ways and that both their arrangements differed from Kennedy's. In any event, our intention is to deal explicitly with change.

The Presidents

Nine men have served as President during the modern era.[5] Since the era has seen not only a new-style presidency but also a period of dominance by the Democratic party in American politics, it is not surprising that there have been more Democratic than Republican Presidents since 1933. At the same time, dominance by the Democratic party has been less strongly reflected in electoral outcomes for President than in outcomes for offices other than President. In fact only a bare majority of the Presidents elected during the modern era − five to four − have been Democrats. The modern Democratic Presidents have served for thirty-two years while the modern Republican Presidents will have served for twenty-four years when Ronald Reagan completes his second term. Viewed from a longer time-scale, it is clear that party competition at the presidential level has been more closely-run since 1932 than during the period of Republican ascendancy which lasted from 1860 to 1932. During the earlier period there were twelve Republican Presidents and only three Democrats.[6]

In the matter of tenure, one comes across remarks about the brevity of tenure of recent Presidents. We are sometimes reminded that no President has served two full terms since Eisenhower. The actual position is that the eight Presidents of the modern era whose incumbencies are complete served an average of 5.9 years. This is significantly longer than the average pre-1933 incumbency, which was 4.9 years.[7] The unprecedented length of Roosevelt's presidency does of course affect the overall position. On the other hand, there has been a spate of incumbencies of irregular length. If Reagan is omitted, only Eisenhower and Carter served uniform terms of four or eight years during the modern era. It may be considered 'normal' for a President to serve for eight years, but in fact only nine of the thirty-

5. A useful compilation of factual information about the thirty-nine individuals who have served as President is found in Joseph Kane, *Facts About the Presidents*, 4th edn, New York, 1981.
6. I am counting Andrew Johnson as a Democrat, although he was elected Vice-President on Lincoln's Republican ticket. The other Democrats were Cleveland and Wilson.
7. Kane, *op. cit.*, p. 325.

Table 1. EXPERIENCE BEFORE ELECTION TO PRESIDENCY

	Vice President	Senator	Representative	Governor	Political executive	Army career
Roosevelt				x	x[a]	
Truman	x	x				
Eisenhower				x		x
Kennedy		x	x			
Johnson	x	x	x			
Nixon	x	x	x			
Ford	x		x			
Carter				x		
Reagan				x		

a Assistant Secretary of the Navy.

nine Presidents have done so, with Eisenhower the only example so far from the modern era.[8]

The backgrounds of the Presidents of the modern era are depicted in Table 1. What generalisations can be made in relation to this information? First, the bias towards congressional experience prior to becoming President remains strong in the modern period as it was earlier on. Secondly, the combination of congressional experience and the vice-presidency is a frequent one. Truman, Johnson, Nixon and Ford fit this mould. Thirdly, a tendency for Vice-Presidents to become President is more common than before 1933. Three of the six men who were elected President after serving as Vice-President accomplished this during the modern era. Repeat dual performances are also more common. On five occasions teams of Presidents and Vice-Presidents were elected twice, four of the occasions being since 1933.[9] Fourthly, there are two kinds of experience which used to be found in Presidents' backgrounds but no longer are. These are diplomatic and Cabinet posts. There were seven examples of the former and nine of the latter before 1933 and none since. Fifthly, a curious circumstance is that the modern Presidents − Johnson and Nixon − with the most elaborate backgrounds in national politics, having served as Representative, Senator and Vice-President before becoming President, got into the most severe difficulties. This

8. Incumbencies can also be looked at from the more inclusive perspective of Presidents who were *elected* to two consecutive terms. After 1860 there were eight such Presidents. Of these, all but one either served during a war (Lincoln, McKinley, Wilson, Franklin Roosevelt and Nixon) or was a war hero (Grant and Eisenhower). The other is Reagan. See H.G. Gallagher, 'The President, Congress, and Legislation', in Cronin and Tugwell, *op. cit.*, p. 275.

9. They were Wilson and Marshall, Roosevelt and Garner, Eisenhower and Nixon, Nixon and Agnew, and Reagan and Bush.

occurred despite, or perhaps because of, the experienced outlooks they brought to the Oval Office.

The most extraordinary incumbencies during the modern era were those of Roosevelt and Nixon. The founder of the modern presidency, Roosevelt, arrived at the White House with no previous experience in national government except as Assistant Secretary of the Navy. Nevertheless, he was elected to an unprecedented four terms while instituting an extended era of dominance for his party in American politics. He is on everyone's list of 'great' Presidents as a consequence of what Burns has called his 'magical personal and political gifts'.[10] Some consider Franklin Roosevelt to be the most astute politician ever to occupy the White House. Schlesinger dissects his techniques in dealing with members of Congress:

He was a master at the art of providing congressional gratification — at the easy first name, the cordial handshake, the radiant smile, the intimate joke, the air of accessibility and concern, the quasi-confidential interview, the photograph at the White House desk, the headline in the hometown newspaper.[11]

Nixon, by contrast, is widely viewed as one of the least suitable individuals ever to serve as President. Barber classified him as an 'active-negative' in his gallery of character types.[12] Such personalities, in Barber's view, are the least desirable and most dangerous type to serve as President. They are 'active' in that they work exceedingly hard at their job, but they are 'negative' in that they don't enjoy it. They strive mightily for political success but find the effort punishing and emotionally unsatisfying. When frustrated, they dig in and refuse to yield, often bringing disaster on themselves. To yield to opposition is to acknowledge their worst fears − that they're weak and inadequate.

Despite these characteristics, Nixon is in the exclusive 60-plus club, i.e. he received more than 60 per cent of the popular vote in the 1972 election. The only others to win so overwhelmingly in the modern era were Roosevelt in 1936 and Johnson in 1964. Barber has said of the Nixon phenomenon:

Nixon demonstrated the vulnerability of the American political system. Throughout his career, his repeated victories after disastrous defeats show with dramatic clarity how the process of evaluating potential Presidents

10. James M. Burns, *Presidential Government*, Boston, 1965, p. 116.
11. Arthur M. Schlesinger, Jr., *The Coming of the New Deal*, Boston, 1957, p. 554.
12. James D. Barber, *The Presidential Character*, 2nd edn, Englewood Cliffs, NJ, 1977.

failed miserably to predict and guard us from the machinations of an expert flim-flam man. The American people had every opportunity to know what they were getting. They elected Nixon despite the most abundant evidence ever available regarding the character of any Presidential candidate.[13]

The only other 'active-negative' in the modern era is Nixon's fellow member of the 60-plus club, Lyndon Johnson.[14]

What other generalisations can be made about the nine Presidents of the modern era? It is of interest that the two most recent Presidents — Carter and Reagan — are the only ones who had no experience of holding office at the national level before becoming President. It is tempting to seize on this similarity. Yet such a consideration may be too broad to be edifying. The behaviour of Carter and Reagan in the White House has in fact been profoundly different. Why? Is serving for two terms as Governor of California better preparation for the presidency than serving one term as Governor of Georgia? Is experience as an actor better preparation than experience as a farmer? While such variables are not insignificant, it would seem that personal qualities, such as those explored by Barber, are much more important.

There has been a significant change in the matter of which states Presidents come from. Prior to Hoover, all the Presidents were born in states east of the Mississippi River. But Hoover, the last pre-modern President, was born in Iowa, and a majority of his successors — Truman, Eisenhower, Johnson, Nixon and Ford — were also born west of the Mississippi River. Eight of the twelve Vice-Presidents in the modern era also came from states west of the Mississippi.[15] It is obvious that as the importance of the West and the Sunbelt has increased, this has been reflected in the geography of presidential availability.

Some things don't change, however. It is still common for Presidents to have obtained their higher education in non-élite institutions. American history is full of presidential backgrounds which include colleges and universities such as Hampden-Sydney, Union, Allegheny, Ohio Central, Southwest Texas State (Lyndon Johnson), Whittier (Nixon) and Eureka (Reagan). At the same time, we should note that five Harvard men have served in the White House.[16]

---

13. *Ibid.*, p. 459.
14. Earlier Presidents classified by Barber as 'active-negative' were Wilson and Hoover.
15. I am counting Mondale as a trans-Mississippi type although the river flows through his home state of Minnesota.
16. The five are the Adamses, the Roosevelts and Kennedy.

The Historical Context

It is useful to consider the development of the modern presidency in the context of the development of the larger social order of which this institution is a part. C.E. Black has discussed the development of the American political system as part of his discussion of patterns of modernisation throughout the world, and his analysis is illuminating for present purposes.[17] Black indentifies three phases of modernisation which occur in nation-states in general and which

Table 2.   PATTERNS OF MODERNISATION

Country	Consolidation of modernising leadership	Economic and social transformation	Integration of society
United States	1776–1865	1865–1933	1933–

Source: Extracted from C.E. Black, 'Phases of Modernization', in Jason L. Finkle and Richard W. Gable, *Political Develonment and Social Change*, 2nd edn, New York, 1971, p. 449.

occurred in the United States (see Table 2) after 1776.

The first phase, which in America ended in 1865, sees the rise of modernising leaders and the securing by them of a basis for support in the country. The period is marked by nation-building. In addition the period is marked by a break with a predominantly agrarian way of life. This break frequently entails a dramatic emancipation of people from traditional agricultural arrangements, taking the form in the United States of the freeing of the slaves. The dual processes of nation-building and agrarian reform are often facilitated by revolts – in the American case by the Revolution and the Civil War.

The second phase, which ended in 1933 in America, sees society transformed from a predominantly rural and agrarian way of life to one that is predominantly urban and industrial. During this transformation the focus in society shifts from the local to the national level. Often, more than half of the workforce moves from agriculture to manufacturing, commerce, transportation and services, and from a rural to an urban environment. This movement is accompanied by a rapid growth in educational provision and medical care. At the same time, value-systems lag behind economic and social development, and throughout this phase minority groups retain many of their disabilities despite changes in their status.

The third and present phase began in 1933 in the United States,

17. C.E. Black, 'Phases of Modernization', in Jason L. Finkle and Richard W. Gable (eds), *Political Development and Social Change*, 2nd edn, New York, 1971, pp. 436–55.

according to Black. The coincidence between its commencement and that of the era of the modern presidency suggests that analysis of the characteristics of this phase may provide clues to the underlying reasons for the changes in the nature of the presidency.

Black characterises the current phase in the modernisation process as the 'integration of society'. In the wake of nation-building, industrialisation, urbanisation and concomitant episodes of violence, there ensues a fundamental reorientation of the social structure in the direction of integration. This occurs at an advanced stage in the life of nations. At the time he wrote (1971), Black's view was that only fourteen countries had entered the integration phase.[18]

Integration arises from the movement of people to urban environments. This movement has the effect of depriving people of their previous connections with regional, occupational and organisational groupings that were relatively autonomous. In exchange they find themselves in highly fragmented, impersonal and isolated situations. This common experience of a mass society results in an integrated social structure in the sense that the previous divisions are diminished. But this is achieved at a price.

In an integrated society the individual is atomized – torn from his traditional community moorings, isolated from all except his immediate family, and left to find his way among the large and impersonal public and private organizations that provide him with his employment, medical care, social welfare, and pension . . . Loneliness, insecurity, and the weakening of close human relationships deprive the individual of an environment suited to psychological stability.[19]

Notwithstanding the above, there are numerous advantages for the individual. There are more consumer goods supplying a mass market. There is a higher per capita national income. There are enhanced educational opportunities. There is a safety-net of social services. Widely-used leisure facilities are available. There are significant advances in social mobility and in social, economic and political equality. Yet despite all this, there are also interludes of social unrest, disorder and economic depression in the integrated society. For example, the question of desegregating black Americans did not become acute until a century after their emancipation from slavery. Prior to the integration of American society, blacks were sufficiently

18. These countries are in Western Europe except for the United States, Canada, Australia and New Zealand. The United States, Switzerland and Germany reached the stage of integration in the early 1930s. The others did so during or after the Second World War. *Ibid.*, p. 449.
19. *Ibid.*, p. 444.

isolated not to be competitively involved with the dominant white majority. But in the context of general social integration, discordant black discrimination could no longer be tolerated. This illustrates the problems that were avoided or compromised in the past but which now had to be confronted.

The point at which one fixes the beginning of the phase of integration is necessarily somewhat arbitrary. The main criterion is the state of the nation's occupational structure. Other criteria that are sometimes mentioned are urbanisation, gross national product, literacy, educational attainment, health provision and means of communication. Broadly speaking, the United States can be considered to have crossed the boundary by 1933.

The new social order cannot help but be reflected in the working of the political system. For example, according to Black, an important characteristic of the new order is that the public service becomes larger and more complex in organisation. In the jargon of development theory, it becomes more differentiated. In his chapter Robert Williams will be advising us on the extent to which this is so in relation to the American national bureaucracy, while John Hart will be looking at this matter from the perspective of presidential staffing.

It would seem reasonable to assume that a transformed society which is in the process of losing its traditional roots and is commencing a transition to national integration will find that its chief executive has a different outlook on his duties from his predecessors. Movement towards integration may require a different style of leadership and a new policy agenda. The President may encounter a significant change in the magnitude and content of the flow of inputs into the political system.[20] This would seem especially likely if, as in Roosevelt's case, he takes office during one of the most severe depressions in the nation's history and has a strong mandate to do something about it. The situation would also seem ripe for change if the chief executive at such a juncture turns out to be, as has been said of Roosevelt, 'the most successful American President of all time'.[21]

20. Gabriel Almond and G. Bingham Powell, Jr., *Comparative Politics: A Developmental Approach*, Boston, 1966, p. 34.
21. Norman Stone, 'A Question of Charisma', *Sunday Times* (London), 30 March 1986, p. 50.

1

THE PRESIDENT AND THE CONSTITUTION

Richard Hodder-Williams

Any consideration of political power in a state must start at least with some examination of the formal distribution of authority in the political system. This is especially true in the case of the United States, since its Constitution has had a greater impact on the real distribution of power than perhaps the constitution of any other country. As Richard Pious has rightly observed, 'not to discuss the formal power of the office in dealing with presidential power is like describing a railroad and not mentioning the tracks'.[1] By the same token, a railroad is more than just the tracks.

Article II of the United States Constitution lays down that 'the executive power shall be vested in a President of the United States of America', and specifies that the President 'shall be Commander-in-Chief of the Army and Navy of the United States, and of the militia of the several states when called into the actual service of the United States . . . may require the opinion, in writing, of the principal officer in each of the executive departments . . . shall have power to grant reprieves and pardons for offences against the United States, except in cases of impeachment . . . shall have power, by and with the advice and consent of the Senate, to make treaties, provided that two-thirds of the Senators present concur . . . shall nominate, and, by and with the advice and consent of the Senate, shall appoint [a number of government officials] . . . shall from time to time give to the Congress information on the State of the Union and recommend to their consideration such measures as he shall judge necessary and expedient . . . shall receive ambassadors and other ministers . . . [and] shall take care that the laws be faithfully executed.' The President can raise no money; he can declare no war; he can proclaim no laws or edicts which are binding upon the people of the United States. These are the prerogatives of Congress. The Senate holds an absolute veto over the President's treaty-making and appointing powers, while the President's veto over congressional legislation can be overridden.

1. Richard Pious, 'Is Presidential Power Poison?', *Political Science Quarterly*, vol. 89 (1974), p. 636.

To have listed the central phrases of Article II is, however, no more than a starting-point. At first sight the slender authority given to a President in these enumerated powers runs in the face of the conventional wisdom concerning the power of modern Presidents, and must raise the question: how have these phrases been translated into the 'imperial presidency' of which Arthur Schlesinger has written?[2] The answer is especially difficult to arrive at when it is remembered that the authors of the United States Constitution consciously devoted Article I to the legislature and relegated the executive to Article II. This symbolised the dominant belief of the day that political authority ought to be located primarily in the legislature and that executive prerogatives were to be much feared. Certainly, Hamilton felt obliged to point out to his New York readers on more than one occasion that their fear of presidential tyranny was misplaced.[3] And yet one of the most striking features of American history has been the steady aggrandisement of presidential power, most notably from the time that Franklin Roosevelt entered the White House in March 1933.

What has happened, quite simply, is that the meaning of Article II has developed over two centuries of rapid political, economic and technological change in the United States and the world. This development of the Constitution's meaning has been due partly to differing expectations on the part of the American people and their leaders and partly to the interpretation of Article II's sparse phrases by the Supreme Court of the United States. Since at least the judgement of *Marbury* v. *Madison* in 1803, the Court has become the final repository of the meaning of the Constitution. Whether this was the intention of the Founding Fathers or not is still a matter of dispute between scholars; but the answer, even if discoverable, is hardly relevant since the American political system now operates on the unchallenged convention that the Supreme Court has the right to find unconstitutional, and therefore declare null and void, the actions of elected national politicians and state executives and legislators. Four years before Franklin Roosevelt entered the White House, Charles Evans Hughes, later to be Chief Justice, published his book *The Supreme Court of the United States*.[4] One of the most quoted passages in it is the assertion that 'the Constitution is what the Justices say it is'.

2. Arthur M. Schlesinger, Jr., *The Imperial Presidency*, Boston, London, 1974.
3. Alexander Hamilton, James Madison and John Jay, *The Federalist*, New York, 1961, letters 68 and 77.
4. Charles Evans Hughes, *The Supreme Court of the United States*, New York, 1928.

Hughes's aphorism encapsulates an important truth; but it is at the same time much less than the whole truth. Americans pride themselves, not without justice, on living under 'a government of laws, not men', thus strengthening the limitations placed upon the exercise of power by the Constitution itself. The Justices of the Supreme Court have largely followed the lead of two of its great Chief Justices − John Marshall at the beginning of the nineteenth century and Earl Warren in the tension-ridden years of the 1960s − in ensuring that the Constitution evolved to meet both contemporary needs and contemporary expectations. So far as presidential power is concerned, this evolution has been based upon the words of Article II and upon the precedents set in earlier years. The consequence is that the precise meaning and reach of some phrases in Article II remain, and must inevitably remain, unclear. Argument continues between those whose interpretations are essentially limiting and those whose interpretations are more expansive; but all agree that there is an element of ambiguity in applying the eighteenth-century document to twentieth-century reality.

The difference of opinion is most clearly illustrated in competing views of the meaning of the very first words of the Article: 'The executive power shall be vested in a President of the United States of America.' Are these words merely descriptive, looking forward to the powers enumerated later? Or do they grant additional authority which is in some way inherently executive? Presidents have answered this question differently, although most recent incumbents of the White House have favoured the broader interpretation. Theodore Roosevelt in his *Autobiography* wrote:

The most important factor in getting the right spirit in my Administration, next to the insistence upon courage, honesty, and a genuine democracy of desire to serve the plain people, was my insistence upon the theory that the executive power was limited only by specific restrictions and prohibitions appearing in the Constitution or imposed by the Congress under its Constitutional powers. My view was that every executive officer, and above all every executive officer in high position, was a steward of the people bound actively and affirmatively to do all he could for the people, and not to content himself with the negative merit of keeping his talents undamaged in a napkin. . . . My belief was that it was not only his right but his duty to do anything that the needs of the Nation demanded unless such action was forbidden by the Constitution or by the laws.[5]

This stewardship theory of the Constitution had its origins in Presidents before Theodore Roosevelt, most notably in Abraham

5. Theodore Roosevelt, *Autobiography*, London, 1913, pp. 388−9.

Lincoln, but its wide acceptance is very much a twentieth-century phenomenon.

Richard Nixon was, therefore, by no means unique in claiming powers for the President which do not appear in the Constitution and which cannot easily be assumed as necessary to the President's enumerated duties. Perhaps one of the most expansive claims was made by President Truman's Attorney-General in the District of Columbia district court in 1952, as the following exchange eloquently testifies:[6]

Judge Pine: And is it . . . your view that the powers of the Government are limited by and enumerated in the Constitution of the United States?

Assistant Attorney-General Baldridge: That is true, your Honour, with respect to legislative powers.

Pine: But it is not true, you say, as to the Executive?

Baldridge: No.

Pine: So, when the sovereign people adopted the Constitution, it enumerated the powers set up in the Constitution but limited the powers of the Congress and limited the powers of the Judiciary, but it did not limit the powers of the Executive. Is that what you say?

Baldridge: That is the way we read Article II of the Constitution.

The Supreme Court did not accept Baldridge's argument but found that President Truman's action — nationalising steel mills to ensure continued production at the height of the Korean War in the face of a threatened strike — was an unconstitutional extension of executive power and therefore impermissible.[7]

Those who have argued against the stewardship theory of presidential powers have tended to be academics or losing politicians rather than Presidents in office. Although William Howard Taft emphatically denied the propriety of expansionist interpretations of Article II in his book *Our Chief Magistrate and his Powers,*[8] he did a good deal as Chief Justice to lend constitutional support to the notion of broad executive power.[9] Legal historians, as well as the politicians trying to persuade their fellow legislators to ratify the Constitution, have tended to side with President Taft rather than Chief Justice Taft. The record of the Convention and the debates on ratification indicate that Article II's first clause was not intended to grant any general authority to Presidents; rather, it was a statement

6. Cited in George Winterton, 'The Concept of Extra-Constitutional Executive Power in Domestic Affairs', *Hastings Constitutional Law Quarterly* (vol. 7, 1979–80), p. 3.

7. *Youngstown Sheet and Tube Co.* v. *Sawyer,* 343 US 579 (1952).

8. William Howard Taft, *Our Chief Magistrate and his Powers*, New York, 1916.

9. For example, *Myers* v. *United States,* 272 US 52 (1926).

to be explained by the powers carefully enumerated afterwards.[10] In a practical sense, this debate is irrelevant to current politics; for the reality is simply that there has been a steady and widely accepted expansion of presidential authority and Supreme Court connivance in this expansion.

The Supreme Court has historically been a nationalising and centralising force, strengthening the central government at the expense of both state autonomy and, on many occasions, individual rights.[11] Attention usually gets drawn to those rare cases which restrain Congress or the President, but this should not distract attention from the Court's more habitual role as the legitimator of the actions of the national government, both Congress and President. For instance the haste with which the 1964 Civil Rights Act and the 1965 Voting Rights Act were tested in the courts well illustrates the importance attached to the Court's legitimising function.[12] As de Tocqueville noted more than a century and a half ago, 'scarcely any political question arises . . . that is not resolved, sooner or later, into a judicial question',[13] and this remains true. The election of Franklin Roosevelt to the presidency marked the beginning of a continuous process of increasing presidential involvement in discretionary actions bearing upon the American people, and consequently the courts have become more involved than ever before in delineating the reach of executive power.[14] The particular tensions raised by the Vietnam War and Richard Nixon's expansionist view of presidential power brought the courts into a more publicised, and more regular, relationship with the executive than had occurred previously. The Supreme Court's treatment of the cases that came before it is a reminder that, although the tendency has been to endorse and thus give constitutional blessing to presidential actions, there is no inevitability in this tradition. The Constitution retains a genuine force to limit the exercise of political power, as it was originally intended.

10. Raoul Berger, *Executive Privilege: A Constitutional Myth*, Cambridge, Mass., 1974, pp. 49–59.
11. Robert G. McCloskey, *The American Supreme Court*, Chicago, 1960; Philip B. Kurland, *Politics, the Constitution and the Warren Court*, Chicago, 1970.
12. *Heart of Atlanta Motel* v. *Katzenbach*, 379 US 241 (1964); *Katzenbach* v. *McClung*, 379 US 274 (1964); *South Carolina* v. *Katzenbach*, 383 US 301 (1966).
13. Alexis de Tocqueville, *Democracy in America*, New York, 1956.
14. As has already been noted, there were precedents upon which Roosevelt built. The best description of the presidency in his time is undoubtedly Edward S. Corwin, *The President: Office and Powers*, New York, 1941. Since 1933, however, there have not been, even under Eisenhower, the sort of retreats from power to be found in the years between Lincoln and Theodore Roosevelt and between Wilson and Franklin Roosevelt.

It is proper, therefore, despite Hughes's aphorism that the Constitution is 'what the Justices say it is', to begin this study with the Constitution itself. I intend in this chapter, first, to record the formal changes made in the Constitution through the amending procedure in the years following Franklin Roosevelt's entry to the White House in March 1933, insofar as they affect the presidency itself.[15] Thereafter, I shall examine the current meaning of the Constitution as expounded by the Supreme Court with reference to the President's role in foreign affairs and in the domestic political arena. This perspective provides the shape, as it were, of presidential power. Precisely what is poured into that shape depends upon individual Presidents and individual Congresses. This distinction between the presidency and the Presidents who have occupied the White House during the last fifty years must always be kept in mind.

Constitutional Amendments and the Presidency

There have been only twenty-six amendments to the United States Constitution in a little less than 200 years, and half of them were passed in two brief moments of activity. The first ten were ratified on 15 December 1791, and the thirteenth, fourteenth and fifteenth amendments were ratified in the wake of the Civil War on 6 December 1865, 9 July 1868 and 2 February 1870 respectively. Congressmen, however, have rarely held back from proposing amendments to the Constitution, and many of these in recent years have related either to the method of electing the President or to the office of President. Everett Brown calculated that by 1953, 4,484 proposals to amend the Constitution had been introduced in Congress. In the six years 1947–53, a proposal to limit the President to a single term of six years was introduced thirteen times, a proposal to introduce proportional representation into the process of electing the President was introduced fifty times and a proposal to empower Congress, through a concurrent resolution expressing lack of confidence, to force the President to resign was introduced five times.[16] Clearly

---

15. The twentieth amendment, proposed during Hoover's presidency, was ratified with remarkable dispatch. It changed the date on which Presidents take office from 4 March to 20 January, thus shortening the transition period considerably. It also made 3 January the date on which the newly-elected Congress begins its new term.
16. Everett S. Brown, *Proposed Amendments to the Constitution of the United States: January 3, 1947–January 3, 1953*, Ann Arbor, 1953.

Table 1.1. PROPOSED AMENDMENTS TO THE
CONSTITUTION, 1969–84

	(a) Number of constitutional amendments introduced	(b) Number concerned with presidential elections	(b) as % of (a)
91st Congress (1969–70)	773	117	15.14
92nd Congress (1971–2)	524	70	13.36
93rd Congress (1973–4)	382	69	18.06
94th Congress (1975–6)	326	46	14.11
95th Congress (1977–8)	373	60	16.09
96th Congress (1979–80)	291	42	14.43
97th Congress (1981–2)	221	23	10.41
98th Congress (1983–4)	161	18	11.18
Total	3,051	445	14.59

Source: Richard A. Davis, *Proposed Amendments to the Constitution of the United States introduced in Congress from the 91st Congress, 1st. Session, through the 98th Congress, 2nd Session, Jan. 1969–Dec. 1984,* Congressional Research Service Report no. 85–36 Gov., 1985.

many people did not then share Hamilton's view in *The Federalist* that the manner of selecting the President, if 'not perfect, [was] at least excellent'.[17]

Twenty years later the same concerns remained. As Table 1.1 indicates, congressmen continued to propose constitutional amendments, the precise number fluctuating with their general propensity to tamper with the Constitution. These amendments covered presidential eligibility, length of tenure, method of nomination and, above all, the reform of the electoral college and the institution of direct popular election of the President. Some issues, like equal rights or a balanced budget, rose and fell in significance; reform of the presidential electoral process continued its steady popularity. In the 91st Congress both houses considered the issue, and the House of Representatives actually voted by 338 to 70 to introduce direct popular elections for the President. But the Senate took no action then; when the issue did reach the floor in 1979 the proposal was voted down by 51 to 48. Throughout this period the issue reached a committee of either house on only eight occasions.[18] Although many congressmen clearly doubted Hamilton's judgement, they did not

17. Hamilton, Madison and Jay, *op. cit.*, letter 68.
18. Richard A. Davis, *Proposed Amendments to the Constitution . . .*, Congressional Research Service Report no. 85–36 Gov., 1985.

feel that reform should be high on their agenda, even after Nixon had been forced to resign.

In the immediate post-war years, however, constitutional reform did become a political issue. Perhaps the major matter confronting congressmen in January 1947 was whether a constitutional limit should be set on the number of terms an individual could serve as President. This was not a new issue. On more than 200 previous occasions an amendment had been proposed which would transform into a constitutional requirement the convention established by Washington and Jefferson that no person should serve more than two full four-year terms. What made the situation in the late 1940s so different, of course, was the fact that Franklin Roosevelt had sought, and won, not merely a third but also a fourth term as President. That the electorate had endorsed him four times at the polls might be interpreted, as indeed it was by some congressmen, as popular support for the convention's death.[19] The New Deal Democrats argued that circumscribing the people's choice by denying them the services of a popular and effective President was to run counter to the undiluted, if hesitant, expansion of popular political rights contained in nearly all the previous amendments to the Constitution. However, the central fact of the 80th Congress which had been elected in 1946 was that New Deal Democrats were now in a minority.

There is little doubt that party politics dominated the debate in early 1947. For the first time since the election of Herbert Hoover in 1928, the Republicans controlled Congress and they used this power, in a fit of pique as it were, to express their longstanding antipathy to the New Deal philosophy of governmental intervention in private and corporate concerns and to its creator, Franklin Roosevelt. Never had the Republicans spent so long in the political wilderness; the Democrats had dominated both the executive and legislative branches of the national government since 1933, and leading members of the Republican Party resented this intrusion into what they had once believed to be the natural order of things. Roosevelt had broken two of their party's cherished beliefs, the inviolability of private property and the principle of limited government. The twenty-second amendment, virtually the first piece of business of the 80th Congress, became the party's retrospective judgement on the New Deal and President Roosevelt. No Republican in either chamber cast a single vote against the proposed amendment.

19. Alan P. Grimes, *Democracy and the Amendments to the Constitution*, Lexington, Mass., 1978, p. 118. The next two paragraphs are drawn from this source.

Although the debates on the issue were often admirable discussions of constitutional principles, the choice of argument was largely
dictated by already formed positions on the proposition that 'no
person shall be elected to the office of President more than twice'. In
the event, the Democrats divided, fifty of their number joining the
solid Republican bloc of 235 votes in the House of Representatives to
make the necessary two-thirds majority, 285 – 121. In the Senate the
vote was 59 – 23, sixteen Democrats favouring the amendment. The
great majority of Democratic defections came from representatives
of Southern and border states – 82 per cent in the House and 63 per
cent in the Senate. The conservative coalition, which was to dominate Congress for the next decade and a half even when the Democrats regained control of both houses, had matured from its origins
in the late 1930s into a formidable force.

Congressional approval was only the first stage; the amendment
now needed the approval of three-quarters of the state legislatures. It
was not until February 1951 that Minnesota became the thirty-sixth
state to adopt the amendment and thus make it part of the Constitution. The delay was partly institutional, in that some state legislatures only met in alternate years; partly ideological, in that the
debate in some states was passionate, with two states voting against
the amendment; and partly a function of that state parochialism
which lies at the heart of American federalism, in that some states
took several years to arrange a debate on the proposed amendment.
In general the post-war years and the development of television and
air transport weakened state parochialism and created a more homogeneous and continent-wide political community; one consequence
has been that states more quickly address themselves to amendments. It was not until the Equal Rights Amendment was introduced
in March 1972 that the states showed any inclination in this period to
provide a constraint. In this instance sufficient states, largely in the
South, so dragged their feet as a conscious act of policy that the
requisite number of states had not ratified the amendment before
time ran out in June 1982.[20] Apart from the ERA, only the twenty-
second amendment has occasioned much passion in the state legislatures in the last fifty years. For the most part, Congress has been
determinate.

While the twenty-second amendment represented mainly a personal judgement on Franklin Roosevelt's 'reign' from 1933 to 1945,
it was also an assertion of a constitutional faith which resisted the
centralisation of executive power. The twenty-second amendment in

---

20. See Janet Boles, *The Politics of the Equal Rights Amendment: Conflict and the
    Decision Process*, London, 1979.

fact has probably done little to curb the growth of the 'imperial presidency'. The bargaining power on which Presidents so much depend for the passage of their favoured legislation depends on the possibility that the incumbent will return to the White House and its source of patronage. Each President entering his second term now is a 'lame-duck' President to the extent that politicians know that another person will occupy the White House in four years' time and inherit the largess theoretically available to its occupant. Yet a President can use that fact to his own advantage. It was Malcolm Moos, one of Dwight Eisenhower's aides, who observed that 'it may be that the President is using the Twenty-second amendment as a political weapon aimed at Congress. In other words, the President can gain support for his policies because he can convince the people he has nothing to gain personally. The amendment eliminates self-interest.'[21] This could be true of an essentially passive, and largely non-partisan President such as Eisenhower, but in the hurly-burly of Washington politics, the claim of impartiality is normally a less powerful weapon in the presidential armoury than the potential ability to reward friends and punish enemies. Since Eisenhower is, at the time of writing, the only President after Roosevelt to complete a second four-year term, it is difficult to judge the effect of the amendment. On balance, as I suspect Reagan would agree, it probably acts as a slight limitation on presidential power and thus exacerbates the difficulty of balancing the popular and personal expectations of a President with the actuality of influence constitutionally available to that President.

The post-Roosevelt concern for the excessive expansion of presidential power was reflected in other proposed amendments to the Constitution, none of which reached the states in the ratification process. But one, known as the Bricker Amendment after its sponsor Senator John Bricker of Ohio, failed by only a single vote to command a two-thirds majority in the Senate in 1954. The purpose behind this amendment was to reassert congressional control over all agreements entered into by the President on behalf of the United States and to ensure that no treaties would be enforceable on American citizens without any new obligations embodied therein being spelled out in federal legislation, itself naturally subject to the Constitution. Had this amendment been ratified, 'it would so restrict the conduct of foreign affairs', Dwight Eisenhower wrote at the time, 'that our country could not negotiate the agreements necessary for the handling of our business with the rest of the world. Such

---

21. Malcolm Moos, 'The President and the Constitution', *Kentucky Law Journal*, vol. 48 (1959), p. 120.

an amendment would make it impossible for us to deal effectively with friendly nations for our mutual defence and common interests.'[22] By 1960 the mood of Congress, which had largely been reflected in a negative attitude towards New Deal economics, internationalism and individual freedoms, altered. The pressure for change now became not a limiting one but an expansionary one. Strong Presidents were widely considered to be what the United States needed.

Franklin Roosevelt may have been thought to have occupied the White House too long. John Kennedy's tenure, by contrast, was cut brutally short. This, too, prompted the passing of an amendment to the Constitution. Just as the twenty-second had a long history, so too had the twenty-fifth. The problems raised by asking what happened when a President was too ill or too incapacitated to carry out the duties of the office were not hypothetical ones. Wilson and Eisenhower had both been gravely ill while in office; Garfield had lived for three months after being shot; Kennedy might, had he survived, have been too injured to continue effectively at the centre of the nation's affairs; more recently Reagan survived an assassination attempt without having his faculties impaired. On sixteen different occasions in the country's history, there has been no Vice-President ready to take up the role of Chief Executive if the need arose. In 1963–4 the role would have fallen to the Speaker of the House, the septuagenarian John McCormack, a man who neither sought the office nor, because of his age, was considered by many to be a suitable choice. There was no partisan conflict over the twenty-fifth amendment. Such disagreement as there was centred, first, on whether a constitutional amendment or a statute was the most appropriate method of dealing with an admittedly serious lacuna in the Constitution, and, secondly, who precisely should certify that a President was incapable of carrying out his responsibilities. It was agreed to leave the decision to the Vice-President and the principal officers of the executive branch; if, however, the allegedly incapacitated President dissented, then Congress had to muster a two-thirds majority in each house in support of the change for the President to be overruled. This amendment, hastened on by fears of what might have occurred after the Dallas shooting, quickly received the approval of the state legislatures. Within two years, forty-seven states had ratified it and none had rejected it.

In less than a decade it became necessary to employ this amendment, although not under circumstances which had originally been

---

22. Quoted in Max Beloff, *Foreign Policy and the Democratic Process*, Baltimore, 1955, p. 119.

envisaged. Section II permitted Richard Nixon to nominate Gerald Ford to the Vice-Presidency after the ignominious resignation of Spiro Agnew, both houses of Congress duly confirming. Section I came into operation when Nixon himself resigned from the presidency in the aftermath of the Watergate revelations. Gerald Ford automatically succeeded him. When the amendment was discussed in the House of Representatives, Congressman Ford had taken little part but he did say: 'The resolution before the House at this time, in my opinion, fulfils a vital need, especially at a vital and turbulent time in our nation's history.'[23] Little did he realise that he would be its first beneficiary and that he would himself appoint his own Vice-President, Nelson Rockefeller, thus establishing the first ever presidential team exercising power without any electoral legitimacy. Not for the first time, therefore, constitution-making and law-making intended to resolve a particular difficulty were used in circumstances which were not considered by the drafters. The American Constitution, with its eighteenth-century core, is well acquainted with such things, and the Supreme Court has, over time, gained much experience in fitting the awkward facts of the real world to the ideals mostly generalised in the Constitution itself.

The turbulent times to which Ford had referred were at the root of other post-war amendments. The twenty-third amendment provided the citizens of the District of Columbia with rights of voting in national elections for President and Vice-President; the twenty-fourth amendment prohibited the payment of taxes as a qualification for voting in federal elections; the twenty-sixth amendment established the minimum age for voting as eighteen. These changes to the Constitution reflected the concern in the 1960s for greater equality and openness in the democratic process and the consequences of drafting eighteen-year-olds to fight in Vietnam. They built on the extension of the franchise begun by the Supreme Court and extended by legislation, and so assisted in the development of a more uniform, nation-wide system of elections. The constituency to which aspiring presidential candidates would now have to attend, therefore, was considerably expanded in the fifteen years following Eisenhower's presidency, and constitutional amendments both assisted and symbolised this development.

The overall effect of these constitutional developments has been paradoxical. On the one hand, it might be argued that they have limited the freedom of a President by strengthening the democratic forces upon which his election depends and by shortening the maximum tenure of office. On the other hand, the same democratic

23. Quoted in Grimes, *op. cit.*, p. 140.

forces give a President greater legitimacy and thus greater authority. Calculating the net effect of these changes is impossible and in any case misses the essential point about any evaluation of constitutional powers: political realities ultimately determine the relative distribution of power. The exigences of world war and cold war, the growing expectations of much of the electorate as to the proper role of a President, the technological changes allowing Presidents to speak directly to the American people on television and radio, and a Congress unable to provide an alternative focus for national leadership have combined to strengthen the position of the President. In the argument of the 1970s over the 'imperial presidency', constitutional provisions became *used* to buttress each side's position and, as we shall see, an equilibrium became established acceptable to all branches of government.

The President and Foreign Affairs

There is little doubt that a President has greater freedom of action in foreign affairs than in domestic affairs. There are good reasons, both constitutional and pragmatic, for this. The Constitution, after all, sets out some plenary powers for a President in making him Commander-in-Chief and effectively chief diplomat. This constitutional grant of authority is buttressed by the commonsense view that relations between the United States and other states are best carried out under the leadership of a single individual. Only in this way, to use John Jay's words, could the necessary secrecy and dispatch be assured.[24] This view was also held as long ago as 1816 by the Senate Foreign Relations Committee, which felt that the President necessarily was competent to determine when, how, and on what subjects negotiations should take place, thus granting him the crucial role of initiation. Believing also that successful negotiations often depended upon speed and secrecy, the committee in effect reduced its role to the examination of agreements once concluded. Initiative, however, is not the same thing as control, and arguments have periodically arisen over the extent of a President's freedom in the field of foreign affairs. Specifically, the debate has tended to concentrate on two areas: agreements with foreign powers and the commitment of American troops to action overseas.

Constitutional blessing for a dominant role in foreign affairs was most famously expressed in Justice George Sutherland's opinion in the 1936 case of *United States* v. *Curtiss-Wright Export Corporation*.[25] He argued that there was a fundamental difference between

24. Hamilton, Madison and Jay, *op. cit.*, letter 64.
25. 299 US 304 (1936).

foreign and domestic affairs in that the United States itself inherited sovereignty when the colonial power was expelled, and thus the Union existed before the Constitution. The investment of the federal government with all the normal attributes of a sovereign state in international matters did not depend upon affirmative grants of the Constitution. There could, therefore, be no question of an invalid delegation of legislative power (such as exercised the minds of a majority of the Justices at this time in domestic matters) since the state — and thus the federal government — already enjoyed all the rights and obligations attributable to independent states. Logically, therefore, whoever decided upon the position taken by the United States in international affairs could draw upon some powers which found no mention in the Constitution. For future generations, Sutherland then had some significant observations to make on this very point:

In this vast external realm, with its important, complicated, delicate and manifold problems, the President alone has the power to speak or listen as a representative of the nation. He makes treaties with the advice and consent of the Senate; but he alone negotiates . . . we are here dealing . . . with . . . the very delicate, plenary and exclusive power of the President as the sole organ of the Federal government in the field of international relations . . . and we must often accord to the President a degree of discretion and freedom from statutory restriction which would not be admissible were domestic affairs alone involved.[26]

These last sentences were no more than dicta, but they came to embody the fundamental assumptions on which most Presidents operated in the field of foreign affairs. The commonsense of the Senate Foreign Relations Committee and the Curtiss-Wright judgement together provide the basis for claims of inherent and extra-constitutional (rather than unconstitutional) powers available to Presidents.

This notion of extra-constitutional power gained some support also from the consequences of reading into the President's duty to take care that laws be faithfully executed the right to employ appropriate means to ensure their execution. Depending upon this duty and his position as Commander-in-Chief, a President can instruct his troops to act in a variety of ways within the United States. The most significant case here is *in re Neagle,* decided in 1890.[27] Justice Field had received threats against his life and the Attorney-General had detailed Neagle, a United States marshal, to be his bodyguard. In the course of his duties, Neagle shot and killed the man who had

26. 299 US 304 (1936), at 319.
27. 135 US 1 (1890).

been making the threats and was promptly arrested and detained by the Californian authorities. Neagle sought his release on a writ of habeas corpus since this was permissible under federal statute 'for an act done or committed in pursuance of a law of the United States'. But no *law* had been passed assigning Neagle to Field, only an executive instruction. The Court, however, decided that the presidential duty to ensure the faithful execution of the law was not limited by the express words of federal law but encompassed also 'all the protection implied by the nature of the government under the Constitution'. Abraham Lincoln had earlier maintained that the preservation of the Constitution might entail action not sanctioned explicitly, indeed denied, by the Constitution and had, of course, acted on this belief in the Civil War. The Supreme Court now gave such an assumption its blessing.

Five years later, in *in re Debs*, the Court confirmed a broad reading of presidential power.[28] What had occurred in this instance was that a railway strike was interfering with the transmission of mails and interstate commerce. President Cleveland thereupon despatched troops to Chicago and obtained an injunction against the strikers. The question was whether the injunction, for violation of which Debs had been jailed for contempt of court, was constitutional since there was no statutory basis for it. The Court decided that the duty of a government to protect the mails and preserve the public interest implied the right to exercise the power necessary to achieve these ends.

Whether the basis for the notion of extra-constitutional authority is grounded in history and law is open to question;[29] but there is little doubt that a presumption exists which permits Presidents to act in the defence of what they consider the national interest, unless there are clear constitutional and statutory provisions contradicting them. The Constitution, as Edward Corwin wrote, 'is an invitation to struggle for the privilege of directing American foreign policy',[30] because both are granted authority in the two most salient areas of foreign relations: the making of agreements and the making of war.

The Constitution sets out the procedure for making treaties. The process is often supposed to fall into two distinct parts – negotiation (the President's prerogative) and ratification (the Senate's prerogative) – but the words of the Constitution in fact make no such distinction. From the beginning of the Union, however, the practice has been to distinguish the two stages, and this convention has

28. 158 US 564 (1895).
29. Winterton, *op. cit.*; Berger, *op. cit.*
30. Corwin, *op. cit.*, p. 201.

become accepted by both sides. Despite the regular consultation that nearly always goes on between the President and congressional leaders, the traditional hostility between Capitol Hill and the White House is on occasions played out in this sphere too. There is no automatic approval of treaties. President Carter had to fight hard to gain approval of his Panama Canal treaties and ultimately was forced to accept amendments to his original proposals. Carter's attempts to get a Strategic Arms Limitation Treaty foundered and never reached the stage of voting. Divided responsibility undoubtedly creates grave problems for the executive branch as well as misunderstanding and frustration on the part of foreign countries who can never be certain that what the diplomats have signed in the name of the United States will be approved by the Senate. Since the final document is often the carefully balanced conclusion of much negotiation, amendments in the Senate can alter that balance and thus its acceptability to the foreign government.

Not all agreements between the United States and other nations are treaties. Some are negotiated, but are never referred to the Senate for its advice and consent, and yet have the same legal authority as a properly promulgated treaty. These executive agreements, as they are called, fall broadly into two categories: first, those which Congress authorises a President, or some other member of the executive branch, to make in advance (such as postal conventions), and secondly, those which a President makes but which are never sent to the Senate for ratification. Some agreements in this second category are of minor significance, such as the exchange of cultural attachés or mutual arrangements for diplomatic staff. Some are of major significance and might involve secret commitments to defend a foreign state against external aggression or establish military bases in a country. What is indisputable is the massive rise in the number of executive agreements over the last half century. In 1930, for instance, the United States concluded twenty-five treaties and only nine executive agreements, while in 1968 it made only sixteen treaties but 266 executive agreements. By January 1972 there were a total of 947 treaties and no less than 4,359 executive agreements to which the United States was a party.[31] This massive rise in executive agreements is, however, almost entirely due to an increase in the first kind,[32] yet it is the second kind which has recently made such agreements a bone of contention.

31. Thomas M. Franck and Edward Weisband, *Foreign Policy by Congress*, New York, 1970, p. 145.
32. Thomas L. Brewer, *American Foreign Policy: A Contemporary Introduction*, Englewood Cliffs, NJ, p. 108; John B. Rehm, 'Making Foreign Policy through

The attraction to a President of the executive agreement is obvious. The failure of the Senate to ratify the Treaty of Versailles and the inability of President Carter to persuade the Senate to take action on his Strategic Arms Limitation Treaty with the Soviet Union give executive agreements a certain political virtue. The Lend-Lease agreement of September 1940, by which Roosevelt exchanged the loan of fifty American destroyers for leases on British bases in the Caribbean, stemmed directly from Roosevelt's fear that an isolationist Senate would disapprove of active support for the anti-Nazi forces. Political convenience, however, should not be enough to give executive agreements, especially ones like those entered upon at Yalta and Potsdam, constitutional blessing. What is also needed is a legal defence, and that was provided in a classic article in the *Yale Law Journal* of 1944—5.[33] Yet the exact status of an executive agreement remains unclear. The courts have not faced the issue square on, even when they could have done,[34] but have, except where an agreement clearly violated a law dealing with a matter enumerated under Article I, section 58,[35] given their blessing to executive action. Despite some legal scholars challenging their constitutionality, the extra-constitutional power alleged to flow from a President's obligations to look after the national interest and from the *Curtiss-Wright*, *Neagle* and *Debs* decisions remains constitutionally intact.[36]

It does not, however, remain politically intact. Rather than challenge the principle in the courts, Congress has chosen to legislate in an attempt to limit presidential freedom in this area. Stung by the realisation in 1972 that the United States was committed, through several secret agreements, to possible action overseas, Congress agreed, despite the different perspectives of the House of Representatives and Senate, to enact the Case-Zablocki bill which required the Secretary of State to submit to Congress within sixty days the text of all executive agreements except where disclosure might be 'prejudicial to the national security of the United States'. In the latter case only the foreign relations committees under an appropriate injunction of secrecy had to be informed. This procedure does not

International Agreement', in Francis O. Wilcox and Richard A. Frank (eds), *The Constitution and the Conduct of Foreign Policy*, New York, 1976, p. 127.

33. Myres McDougal and Asher Lans, 'Treaties and Congressional-Executive or Presidential Agreements: Interchangeable Instruments of National Policy', *Yale Law Journal*, vol. 54 (1944—5), pp. 181—351 and 534—615.
34. *B. Altman & Co.* v. *United States*, 224 US 583 (1912); *United States* v. *Belmont*, 301 US 324 (1937).
35. See Franck and Weisband, *op. cit.*, pp. 146—54.
36. Louis Fisher, *Constitutional Conflicts between Congress and the President*, Princeton, NJ, 1985, pp. 272—9.

permit Congress to reject or amend such agreements, nor did it entirely do away with secret agreements.

Although the Case-Zablocki Act, and other Acts such as the Trade Act of 1974, have brought some pressure to bear on the executive branch and resulted in some congressional oversight, the General Accounting Office in 1976 still found that many agreements were not submitted to Congress within the stipulated sixty days and that there were still several agreements (such as the thirty-four between the United States and South Korean intelligence agencies) which had never been shown to the State Department or reported to Congress.[37] The Supreme Court has shared the executive's view that in certain circumstances the President *must* act unilaterally. When Carter agreed — as part of a bargain with the Iranian government after the fall of the Shah to release American hostages — that the United States would transfer billions of dollars in frozen assets to the Bank of England for later transfer to Iran, the Reagan administration upheld this policy, which directly affected many American companies' claims to Iranian assets, and the Supreme Court in *Dames and Moore* v. *Reagan* agreed.[38] As Justice Rehnquist explained, 'where, as here, the settlement of claims has been determined to be a necessary incident to the resolution of a major foreign policy dispute between our country and another and where, as here, we can conclude that Congress acquiesced in the President's action, we are not prepared to say that the President lacks the power to settle such claims.' As is so often the case, the President enjoys any benefit of the doubt, especially when Congress remains silent.

Treaties and agreements are the bread and butter of foreign relations; but military action is the ultimate weapon. It is well-established that Presidents have a duty to repel invasions without recourse to a congressional declaration of war. But this does not appear to grant any right to involve troops overseas on the President's own instigation. Indeed a careful reading of the Constitution suggests that it is Congress, rather than the President, who ought to dominate in the commitment of troops overseas. For Congress has a formidable list of enumerated powers which would seem to make it the prime power in the matter of war-making. Congress is authorised to provide for the common defence, raise and support armies, provide and maintain a navy, make rules for the government and regulation of the land and naval forces, and make all laws necessary and proper for carrying into execution these powers. Since Congress also appropriates funds (military appropriations

37. Fisher, *Constitutional Conflicts, op. cit.,* p. 278.
38. *Dames and Moore* v. *Reagan*, 453 US 654 (1981).

constitutionally require renewal every two years), it clearly has the constitutional authority to determine the extent and form of American involvement in war. Yet it has been the President in recent years who has actually been the determining influence.

The reason for this is essentially political, although the Constitution, as is to be expected in the American system, has been artfully employed to buttress consecutive Presidents' positions. The role of Commander-in-Chief is frequently cited as a source of power, but such a role has expanded dramatically since the days of Alexander Hamilton, who viewed the Commander-in-Chief's powers as amounting 'to nothing more than the supreme command and direction of the military and naval forces'.[39] There is no doubt that a President has the authority, either personally or through his subordinates, to give orders to his military forces. During the Cuban missile crisis nobody challenged President Kennedy's right to speak directly to senior officers and give them instructions; indeed, he was obliged to do so when he encountered a lack of cooperation from a senior subordinate.[40]

In a hierarchical organisation such as the Army the Commander-in-Chief can dismiss whom he pleases. When President Truman dismissed General MacArthur in April 1951, the sense of outrage in some quarters was reflected in the establishment of a Joint Senate Committee which unanimously accepted the proposition that the President had the constitutional power to act as he did, although some of its members thought he had acted unwisely. More recently, when a naval officer was summarily removed from the command of a ship by his superiors, the District Court held that 'military decisions concerning internal duty assignments and promotions must be left, absent of Congressional regulation to the contrary, to the judgement of the chain of command under the President as Commander-in-Chief.'[41] But the military is not a watertight compartment. The Constitution controls much of what occurs in the armed services. Thus, the Court has held that Congress had no power to subject a discharged serviceman to trial by court-martial for offences committed by him while in service since this would deprive him of the constitutional safeguards available to him in the civilian federal courts.[42] The Court has also held that serving officers should receive the same privileges regardless of sex.[43]

39. Hamilton, Madison and Jay, *op. cit.*, letter 69.
40. Graham Allison, *Essence of Decision: Explaining the Cuban Missile Crisis*, Boston, 1971, pp. 128–32.
41. *Arnheiter* v. *Ignatius*, 292 F. Supp. 911 (1968); *affirmed* 435 F. 2d. 691 (1970).
42. *O'Callaghan* v. *Parker*, 395 US 258 (1969).
43. *Frontiero* v. *Richardson*, 411 US 676 (1973).

The rise of the United States to the status of a superpower and the changed nature of war and international relations has clearly strained the constitutional fabric. Presidents are expected, by foreigners and nationals alike, to act rapidly and decisively in foreign affairs, even to the extent of using the armed forces they command by virtue of their position as Commander-in-Chief. It was the Vietnam War which brought this issue very much on to the public agenda. However, sending American troops into battle was not new. Dean Acheson unearthed eighty-seven instances before 1950 in which American Presidents had done so. For the most part Presidents came to Congress afterwards for retrospective approval.

Franklin Roosevelt and Woodrow Wilson made a point of getting authority from Congress to involve American troops in the two World Wars. Roosevelt asked Congress for a declaration of war against Japan, retroactive to the date of the Pearl Harbor attack, to which Congress promptly acceded. It was only after Germany and Italy formally declared war against the United States that Roosevelt petitioned Congress for formal declarations of war and Congress responded that day. Harry Truman, however, committed American troops to the defence of South Korea without any explicit congressional authorisation. Lyndon Johnson and Richard Nixon presided over lengthy military involvement in Vietnam, again without formal congressional blessing. In both conflicts, however, the facts made a formal declaration of war difficult. Truman, in theory, was assisting the United Nations in its peace-keeping activities, and the United States, as a sovereign state, was not at war with North Korea. In Vietnam the American involvement began as military assistance and advice which escalated incrementally into full-scale war. Not only was it difficult to pinpoint the moment at which the United States was at war in Vietnam; it was problematic deciding exactly with which state the United States was supposed to be at war. Yet the deployment of 500,000 troops, many of them drafted, over a substantial period of time in active combat thousands of miles from the United States looked uncannily like a war. Yet no war had been declared by Congress, the body clearly specified in the Constitution as the agency empowered to commit the United States to war.

The Vietnam War was undoubtedly a very special case. In the first place, Congress had implicitly lent its approval to the President's actions. It did this through the Gulf of Tonkin Resolution in 1964, whose phraseology is significant, for Congress approved and supported 'the determination of the President, as Commander-in-Chief, to take all necessary measures to repel any armed attack against the forces of the United States and to prevent further aggression'. It continued its implicit support with legislation providing massive military appropriations for the escalating action. It could be argued, then, that the Vietnam War was merely a very much larger and longer operation than any other undeclared war. In the second place, however, it came to arouse an unprecedented degree of hostility among many Americans. Whereas Presidents in the past had anticipated popular opinion or acted where public opinion was unformed, by the late 1960s there was a large and vocal minority in the United States bitterly opposed to the war. It is only under these conditions that the constitutionality of presidential action is generally challenged.

As Americans so often do, they litigated. They held that the draft was not binding on those it called up because the war was an unconstitutional war. But the Supreme Court justices never pronounced authoritatively on the issue, although it clearly occupied a considerable amount of their time.[44] Ultimately, however, not enough of the justices were prepared to face the problem head-on. For some, the marvellously plastic concept of 'political questions' saved them that uncomfortable task as they argued that the dispute was neither amenable to judicial resolution nor the proper province of the courts. A little later they were faced with another difficult problem when Senator Barry Goldwater claimed that President Carter had exceeded his constitutional authority in terminating a treaty with Taiwan without gaining Senate approval. If a President can terminate a treaty at will, a good deal of the Senate's authority in this area is conceded. Once again, the Court decided not to face the issue, but the longest and most interesting opinion held that the issue was manifestly one over which the courts had jurisdiction, but one in which Congress itself should have been a party.[45] Since there was no dispute between Congress and the executive branch, there was no occasion for entering so complex and potentially entangling a thicket. So the issue remained unresolved.

Just as the delicate question of where the line should be drawn between constitutional and unconstitutional executive agreements was never litigated in the courts, but addressed through legislation, so it was in the case of the war powers as well. In October 1972 Congress passed legislation, over President Nixon's veto, which attempted to recapture some of the authority for making war. The

44. See, for example, *Mora* v. *McNamara*, 389 US 93 (1967), *certiorari denied*, and *Massachusetts* v. *Laird,* 400 US 886 (1970), *certiorari denied*, Douglas J. dissenting; Bob Woodward and Scott Armstrong, *The Brethren: Inside the Supreme Court*, New York, 1979, pp. 125–7.
45. *Goldwater* v. *Carter*, 444 US 996 (1979), where Powell's quasi-opinion is a call for a genuine controversy between the two branches of government before the Court can act, such as existed in *Powell* v. *McCormack*, 395 US 486 (1969).

War Powers Resolution, as it was called, required Presidents to inform Congress within 48 hours whenever troops were employed in active service abroad, limited the use of those troops to sixty days (with a thirty-day extension in exceptional circumstances) unless Congress expressly authorised continuing activity, and permitted Congress to terminate any operation by a concurrent resolution. A Vietnam situation, it was hoped, could never occur again.

Since the passage of the War Powers Resolution, Presidents have on several occasions committed American troops in situations where lives have been lost. In May 1975 President Ford, responding to the Cambodian seizure of the American container ship *Mayaguez*, directed the marines to rescue the ship and the crew. Cambodian gunboats were sunk and a Cambodian oil depot was bombed. Forty-one Americans were killed and seventy-one were injured in the process of assaulting an island where the crew were thought to be held and recapturing the empty ship. Ford informed Congress but certainly did not consult; to the extent that there was any communication, Ford acted 'taking note of', not 'acting pursuant to', the War Powers Resolution. In September 1982, shortly after introducing marines into Beirut as part of a multinational peacekeeping force, Reagan sent a note to the Speaker of the House and the President *pro tempore* of the Senate, but once again this was not done in line with the War Powers Resolution's requirements.[46]

On the morning of 25 October 1983 American troops were involved in an attack on the island of Grenada; 18 soldiers were killed and 116 were wounded. This is a textbook case of the Resolution's weakness. Reagan did not consult in advance, although the executive branch for several days considered a range of options, so that no collective judgement of both Congress and the President could be brought to bear. The President 'consistent with the War Powers Resolution' informed the leaders of each House of Congress of his action which was taken 'pursuant to my constitutional authority with respect to the conduct of foreign relations and as Commander-in-Chief of the United States Armed Forces'. But because he did not follow the precise requirements of the War Powers Resolution, the sixty-day clock was not triggered. The experience of Grenada highlighted several things, not least the ambiguous drafting of the Resolution.[47] Above all, however, it stressed the paramountcy of political factors, especially in low-intensity con-

46. Franck and Weisband, *op. cit.*, pp. 61–6.
47. Michael Rubner, 'The Reagan Administration, the 1973 War Powers Resolution, and the Invasion of Grenada', *Political Science Quarterly*, vol. 100 (1985–6), pp. 627–47.

flict situations. A popular President, acting in a way that was widely seen to be popular, *can* call upon inherent authority, extra-constitutional for sure, but real nonetheless. The prerogatives of Congress provide it with some potential constraint, but the ultimate constraint remains the power of the purse. Whether that could be exercised if, say, American troops became enmeshed in a Central American war of attrition remains to be seen.

There is little doubt that the Constitution as it is currently understood grants certain extra-constitutional or inherent powers to a President. But it is also true that these powers are limited. Richard Nixon offered no resistance to the repeal of the Tonkin Gulf Resolution in January 1971 because he believed that his actions did not require such congressional blessing. The Court was never to pronounce on his reading of the reach of inherent powers, but it has regularly asserted that Sutherland's dicta, although expressing a general presumption of the dominance of the President in foreign affairs, do not constitute an absolute grant of power. Presidential claims that threats to the security of the state permit them to act in any manner they believe necessary to meet such threats have fallen on deaf ears. In the Steel Seizure case, the Court, although it spoke with several voices, clearly agreed that the President's actions were subject to judicial review and that there were no inherent powers which could justify the seizure of the steel mills.[48] In the Pentagon Papers case, again, claims that national security required an injunction against the publication of a classified study of the Vietnam War were not upheld. Hugo Black, in a passionate defence of the first amendment right to freedom of information, made it quite clear that the President could not be above the law.[49] Nor can a President, in the name of national security, tap the telephones of suspected subversives without getting proper authorisation.[50]

The relationship between the Constitution and a President's authority in the realm of foreign affairs is a special one, dependent much more on the relative power of individual Congresses and Presidents than on the exegesis of justices of the Supreme Court. What a President now appears able to do by virtue of his office is markedly different from the expectations of the Founding Fathers and a literal reading of the Constitution. But an attack on the aggrandisement of presidential power such as was launched by Arthur Goldberg, once a Supreme Court Justice himself, misses the point that in the real world of politics the dominant forces in this area of activity are the

48. *Youngstown Sheet and Tube Co.* v. *Sawyer*, 343 US 579 (1952).
49. *New York Times* v. *United States*, 403 US 713 (1971).
50. *US District Court* v. *US*, 407 US 297 (1972).

politicians and their appreciation of United States interests.[51] Sometimes these coincide to yield results which shift the balance of power
from one branch to another, and history teaches that, where this is
generally agreed, the Supreme Court endorses the change.[52] In the
realm of domestic politics, where individuals have personal interests
at stake on which to litigate and where politicians have constituency
pressures to bear in mind if they are to survive in Washington, the
opportunity and readiness to challenge a President are greater; and
here, additionally, a President's constitutional basis for exercising
power is more limited.

The President and Domestic Affairs

Reaching the White House at all involves a long and strenuous path,
the rules of which are subject to the Constitution and thus to
Supreme Court overview. Attempts to limit participation in the electoral process have been largely negated by the Supreme Court and
recent constitutional amendments. Parts of the laws controlling
campaign expenditures have in their turn been overturned by the
Supreme Court. The seating of rival delegations at a party convention or the right to get a name on the ballot in some states have also
been subject to review by the justices of the Supreme Court.[53] Every
presidential hopeful needs a bevy of lawyers to pick his way through
the increasingly complex legislative and constitutional framework
within which elections now take place. Having reached the White
House, there is still a need for lawyers, for a President is confronted
with a Constitution whose words hardly encourage the sort of
dynamic leadership expected by Americans and desired by
candidates.

The Founding Fathers, after all, envisaged Congress as the body
most appropriate for leadership in domestic affairs. A President
may require the opinion, in writing, of the principal officer in each
of the executive departments, pardon criminals except for those who
have been impeached, nominate people to various offices subject to
senatorial ratification, fill vacancies in the Senate, give Congress
information on the state of the Union, convene extraordinary
meetings of Congress and take care that the laws be faithfully

51. Arthur Goldberg, 'The Constitutional Limits on the President's Powers',
    American University Law Review, vol. 22 (1972–3), pp. 667–716.
52. Walter Murphy, *Congress and the Court*, Chicago, 1962.
53. Richard Claude, *The Supreme Court and the Electoral Process*, Baltimore, 1970;
    Buckley v. *Valeo*, 424 US 1 (1976); *Cousins* v. *Wigoda*, 419 US 447 (1975).

executed. It does not amount to much of a grant of power. Yet modern Presidents are central figures in domestic affairs and exercise power far in excess of that suggested by a literal reading of Article II.

Schlesinger's classic account of the 'imperial presidency' stresses the growth of presidential power in the field of foreign affairs. But there is little doubt that Franklin Roosevelt considerably enlarged the presidential domain in the field of domestic affairs too. He believed in the necessity of strong, central leadership at a time of crisis, and the Congress elected in 1932 apparently agreed with him. In the first few months of the New Deal, a number of laws were passed which granted to the President considerable discretion and delegated to him the responsibility for making regulations which clearly contained policy implications. A majority of the justices of the Supreme Court believed that this delegation transgressed the principle of the separation of powers implied in the Constitution, and they found parts of the New Deal programme unconstitutional. This provoked one of the classic confrontations between Court and presidency, as Roosevelt attempted to circumvent the judgement by appointing additional justices to the Supreme Court. However, a combination of factors − judicial retreat, the retirement of a justice, a Congress less amenable to presidential dominance − frustrated Roosevelt's design. Although he lost the battle, he won the war. The Supreme Court came to accept Congress's right to choose its own preferred method to combat economic and social problems and it thus acknowledged that it might be necessary and proper, in the process, to delegate considerable powers to the executive branch.[54]

Delegated legislation clearly meets some of the needs of efficient government in an age of regulation, but it also reduces the ultimate authority of the legislators thereby. So Congress included in a number of laws what came to be called a 'legislative veto'. This permitted Congress as a whole (or one of its two chambers in some instances) to negate an executive decision of which it disapproved by passing an appropriate resolution expressing its opposition. In the 1970s, when conflict between Nixon and Congress became acute, the legislative veto was incorporated into major legislation such as the Budget and Impoundment Control Act, the War Powers Resolution and the Arms Export Control Act. By the 1980s more than 200 laws included such provisions. Although there were some doubts about the constitutionality of the legislative veto, the legislative and executive branches did not test the issue in the courts (which had traditionally indicated an unwillingness to arbitrate in such disputes

---

54. *United States* v. *Darby Lumber Co.*, 312 US 100 (1941).

unless absolutely necessary) and no opportunity arose for an individual with a grievance to raise the issue in the 1970s.

But in the early 1980s there was such an individual, Jagdish Chadha. A Kenyan Asian carrying a British passport, he had been served with a deportation order when his student visa expired but had mounted several appeals against this decision until the Attorney-General ultimately permitted him to stay. Under the immigration legislation, the names of those whom the Attorney-General has in his discretion decided to treat differently from the Immigration and Naturalisation Service are sent to Congress, and Congress (in this case the Chairman of the House Judiciary Subcommittee on Immigration) decided to use the legislative veto to overrule the Attorney-General. Chadha appealed through the federal courts, claiming that the exercise of the legislative veto was unconstitutional. In *Immigration and Naturalisation Service* v. *Chadha* the Supreme Court in 1983 upheld his case and, at a stroke, invalidated parts of more federal laws than the Court had invalidated throughout its history.[55]

What this decision appears to mean, then, is that power once delegated by Congress cannot be reclaimed. The separation of powers may, in other words, permit Congress to grant the executive discretionary power to assist in the efficient administration of a programme, but it forbids what is in effect concurrent responsibility. One of the central features of the War Powers Resolution seems therefore inoperative. Had *Chadha* been decided two years earlier, President Reagan would have avoided the need to lobby so assiduously to ensure that the Senate did not veto his sale of AWACS aircraft to Saudi Arabia. Although much has been said about the effect of *Chadha*, especially in relation to its applicability to the War Powers Resolution and the invasion of Grenada, there has been little action on Capitol Hill. New legislation continues, in some instances, to include the equivalent of the legislative veto by writing in limitations on executive discretionary power that require the President to persuade both houses of Congress to enact his wishes. The central point is that, given the extent to which legislation must provide the executive branch with some freedom of action in its administration of laws, Congress will find some way to keep an eye on that discretion. As Louis Fisher has written, 'call it supervision, intervention, interference, or just plain meddling, Congress will find a way.'[56]

55. *Immigration and Naturalisation Service* v. *Chadha*, 103 S. Ct. 2764 (1983). See also Fisher, *Constitutional Conflicts, op.cit.*, pp. 162–83, and Christopher Pyle and Richard Pious (eds), *The President, Congress and the Constitution: Power and Legitimacy in American Politics*, New York, pp. 195–218.
56. Fisher, *Constitutional Conflicts, op. cit.*, p. 183.

In dealing with Congress, the President enjoys one clear constitutional weapon, the veto. But it is a blunt weapon, for its use negates the whole bill, even those points of which Presidents approve. Politicians know this and include in bills which Presidents dislike provisions they might find hard to veto. Naturally Presidents have sought an item veto, a power to veto only parts of a bill. No one has been more assiduous than Reagan in seeking this advantage, but he has not succeeded because it would radically alter the subtle balance between executive and legislature to the executive's advantage. The pocket veto, the process by which Presidents kill legislation by withholding their signature to a bill at the end of a session, has recently created friction. Nixon's attempt to use this device in the middle of a session was found unconstitutional by the Court (for it was possible to return the bill to Congress with his reasons for refusal), and Reagan's attempt to act similarly on a bill requiring certification of a good human rights record in El Salvador as a prerequisite for any military aid was being considered by the Supreme Court at the time of writing.[57]

Conflict between executive and legislature is one of the central facts of American political life, and both branches of government sometimes push their claims to the very limit of constitutional propriety and occasionally beyond. For the most part they work amicably enough, aware of the strengths and rights of each other. At the end of 1985, with budget deficits rising alarmingly and no sign of a satisfactory compromise being worked out, an amendment (the so-called Gramm-Rudman amendment) was attached to a bill raising the ceiling for the national debt. This amendment established an automatic process intended to force the budget deficit to fall to $144 billion in fiscal 1987 and then by a further $36 billion each year until it balances in 1991. The cuts are divided equally between non-excluded domestic programmes (social security, Medicare and debt interest are inviolate) and defence programmes. Once the process is triggered by the General Accounting Office, there is no discretion left for either the executive or the legislature in where to make cuts. At the time of writing, the District Court in Washington had already found the process unconstitutional and the Supreme Court is to hear the appeal. When Congress and the President fail to negotiate an acceptable compromise, the Constitution, with its separation of powers granting power to both branches, can easily thwart radical solutions to the incipient immobilism contained in the nation's constitutional arrangements.

The increased incidence of delegated legislation is one sign of the

57. Pyle and Pious, *op. cit.*, pp. 221–2.

enlarged role played by government generally since 1933. Another sign is the massive increase in the size of the executive branch, not only in the great departments of state but also in the burgeoning number of regulatory agencies. Many members of this bureaucracy hold office under statutes with strict qualificatory criteria and rights. They are responsible to the President in his capacity as head of the executive branch but they are not necessarily subject to his discipline.

The right of a President to dismiss subordinates has been discussed since the First Congress addressed itself to the question. The generally accepted view was that, although the Senate had to confirm nominations, one of the central features of executive power was the ability to dismiss subordinates who lacked the skill, temperament or commitment to carry out policy. This view was well expressed by John Lawrence in the First Congress who declared: 'I contend that every President should have those men about him in whom he can place the most confidence, provided the Senate approve his choice.'[58] The rule at the beginning of the Roosevelt presidency was that laid down by Chief Justice Taft in the *Myers* case.[59] As President, Taft had held a minimalist view of presidential power. As Chief Justice, by contrast, he asserted in 1926 that 'the power to remove superior officers is an incident of the power to appoint them, and is in its nature an executive power.' Although the Senate had confirmed the appointment of Myers to his Oregon postmastership, the President alone now had the authority to remove him. What, then, if any, were the limitations on this power of dismissal, of which the Constitution itself made no mention?

The answer came in 1935.[60] William Humphrey had been nominated to the Federal Trade Commission by President Hoover, confirmed by the Senate and duly commissioned for a seven-year term. This had run less than two years when President Roosevelt sent him a letter saying that 'the aims and purpose of the Administration . . . could be carried out most effectively with personnel of my own selection.' The letter made it clear that Humphrey's competence was not at issue. A month later Roosevelt wrote again, urging Humphrey to resign, but to no avail. In October 1933 Roosevelt wrote to Humphrey once more: 'Effective as of this date', the letter said, 'you are hereby removed from the office of Commissioner of the Federal

---

58. Quoted in Joseph P. Harris, *The Advice and Consent of the Senate*, Berkeley, 1953, p. 32; see also pp. 30–5.
59. *Myers* v. *United States*, 272 US 52 (1926). See especially on this case Charles A. Miller, *The Supreme Court and the Uses of History*, Cambridge, Mass., 1969, pp. 52–70.
60. *Humphrey's Executor* v. *United States*, 295 US 602 (1935).

Trade Commission.' Humphrey died not long afterwards, never having accepted his removal from office, and his estate's executors sued for back pay. The Court addressed itself to two questions. First, it examined the Federal Trade Commission Act which established seven-year terms of office and stated that commissioners might be removed by the President for 'inefficiency, neglect of duty, or malfeasance of office'. It found that the causes for removal in the Act were definitive and unambiguous and that, as Roosevelt's letter admitted, Humphrey was guilty of none of them. Secondly, it considered whether, following *Myers*, the chief executive had an inherent right to dismiss members of the executive branch. Here the Court distinguished between the Oregon postmaster, who was an executive officer, and Hoover's appointee, who was an officer of a quasi-judicial and policy-making agency established consciously by Congress to operate as far as possible in a non-partisan and continuing manner. A presidential right to dismiss such men would destroy the purpose of the offices created by Congress. This view was confirmed in 1958 in a case very similar to the Humphrey case.[61] Myron Wiener had been nominated to the War Claims Commission by President Truman, confirmed by the Senate, asked to resign by President Eisenhower and then removed against his will. Nobody had been confirmed in his place, although Eisenhower had sent the name of a successor to the Senate before the War Claims Commission was abolished. Wiener claimed recovery of his salary and the Supreme Court supported him.

Although there are limitations, therefore, on the chief executive's complete control of the bureaucracy broadly defined, his position as chief executive gives him both political and constitutional power to advance his own policies. By their nature bureaucracies exercise power in the process of administering laws. In the second half of the twentieth century, there is considerable 'political space' which permits executive officers discretion in ordering priorities, allocating funds, appointing subordinates and supervising programmes.[62] Congress remains the dominant body ultimately, but Presidents have often tried, and succeeded, in 'legislating' through their control of the executive. Sometimes this is done through executive orders. Kennedy prohibited racial discrimination in housing supported by federal loans or guarantees (Executive Order 11063 of 1962), and Johnson regulated large segments of industry by prohibiting

61. *Wiener* v. *United States*, 357 US 349 (1958). See generally Pyle and Pious, *op. cit.*, pp. 195–218.
62. G. Calvin Mackenzie, *The Politics of Presidential Appointments*, New York, 1981.

discrimination among employees by government contractors on grounds of race or sex (Executive Orders 11246 of 1965 and 11375 of 1967). Sometimes this is done by reordering priorities, as Nixon did when he effectively reduced the attention given to civil rights issues by the Justice Department. More frequently, it is done through control of programmes and expenditure. Nixon, faced with a Congress whose policy preferences conflicted with his own, sought to outflank the legislature by administrative means.[63] Foremost among his techniques was the refusal to spend funds allocated by Congress for specific programmes.

'Impoundment', as this is called, was not entirely new. There had, traditionally, been four kinds: routine actions taken for the purpose of efficient management where savings did not interfere with the programmes; withholdings that have statutory support; withholdings that depend upon constitutional arguments, especially the Commander-in-Chief clause; and the impoundment of domestic funds as part of executive policy-making.[64] Common sense and the Supreme Court have always acknowledged that a President was the chief executive rather than the chief clerk of the nation and therefore enjoyed some discretion in the handling of public funds. Nixon, however, extended this legitimate discretion to illegitimate extremes in cutting a veritable swathe through congressional appropriations after his resounding electoral victory in 1972. Although it is possible to discover a few previous examples of isolated presidential impoundments for policy purposes, no President attempted to use impoundment to the extent, and with the potentially significant consequences, that Richard Nixon did. Approximately $17.7 billion were effectively impounded, much of it being excised from programmes where the cuts were peculiarly serious. The Defence budget escaped comparatively lightly, while those of Agriculture and Housing and Urban Development were badly mauled.

Since the effects on local government and on individuals were immediate and noticeable, litigation was soon embarked upon. From the beginning, the lower courts took what was, to some observers, a surprisingly tough line, well represented in the following opinion of the Fourth Circuit Court of Appeals:

The power to spend rests primarily with Congress under the Constitution; the executive, on the other hand, has the constitutional duty to execute the law in accordance with the legislative purpose so expressed. When the execu-

63. Richard P. Nathan, *The Plot that Failed: Nixon and the Administrative Presidency*, New York, 1975.
64. Louis Fisher, *Presidential Spending Power*, Princeton, NJ, 1975, p. 148.

tive exercises its responsibility under appropriate legislation in such a manner as to frustrate the Congressional purpose, either by absolute refusal to spend or by a withholding of so substantial an amount of the appropriation as to make impossible the attainment of the legislative goals, the executive trespasses beyond the range of its legal discretion and presents an issue of constitutional dimensions which is obviously open to judicial review.[65]

When the issue was raised before the Supreme Court, the justices unanimously upheld the City of New York's complaint that money authorised under the Federal Water Pollution Control Act of 1972 had to be allocated in full and that Russell Train, the Administrator of the United States Enviromental Protection Agency, had improperly withheld $3 billion of the $5 billion appropriated for the fiscal year 1973 for improvements to municipal sewers and sewer treatment works.[66] Current sewer problems are better instigators of litigation than the potential difficulties inherent in some executive agreements. Congress, as it had done in the case of military involvement, turned to legislation as a method of establishing the rules for impoundment, and in 1974 passed the Impoundment Control Act. This has been broadly effective both in making Presidents defend their failures to spend allotted money and in permitting Presidents a degree of flexibility necessary for sensible and efficient government.[67] The chief executive, it should be said again, is not the chief clerk.

The disputes revolve round the exact line of demarcation between the two poles of leader with inherent executive powers and administrator of legislative policies and priorities. Most Presidents have in recent years attempted to stress the powers that are claimed to be inherently executive, but nobody attempted to do this more than Nixon. Apart from claiming virtually plenary power in foreign affairs and a very expansive reading of the Constitution to legitimise his impoundments, he sought to erect a degree of separation of executive from legislature (in sharp distinction from his readiness to ignore the separate role laid down for the legislature in Article I) which had few earlier parallels. By using 'executive privilege' he tried to limit to the minimum the extent to which the executive branch could be accountable to Congress.

Executive privilege has a long history. Many Presidents have refused to divulge information to Congress when asked to do so, but this refusal was defended for the first 150 years of the Union on the grounds that there are some facts – the names of advisers on

---

65. *Campaign Clean Water Inc.* v. *Train*, 489 F. 2d 492 (1973).
66. *Train* v. *City of New York*, 420 US 35 (1975).
67. Pyle and Pious, *op. cit.*, pp. 224–30.

particular policies, for instance − which rightfully belonged exclusively to the President. Few matters of substance were withheld. The more extravagant doctrine to which Nixon had recourse begins with President Eisenhower.[68] On the same day on which the Supreme Court handed down its famous decision in the case of *Brown* v. *Board of Education of Topeka*, Eisenhower wrote to his Secretary of Defence directing him to tell all his subordinates not to testify about advisory communications during the hearings of a special subcommittee of the Senate Government Operations Committee. Kennedy exercised 'executive privilege' on four occasions, Johnson on two occasions, and Nixon on fifteen occasions during his first term of office alone. The issue, which at this stage was merely a cause of congressional annoyance, became of greater public concern as the Watergate entanglement unfolded in the summer of 1974. The details need not concern us here. What was essentially at issue was the right of the President to withhold from a grand jury some tape-recordings made in the White House which, it was thought, might have a direct bearing on the criminal case being investigated. Nixon maintained that the separation of powers doctrine and the right to executive privilege permitted him alone to decide what information available to the executive branch could be released to another branch. The Court disagreed.

The Supreme Court's unanimous judgement in *Nixon* v. *United States* [69] is significant for two points. First, it reminds us that the ultimate arbiter of the Constitution is the Supreme Court. The separation of powers is a fine phrase, but the United States constitutional system in fact institutes coordinate powers, and no branch of government is entirely free from constraints exercised by another. Precisely where the line is to be drawn when two branches disagree over the extent of one branch's powers is a matter for the Supreme Court. Although the justices have tended to look in a friendly way towards Presidents, they have been ready to exercise their undoubted powers, as in the Steel Seizure case and in various limitations on President Nixon. The second point was this: although Nixon was not granted the right to withhold the tapes from the grand jury, Presidents were generally acknowledged to have a limited degree of executive privilege, the first time this had been authoritatively stated by the Court. It was accepted that the executive branch needed, when considering policy options or negotiating with foreign powers, a degree of privacy beyond the reach of congressional

68. *Study Prepared by the Government and General Research Division of the Library of Congress*, reprinted from *Congressional Record*, H. 2243−6 (28 March 1973) in Berger, *op.cit.*, pp. 373−86.
69. 418 US 683 (1974).

demands. But in the case before the Court, 'the generalised assertion of privilege must yield to the demonstrated, specific need for evidence in a pending criminal trial.' Not for the first time, the Court shied from enunciating an absolute rule, and thus retained for itself discretionary power to decide precisely when executive privilege was constitutionally permissible. It is this calculated determination not to foreclose issues that allows the Constitution the flexibility to evolve as new demands are made upon it.

If the emphasis in this section is heavily on the constraints imposed by the Constitution, it should not obscure the opportunities for the exercise of power offered by that same Constitution. The provision for a State of the Union message, abetted by a fragmented Congress unable or unwilling to provide coherent leadership, has made Presidents become chief legislators; the growth of the executive branch itself and the readiness of Congress to delegate authority has created additional sources of influence; and the right to nominate to a vast range of important and influential posts, although subject to senatorial approval, confers still further power on the chief executive. A shrewd and able President can employ these resources to great advantage; an inept President can make little of them. It is an exaggeration, but a useful one, to hold that the presidency is what a President chooses to make of it, subject to congressional acceptance.

The reach of presidential power may be seen essentially as a function of political forces. But the Constitution, or rather what litigants and the justices of the Supreme Court make of the Constitution, is a constant reminder of the formal limitations on a President's power. Yet the Constitution also provides an opportunity for influence. Presidents who find Congress antagonistic to their goals sometimes use the courts to advance their policy preferences. This was true to some extent in the area of civil rights, where the executive branch was a major litigant using the Constitution to assist in achieving its goals. Moreover, one of the most powerful *amicus curiae* briefs in the case arguing that the courts had jurisdiction in suits challenging the gross inequalities in the size of congressional and state constituencies was written by the Justice Department.[70]

The more normal method by which Presidents influence the meaning of the Constitution is to use the appointing power to alter the ideological balance of the justices and thus precipitate a reinterpretation of the Constitution to their liking. Franklin Roosevelt chose his nominees for the highest Court almost entirely on their

---

70. *Baker* v. *Carr*, 369 US 186 (1962). See also Victor Navasky, *Kennedy Justice*, New York, 1971; and R. Huston (ed.), *Roles of the Attorney-General of the United States*, Washington, DC, 1968.

view of the Constitution's grant of power to the legislature and executive. It is not always easy for Presidents to achieve desired aims, although Roosevelt was notably successful in his fundamental aim; but what he did not realise was that agreement on one issue does not obviate disagreements on others. The Roosevelt Court was one of the most divided in American history.[71] And men once appointed to the Court can become unexpectedly independent and act in ways which horrify their nominators. Richard Nixon, who nominated four men to the Court, also attempted to 'pack the Court'. There is some dispute over the extent of his success, but there is no escaping the fact that a unanimous Court forced him to surrender the most incriminating Watergate tapes and thus hastened his resignation. Presidential power is always a fragile thing, to be carefully cherished in the face of a traditionally competitive Congress and a Supreme Court whose perception of a President's constitutional power is rarely static and often unpredictable.

Conclusions

The stewardship theory of the presidency propounded by Theodore Roosevelt has found fertile soil in which to develop during the twentieth century. There has been a tendency since the 1930s for central government to play a major economic and social role, and the President – because of Congress's inability to provide coherent leadership and the rise of the United States as a world power – has been drawn into the centre of the political stage. The media's increased political significance and its ability to permit Presidents largely to set the political agenda have further enhanced this development. The Constitution as a document has contributed only a little to this aggrandisement. The Constitution as interpreted by the Supreme Court, however, has been flexible enough to permit such changes.[72]

But the Supreme Court does not always speak with a clear voice, and the principle of separation of powers (in reality, the principle of cooperation between analytically separable powers) calls for creative tension. It produces tension because more than one branch of government has some claim to authority in a given area, and it requires creativity because only by voluntary cooperation can the United States political system function effectively at all. By delibe-

---

71. Charles Herman Pritchett, *The Roosevelt Court*, London, New York, 1948.
72. For a short history of the period, see John D. Lees, *The President and the Supreme Court: New Deal to Watergate*, British Association for American Studies, 1980. Generally, consult *Law and Contemporary Problems* (Spring 1976), pp. 3–86, and (Summer 1976), pp. 86–105.

rate choice, the legislature and the executive have only rarely litigated in order to resolve their differences, so the Supreme Court's role in demarcating the precise division of powers has been slight. There have been few direct clashes. And where these might have occurred, as with the Vietnam War, the Court of last resort has chosen not to act. Yet the Court has acted often enough – for example in Humphrey's Executor's case, in the Steel Seizure case, in the White House tapes case, in the impoundment case – to remind Presidents that it can, and will, draw a definite line to limit the reach of executive power.[73] There has been a definitive accretion of power, but the advance has been erratic and discontinuous. Watergate was a constitutional crisis which reminded the American people that they are supposed to live under 'a system of laws, not men' and that claims to inherent powers are suspect. It provided a check to the growth of presidential power; it did not dramatically reverse it.

Because the Constitution and its interpreters – the nine justices of the Supreme Court – do not generally play a major role in defining the bounds of presidential power, the interplay of political forces does so. The reality of relative power (and both legislature and executive are more involved in world and domestic affairs than they were in the 1930s) depends essentially upon the balance between Congress and President, the subject of a later chapter. It has been argued that congressional action in the 1970s 'radically redistributed' the powers of the presidency, especially in the field of foreign affairs.[74] This may be so, although the redistribution does not appear to have been very radical in effect. Clearly, however, such a revolution (if revolution there be) flowed not from alterations to the Constitution or changes in the Supreme Court's understanding of it, but from Congress's deliberate reassertion of its potential. The words of the Constitution were freely used in the hope of adding legitimacy to participants' arguments, but they were not tested in the courts, at least by the major protagonists. The Constitution thus casts its shadow over all of Washington's politics and it is pierced from time to time with startling and far-reaching results. The 1960s remembered Truman's failure to seize the steel mills; the 1970s remembered the expansionary interpretations of the Warren Court; the 1980s remembered how a President fell when the Court denied him privileged access to incriminating tapes; the 1990s will probably remember how a Kenyan student destroyed the legislative veto and thus one of Congress's techniques for checking the executive branch.

73. The Court has been much more active in restraining Congress. Its generally restrictive view of its role *vis-à-vis* the executive branch is more clearly perceived if this relative activism in other areas is remembered.
74. Franck and Weisband, *op. cit.*, p. 3.

2

THE PRESIDENT AND HIS PARTY

John D. Lees

The nature of relations between Presidents and political parties is strongly affected by certain important factors. First, the party role of the President, in particular that of party leader, has been grafted on to the presidency rather than being one of the constitutional obligations or responsibilities of the office. As a result, whether and how this role is performed depends very much on the attitudes of particular Presidents and the particular political situation. Secondly, the presidency was conceived as an office in which qualities of statesmanship and the capacity to unify were considered to be pre-eminent, and these considerations remain important regulators of the behaviour of individual Presidents. Presidents therefore face the dilemma of being unable to ignore the demands of party, yet often believing that acting in a partisan manner and responding to party pressures may be disadvantageous. Thirdly, the framers of the Constitution believed that relations between the President and Congress should consist of checks and balances rather than cooperation or executive leadership, and to this end they divided the powers of the national government between the President and Congress. In practice, however, any President has to try to work with Congress, and as party leader gain the support of as many as possible of the members of Congress of his own party, if he is to induce Congress to adopt many of his political initiatives.

Every President since George Washington has been a member of a political party, and the relationship between political parties and Presidents may be simply summarised as one of reciprocal needs and mutual dependence. In order to become President, an aspirant needs the approval of one or other of the major parties by becoming its nominated candidate, and in office he normally finds it advantageous to maintain a close relationship with members of his party in Congress. A President also needs the continued support of his party if he is to seek and gain re-election. In turn, party success depends in large measure on a capacity to recruit presidential candidates who can win the presidency, as presidential elections have become a central test of party strength. Control of the presidency may also bring rewards to party members in the form of patronage because of the many political appointments or nominations which Presidents

46

can make. Moreover, the growth of executive influence and leadership over public policy helps to satisfy the appetites of those party supporters who seek changes in national policy.

The role of the President as leader of his party more clearly than any other illustrates the changes which have occurred in the original conception of the presidency. The role emerged as a result of changes in the process of electing Presidents and has become an inescapable responsibility. At the beginning of the twentieth century Woodrow Wilson, later to become President himself, summarised the nature of this role as follows: 'He cannot escape being the leader of his party except by incapacity and lack of personal force, because he is at once the choice of the party and of the nation.'[1] Yet the nature of the relationship between President and party may be more readily understood in terms of game theory rather than development theory, both with respect to the problems of gaining election and retaining office and in becoming an effective President. This has been recognised by two distinguished students of the development of the presidency. Richard McCormick, in his study of the origins of presidential politics, concludes that 'by 1844 the presidential game had become the party game . . . Every element of this game was at variance with the republican ideology that had shaped the actions of the Framers when they contrived their process of presidential selection.'[2] Louis Koenig, in assessing Presidents as party leaders, states that success in party affairs 'is a mixture of many things: his own personality, his public popularity, his skill at maneuvring, his intuitive sense. It is a game played not with rules but with a master's instinct for the shifting sources of power.'[3] Equally, it is an area of presidential behaviour in which exchange theory, involving strategies such as transactions, bargaining and coalition-building are likely features.[4] Hence, while there are stable features of this relationship, its precise nature depends on factors such as the existing political situation and the attitudes and perceptions of their responsibilities of particular Presidents. The stable features include the President as candidate for office, as partisan politician needing maximum party support in Congress in order to achieve policy goals, and as leader of a national party organisation.

The significance of the relationship between the President and his

---

1. Woodrow Wilson, *Constitutional Government in the United States*, New York, 1908, p. 67.
2. Richard P. McCormick, *The Presidential Game: The Origins of American Presidential Politics*, New York, 1982, p. 205.
3. Louis W. Koenig, *The Chief Executive*, 3rd edn, New York, 1975, pp. 126–7.
4. For development of this point, see Robert J. Sickels, *Presidential Transactions*, Englewood Cliffs, NJ, 1974.

party is also influenced by changes in the role played by national parties with respect to presidential elections, as links between elected national officials and the electorate, and as a possible bridge between elected officials in the executive and in Congress. Assessing the nature of the relationship in the presidencies from Franklin Roosevelt to Ronald Reagan involves identifying and evaluating evidence relating to particular Presidents and significant new trends or developments. As this study is concerned primarily with an analysis of Presidents as office-holders, less attention will be given to the initial links with party made in order to become President, except where they are of significance in explaining activity while in office. Relations at this pre-presidency stage involve a high degree of bargaining and the cultivation of support within the party at all levels, and may affect the way in which a President tries to lead his party from the White House. For example, President Carter did not establish close links with, or obtain strong support from, Democratic party leaders and elected officials before his election in 1976. They could not prevent him from becoming the presidential candidate but they did not give him enthusiastic support. His subsequent disinclination or inability to strengthen party ties while in office contributed to his ineffective performance as President and possibly to his re-election defeat in 1980. The contrast with Eisenhower is instructive. Despite Eisenhower's unique personal attributes as a candidate and his public reputation as a non-partisan leader, it is evident that he tempered his political attitudes in a serious effort to improve electoral support for the Republican party and its candidates as well as strengthening its internal organisation.[5]

The Emergence of the President as Party Leader

The major areas of activity as party leader nowadays include relations with the national party committee and its chairman, relations with party leaders and members in Congress, campaigning for party candidates at elections, and rewarding party supporters by appointing them to positions in the federal government and judiciary. Participation in party fund-raising is also expected, and if a President intends to seek re-election there is much that must be done to help ensure renomination.

While the party role for the President is not a fixed one, the

5. For examples, see Fred I. Greenstein, *The Hidden Hand Presidency: Eisenhower as Leader*, New York, 1982, pp. 50–4; also Cornelius P. Cotter, 'Eisenhower as Party Leader', *Political Science Quarterly*, Summer 1983, pp. 255–83.

essential features of that role had been established well before Franklin Roosevelt assumed the office. As early as the presidency of Thomas Jefferson, the emergence of party organisations to compete for the presidency began to change the nature of the office and demonstrated the potential value of the authoritative exercise of party leadership in strengthening executive influence on policy issues. Jefferson obtained the support of state and local party organisations and used the party as an instrument of majority rule, working with and through his party supporters in Congress. He employed patronage to obtain cooperation from legislators and ensure loyalty to his policies within the executive. He demonstrated that party leadership by the President could be a source of strength for the chief executive. His immediate successors did not follow his example, but the election of Andrew Jackson in 1828 led to a resurrection and strengthening of the party leadership role. Jackson used his power of appointment and removal in a partisan manner in order to strengthen his control over Congress and over his administration. He built up support for himself and his party at the state and local levels and welded together an effective national party organisation.

The establishment of the national party conventions as the vehicle for the selection of presidential and vice-presidential candidates also facilitated the development of the President as party leader. Jackson was able to mould the Democratic party in his own image and control party policies, and in 1836 was able to dominate the party convention and obtain the presidential nomination for Van Buren. Jackson demonstrated how the office of President could be a powerful party leadership position as well as an instrument for achieving popular control over governmental policy. For a variety of reasons, his successors did not or could not develop the role of party leader.

The Democratic party established its first national committee in 1848, and the new Republican party which emerged in 1854 set up the predecessor of the Republican National Committee at its first national convention in 1856. Abraham Lincoln's election in 1860 as the first Republican President could have led to the revitalisation of presidential party leadership, but the threat of the dissolution of the Union forced him into the role of non-partisan statesman. Following the Civil War, control and initiative in shaping national party policies shifted to congressional party leaders until the presidencies of Grover Cleveland, William McKinley and Theodore Roosevelt. The last-named in particular demonstrated the capacity of the chief executive to provide party leadership, prompting Woodrow Wilson to make his forceful statement of the President's obligation to act as party leader and to give expression to this later when he became President in 1913. Wilson provided effective political leadership of Congress in his first term and used patronage to further party and personal goals. Yet he was never able to fashion the state and local organisations of the Democratic party into an effective political organisation or build a strong national party in Washington, despite his emphasis both as political scientist and as politician on the importance of the role of party. In 1920 his party suffered one of its heaviest defeats.

There was little evidence of party leadership by the Republican Presidents in the 1920s, but the election of Franklin Roosevelt in 1932 brought to the White House a man who many observers believe was the most powerful of the modern Presidents and 'the most assertive as party leader'.[6] Renominated three times by his party and building on his personal electoral support, Roosevelt attempted a drastic renovation of his party. By the end of his long presidency, his party had become the majority party in the country, controlling Congress if not the presidency almost without exception through the period up to the election of Ronald Reagan. Apart from a two-year period in the Truman presidency (1947–9) and at the beginning of the Eisenhower administration (1953–5), the Republican party has remained the minority party in both houses of Congress, although in 1980 it did succeed in gaining a majority in the Senate. This phenomenon has had important implications for Republican Presidents in dealing with Congress, just as the Roosevelt presidency had a major influence on the nature of the modern presidency and on how Presidents since his time have acted with respect to partisan leadership.[7]

By the 1930s, then, the parameters of the relations between Presidents and their parties could be summarised as follows: There had developed a clear and important electoral connection in which party became the vehicle through which individuals reached the White House. The President in turn could use his power of appointment to sustain and strengthen loyalty among party members and obtain support for policies from fellow party members in Congress. As party leader he could also appeal for support for policy initiatives through his congressional party leaders, seek to influence the electoral fortunes of other members of the party, and strengthen overall party organisation by working closely with the party in the country as represented by the national party committee and its

6. Koenig, *op. cit.*, p. 131.
7. For elaboration of this point, see William E. Leuchtenburg, *In the Shadow of FDR: From Harry Truman to Ronald Reagan*, Ithaca, NY, 1983.

national chairman. However, it is also evident that there was no guarantee that every President would wish to assume all or any of these party responsibilities or that the assumption of such responsibilities would be successful or would necessarily contribute to his effectiveness as President. If this was the case when Franklin Roosevelt was President, it is no less likely to be so for those who succeed Ronald Reagan.

Presidents, Partisanship and Conditioning Factors

In assessing the performance of Presidents from Franklin Roosevelt to Ronald Reagan as party leaders, it is necessary to identify several factors which condition presidential decisions on how to play the party game. It is significant that partisan activity is only one of several strategies which Presidents may employ in seeking to achieve political objectives.

The President is the titular leader of his party, yet existing structures and relationships within the national political parties are anti-presidential. Party members have some incentive to work with and support their leader, yet the President cannot control members of his party in Congress because he is institutionally and electorally separated from them, and there are no national party mechanisms to bind the congressional party to him. Moreover, even if a President can establish a good relationship with his party leaders in the House and Senate, they cannot guarantee the full support of the congressional party in getting his policy initiatives approved by Congress. This means that there are few issues on which a President does not need some support from members of the opposition party. This has been a particular problem for the four Republican Presidents since the 1930s, for only Eisenhower enjoyed a Congress with Republican majorities in both the House and Senate, and that for only the first two of his eight years in the White House.

Some Presidents find the role of partisan leader incompatible with their responsibilities and their political instincts, Jimmy Carter being the best example among recent Presidents.[8] Equally, Presidents find that they have only limited control over their party organisations. They have limited influence over the selection of party candidates for Congress or the selection of party leaders in Congress. They can determine who will be the national committee chairman, but have

8. See the discussion of Carter in Charles O. Jones, 'Presidential Negotiation with Congress', in Anthony King (ed.), *Both Ends of the Avenue: The Presidency, the Executive Branch and Congress in the 1980s*, Washington, DC, 1983, pp. 118–23.

limited influence on the way the chairman and the national committee try to control the party in the country, given the autonomy enjoyed by state parties. This autonomy may be weakened by the use of presidential patronage, either by appointing party nominees to positions in the federal government or channelling government grants and contracts to particular states or congressional districts. Presidents, however, have to consider other factors as well as party obligations in using their patronage powers. They may have to satisfy demands from other potential political supporters of their policies.

These are some of the permanent influences conditioning the partisan role of Presidents since 1932. After looking at the behaviour of particular Presidents, it may be possible to assess how they, and other new factors which have emerged in the period, have affected the relationship of the President in office with his party. As the nature of relations between Presidents and Congress is the subject of another chapter, this important political relationship will be considered only in terms of the partisanship dimension.

Given what has been said already it should not be too surprising to find that, in most analyses of the modern presidency, little attention is given to the partisan relationship when assessing the effectiveness or otherwise of Presidents. In order to put the role of partisanship into perspective, we may note the subjective assessment of Austin Ranney.[9] Ranney suggests that in ranking twentieth-century Presidents (excluding Reagan) on a scale of partisanship ranging from the least partisan (0) to the most partisan (100), it is possible to imagine that the only Presidents who would score close to 50 would be Woodrow Wilson and Franklin Roosevelt. Among the lowest rankings would be Jimmy Carter. In short, the role of partisan executive or party leader is not an easy one to perform. If a President is too visibly or actively partisan, he risks criticism for using his office improperly. Yet if he neglects or ignores party or partisan obligations, he may lose the confidence and support of his party in Congress and in the country. If a President maintains a high level of personal popularity, this may help to override party disquiet; if he does not, then he risks being abandoned not only by the nation but also by his party.

In considering the record of Presidents since 1932, we will review in turn individual Presidents in the period up to the election of John

9. Austin Ranney, 'The President and His Party', in King, *ibid.*, pp. 148–9. For a similar evaluation with particular respect to relations with the party in Congress, see Randall B. Ripley, *Congress: Process and Policy*, 2nd edn, New York, 1978, pp. 308–23.

Kennedy in 1960, and then from Kennedy through to Reagan. This is not to suggest that 1960 marks a significant watershed in terms of presidential relations with party. Rather it is relevant in that since 1960 only two Presidents have succeeded in being re-elected, and (at time of writing) no President has served two full terms, in marked contrast to the period from 1932. Also, many of the changes in presidential elections, presidential responsibilities and party procedures, some of which were evident before 1960 or were a consequence of changes in the executive as a result of the presidency of Franklin Roosevelt, are more clearly identifiable after 1960.

Franklin Roosevelt and the Democratic Party

When Roosevelt accepted the presidential nomination of the Democratic party in 1932, he had already learned much about the weaknesses of his party at all levels and something of the delicate relationships of party and faction to different types of election. He had seen his cousin Theodore Roosevelt and his mentor Woodrow Wilson dominate their national parties yet fail to unite or strengthen them. As vice-presidential candidate in 1920 he experienced at first hand the deficiencies within the Democratic party organisation which contributed to its massive defeat. After the subsequent defeat in 1924 Roosevelt sought without success to reform the finances and organisation of his party. His narrow victory in the election for Governor of New York in 1928 enabled him to obtain valuable executive experience and also to lead his state party and put loyal supporters such as Ed Flynn and James Farley into state party leadership positions. In 1932, by the time his party supporters had bargained and brokered the presidential nomination for him on the fourth ballot, he recognised the obvious necessity for a party victory in the November election. At the same time, he recognised that it would be achieved largely by his own personal organisation and his particular personal appeal.

The election proved to be a personal *and* a party victory. Roosevelt won easily, while the Democrats gained comfortable majorities in the House and Senate. His close adviser James Farley was made chairman of the Democratic national committee, where he served until 1940, to be succeeded by Ed Flynn. However, Roosevelt's political successes during much of his first term were achieved by acting as a non-partisan head of the nation, rather than by emphasising his position as Democratic party leader. While he supported Democratic candidates in the 1934 congressional elections, he did not intervene in a totally partisan manner. The outcome was that his party increased its majorities in the House and Senate.

Roosevelt was working to build an electoral coalition broader than the existing Democratic coalition, which might in due course coalesce to become a permanent party majority in the electorate. He led Congress by the use of adroit and highly personal appeals and by exploiting the national economic crisis and winning the support of conservative committee leaders for New Deal programmes while not particularly building up support among new rank-and-file Democrats. He made little use of the Democratic Steering Committee, which was the formal link between the President and his party in the House of Representatives. These tactics were successful in Roosevelt's first term, although there was evidence in the 1935 session of Congress, during the consideration and passage of the Second New Deal legislation, of some resistance and resentment within his party in Congress.

The 1936 landslide election victory of Roosevelt, and its coat-tail effect in giving the Democrats massive majorities in the House and Senate, together with major gains in state and local elections, were achieved as much by the personal appeal of Roosevelt and the New Deal policies as by any coherent party campaign. Moreover, the party platform in 1936 was one which Democratic members of Congress played little part in drafting. The fragility of the attempt to fashion a new majority party coalition and a new progressive Democratic party through essentially personal appeals became evident in Roosevelt's second term when he sought party support for his Supreme Court reorganisation in 1937 and executive branch reorganisation in 1938. Defeat over these measures, and in particular the defections of senior conservative Democrats, led Roosevelt to intervene directly in the Democratic primaries in 1938 as well as the subsequent congressional elections in an attempt to reassert his position as party leader and make the party the instrument of a popular majority.[10]

The result was failure. Most of the Democrats Roosevelt opposed in the primaries won, and the Republicans made significant gains in the House and Senate elections and in elections for governor. In 1939 the international situation prompted Roosevelt to return to his earlier role of President of the people and later to emphasise his role as Commander-in-Chief. Not until 1944 did Roosevelt make a further effort to effect a clear realignment of his party. In the first congressional elections after his death the Republicans recaptured control of both the House and Senate.

10. For detailed analyses of these events, see James M. Burns, *Roosevelt: The Lion and the Fox*, New York, London, 1956, esp. pp. 358–80; and Koenig, *op. cit.*, pp. 131–5.

This summary of Roosevelt's relations with his party illustrates some of the dilemmas that have affected the behaviour of many of his successors. While in the course of time his electoral success transformed the Democratic party into the new majority party in the country, and his supporters effected significant changes in the balance of influence in the national party committee, Roosevelt did not succeed in creating a unified party coalition in Congress committed to a coherent programme.

The experience of Roosevelt illustrates the problems facing any President, however popular, who seeks to act as party leader. There are particular difficulties if he attempts to be active in party affairs at all levels – actively campaigning for the party ticket at elections, working closely with party leaders in Congress to get party programmes accepted, and seeking to leave his party in the best possible condition to win elections after he has left the White House. These problems are the result of weaknesses in the nature of national political parties in the United States, the most significant being the realities which follow from a federal system and the formal separation of the executive and the legislature. National parties, as is often noted, are loose coalitions of state parties, with distinct presidential and congressional party organisations. Writing at the end of the 1950s, Clinton Rossiter summarised the problem for Presidents as follows: 'Franklin Roosevelt, supposedly the most dominant of party leaders, felt the drag of his own party through most of his years in office . . . The party that makes him also brakes him: this is the lot, not entirely unhappy, of the modern President.'[11]

While Roosevelt has often been portrayed as a great party leader, such a judgement is inevitably a relative one. James MacGregor Burns indicates the difficulty, even for as skilful a President as Roosevelt, of being a successful President *and* a successful party leader. The latter would have required a comprehensive, long-term effort to reform state party organisations. Burns summarises the situation as follows:

Perhaps he saw the difficulties better than some of his advisers, or perhaps he missed a great opportunity. In any event, Roosevelt was the prisoner of the concessions he had made to the regulars – especially Southern Democrats – in gaining the nomination. He had recognized and hence strengthened conservative Democrats in Congress who had gone along with his program . . . As a pragmatic politician eager above all to win office, he was reluctant to divert the political effort necessary to improve the disheveled party organization. The personal traits that made Roosevelt a

11. Clinton Rossiter, *The American Presidency*, New York, 1960, p. 64.

brilliant tactician ... were not the best traits for hard, long-range, purposeful building of a strong party behind a coherent political program.[12]

The experiences of Roosevelt also highlight a development which came to affect later Presidents. This is the tension created by the emergence of the institutionalised presidency. It began with the 'brains trust' formed during Roosevelt's governorship of New York, who became his inner circle of advisers after his inauguration as President. Almost from the outset this group had an uneasy relationship with James Farley and other Democratic politicians in Congress and at the state and local level. Relations became strained at the beginning of the second term when Farley attacked the White House aides as zealots who mocked party loyalty and were devoted only to Roosevelt. The cleavage was exacerbated with the struggle over the Supreme Court legislation in 1937 and the ill-fated efforts of Roosevelt to purge congressional and senatorial candidates in 1938. Farley and the party professionals opposed the latter, seeing it as an attempt by Roosevelt to create a personal party and to shape the Democratic party in Congress and the country into a mould set by a White House faction. By the 1940 election, while the public issue was that of the legitimacy of a third term, the underlying issue was the battle for control of the party between a White House group headed by Harry Hopkins and the party professionals led by Farley. At issue was whether the presidential party would succeed in reshaping the Democratic party organisation.

The issue emerged again in 1944 and reflected the tensions that had developed between the presidential party, the party in Congress and the party at the state and local levels. This tension was not resolved by Roosevelt's successor, Harry Truman, who in 1948 found himself supported principally by presidential advisers. These advisers fashioned a programme on which he won nomination and election, while other elements of the party, including leading party professionals, were prepared to abandon him and seek out a vote-getter such as Eisenhower.[13]

12. James M. Burns, *The Deadlock of Democracy: Four-Party Politics in America*, Englewood Cliffs, NJ, 1963, p. 173.
13. For extended discussion of the implications of the institutionalised presidency for the party leadership role, see Lester Seligman, 'The Presidential Office and the President as Party Leader' (with a postscript on the Kennedy-Nixon era), in Jeff Fishel (ed.), *Parties and Elections in an Anti-Party Age*, Bloomington, 1978, pp. 295–302.

Harry Truman — the Accidental Partisan

Truman became President in part because he was a loyal partisan Democrat, and this loyalty and partisanship influenced his actions as President. A product of the Pendergast political machine in Kansas City, he was throughout his political career a party man who 'accepted the logic of patronage while rejecting the necessity of graft'.[14] He was both a Roosevelt Democrat and a party loyalist, a useful combination in 1944 for preventing factional conflict within the party when Roosevelt abandoned Henry Wallace and sought a new candidate for the vice-presidential nomination. On the death of Roosevelt in 1945, Truman became President at the age of 60. He inherited a presidency which had been changed by both the personal achievements of Roosevelt and the realities of the new responsibilities placed on the United States by the Second World War. The presidency was to change again during Truman's incumbency with the political realities of the cold war. At home there were economic problems to resolve in the face of an often hostile Congress, where in 1947 and 1948 the Republicans were in the majority for the first time since the 1920s.

Truman was conscious of his role as party leader and of his inheritance from Roosevelt of the New Deal, internationalism and a new political coalition. However, he saw these as an inheritance to maintain rather than expand by dint of any distinctive personal innovations. His job as President 'was to make decisions and take initiatives; those were the duties of the boss-and-spokesman.'[15] To this extent he saw his job as party leader as a necessary responsibility, but not one in which he could or should exert any special personal influence.

Truman was more a partisan President than a party leader in the sense of actively encouraging and developing party organisation, soliciting public support for party candidates or working closely with party leaders in Congress. As a former Senator, he did not feel that the President should try to influence too directly the decisions on legislation made by his fellow Democrats in Congress. His strategy in dealing with Congress was also affected by the situation he faced with the 80th Congress, where he encountered opposition from both the Republican majority and conservative Democrats.[16]

14. Robert J. Williams, 'Harry S. Truman and the American Presidency', *Journal of American Studies*, Dec. 1979, p. 394.
15. Richard E. Neustadt, *Presidential Power: The Politics of Leadership from FDR to Carter*, New York, 1980, p. 243.
16. See Susan M. Hartman, *Truman and the 80th Congress*, Columbia, Missouri, 1971.

In this situation he preferred initially to present legislation, attack the opposition in Congress and use his veto power rather than work through intense liaison in order to obtain legislative support. Hartman observes that 'the Administration cooperated poorly with congressional Democrats. There was no consultation before the presentation of Truman's tax and civil rights bills in 1948.'[17] Other bills either were not available for sympathetic congressmen or reached them too late. Not until April 1948 did Truman begin to work closely with his party leaders in Congress.

Part of the difficulty lay in the fact that on major foreign policy issues such as the European Recovery Act (the Marshall Plan) bipartisan support was vital, while on domestic issues bipartisan support was unobtainable and partisan support was insufficient. Only during and after the special session of Congress called by Truman when he was nominated at the 1948 Democratic convention did he try to rebuild the links between his administration, Democrats in Congress and the Democratic national committee. Truman's partisan attacks on the 'do-nothing' 80th Congress, in which he blamed the Republicans for its failings and informed the electorate of the Democratic legislative programme, were important factors in his narrow electoral victory in 1948. The Democrats made large gains in the House and Senate elections, recapturing control of Congress, but many Democrats obtained more votes than Truman and did not feel that they owed very much to their party leader.

Truman's campaign strategy in 1948 was devised and implemented primarily by a key White House aide, Clark Clifford. It was influenced by the candidacies of Henry Wallace and Strom Thurmond, representing defections by the radical and Southern conservative wings of the Democratic coalition. While at one level the result could be interpreted as a major victory for the Democratic party, it was not a united party or one which had great faith in, or loyalty to, its leader in the White House.

Truman did not help his poor standing as party leader among significant groups of rank-and-file Democrats by choosing mediocre national committee chairmen.[18] Robert E. Hannegan was a product of the St Louis machine and an indifferent head of the national committee. His successor in 1947, J. Howard McGrath, while playing an important part in the 1948 campaign, used patronage to reward Truman supporters but did little to bring dissident Southern Democrats back into the party. He was succeeded in 1949 by William

17. Hartman, *ibid.*, p. 212.
18. For 'profiles' of these chairmen, see Jules Abels, *The Truman Scandals*, Chicago, 1956, Ch. 5.

Boyle, another product of the Pendergast machine and a close friend of Truman. Boyle became involved in one of several conflict-of-interest scandals which plagued the Truman administration, and resigned in 1951. His replacement, Frank McKinney, was an Indiana political boss who made little impact. None of these appointees did very much to complement Truman in building and improving relations within the party. They had similar attitudes and political backgrounds to Truman, seeing party loyalty as something to be expected and rewarded rather than created.

Truman, in short, was a natural partisan politician who did not use his position as President or his personal influence to provide party leadership. He expected fellow Democrats to be loyal to the party and to him as party leader. Just as his loyalty to personal friends whom he appointed to positions in government caused him embarrassment when they became the subjects of scandals and investigations and affected his leadership in domestic affairs, so too his unwillingness to exploit his position as President to lead his party was a contributory factor in the failure of the Democrats to retain control of the presidency and Congress in 1952.

Dwight Eisenhower — the 'Hidden Hand' Party Leader

To many observers Eisenhower was the epitome of the non-partisan or bipartisan President. Koenig, for example, has suggested that Eisenhower 'eschewed partisan conflict . . . and avoided it if possible as activity that was troublesome and petty' and 'never wore his hat as party chieftain gladly'.[19] His close aide, Sherman Adams, has noted Eisenhower's 'distaste for partisan politics' and his 'lack of any firm or militant command over the Republican party. He preferred to leave the operation of the political machinery to the professionals.'[20]

Recent studies, based on analyses of personal and confidential sources which document Eisenhower's daily activities, challenge this conventional interpretation and provide strong evidence that Eisenhower was 'the most constructive and consistent intervener in party organizational matters of any president after Franklin D. Roosevelt'.[21] This new evidence suggests that, far from being

19. Koenig, *op. cit.*, pp. 135, 137.
20. Sherman Adams, *First-Hand Report: The Story of the Eisenhower Administration*, New York, 1961, p. 25.
21. Cotter, *op. cit.*, p. 256. See also Fred I. Greenstein, 'Eisenhower as an Activist President: A Look at New Evidence', *Political Science Quarterly*, Winter 1979–80, pp. 575–99.

'allergic to the responsibilities of party leadership',[22] Eisenhower deliberately sought to exert considerable influence over the Republican party, accepted a party leadership role and had a coherent theory of how the party should relate to the presidency.

There are many sound reasons why Eisenhower might have eschewed the role of party leader. Before gaining the Republican presidential nomination in 1952, he had no record of party involvement and his successful election campaign relied heavily on the non-party work of the Citizens for Eisenhower movement. For six of his eight years as President the House and Senate were controlled by the Democrats, making it sensible tactically to avoid a partisan appeal to Congress. Eisenhower also had the unquestioned advantage of being a war hero, and this, plus the high level of personal popularity he enjoyed throughout his presidency, made the role of chief of state a more rational one to occupy when seeking political goals rather than any partisan or party leadership activity. Moreover, the 1952 presidential election was a transitional one in which the beginnings of a decline in the influence of party can be discerned. It also marked the beginning of televised national conventions and election campaigns, the emergence of citizen groups to aid both candidates in their election campaigns, and a general shift towards the popularisation of the selection of presidential candidates. Eisenhower himself had captured the party nomination at the expense of the favourite of the party loyalists, 'Mr Republican' Robert A. Taft. Finally, voting studies were later to reveal the consolidation of an identification with the Democratic party among a majority of the electorate in the 1950s.

Not surprisingly, therefore, Eisenhower's performance as party leader and his playing of the party game was often latent and covert and done primarily out of a sense of duty to his 'adopted' party. It consisted of a persistent effort to improve the electoral support and organisational strength of the party and give it a more progressive and internationalist cast. This was seen as more important than seeking major changes in public policy or using personal popularity to achieve Eisenhower's personal political goals. To further this end, Eisenhower was prepared to be a pragmatic party politician. He used patronage to satisfy the Taft party regulars and at the same time tried to put his 'citizen' activists into leading positions in Republican national and state party organisations. He sought to strengthen the party in the South — where it was very weak — while also improving the national party organisation.

In his first term he appointed Arthur Summerfield and Leonard

22. George H. Mayer, *The Republican Party 1854–1964*, New York, 1964, p. 496.

Hall to chair the national committee, both men with reputations as talented political organisers. A high percentage of his sub-cabinet appointments and his staff in the White House Office were persons with records of active party and campaign service. His appointees as national committee chairmen in his second term, Meade Alcorn and Senator Thruston Morton, were men with extensive loyal service on the national committee and in the congressional party respectively. Eisenhower knew his party chairmen well and saw them often, involving them in Cabinet and other White House meetings.[23]

Eisenhower's military training and experience gave him an instinctive preference for order and structure in making decisions. The party was seen as an organisation for pursuing the goals of his administration and as a vehicle for garnering votes in Congress and mobilising electoral support in the states. The Republican national organisation had developed during the period of Democratic control of the executive and Congress from a skeletal to a well-staffed unit, and the Eisenhower victory provided the first opportunity to adapt to the requirements of a Republican President.

Despite his public stance of disliking the patronage aspects of party politics, Eisenhower privately encouraged the use of patronage to weld together the disparate elements of the party he sought to lead – his citizen activist supporters; Republican organisations at the national, state and local levels; political executives; and Republicans in Congress. The national party headquarters came to play an important role with respect to patronage, although relations with the White House staff were not always smooth.[24] On occasions Eisenhower was directly involved in recruiting individuals to the Republican national committee staff. His style of intervention differed from that of his immediate Democratic predecessors, but it was as intensive. Unlike Roosevelt, he did not have close associations with national committee staff, nor did he emulate Truman and place long-term political associates on the staff. He did, however, try to get his citizen activist supporters on the national committee, and he saw the job of chairman of the national committee as a full-time responsibility for someone who should be in full control of the national party organisation.

Eisenhower was willing to use the prestige of the White House to further the needs of party. Members of the national committee were invited to his informal but regular 'stag dinners' for business and

23. Cotter, *op. cit.*, Table 1, p. 263.
24. For an example of efforts by the White House staff to make department and agency positions available to loyal Republicans, see Arthur Maass, *Congress and the Common Good*, New York, 1983, p. 178.

party leaders,[25] the most formal manifestation of Eisenhower's less visible partisan activities. He received many party delegations at the White House and made at least one visit to the national committee headquarters. He also sought national committee help with congressional liaison. He took an interest in party finance and used his personal influence to set up fund-raising organisations for specific campaigns, most notably Nixon's presidential campaign in 1960. He also assumed that he would be involved in the off-year congressional election campaigns. He campaigned extensively in 1954, thereby perhaps helping to avert a predicted Democratic landslide, but not preventing the Democrats from regaining control of the House and Senate. In 1956 the national committee was the central organiser of his successful re-election campaign, and he took a strong partisan line when campaigning in 1958 in an unsuccessful effort to avert heavy Democratic congressional gains. These losses prompted Eisenhower to request the national chairman to set up a committee to define the policy goals of the Republican party, and the resulting committee chaired by Charles Percy got useful media attention in 1959.[26] Eisenhower's concern for the image of the Republican party continued after he ceased to be President. In 1962 he initiated the National Republican Citizens Committee.

Eisenhower also encouraged Leonard Hall to work with state party organisations to promote support for the Republican administration. He was especially concerned to use patronage to improve party organisations in the Southern states. By 1957 the national committee had established a Southern Division to handle all patronage to state parties in the South. Ironically, this and other activities by Eisenhower tended to strengthen the ranks of conservative elements who regained control of the party in 1964.

Eisenhower also used the Cabinet for discussion of party business, especially concerning relations with Republicans in Congress, and he met weekly with Republican congressional party leaders. These meetings often included the formal leadership, other leaders, legislative liaison aides and appropriate Cabinet members. Eisenhower consulted with Senate Majority Leader Taft regularly and insisted that he be free to enter the Oval Office unannounced. His relations with Taft's successor William F. Knowland were less harmonious, but he established close links with Everett Dirksen when he became leader of the Senate Republicans. In the House he maintained an

---

25. Dwight D. Eisenhower, *Mandate for Change, 1953–1956*, Garden City, NY, 1963, pp. 264–5; and Greenstein, *The Hidden Hand Presidency*, pp. 149–50.
26. Cornelius P. Cotter and Bernard C. Hennessy, *Politics Without Power: The National Party Committees*, New York, 1964, pp. 195–204.

informal working relationship with Charles Halleck as well as the aged Republican leader Joseph Martin. He tried to educate Republicans in Congress, unused to a President of their own party, on how to work together constructively.[27]

All these activities were part of Eisenhower's continuous efforts to 'broaden, unify, strengthen, and modify the Republican party, notwithstanding his simultaneous efforts to convey the impression of nonpartisanship'.[28] He was President during a period of important changes in the nature of presidential elections and party influence in elections. Visible partisanship was eschewed by Eisenhower because it might interfere with his attempts to get the necessary bipartisan support in Congress.[29] Efforts directed at strengthening the influence of moderate or centrist groups within the party, if made too overtly, might have provoked greater factional conflict. Eisenhower also believed that he should be seen as representing the entire American population, not just one party, yet his concern to improve the electoral and organisational strength of the Republican party was a genuine one. The hidden rationale for not publicising his party activity was a distinguishing feature of Eisenhower's style of presidential activism.

President and Party after 1960

From 1933 to 1960 three Presidents presided over the affairs of the nation in distinctive ways, and relations with their parties provided more contrasts than continuities. Roosevelt was an active party leader in almost all respects, yet not a totally successful one. Truman was an aggressive partisan but an ineffectual party leader. Eisenhower was publicly a non-partisan leader who did much covertly to help strengthen and unify his party in government and in the country. The election in 1960 of Democrat John Kennedy marked the beginning of a period in which the disincentives of overt party leadership by Presidents became greater as party loyalty among voters began to decline, as party structures became even more fragmented, as Presidents needed to reach out beyond the confines of party in order to create electoral and governing majorities, and as the ever-present tensions between partisan demands and presidential responsibilities increased. The factors which may have diminished

27. Greenstein, *The Hidden Hand Presidency*, pp. 78, 104.
28. Greenstein, 'Eisenhower as an Activist President', p. 579.
29. For a study of Eisenhower's relations with Congress in 1953–4, when there were Republican majorities, see Gary Reichard, *The Reaffirmation of Republicanism: Eisenhower and the Eighty-Third Congress*, Knoxville, Tenn., 1975.

John D. Lees

the utility of the constructive use of party structures and vigorous party leadership may be summarised as: the decline in party identification and party voting in the electorate,[30] the consequences of a period of reform of party procedures for selecting presidential candidates (especially in the Democratic party),[31] and the decentralising of power and influence within Congress.

Since 1960 there have also been significant changes in the position of the President in office. The first decade saw the development of what James MacGregor Burns called 'presidential government' and Arthur Schlesinger termed the 'imperial presidency'.[32] This was followed by the decline of presidential power in the 1970s in the wake of the Vietnam War and the Watergate scandals. Also during this period the increased importance of television and its 'exploitation' by Presidents, the increased 'independence' of Presidents as reflected in the growth in size and responsibilities of the White House Office, and changes in the nature of election campaigns all served as potential disincentives to close links between Presidents and their parties. Yet the party game remained a factor prompting some degree of party activity, for Republican no less than Democratic Presidents. As the evidence relating to Eisenhower suggests, there seems to be no significant distinction in this between Republican and Democratic Presidents. The former have been as conscious of party as their Democratic counterparts in the period since 1960.[33] These examples suggest that long-term strategic factors continue to influence the nature of the interaction between Presidents and their parties.

John Kennedy — Partisan Party Leader

John F. Kennedy's abbreviated tenure as President was characterised by a combination of partisan and party leadership. This was a consequence of several factors, both personal and situational. Kennedy was a member of a highly politicised family, and his

30. William J. Crotty and Gary C. Jacobson, *American Parties in Decline*, Boston, 1980.
31. See in particular Nelson W. Polsby, *Consequences of Party Reform* (New York: Oxford University Press, 1983); and the chapters by Austin Ranney, Fred Greenstein and Samuel C. Patterson in Anthony King (ed.), *The New American Political System*, Washington, DC, 1978.
32. James M. Burns, *Presidential Government: Crucible of Leadership*, Boston, 1965; Arthur M. Schlesinger, Jr., *The Imperial Presidency*, Boston, London, 1974.
33. For the development of this and other arguments, see Roger G. Brown and David M. Welborn, 'Presidents and Their Parties: Performance and Prospects', *Presidential Studies Quarterly*, Summer 1982, pp. 302–16.

political career was based on the Irish-Catholic Democratic organisation in Boston which had, especially since the party realignment of the 1930s, come to dominate Massachusetts politics. He became a senator largely as a result of this party strength, though he was not a highly partisan member of the Senate. His family background, however, was one which emphasised loyalty and activity. This combination of family and political environment was evident in the planning of his strategy to gain the Democratic presidential nomination, which began with a trial run for the vice-presidential nomination in 1956. He used the financial and other resources of his family to build a personal organisation which permitted him to campaign effectively within his party for the nomination. His youth and energy, his ethnic and religious roots in the urban northeastern wing of the party, and his ability to win the support of Democratic organisations in most of the larger cities and states helped him to gain the nomination. His capacity to weld his personal organisation to that of the party in turn became an important factor in his narrow election victory in 1960, despite the possible handicap of being a Catholic.

Kennedy's recognition of the importance of sustaining the Democratic party organisation in the country is reflected in his choice of John Bailey as national chairman after his inauguration. Bailey was not the archetypal party boss but a professional party organiser. His experience and talents were directed at the mechanics of party organisation, the development and maintenance of electoral machinery, and the inevitable bargaining with different party groups. He was never a close friend of Kennedy, but he was a member of the group which planned the 1960 campaign, many of whom became key advisers in the Kennedy White House. He had done much to consolidate the support of the big-city Democratic organisations in 1960, and he was now useful in smoothing over the difficulties which emerged between the so-called 'Irish Mafia' in the White House and the party in the country and in Congress. This was of particular importance with respect to patronage and presidential appointments, which now constituted a much more complex task than that undertaken for Roosevelt by James Farley. Bailey also worked hard to strengthen the central control of the national committee and improve its capacity to help Democratic congressional candidates in fund-raising and campaign organisation. In 1962 these endeavours helped to keep down party losses in the House elections and to gain some seats in the Senate.[34] However, as the Kennedy

---

34. Joseph I. Lieberman, *The Power Broker: A Biography of John M. Bailey, Modern Political Boss*, Boston, 1966, esp. Chs 15 and 16; also Stan Opotowsky, *The Kennedy Government*, New York, London, 1961, Ch. 17.

administration settled down, more and more party liaison and patronage decisions were effected by members of the White House staff rather than the national committee.[35] During the Kennedy presidency close to 600 appointments were made, 70 per cent of which went to Democrats.

Throughout his presidency Kennedy voiced his loyalty and commitment to the Democratic party and the idea of partisanship. This was reflected in his approach to Congress. He was aware of the reality of opposition to many of his policy goals, such as civil rights legislation, among senior Southern Democrats. He dealt with this by tactics such as the successful effort to change the size of the House Rules Committee to make it less independent of the House Democratic leadership.[36] Kennedy's relatively modest record of legislative success is in part attributable to his decision to employ a long-term strategy of not modifying legislative demands in order to obtain bipartisan support.

Kennedy intervened in a partisan manner in the 1962 congressional elections and achieved the best mid-term result for the President's party since 1934, and better than any President since. He also made pointed interventions in party affairs, using the Democratic national committee to influence the activities of state and local parties in the big industrial states which had been so crucial in his 1960 victory and would have been again in 1964.[37] This desire to make the Democratic party a more effective national organisation is evidenced by his numerous appearances at fund-raising gatherings (eight in 1961) for the national party. He also tried, against the opposition of some congressional Democrats, to centralise party fund-raising in the national committee and to use such funds to help candidates who were committed to the party programme.[38] Moreover, Theodore Sorenson indicates that shortly before his assassination Kennedy supported efforts to reform party convention rules and give greater delegate representation to states where the Democratic party was strong.[39]

Kennedy's partisanship and his serious efforts to lead his party obscured the development of certain trends. These related to his nomination and election and his expansion of the White House staff and formal liaison links with Congress. Such trends might

35. Cotter and Hennessy, *op. cit.*, pp. 141–3.
36. Douglas M. Fox and Charles P. Clapp, 'The House Rules Committee and the Programs of the Kennedy and Johnson Administrations', *Midwest Journal of Political Science*, Nov. 1970, pp. 667–72.
37. For evidence of direct personal influence on state parties, see Koenig, *op. cit.*, pp. 138–41.
38. David S. Broder, *The Party's Over*, New York, 1971, p. 38.
39. Theodore C. Sorenson, *Kennedy*, New York, 1966, p. 848.

lead his successors to feel less sensitive than Kennedy about party obligations.

Lyndon Johnson – the Consensus Democrat

It is ironic that Johnson, who at the age of fifty-five became President on Kennedy's assassination and went on to win a landslide victory in 1964, proved to be a less partisan and less attentive party leader than his young predecessor. This is explained in part by the circumstances in which he became President, the special situation in 1964 and his prior political experience. Johnson was a committed New Deal Democrat whose political base was the strongly Democratic state of Texas. His long career in Congress, especially in the Senate, made him 'a child of Congress',[40] skilled in dealing with and getting the support of its members. It is significant that, as leader of the Senate Democrats in the 1950s, he spent much of his time in bipartisan negotiation with a Republican President. In 1960, despite his status as a congressional leader, Johnson did not have sufficient party support to prevent Kennedy capturing the presidential nomination, but he accepted the vice-presidential candidacy.

In the early weeks of his presidency and up to the 1964 election, relations between the President and members of Congress, Democrat and Republican, were closer than at any time in memory.[41] Exploiting the memory of the dead President, Johnson acted swiftly and persistently to obtain the passage of legislation which Kennedy had been struggling to get Congress to accept. Tax, civil rights and poverty legislation was obtained by a deliberate strategy of consensus politics and a personal appeal for bipartisan support. Such an approach also became appropriate and successful in the 1964 presidential campaign, where Johnson was opposed by a Republican, Barry Goldwater, who made no attempt to hide or modify his radical conservative views. Johnson was able to make his opponent a major campaign issue and campaign in a non-partisan manner for electoral support to continue his stewardship. His massive victory also helped to increase the Democratic majorities in Congress, providing the opportunity for him to initiate and obtain further legislation from the 89th Congress. Again, however, this was achieved by the exercise of skills which were not rooted in an overtly partisan strategy. While Johnson's number of victories and level of support in Congress were higher in 1964 and 1965 than any

40. Jones, 'Presidential Negotiation with Congress', *op. cit.*, p. 110.
41. Rowland Evans and Robert Novak, *Lyndon B. Johnson: The Exercise of Power*, New York, London, 1967, Ch. XVII.

other President's from Eisenhower to Carter, data on presidential support indicate that Kennedy received more support in the House from both Northern and Southern Democrats than Johnson, who received more support from Republicans. In the Senate Kennedy also did better than Johnson among Northern Democrats, and worse than Johnson only among Republicans.[42] Johnson's success in achieving domestic legislative goals was achieved as much by personal as by party leadership strategies.

Johnson avoided a close relationship with the national party organisation. His personal relations with John Bailey and his successors were much less cordial than with his personal advisers on the White House staff. He made some fund-raising appearances in 1965, but maintained liaison with the Democratic national committee from 1964 to 1966 through his fellow Texan, Clifton Carter. He used the advice of his White House staff rather than the national committee in deciding on appointments, and greater emphasis was placed on loyalty to the President and his administration than on partisan service or party organisational interests. Johnson took a close interest in such appointments, but he scores lowest of the Presidents since Eisenhower in the use of appointments as a technique of party leadership and for paying party debts.[43] Despite visits to several campaigns in the 1966 congressional elections, Johnson remained largely aloof, endorsing no Democratic candidates. The Republicans made significant gains, and Johnson's apparent indifference damaged his relations with party leaders in Congress and in the state and local parties.

After 1966 Johnson made some attempts to improve his relations with his party. At a meeting with Democratic governors he received complaints about a failure to consult or inform them about the implementation of many of the Great Society programmes in the states. The Governors also mentioned the decline in the services and links provided by the national committee. Johnson responded to these and other complaints from within his party but did little personally to improve his reputation as party leader.[44]

The limitations of Johnson's personal approach in dealing with Congress over domestic legislation, and his style of consensus politics, became evident after 1966 in his handling of American involvement in Vietnam. He was forced to devote less time to relations with Congress. As his personal popularity declined with the

42. George C. Edwards, *Presidential Influence in Congress*, San Francisco, 1980, Tables 3.1 and 3.2, pp. 59−60, and Tables 7.1 and 7.2, pp. 191−2.
43. Brown and Welborn, *op. cit.*, p. 310.
44. Koenig, *The Chief Executive*, p. 143.

growing concern in the country over Vietnam, so it became more difficult for Johnson to retain support in Congress. Democrats on the Senate Foreign Relations Committee began to question the support they had given him in the Gulf of Tonkin resolution in 1964. Loyalty to Johnson within the Democratic party as a whole weakened as the 1968 election neared, and his support deriving from 'consensus' also crumbled. The emergence of an anti-Vietnam movement within the party led by Senator Eugene McCarthy, and its challenge in the presidential primaries to Johnson's renomination, led Johnson to announce that he would not seek another term.

Johnson was never fully accepted by the liberal wing of his party, despite his success in translating many of their domestic policy goals into law. The replacement in 1964 of the Kennedy 'Irish Mafia' by his own less respected 'Texas Mafia' did not help to improve his relations with the party. In the end the strategies which made his presidency so successful on the domestic front weakened his capacity to respond to the very different problems of foreign policy.[45] The inadequate attention he paid to maintaining personal support within the party and his failure to employ techniques used to gain support in Congress in the more mundane arena of party affairs put Johnson in a vulnerable position when his personal popularity waned.[46] The Johnson experience, albeit in rather special circumstances, nevertheless suggests that an incumbent is well-advised to maintain personal and organisational support within his party in order to avoid being challenged for the party nomination at the next election. After effectively denying Johnson renomination in 1968, the party still lost the presidential election. In 1980 Jimmy Carter survived another pre-convention challenge but failed to be re-elected. The evidence suggests that the reciprocal nature of President-party relations remains an important factor affecting both personal and organisational success or failure.

Richard Nixon — the Ambivalent Partisan

Johnson's Republican successor in 1968 had 'brooded, dreamed and schemed for the Presidency for the last sixteen of his fifty-five years'.[47] As a member of Congress and as Vice-President under Eisenhower, Richard Nixon was openly partisan in his political

45. See Doris Kearns, *Lyndon Johnson and the American Dream*, New York, 1976, esp. postscript, pp. 369—400.
46. For a critical view of Johnson's anti-party style of leadership, see David Broder, *The Party's Over*, Ch. 3.
47. Rowland Evans and Robert Novak, *Nixon in the White House: The Frustration of Power*, New York, 1971, p. 9.

activities. In seeking the presidency in 1960 his party loyalty gained him the support of national party leaders, and his partisan instincts prompted him to campaign not only for himself but also for congressional and local Republican candidates. The latter occurred despite Nixon's need to win over more than just Republican voters in order to defeat Kennedy.[48]

His narrow defeat in 1960, and the failure to become Governor of California in 1962, left Nixon with little national political visibility, but he continued to work for the party and its candidates. He received much credit for campaigning in the 1966 congressional elections when the Republicans made significant gains. This gave him strong grassroots support in the aftermath of the disastrous Goldwater performance in 1964, helping him to regain the Republican nomination for President in 1968. During his successful campaign in 1968 his partisan instincts remained in evidence.

On becoming President, however, Nixon's personal approach changed. This was in part due to the particular political situation, but also because of certain traits in his political character. Nixon and Johnson provided a marked contrast in experience and attitudes. Nixon was far more interested in, and knowledgeable about, foreign affairs. He faced a Congress controlled by Democrats, who were anxious to preserve programmes which he was pledged to change or terminate. If Nixon indeed sought to overturn the Roosevelt political legacy, reversing the developments in domestic policy begun in the 1930s, as well as to replace the Democrats' majority electoral coalition, then it was necessary as President to maximise and emphasise executive authority backed by public support. Party leadership was of limited use in getting programmes through the Democratic Congress, in mobilising public and electoral support, or in gaining control of the federal bureaucracy while changing both its attitudes and procedures.

This is not to say that Nixon ignored party or partisan responsibilities; rather that they became less important as his administration came to exercise executive responsibilities. His overall record on appointments included a high percentage (around 70 per cent) of Republicans, but the partisan commitment of many of these appointees was often weaker and less important than their administrative experience and policy attitudes. The national committee was almost entirely shut out of the selection process and was in any case poorly equipped to handle patronage.[49] The state-

48. Richard M. Nixon, *Six Crises*, New York, 1962, pp. 304–22.
49. John S. Saloma and Frederick H. Sontag, *Parties: The Real Opportunity for Effective Citizen Politics*, New York, 1973, p. 197.

ment of Frederick Malek, head of the White House personnel operation created in 1970, that 'the kind of guy we're looking for doesn't
hang around party offices'[50] summarises the tone and emphasis of
the Nixon administration. Nixon dissociated himself from the
process, despite complaints from congressional Republicans at the
failure of the administration to find jobs for their favoured candidates. The centralisation of the appointment process for political
executives and its control by the White House staff was only one
aspect of the way in which the national party organisation was
ignored or by-passed by the infamous 'palace guard' who had helped
with Nixon's campaign in 1968 and were now key members of his
White House staff.

Beginning with the controversial replacement of Ray Bliss as
national committee chairman by Rogers Morton in 1968, the gap
between the White House and the national committee widened. By
the 1972 election campaign the regular party organisation had
become almost irrelevant, with the establishment of the Committee
to Reelect the President. In 1970 Morton was succeeded by Senator
Robert Dole, who found himself unable even to get an appointment
to see the President at the time of the 1972 campaign. The emergence
of an alternative electoral organisation was part of Nixon's attempt
to become a 'superpartisan' President. In the 1972 election he would
create a new majority while obtaining maximum support for his
candidacy and a popular mandate which would weaken the
legitimacy of the opposition.

In 1968 he tried to strengthen support for the party in the Southern
and border states, beginning with his choice of Spiro Agnew of
Maryland as his running-mate. During the first term Agnew made
several partisan speeches, and in 1970 both he and Nixon campaigned for Republican candidates in more than twenty states. The
Democrats gained seats in the House and won eleven governorships,
while the Republicans gained two Senate seats. Nixon raised $20
million through a special campaign fund, but this money was only
apportioned to loyal Nixon supporters, and he refused to endorse
some Republican candidates.

The establishment of the Committee to Reelect the President
marked the end of Nixon's efforts to help and work with the party.
Through the Committee, Nixon hoped to build a new 'American' or

50. Quoted in G. Calvin Mackenzie, *The Politics of Presidential Appointments*, New
York, 1981, p. 198. See also pp. 40–56 and 195–9 for discussions of the decline
in the role of the President's party in influencing appointments. For a different
interpretation, see Martin and Susan Tolchin, *To the Victor: Political Patronage
from the Clubhouse to the White House*, New York, 1971, Ch. 6, esp.
pp. 250–68.

'Nixonian' majority. The Committee was run primarily by key presidential aides, few of whom had much party experience or party loyalty. It marked the ultimate step in the separation of a President from his party. The Committee was headed by John Mitchell, who had been Nixon's campaign manager in 1968 and who had been rewarded with appointment as Attorney-General, a position he gave up to take charge of the Committee. The Committee was very different from other citizen or non-partisan organisations in that it was staffed by administration 'insiders', like Mitchell, who owed nothing to the Republican party and everything to Nixon. Their knowledge and influence as 'insiders' were used to press organisations or groups to give money to help Nixon get re-elected in order to get favoured treatment or avoid punitive action from the administration. The Committee (together with its companion the Finance Committee to Reelect the President) was unique in the massive sums of money it obtained and spent, much of it without having to record who the donors were or how the money was used. Almost all of its funds went to sustain the Nixon campaign.

Had Nixon seriously wanted to help the Republican party, a rational strategy would have been to channel a good deal of this money to Republican candidates and their congressional campaigns. From the outset, however, the Committee was not seen as a partner to the Republican national committee but as an autonomous unit and a creature of the White House in origins and personnel. In the words of the Ervin Committee, the Senate select committee which later investigated the 1972 presidential campaign, it was 'a White House product, answerable to top White House leadership'[51] and indifferent to the Republican national committee. It actually withdrew support from 100 Republicans challenging incumbent Democrats who had supported Nixon over the Vietnam War.

The Committee to Reelect the President was in name and action an anti-party, non-party national political machine, which in no way relied on state or local parties for its operational efficiency. It was dominated by party 'outsiders' who lacked the experience and the mores of professional politicians accustomed to working through established party structures. Because of this they had no sense of the informal conventions and limitations within which party campaign organisations normally compete for votes. It was this, together with their belief in the absolute necessity of a Nixon landslide victory if a new electoral realignment was to be achieved, which led to illegalities and corrupt activities in 1972, including the burglary of the head-

---

51. *Final Report of the Senate Committee on Presidential Campaign Activities*, 93rd Congress, 2nd Session, Washington, DC, 1974, p. 18.

quarters of the Democratic national committee in the Watergate office complex in Washington in May.

Attempts to cover-up the involvement of the 'President's men' and later the President himself in approving and planning this and other illegal acts led to congressional investigations, with the House Judiciary Committee initiating procedures to impeach Nixon. These and other developments severely strained relations between Nixon and his party in Congress and in the country. Some Republicans in Congress called for Nixon to resign, as did a few local party officials. Large segments of hard-core conservative Republicans continued to support Nixon personally and out of party loyalty, but ultimately all the Republicans on the House Judiciary Committee voted for impeachment on a charge of obstruction of justice, and it was soon evident that Nixon had lost the support of most Republican senators. Nixon finally resigned in August 1974, but only when it was clear that he no longer had any support from within his party.

The consequences for the Republican party of the events that culminated in Nixon's resignation were considerable in the short term. Despite his landslide victory in 1972, the Republicans lost seats in Congress and at the state level in that year. At the mid-term elections in November 1974 the party suffered severe losses at all levels.

It is not feasible to discuss other activities of the 'revolutionary' presidency of Nixon which prompted the aberrant actions of his administration.[52] What the Nixon experience does demonstrate, however, is the potential danger of the absence of checks on a President by his party and the consequences of an excessive independence of Presidents from the constraints of party and its mediating influence. There were several factors which helped to create this situation, such as the absence of effective laws regulating campaign finance, the temptation for a reasonably popular President to try to build a new governing majority, and the weakness of the Democratic opposition following reforms in party procedures for selecting presidential candidates. In general, the fall of Nixon provides a warning as to the possible consequences of the decline of party influence on Presidents.

Gerald Ford — the Unelected Partisan

Ford became President, as he had become Vice-President, in very special circumstances. Having served in the House of Represen-

---

52. See on this Arthur M. Schlesinger, Jr., *The Imperial Presidency*, pp. 205–68; also Theodore H. White, *Breach of Faith: The Fall of Richard Nixon*, New York, 1975; and Jonathan Schell, *The Time of Illusion*, New York, 1976.

tatives for twenty-five years, he was nominated by Nixon in October 1973 as the first Vice-President to be selected, under the terms of the 25th amendment, by votes in the House and Senate. Then he became the first non-elected President following the resignation of Nixon in August 1974, assuming the office at a very difficult time for the presidency and the Republican party.

Finding himself in an unprecedented situation, Ford chose to be both a partisan President and one who would try to restore faith and trust in the presidency.[53] He was reasonably successful in both of these objectives, yet he failed to win election for a full term in 1976 or to improve the fortunes of his party in Congress. He was partisan because his whole political career had been based on loyalty to his party. His experience as minority leader in the House after 1965 taught him how to maintain the support of fellow Republicans and also to fashion majorities in support of Republican initiatives or against Democratic programmes.

In his relations with Congress, therefore, Ford applied the only methods he knew. He was accessible and worked closely with party leaders in the House and Senate and with his own legislative liaison staff. He took members of Congress seriously and recognised their importance. He also took his role as party leader seriously, especially the need to strengthen and rebuild Republican party organisations in the states. He campaigned in twenty states for Republican congressional candidates in the 1974 elections, arguing strongly for the need to keep sufficient Republicans in Congress to sustain his use of the veto power. Inevitably the Democrats made substantial gains, but Ford continued to work for his party. In 1975 he attended many fund-raising rallies and dinners to improve the finances of state and local parties. When he announced the appointment of Mary Louise Smith as chairman of the national committee in 1974, he stated his desire to work closely with the national committee and to have the committee run his 1976 presidential campaign. In the end Ford created an independent group to run his campaign, but his reputation as a party loyalist helped him to overcome the serious challenge of Ronald Reagan for the party nomination. This challenge did, however, weaken his effort to retain the presidency.

The most significant feature of the brief Ford presidency in terms of party relationships was the fact that he did not feel that the special circumstances of his accession precluded him from being, as his political career had always led him to be, a partisan and loyal party leader. In this respect, as in others, he was a very different

53. See Richard Reeves, *A Ford, not a Lincoln: The Decline of American Political Leadership*, New York, London, 1976.

Republican President from Nixon and different also from his Democratic successor.

Jimmy Carter — the Nonpartisan Amateur Democrat

Throughout his presidency Carter retained the distrust of party and party-related activities which had characterised his previous political career. Despite having been leader of the Georgia Young Democrats, Democratic Governor of Georgia and in 1974 head of the congressional campaign organisation for the Democratic national committee, he had always been an 'outsider' within the party. He became a state senator in Georgia despite the opposition of the local Democratic organisation, and gained the governorship on the strength of his independence from the party organisation. Before becoming President, he had no elected experience in national politics or any ties with the Democrats in Congress.

He gained the Democratic presidential nomination in 1976 by taking advantage of the new procedures for selecting delegates to the national convention and through his appeal as an independent anti-Washington candidate of the people rather than the choice of party professionals. His election campaign against Ford was run primarily by his personal campaign organisation and stressed his independence. Such tactics were not inappropriate in the context of public attitudes towards the presidency at the time, but his victory reinforced his belief that the strategies which had brought him to the White House might also be appropriate for governing in Washington.

This was evident in Carter's approach to the selection of his administration and his political appointments.[54] He sought to bring new faces into government, establishing procedures which depoliticised the selection process. Carter had become President by capturing the party, not by cultivating the support of party professionals. He therefore saw little need to consult party officials over appointments. In April 1977 the Democratic national committee adopted a resolution rebuking Carter for failing to consult state party officials over political appointments. Later in the year the national committee chairman Kenneth Curtis resigned; he complained about day-to-day meddling in national committee operations by White House staff. Party officials were also unhappy about the influential role played by presidential aide Hamilton Jordan in

---

54. Bruce Adams and Kathryn Kavanagh-Baran, *Promise and Performance: Carter Builds a New Administration*, Lexington, Mass., esp. Chs 2 and 13; see also Mackenzie, *op. cit.*, pp. 62–9.

filling government positions and the failure to consult Democrats in Congress regarding appointments.

The successor to Curtis, John C. White, made some effort to prevent the national committee becoming a political wing of the White House and outlined presidential plans for fund-raising and participation in the 1978 elections, but relations between Carter and the party in the country remained uneasy. In response to pleas by Vice-President Mondale and others, Carter participated in the campaign in 1978. However, some Democratic candidates were ambivalent about getting Carter's blessing until his public standing improved in the summer of 1978 following the Camp David accords. The Democrats lost twelve House seats and three Senate seats overall, a reasonable enough performance, but Carter was given little credit for this.

Carter seemed interested in party affairs only where they might affect his chances of being renominated. He and his staff took a close interest in the work of a special party panel on delegate selection and succeeded in preventing major alterations in nominating procedures for 1980 at the Democratic mid-term convention. As the presidential primaries approached and his public approval declined, Carter belatedly tried to mend some party fences, but his poor relations with the congressional party and with liberals in the party led to a serious challenge to his renomination by supporters of Senator Edward Kennedy. In the end Carter was able to overcome this challenge, but the strength of opposition within the party at the national convention weakened his re-election campaign. A final demonstration of his lack of party loyalty and leadership came on election day when he conceded defeat to Reagan before the polls had closed in the Western states — to the chagrin of several Democrats from those states who lost their congressional seats by narrow margins.

If Carter was insensitive or indifferent to his obligations to the party in the country, he was inept in dealing with his party majority in Congress. He offended congressional Democrats unnecessarily by his opposition to traditional patronage in the form of public works projects, and he lost their respect through the inadequacies and inexperience of his legislative liaison staff. While it may be true that the large majorities in Congress after 1976 were very different in attitude and approach from those enjoyed by Roosevelt and Johnson in 1933 and 1965,[55] these differences can be exaggerated.[56] There were fewer incentives for Democrats in Congress to support

55. Eric L. Davis, 'Legislative Reform and the Decline of Presidential Influence on Capitol Hill', *British Journal of Political Science*, Oct. 1979, pp. 465–79.
56. Polsby, *The Consequences of Party Reform*, pp. 105–14.

Carter; they had played little or no part in his nomination, and few of them felt they owed their seats to his narrow victory in 1976. At the same time, however, Carter did little to help himself, either in building and sustaining a close personal relationship with his party leaders in the House and Senate or in creating coalitions of support within his party by political bargaining or personal appeals.[57]

Carter did succeed in mobilising Democratic support to avert a possible humiliation in the Senate over the Panama Canal treaties, and indeed his average presidential support scores from congressional Democrats were not significantly lower than those of Kennedy or even Johnson and were actually better with respect to the Senate.[58] Yet average support scores can be misleading. Much of this support was lukewarm and given almost in spite of rather than because of any coherent effort by Carter to use his position as party leader to help him deal with Congress. His poor personal relations with his party on Capitol Hill was a direct result of his reluctance 'to adopt the members of his own party as full partners in the development of legislative alternatives and in the assignment of priorities to them'.[59]

While a strong partisan approach by the Carter administration might have been counter-productive in the context of the post-Watergate presidency, quite apart from being inconsistent with Carter's style, his loss of public support and his vacillations in dealing with economic problems and with the embarrassing issue of the American hostages in Iran made him electorally vulnerable. As we have said, Carter seemed interested in the party organisation and the national committee only to the extent of ensuring that he was renominated in 1980. In all other respects he neither understood nor acknowledged his party obligations, nor did he try to sustain party unity. His defeat in 1980, together with the loss of control of the Senate to the Republicans, meant that the Democratic party paid a high political price for the luxury of having a non-partisan Democratic President who refused to play the party game.

Ronald Reagan — the Autocue Partisan

The first term of the Reagan presidency was a marked contrast to the tenure of his predecessor. Reagan differs in style, ability and philosophy from Carter, not least in his sense of the importance of

57. Edwards, *op. cit.*, pp. 173–80.
58. *Ibid.*, Tables 7.3 and 7.4, pp. 192–3.
59. Nelson W. Polsby, 'Presidential-Congressional Relations', in King, *The New American Political System*, *op. cit.*, p. 17.

partisanship. While Reagan is not an aggressive partisan or party leader, he has used his personal experience in dealing with the media and his political acumen to avoid some of the errors made by the Carter administration in party matters in an attempt to make the Reagan presidency both a personal and a party success.

With a style and sense of political tactics more reminiscent of Roosevelt than of recent Republican Presidents, Reagan proved to be an effective President in his first year. He was helped by party activities which were not entirely of his own making. In January 1977, in the wake of Ford's defeat, there was a fierce contest for the chairmanship of the Republican national committee between Bill Brock, a Ford supporter and former senator, and Richard Richards, a Reagan supporter. Brock won and became an active and successful head of the national committee. Among other things he was the principal architect of the Republican gains in Congress and the state legislatures in 1978 and 1980, achieved primarily by diverting funds and party resources to sustain congressional campaigns. These efforts were most important in leading to the recapture of control of the Senate in 1980, which was as significant for the Republicans as was Reagan's presidential victory. It allowed Reagan and other Republicans to claim that the 1980 election marked the beginning of a new party realignment, made it easier for Reagan to gain significant successes in Congress in 1981 and helped him to obtain a very high level of party support in both the Senate and the House. All this did not, however, preclude Reagan from exercising his prerogative as party leader in January 1981 when the national committee voted to replace Brock by Richards.

In contrast to Carter, Reagan was more aware of the need to take into account partisan and ideological factors in making initial appointments to his administration. To deal with Congress, he set up a transition liaison office, composed of experienced congressional lobbyists. As a candidate he had gone out of his way to link his own campaign with that of congressional Republicans, and after the election he met with Republican leaders and made a real effort to give them a say in Cabinet and other executive appointments. A former congressional liaison aide for Ford, Max Friedersdorf, was appointed to head the White House congressional liaison office, and an office of political affairs was set up to help with requests from Republican legislators. A simple set of legislative objectives was mapped out, and strong efforts were made to obtain a partisan majority in the Senate and maximum Republican support in the House.[60]

60. Stephen J. Wayne, 'Congressional Liaison in the Reagan White House: A

Reagan capitalised on the psychological impact of the Republican successes in 1980, and succeeded in fusing high Republican support with sufficient defections by conservative Democrats in the House to obtain his budget and tax cut initiatives. When necessary, he used direct personal persuasion to obtain support from Republican waverers, as in October 1981 when he won a crucial Senate vote on his proposed sale of aircraft and other advanced military equipment to Saudi Arabia.

Reagan's success in 1981 in getting support in Congress was considerable, but it proved more difficult to achieve in 1982 and after the 1982 mid-term elections. His partisan approach relied more and more on his capacity to sustain personal support through his skills at communicating with the public. He sought to be an active and relatively successful partisan leader rather than a strong party leader, but he could not prevent the normal reaction against the party in power in the White House in the 1982 mid-term elections. Here the Democrats made substantial gains in the House and at the state level, but the legacy of Brock in the form of well-financed and organised Senate campaigns enabled the Republicans to retain majority control in the Senate.

The Reagan record in the first term suggests that it is still advantageous in certain circumstances for a President to act in a predominantly partisan manner. While Reagan was not a persistent and strong party leader, he was conscious of his obligations to strengthen the Republican party as long as such activity did not conflict with his major objective of staying in the White House. He did not satisfy many conservative Republicans, but he retained considerable personal support within the party at all levels.

Nevertheless, the Republican party could not capitalise on Reagan's personal re-election landslide in 1984, even though the national party organisation was at least as strong as in 1980. The Reagan re-election campaign was organised from the White House and not by the Republican national committee, despite the fact that the latter was an impressive fund-raising and campaign management organisation. The 'separate' nature of Reagan's 1984 campaign led to complaints from Republicans such as the House minority leader, Robert Michel. He blamed Reagan's personal campaign for the disappointing party performance in the House elections and accused Reagan of not helping enough to ensure more Republican gains in

Preliminary Assessment of the First Year', in Norman J. Ornstein (ed.), *President and Congress: Assessing Reagan's First Year*, Washington, DC, 1982, pp. 44–65.

the congressional elections.[61] Thus, despite the fact that the Republican national committee organisation is stronger and more professional, it is unlikely that Reagan will leave his party in 1988 in a better electoral position than in 1981. The communicating skills and political success exemplified by Reagan are not readily transferable from the individual to the party as a whole.

Conclusions

The evidence of presidential activity since the accession of Roosevelt indicates that it is difficult for Presidents to be successful chief executives *and* strong party leaders. Yet most Presidents have felt the need for different reasons to be attentive to party affairs, despite a certain ambivalence towards the public role of party leader. Part of the reason for this ambivalence has been strategic, because the period since Roosevelt has been one in which several factors have made the performance of a consistent party leadership role potentially counter-productive. Style, personality and previous political experience may account for Presidents such as Kennedy and Ford being more partisan and playing a stronger party leadership role than political circumstances might have warranted, with others such as Johnson and Carter being less partisan. This suggests that a President's relations with his party depends on the strength of partisan disposition, together with a strategic assessment of the utility of playing the party game in order to achieve certain goals. Eisenhower had a low partisan disposition but a strong sense of obligation to help his party. Strong partisan disposition appears to have led certain Presidents to do more for their party than was strategically profitable, or in the case of Carter weak partisan disposition led to an inability to maximise the potential advantage from greater party activity. In very different ways both Carter and Reagan also demonstrate that Presidents as campaigners for their parties are likely to be motivated by self-interest rather than any altruistic desire to improve party performance.

While the rules of the party game have changed since 1932 in ways which may have weakened some of 'the ties that bind' President and party, it is possible to undervalue their mutual needs in relation to achieving a successful presidency. Presidents need the minimal unity and political support which party ties may still provide.[62] Moreover,

---

61. See Richard Viguerie, 'Reagan's Campaign Double-Crossed the GOP', *New York Times*, 12 Nov. 1984, p. A19.
62. For more details, see Robert Harmel (ed.), *Presidents and Their Parties: Leadership or Neglect?*, New York, 1984.

the party connection imposes a degree of public accountability on individual Presidents, which, if it had been operative during the Nixon years, might have avoided the damage to the presidency caused at that time. The evidence does not suggest any particular behavioural pattern to distinguish Democratic from Republican Presidents, but some general patterns of development appear to exist.

First, the decline in the influence of party in determining the responses of voters to presidential candidates during the period may account for the diminished importance of party to Presidents such as Johnson, Nixon and Carter. Evidence also of the lessening of presidential coat-tails, and the increased electoral independence of members of Congress, may help to explain the limited and largely unsuccessful presidential interventions in mid-term elections.

Secondly, there is the matter of relations with the national party committee. While Presidents continue to have strong control over the selection of the chairman of the national committee, the committee is likely to remain only one of several channels through which Presidents will work to maintain political support in the country.[63] Similarly, while Presidents remain sensitive to the demands of their parties with respect to patronage appointments, party advice will be only one of several considerations influencing decisions on appointments.

Thirdly, it can be said that perhaps the most important change since the 1930s which has affected relations between Presidents and their party is the development of the White House Office as the President's central organisation for advice and strategy while in office. The period has been marked by tension between the White House staff and those more closely linked with the party. The dangers arising from this development were most evident in the events which led to the resignation of Nixon, yet this personal organisation is likely to remain more important than party-related organisations in influencing presidential behaviour in the future.

Fourthly, there is the matter of relations between the President and his party in Congress and in particular the crucial presidential need to obtain support for his programmes in the House and Senate. Here the evidence indicates that most recent Presidents have placed great importance on close liaison between the White House and party members in Congress. At the same time, there have been no significant changes in the long-term overall level of support for the

63. William Crotty, 'The National Committees as Grass-Roots Vehicles of Representation', in William Crotty (ed.), *The Party Symbol: Readings on Political Parties*, San Francisco, 1980.

President from members of his own party in Congress. Clearly it is important for Presidents to hold regular meetings with congressional leaders of their own party. Yet any President can normally expect to obtain between 60 and 70 per cent support from his own party in votes in Congress. Statistical evidence on support for the President's position by his party between 1954 and 1981 indicates that in no year did any President received *less* than 59 per cent support in the House and 64 per cent in the Senate or *more* than 84 per cent in the House and Senate.[64] The low House score was experienced by Ford in 1974 in the immediate aftermath of Nixon's resignation; and the low Senate score by Johnson in 1968. The high scores were obtained by Reagan in the Senate in 1981 after the Republicans took control of that chamber and in the House by Johnson in 1964 after his landslide election victory. Even Carter, despite his reputation for not getting on with his party in Congress, won seven out of eight key votes in the House and five out of nine in the Senate in 1977, with an average Democratic support score of 64.6 per cent in the House and 74.1 per cent in the Senate. Carter's overall average support score in 1980 among House and Senate Democrats was around 70 per cent.

While the degree of party support may be affected by the size of a party's representation in Congress at any one time, the general level of support for Presidents does not appear to depend on presidential party leadership but on specific strategic decisions made by members of Congress. Where party appeals on the part of the President may be important and where good liaison with party members in Congress may pay off is in ensuring maximum support on key votes. This is important for Republican Presidents who more often than not have found their party in the minority in Congress, but also for Democratic Presidents who have had to contend with defections by Southern Democrats. There is therefore an important strategic quality to the use of party cues or ties by individual Presidents as a means of maximising political support in Congress to achieve policy goals. Yet for all kinds of reasons it remains very difficult in practice for Presidents to act as genuine party leaders in Congress.

Whether they like it or not, however, Presidents and their parties are too interrelated to permit one to disown or divorce the other. Presidents in the future may become more selective about their participation in party activity, but they are unlikely to ignore entirely the obligations or indeed the benefits of this relationship.

64. Norman J. Ornstein *et al.*, *Vital Statistics on Congress, 1982*, Washington, DC, 1982, Table 8.2, pp. 166–7.

3

THE PRESIDENT AND CONGRESS

David Mervin

Modern Presidents, unlike their nineteenth-century counterparts, are expected to play a major part in the legislative process. Both Congress and the people now look to the White House for a comprehensive legislative agenda. The President is expected to set legislative priorities, submit drafts of bills, mount an effective legislative liaison operation and see his legislative proposals through to completion. If he fails in these undertakings, a modern President will be found wanting, for, since the time of Franklin Roosevelt at least, 'the classic test of greatness in the White House has been the chief executive's capacity to lead Congress.'[1]

The President is expected to lead Congress, yet some formidable obstacles stand in the way of his meeting that obligation. The most important of these is the Constitution, which requires that the President share his power of appointment with the Senate, places the purse-strings in the hands of Congress, and obliges him to struggle with the legislative branch for 'the privilege of directing American foreign policy'.[2]

The attempts of modern Presidents to establish ascendancy in the field of foreign policy has been the subject of much attention, yet there has been a certain inevitability about the enlargement of the President's role in this area. From the beginning he was accorded a major role in the making of foreign and defence policy; the Constitution identifies him as the Commander-in-Chief and gives him the primary role in the making of treaties. The Commander-in-Chief clause has been used repeatedly to justify the commitment of armed forces overseas, notwithstanding the theoretical constraints imposed by congressional prerogatives with regard to declarations of war.[3] In recent years – despite the traumas of Watergate and Vietnam, the passage of the War Powers Act and widely expressed concerns about excessive presidential power – Presidents Carter and Ford were

1. James MacGregor Burns, *Roosevelt: The Lion and the Fox*, New York, London, 1956, p. 186.
2. Edward S. Corwin, *The President: Office and Powers*, New York, 1957, p. 171.
3. See Aaron Wildavsky, 'The Two Presidencies', in Ronald C. Moe, *Congress and the President*, Pacific Palisades, 1971, p. 124.

able to use military force without congressional approval. Furthermore, they did so without provoking an adverse reaction in Congress, and they improved rather than weakened their standing in public opinion as a consequence.

The passage in the Constitution dealing with treaty-making similarly strengthens the President's position. In other words, with regard to the crucial questions of foreign and defence policy, although the chief executive's authority to act has periodically been subject to challenge, there has never been any real doubt as to the potential importance of the presidential role. Once the United States began its movement from the edge to the centre of the world stage at the end of the nineteenth century, it was inevitable that the power of the President in this area would be significantly enhanced.

There was no such constitutional inevitability involved in the President's emergence as chief legislator, for the legislative powers granted to him in the Constitution are paltry. The first article of the Constitution states that 'All legislative Powers herein granted shall be vested in the Congress of the United States', and much subsequent detail is devoted to spelling out the nature of the powers granted to Congress. The President, by contrast, is conceded the negative power of the veto, and is also authorised 'from time to time to give to the Congress Information of the State of the Union, and recommend to their Consideration such Measures as he shall judge necessary and expedient'. James Bryce, writing in 1893, noted that Congress was under no obligation to act on such communications from the chief executive. A presidential message was likely to have little more impact than 'a shot in the air without practical result. It is rather a manifesto, or declaration of opinion and policy, than a step towards legislation. Congress need not take action: members go their own ways and bring in their own bills.'[4] Bryce, reasonably enough for a nineteenth-century commentator, believed that the only really important legislative power available to the President was the veto.

The authority of modern chief executives in the legislative field clearly owes little to the Constitution and much to the vision, determination, resourcefulness and political good fortune of a number of Presidents. The establishment, consolidation and development of the legislative leadership role has involved a long and difficult contest with the legislature. It is on this 'struggle' that this chapter is mainly focused.

In the following section, in which we consider the development of

---

4. James Bryce, *The American Commonwealth*, New York, 1915, vol. I, p. 58.

the President's role as legislative leader in domestic policy, particular attention will be given to those Presidents who have contributed most to that development. Then we will endeavour to place these contributions in perspective. The concluding section will be concerned with legislative leadership in the post-Johnson era.

Development of the President's Legislative Leadership Role

Franklin Roosevelt was, arguably, the first modern President. During his administration the office was brought to new heights of power and responsibility, and he effected a fundamental shift in the balance of powers between the executive and legislative branches of the federal government. In particular, Roosevelt's presidency, once and for all, established the chief executive's legislative role. However, Roosevelt's conception of the presidency was much influenced by two of his predecessors – his cousin Theodore and Woodrow Wilson, in whose administration he served as Assistant Secretary of the Navy.

Theodore Roosevelt's contribution to the development of the President's legislative role was considerable in terms of innovation. Jackson and Lincoln had ventured into the legislative realm, but Jackson's influence on Congress was largely negative, whereas Lincoln's assumption of legislative power occurred in an atmosphere of high crisis.[5] Theodore Roosevelt, on the other hand, was President during a normal rather than a crisis period, and he successfully claimed for his office a positive legislative role. Roosevelt wrote in his autobiography, 'In theory the Executive has nothing to do with legislation. In practice, as things now are, the Executive is or ought to be peculiarly representative of the people as a whole . . . Therefore a good Executive under present conditions of American life must take a very active interest in getting the right kind of legislation in addition to performing his Executive duties with an eye single to the public welfare.'[6] In keeping with this and working closely with Joseph Cannon, the Speaker of the House of Representatives, Roosevelt as President fashioned an unprecedented record of legislative achievement.

Woodrow Wilson came to the White House with an even more carefully developed view of presidential responsibilities and with legislative leadership at its very centre. As he saw it, the modern President was obliged to be leader of his party and chief administra-

5. Robert Dahl, *Pluralist Democracy in the United States*, Chicago, 1967, pp. 93–4.
6. Wilfrid Binkley, *President and Congress*, New York, 1947, p. 238.

tor, but above all else, 'He must be prime minister, as much concerned with the guidance of legislation as with the just and orderly execution of the law.'[7] In the early years of his administration, Wilson proved to be an exceptional legislative leader who indeed operated much in the manner of a prime minister. He developed techniques of legislative leadership that his successors have copied.

One of Wilson's first and symbolically most important acts was his revival of the long-lapsed custom of the President delivering messages to Congress in person. His appearances on Capitol Hill made a considerable impact and were interpreted, as he intended, as tangible evidence of his determination to direct and dominate the work of Congress. 'It was Woodrow Wilson's great contribution to the Presidency to have made the provision of the Constitution for the Presidential message to Congress the basis of dynamic legislative leadership.'[8]

Wilson also made considerable use of party machinery as a means of furthering his legislative objectives, and this has been seen as consistent with his earlier ruminations on the advantages of responsible party government. In fact Wilson, in the early stages of his presidency, showed some disinclination to make use of party. Initially, he expressed a preference for working through the progressives in Congress rather than through conservative Democratic leaders. At the outset he was also reluctant to use patronage as a means of lubricating the wheels of party, and was dubious about working through the party caucus. However, fortunately for Wilson's place in history, he was persuaded to set aside these reservations, and ultimately his skilful use of the machinery of party was an essential ingredient of his legislative success.

Wilson's outstanding personal qualities are important to an understanding of his part in the development of the President's role as chief legislator. In office he displayed some of those qualities of heroic leadership that he had so admired in his youth. On a public platform he conveyed an impression of great intellectual power, combined with moral authority and unwavering conviction. On innumerable occasions he displayed a rare ability to stimulate and arouse audiences and to mobilise public opinion on behalf of his objectives. He was less effective in situations with small groups or individuals, although even in those circumstances many were swayed by his strikingly evident intellectual gifts, his personal magnetism and his commanding presence.

7. Arthur S. Link (ed.), *The Papers of Woodrow Wilson*, Princeton, NJ, 1966, vol. 27, pp. 99–100.
8. Wilfrid Binkley, 'The President as Chief Legislator', in Moe, *op. cit.*, p. 57.

These and other strengths enabled Wilson to preside over the passage of an impressive legislative programme, including major tariff reform, the Federal Reserve Act, the act setting up the Federal Trade Commission and the Clayton Anti-Trust Act.[9] These were hardly Wilson's accomplishments alone, but he was the essential catalyst. His example of dynamic legislative leadership was not lost on his young Assistant Secretary of the Navy, who in 1932 would himself be elected to the presidency.

Any assessment of Franklin Roosevelt must take account of the fact that he took office in circumstances especially favourable to strong leadership from the White House. He won an enormous victory in the electoral college which was paralleled by sweeping gains for the Democratic party in the House and Senate. In addition, when he took office there was a massive leadership vacuum at the centre waiting to be filled, and furthermore the foundations of the American capitalist system appeared to be crumbling, with 25 per cent unemployment, national income in steep decline, and banks throughout the country closing their doors. 'It was now not just a matter of staving off hunger. It was a matter of seeing whether a representative democracy could conquer economic collapse. It was a matter of staving off violence, even (at least some thought) revolution.'[10]

This was one of those relatively rare moments when the American people craved strong leadership. At this juncture, the gravest national emergency since the Civil War, traditional fears of executive tyranny and concern for constitutional purity were, for the time being, laid aside. Eleanor Roosevelt, commenting on the rapturous reception accorded her husband at his inaugural, said, 'The crowds were so tremendous, and you felt that they would do anything — if only someone would tell them what to do.'[11]

In his inaugural Roosevelt struck the right notes of confidence and leadership and, in particular, made very clear his intention to exercise legislative leadership. 'I am prepared under my constitutional duty to recommend the measures that a stricken nation in the midst of a stricken world may require. These measures or such other measures as Congress may build out of its experience and wisdom, I shall seek within my constitutional authority to bring to speedy adoption.'[12] True to his word, in the first three months of his

9. Arthur S. Link, *Wilson: The New Freedom*, Princeton, NJ, 1956, *passim*.
10. Arthur M. Schlesinger, Jr., *The Coming of the New Deal*, New York, London, 1957, p. 3.
11. Burns, *op. cit.*, p. 165.
12. *The Public Papers and Addresses of Franklin Roosevelt*, New York, 1966, vol. 2, p. 15.

administration Roosevelt pushed through Congress a stunning programme of legislation. Within hours of Congress convening, emergency banking legislation was passed. During the next 'hundred days' fifteen major bills were enacted, including legislation providing for a national agricultural policy, the establishment of the Tennessee Valley Authority, the Federal Emergency Relief Act and the National Industrial Recovery Act.[13] As Binkley remarked, 'President Wilson, the exponent and practitioner of the parliamentary theory of American government, had never come as close as this to the realisation of his ideas.'[14] However, the extraordinary legislative output of the first 'hundred days' owed much to the atmosphere of crisis in which Roosevelt took office, with Congress virtually throwing itself into his arms. The situation was quite unlike 1913 when Wilson had to battle every inch of the way to wring his legislative achievements from Congress. Roosevelt's later legislative successes are probably more important than the early ones in considering the development of the presidency. During the so-called 'second hundred days' of 1935 Roosevelt demonstrated, in less fortuitous circumstances, a considerable mastery of Congress in putting through a number of key New Deal measures, including the Wagner Labor Relations Act, the Social Security Act and a major tax reform bill.

With a vigour and determination not seen since the days of Wilson, Roosevelt in his first term seized the initiative from Congress and played a major role in the passage of an impressive programme of reform legislation. As we shall see, his record as legislative leader was not without its blemishes, but for the moment we are concerned with the positive aspects of his performance, and in particular those that contributed to the development of the President's role as chief legislator.

Roosevelt not only confidently reasserted a role that had fallen into disuse during the administrations of Harding, Coolidge and Hoover, but he also dramatically extended the range of presidential legislative activity far beyond anything that had gone before. It was this expansion that was probably FDR's most important contribution to development rather than any innovation in methods, although there were some of these as well.

No doubt mindful of Wilson's example, Roosevelt renewed the practice of addressing Congress in person, and in support of his messages to Congress he provided draft bills and made arrangements for them to be introduced by administration supporters. When

13. Rexford G. Tugwell, *The Enlargement of the Presidency*, New York, 1960, p. 415.
14. *President and Congress, op. cit.*, p. 296.

Lincoln sent the draft of a bill with one of his messages to Congress, the legislature responded angrily to such presumption, but since the days of Franklin Roosevelt this has become an accepted practice.[15]

A substantial extension of the range of legislative clearance was undoubtedly one of Roosevelt's most important innovations, for it significantly strengthened the President's control over the legislative process. Clearance and coordination of legislative requests and recommendations through the Bureau of the Budget, acting on behalf of the President, had already been developed with regard to appropriations. But Roosevelt at an early stage in his first term made clear his determination to gain similar control over the substance of all legislation emanating from the departments and agencies.

The Roosevelt clearance system, thus established, incorporated its financial precursor but was no mere extension of the budget process. On the contrary, in form and fact and terms of reference this was Roosevelt's creation, intended to protect not just his budget, but his prerogatives, his freedom of action, and his choice of policies, in an era of fast-growing government and of determined presidential leadership.[16]

Roosevelt also widened the role of the Bureau of the Budget as an advisory and coordinating mechanism for dealing with bills emerging from Congress. For some years the Bureau had been advising Presidents on whether they should veto appropriation bills, but during the FDR years this responsibility was extended to include all manner of bills coming from Congress. By this means the presidential veto power became immeasurably more effective in line with Roosevelt's belief that the 'veto power was among the presidency's greatest attributes, an independent and responsible act of participation in the legislative process, and a means of enforcing congressional and agency respect for presidential preferences or programs.'[17] Before Franklin Roosevelt became President, the veto power had been used relatively sparingly with the notable exception of Grover Cleveland, who had deployed it extensively to turn back private relief bills. In the twentieth century before 1933, Presidents had vetoed on average about nine bills per year whereas FDR, during his twelve years of office, vetoed no less than 635 bills. Pocket vetoes accounted for 263 of these, but in relation to the remaining 372 bills Roosevelt was only overridden on nine occasions.[18]

15. *Ibid.*, p. 298.
16. Richard Neustadt, 'Presidency and Legislation: The Growth of Central Clearance', *American Political Science Review*, vol. 48, no. 3 (Sept. 1954), p. 650.
17. *Ibid.*, p. 656.
18. Louis Fisher, *The Politics of Shared Power: Congress and the Executive*, Washington, DC, 1981, p. 26.

Roosevelt's personality and the qualities of temperament that he brought to his job contributed much to his consolidation and enlargement of the President's role as chief legislator. As Oliver Wendell Holmes said of Roosevelt, 'A second class intellect, but a first class temperament'.[19] Intellectually Wilson was probably Roosevelt's superior, but temperamentally the positions were reversed. Unlike his gloomy, insecure and intensely introspective predecessor, Roosevelt revelled in the challenges of the presidency and derived vast satisfaction from his work.[20] In addition he displayed a brilliant intuitive understanding of human psychology. Taken together, these attributes proved to be considerable assets in his dealings with public officials and the press, besides contributing much to his popularity with the American people.

Legislative leadership requires skill in dealing with legislators directly, plus an ability to bring pressure to bear indirectly. Roosevelt was particularly adept at both. In his face-to-face encounters with members of Congress he demonstrated a rare ability to tend the egos, smooth the feathers and to express understanding of the preferences and perspectives of legislators. 'He was a master at the art of providing congressional gratification — at the easy first name, the cordial handshake, the radiant smile, the intimate joke, the air of accessibility and concern, the quasi-confidential interview, the photograph at the White House desk, the headline in the hometown newspaper.'[21] In the early years of his administration, at least, Roosevelt's relations with Congress were studiously collaborative, with the President showing himself keenly aware of the dangers of appearing to relegate Congress to 'rubber-stamp' status and careful to consult widely with party leaders, committee chairmen and other legislators of importance.

The principal means of bringing indirect pressure to bear on legislators is through the manipulation and marshalling of public opinion, and FDR carried the presidency to new heights in this respect. Most Presidents in this century have recognised the importance of establishing a good relationship with the press, yet very few have succeeded in that objective and certainly none have excelled Roosevelt. That same mastery of the arts of managing people that served him so well in his dealings with members of Congress and administrators greatly aided him at his press conferences, which were, quite remarkably, held roughly twice a week

---

19. Burns, *op. cit.*, p. 157.
20. James Barber, *The Presidential Character*, Englewood Cliffs, NJ, 1977, Ch. 7.
21. Schlesinger, *op. cit.*, p. 536.

throughout his presidency.[22] Schlesinger has provided us with a graphic picture of these virtuoso performances:

There he sat, his cigarette fixed in his holder, his eye friendly but vigilant, his manner jovial but ever so slightly on his guard, his whole bearing that of a man awaiting with relish an impending battle of wits. Then the questions began to fly. The President answered some plainly and soberly, used others as pretexts for a display of his grasp of administrative or topographical detail, turned away others with jokes or diplomatic avowals of ignorance, put others off the record, on occasion reproached or scolded reporters for asking others.[23]

Roosevelt's consummate skill in handling the press added a powerful new dimension to the art of legislative leadership. In addition, he was the first President able to take advantage of the opportunities offered by broadcasting, and his seizing of that opportunity was no less outstanding. As Governor of New York he had counteracted legislative opposition by the use of radio addresses, and he now developed this revolutionary new technique even more fully with enormously skilled and effective 'fireside chats'.[24]

All in all, Roosevelt's contribution to the development of the President as chief legislator can only be described as vast. He brought to the presidency a phenomenal combination of understanding, temperament and ability that enabled him to build on the groundwork provided by Theodore Roosevelt and Woodrow Wilson in consolidating and massively expanding the President's legislative role. 'Beginning with Franklin Roosevelt, legislative policy making became an important expectation of the presidency, and influencing the Congress became a necessity if the executive's domestic priorities were to be achieved.'[25]

Harry Truman very much aspired to legislative leadership in the Roosevelt manner, but the circumstances of his presidency were much less propitious. By the time he became President, disillusionment with strong executive leadership had set in, Congress was in one of its reassertive phases, and Truman was never able to command public support at the levels enjoyed by Roosevelt. Truman nevertheless bombarded Congress with legislative proposals, even though he was notably unsuccessful in getting them passed. One of his innovations, however, did contribute to the development of the President's legislative role. In 1948 he began the practice of

22. Richard Neustadt, *Presidential Power*, New York, 1976, p. 284.
23. Schlesinger, *op. cit.*, p. 543.
24. *Ibid.*, pp. 540–1.
25. Stephen J. Wayne, *The Legislative Presidency*, New York, 1978, p. 23.

submitting an annual programme of legislation to Congress, a practice that his successors have followed.[26]

The election of Dwight Eisenhower in 1952 brought to the White House a man whose conception of the presidency differed sharply from that of Roosevelt and Truman. Even if the opportunities had been available, he would have been reluctant to seize the reins of legislative leadership fashioned by Roosevelt and others. Eisenhower believed that FDR had usurped the powers of Congress and was anxious to restore the constitutional balance.[27] It follows that Eisenhower has not been regarded as a legislative leader of any great distinction, and has in fact generally been given very low ratings by students of the presidency. Thus the Schlesinger poll of 'presidential greatness' in 1962 placed him 22nd out of thirty-one Presidents, level with Chester Arthur. Another evaluation some years later placed Eisenhower 23rd on a scale of presidential activeness, 20th in terms of the accomplishments of his administration and 19th on a scale of general prestige.[28] However, as we shall see later in this chapter, earlier assessments of Eisenhower's presidency have been challenged in recent years.

In the 1960 election campaign John Kennedy sought to exploit the supposed inactivity of the Eisenhower administration, and he entered the White House with a determination to be an activist President in the Roosevelt mould, even though the realities of office, particularly his lack of support in Congress, obliged him to settle for much less in terms of legislative achievement. Kennedy did, however, contribute to the development of presidential-congressional relations by his establishment of a high-powered and professional legislative liaison operation. Earlier Presidents had recognised the need for involvement by intermediaries in the legislative process. Roosevelt's emissaries were very active on Capitol Hill during the New Deal years, and Truman had set up a small White House unit specifically for legislative liaison purposes.[29] However, Truman's unit was confined to relatively trivial liaison tasks, and its staff never acquired great standing in either the executive or the legislature. The first serious institutionalisation of legislative liaison occurred under Eisenhower, who set up a unit headed initially by General Wilton Persons and subsequently by Bryce Harlow. These were figures of substance on the White House staff, reflecting the high priority that Eisenhower gave to developing good relations with

26. *Ibid.*, pp. 19–20.
27. Emmet Hughes, *The Ordeal of Power*, New York, London, 1963, p. 128.
28. Gary Maranell, 'The Evaluation of Presidents: An Extension of the Schlesinger Polls', *Journal of American History*, vol. 57 (June 1970).
29. Wayne, *op. cit.*, p. 141.

Congress. On the other hand, Eisenhower, as we have seen, had a marked sense of constitutional propriety and was unwilling to give any impression of interfering in congressional politics. It was not surprising therefore that Persons, Harlow and their staffs should adopt a low profile and a restrained, cautiously bipartisan approach to their work. No such inhibitions hindered the activities of Lawrence O'Brien, who, as head of legislative liaison, became a major figure in the Kennedy administration.[30]

In line with Kennedy's desire to be a reforming President and in contrast with what happened in the 1950s, 'The congressional liaison staff became more active and more assertive. There was greater presidential involvement and, throughout, a clear sense of both general and specific goals. Kennedy wanted a well-organised, well-run, aggressive operation, one that would vigorously push his program.'[31] O'Brien provided Kennedy with this, replacing the relatively modest legislative liaison of the Eisenhower years with a considerably more ambitious approach. From the beginning O'Brien threw himself wholeheartedly into the vital struggle to increase the size of the House Rules Committee, thereby involving the executive in matters concerning the internal organisation of Congress, a step that Eisenhower would never have allowed. When it came to the formulation of policy in the Kennedy administration, the liaison staff played a major role. Once the requisite legislation was submitted to Congress, the role of the liaison staff became even more crucial. They sat in on strategy meetings with congressional leaders and effectively supervised the legislative process on behalf of the President. Kennedy, for his part, gave O'Brien his wholehearted support. He tried to ensure that congressional requests and communications were routed to him via the liaison office and left no one in any doubt that O'Brien spoke for the President on Capitol Hill.[32]

The importance of a well-oiled legislative liaison machine was also very apparent to Lyndon Johnson, although his consuming interest in the detailed work of Congress led him to keep Lawrence O'Brien on a shorter leash than had been the case during the Kennedy years. Johnson too was desperately anxious to emulate Roosevelt. As a young man he had idolised FDR and had studied his performance as chief legislator. Later he had supplemented this with his own long and distinguished service in Congress.[33] On the face of it, Johnson

30. *Ibid.*, p. 147.
31. *Ibid.*, p. 146.
32. *Ibid.*, p. 147.
33. Rowland Evans and Robert Novak, *Lyndon B. Johnson: The Exercise of Power*, New York, London, 1967, p. 10 and Ch. 6.

was supremely well qualified for the legislative leadership role. He skilfully used many of the techniques employed by Roosevelt, in conjunction with his own extraordinary persuasive skills. Johnson masterminded the passage of a formidable programme of legislation. This included reforms that had for years been on the liberal agenda, such as the civil rights bills of 1964 and 1965 and the federal aid to education act of 1965.

One of Johnson's greatest strengths as legislative leader, in the early years of his presidency, was his profound understanding of the innermost workings of Congress. To an extent that even Roosevelt could not have equalled, Johnson 'knew the deck' in Congress. 'He knew where every wire of power ran, whose influence was waxing or waning, the rules and habits of the committees, what each had done three years before and wanted to do next year, the skeletons and hopes in scores of closets.'[34] Johnson understood fully the preoccupation of congressmen with the problems of their reelection.

The decades of congressional life, the national campaigns, the photographic memory, the voracious interest in political situations all counted. He had studied not only congress but the circumstances surrounding congressmen . . . he had a surgical knowledge of states and districts, the political strengths and weaknesses of individual congressmen, their supporters back home, their allegiances, apprehensions and ambitions.[35]

This was a level of understanding of the minds of congressmen that no other President has been able to equal, and, in the short term, Johnson used it to devastating effect.

There is another sense in which Johnson went even further than Roosevelt. The latter had been well aware of the need of a President to come to grips with the detail of legislation, but Johnson's immersion in detail was phenomenal. 'Other Presidents have paid close attention to the congress but the scope and intensity of Lyndon Johnson's participation in the legislative process were unprecedented.'[36] President Johnson also broke new ground by drawing members of Congress into the processes of formulating legislative proposals in the executive branch. At the earliest stages of preparing legislation, secret discussions took place with key congressmen, and then, before the sending of presidential messages to the Hill, committee and party leaders received special briefings.

Johnson later explained his view of the appropriate relationship

---

34. Eric Goldman, *The Tragedy of Lyndon Johnson*, New York, 1968, p. 70.
35. *Ibid.*, p. 73.
36. Doris Kearns, *Lyndon Johnson and the American Dream*, New York, 1976, p. 236.

between the legislative and executive branches. 'If it is really going to work, the relationship between the President and the Congress has got to be almost incestuous. He's got to know them even better than they know themselves. And then, on the basis of this knowledge, he's got to build a system that stretches from the cradle to the grave, from the moment a bill is introduced to the moment it is officially enrolled as the law of the land.'[37] For a while, at least, Johnson came close to meeting these conditions, and for a short while he had a grip on the legislative process that even a British prime minister might envy.

Legislative Leadership in Perspective

The discussion in the previous section on the evolution of the President's role as legislative leader has tended to portray Woodrow Wilson, Franklin Roosevelt and Lyndon Johnson in a particularly favourable light, and there is little doubt that these Presidents contributed substantially to the development of that role. However, our presentation so far has been rather selective. We have deliberately emphasised the positive with regard to development at the expense of some distortion of the historical record.

In placing the achievements of these outstanding legislative leaders in perspective, we must first of all take account of some of the considerable advantages they enjoyed. Woodrow Wilson, for instance, went to the White House on a wave of progressive reform. Moreover, his electoral success was a consequence of chronic divisions among the Republicans, and his party won a sweeping victory in the House and also gained control of the Senate. Taken together, the election results of 1912 represented an impressive mandate for progressive reform and presented Wilson with an exceptional opportunity for leadership from the White House.

Franklin Roosevelt was the beneficiary of even more advantageous circumstances. His election in 1932 was a landslide, and subsequent congressional and presidential elections consistently provided him with considerable electoral support. Furthermore, as we have seen, many of Roosevelt's legislative achievements were accomplished at a moment of desperate national emergency when many of the normal constraints were in abeyance and the American people and Congress were clamouring for leadership. In all probability no President in history has been presented with a more compliant Congress than the one that faced Roosevelt when he took office.

37. *Ibid.*, p. 236–7.

Similarly, a balanced evaluation of Lyndon Johnson's success as legislative leader must take account of the advantages he enjoyed, at least initially. He too became President at a moment of crisis and in addition was heir to the formidable legacy of his martyred predecessor. President Kennedy's rhetoric and the legislative groundwork of his administration in combination with the wave of popular emotion that followed his assassination were essential prerequisites of Johnson's remarkable legislative record in the early years of his presidency. This is not to undervalue Johnson's own contribution, which was considerable, but to recognise that he was presented with opportunities available to few other chief executives in history.

Presidents Wilson, Roosevelt and Johnson all entered the White House at a particularly opportune moment: when the need for change was widely accepted; after a period of congressional dominance; and at a point in American history when the people laid aside their prejudice against centralised power in favour of executive leadership. It may have required exceptional leaders to take advantage of the opportunities presented, but recognition of their good fortune is necessary to an evaluation of the Presidents under discussion. Such evaluations also need to take account of the fact that each of these Presidents enjoyed outstanding legislative success for only a relatively brief period. Eventually, each faltered badly in his dealings with Congress.

In the case of Wilson, his relations with Congress underwent a severe deterioration, culminating in the defeat of the Treaty of Versailles by the Senate. This was not only a devastating rebuff for Wilson personally but also a disastrous institutional defeat for the presidency from which it did not recover until the election of Roosevelt in 1932. This drastic reversal in Wilson's fortunes as legislative leader had many causes, including his illness and the seemingly inevitable cyclical swing in the balance of power back to the legislature after a period of presidential dominance. In addition, it may be that in the end his qualities of legislative leadership left something to be desirèd. He had never really understood Congress or sympathised with its members. At the outset these predispositions had been concealed behind a mask of geniality, but in the face of illness and the heat of a bitter constitutional battle his true feelings were laid bare. In his dealings with the Senate he became cold, austere, uncommunicative, domineering and, above all, inflexible.

Roosevelt was probably the most gifted legislative leader of all, but even his mastery of Congress in domestic affairs was eventually weakened. By the end of 1938 his relations with the legislature were at a low ebb, and, writing of the 1940s, Rexford Tugwell spoke of the 'crippling of Roosevelt as chief legislator'.[38] These developments were partly due to the President's preoccupation with the conduct of the war and also to the same cyclical shift that afflicted Wilson. However, Roosevelt also brought some of these difficulties on his own head, and, in a manner not dissimilar to Wilson's over the Treaty, he catastrophically overreached himself with his plan to pack the Supreme Court.

Emboldened by his massive victory in the 1936 election, Roosevelt chose to take on the Supreme Court, seeking to circumvent its resistance to the New Deal by a bill that would have enabled him to appoint a number of new justices. However, the President's much-vaunted skill in dealing with Congress and marshalling public opinion seems to have deserted him at this stage. His collaborative approach towards Congress was abandoned as he suddenly produced a full-blown judiciary reorganisation bill, much to the chagrin of congressional party leaders, committee chairmen and rank-and-file Democrats. Many legislators saw the bill as evidence of a President wilfully overstepping the boundaries of the Constitution, and Roosevelt's long-running battle with the Supreme Court now became a President-versus-Court-and-Congress contest.[39]

Even more surprising, perhaps, was the President's loss of his command of public opinion as it became increasingly apparent that the American people did not approve of this executive assault on the judiciary. In short, the court-packing plan fed the ever-present suspicions among congressmen of executive usurpation, divided the Democratic party, alienated progressives and dissipated Roosevelt's public support.

Early in 1965, Lyndon Johnson drew on the examples of Wilson's defeat over the Treaty of Versailles and Roosevelt's rebuff over the court-packing plan to illustrate his awareness of the tendency of Congress to reassert itself after periods of presidential dominance. 'I have watched the Congress from either the inside or the outside, man and boy, for more than forty years', he said, 'and I've never seen a Congress that didn't eventually take the measure of the President it was dealing with.'[40] Johnson's keen understanding of presidential-congressional relations helps to explain the frenetic pace of his legislative activity in the early years of his presidency. However, his knowledge of the fate that had befallen his predecessors did not prevent him from making similar mistakes. Like the others, Johnson

38. Tugwell, *op. cit.*, p. 442.
39. Leonard Baker, *Back to Back: The Duel Between FDR and the Supreme Court*, New York, 1967.
40. Evans and Novak, *Lyndon B. Johnson: The Exercise of Power, op. cit.*, p. 490.

in the end overreached himself, not in as dramatic a fashion, yet in the long run with no less disastrous results. Despite Johnson's keen understanding of the needs and ambitions of his former colleagues, it was not long before resentment against his forceful legislative leadership flared into open rebellion. With regard to domestic policy Johnson pushed too far and too fast, becoming impatient with congressional delays. As early as the autumn of 1965 his hold on Congress began to weaken and in subsequent years his credit plummeted even further in the wake of disillusionment with his conduct of an undeclared and increasingly futile war in South-East Asia.

Like Wilson and Roosevelt before him, Johnson was an outstanding legislative leader, yet his mastery over Congress was similarly brief. Like his predecessors, Johnson's spectacular successes were much dependent on the combination of fortuitous circumstances that came together as he took office, making it possible for him to extract a number of important reform measures from Congress. In the words of Johnson's most important biographer:

In the first years of Johnson's Presidency, as twice before in the twentieth century – during the New Freedom and the New Deal – special circumstances produced a blend of interests, needs, convictions, and alliances powerful enough to go beyond the normal pattern of slow incremental change. But if the resources of change were provided by the circumstances Lyndon Johnson played the dominant role – as Wilson and Roosevelt had before him – in transforming opportunity into achievement.[41]

There is no denying that Lyndon Johnson made good use of the opportunities available to him in the early years of his presidency. Nevertheless, in evaluating his record and in comparing it with that of other Presidents in recent years it is important to bear in mind his advantages. The wave of public sympathy generated by Kennedy's assassination plus the ill-fated candidacy of Barry Goldwater obtained for Johnson a formidable standing in the public opinion polls, a landslide victory in the 1964 election and massive support in Congress.

Public approval, electoral success and party support in Congress constitute the 'capital' that a President needs if he is to exercise leadership, and the last of these is, without doubt, the most important. 'Party support is the chief ingredient in presidential capital; it is the "gold standard" of congressional support.'[42]

41. Kearns, *op. cit.*, p. 222.
42. Paul Charles Light, *The President's Agenda: Domestic Policy Choice from Kennedy to Carter*, Baltimore, 1982, p. 27.

Members of the same party are likely generally to share the President's policy preferences, and, despite their notorious indiscipline, most pay heed to calls on their party loyalty. A large party in Congress is no guarantee of a President's legislative success, but without it he is seriously handicapped. According to a member of Johnson's legislative liaison staff: 'You can cajole Congress and try to buy the votes, but if you don't have your party on board, there isn't much hope. The President's legislative success starts with party. It's that simple.'[43]

Presidential support scores published in *Congressional Quarterly* have been widely used as a measure of the success of Presidents in their dealings with Congress, but one of the problems with such calculations is that they take no account of the party strength that a President may or may not have in Congress.[44] Such scores are no more than 'a rough measure of the comity between Congress and the President – how often Congress voted the way the President wanted or, conversely, how often he endorsed what Congress did.'[45] Such scores do not measure a President's success with his legislative programme. Furthermore, they do not distinguish between major and minor issues, between unanimous votes and those that succeed or fail by small margins, between administration proposals and congressional initiatives.

An examination of 'support scores' confirms some of the conventional wisdom with regard to legislative leadership in recent years. They illustrate Johnson's dominance from 1963 to 1965; they give an impression of the collapse of presidential influence in Congress in the wake of Watergate; and they provide some idea of Reagan's early successes in his relations with Congress. However, because these figures ignore differences in congressional party strengths, no distinction is made between, say, the 89th Congress when Johnson had a majority in his favour of 36 seats in the Senate and 155 seats in the House as against the 92nd Congress when Nixon's party was in a minority by 12 seats in the Senate and 75 seats in the House. Eisenhower's record in congressional relations looks decidedly better when account is taken of the modest representation of the Republican party in Congress in the 1950s. Similarly, Johnson's legislative achievements in 1964 and 1965 are seen in perspective against his massive congressional majorities. Despite the rebuffs that Nixon

43. *Ibid.*
44. Extensive use of these scores is made by George C. Edwards, *Presidential Influence in Congress*, San Francisco, 1980.
45. *Congressional Quarterly Weekly Report*, 2 Jan.1982, p. 18.

suffered at the hands of Congress in the early years of his presidency, he can be seen to have enjoyed a degree of success when party strength is taken into account.

In examining legislative leadership in perspective, it needs finally to be borne in mind that in the literature on the presidency there tends to be a built-in bias in favour of liberal, reforming Presidents. Chief executives like Roosevelt and Johnson are highly regarded whereas Eisenhower, as we have seen, is not. However, in recent years scholars such as Fred Greenstein have made necessary some re-thinking about the Eisenhower presidency.[46] They have denied that the 1950s was a period of drift and stagnation sorely lacking in firm direction from the executive branch. It is now argued that Eisenhower exercised effective leadership, although the style of that leadership differed fundamentally from that of other Presidents.

There has been a tendency to reserve the label of 'activist' for liberal, innovating Presidents whereas Greenstein argues that Eisenhower, although a conservative, was an 'activist' in the sense of seeking to 'restrain policy change'.[47] Furthermore, in contrast to the flamboyant and aggressive leadership styles of other Presidents, which in any case often came unstuck, Eisenhower worked quietly but effectively behind the scenes to secure his objectives. Unlike a Wilson or a Roosevelt obsessed with maximising influence in the political system, Eisenhower was endowed with a keen sense of constitutional propriety. He was meticulously respectful of the separation of powers. In his dealings with legislators he was carefully deferential, consulting with a wide range of congressional leaders on crucial issues and taking pains to avoid any impression of imposing his will. Such tactics, rather than reducing the President to a cypher, allowed him to influence events in a manner that would not otherwise have been possible. Thus rather than ducking the McCarthy issue − as hostile observers have been inclined to believe he did − the President was in fact covertly manoeuvring in colla-boration with his allies in Congress to bring about the Wisconsin Senator's defeat.

President Eisenhower's constitutional fastidiousness and his 'hidden hand' style of leadership were important in allowing him to retain his credibility and effectiveness throughout his two terms, thereby avoiding the severe collapse of public confidence that almost every other post-war President has suffered. Eisenhower's approval rating in Gallup polls averaged more than 60 per cent

46. Fred I. Greenstein, *The Hidden Hand Presidency: Eisenhower as Leader*, New York, 1982.
47. *Ibid.*, p. 58.

during the eight years of his presidency and only briefly went as low as 50 per cent, in stark contrast to the disastrously low poll scores of Presidents such as Truman, Johnson, Nixon and Carter at the end of their periods of office.[48]

Richard Neustadt's classic study of presidential power has Franklin Roosevelt as its hero whereas Dwight Eisenhower is depicted as representing much of how Presidents ought not to behave if they want to exercise effective leadership.[49] Greenstein, by contrast, suggests that the Eisenhower presidency has much to contribute to our understanding of the office. Every President is required to be both chief of state and chief policy-maker. The former role obliges Presidents to act as a symbol of national unity, and requires a broad base of public approval. On the other hand, the policy-making responsibilities of the President as prime minister and legislative leader involve him in intensely political and divisive activity. His efforts in the latter area are likely to undermine his position as chief of state, but in the case of Eisenhower he succeeded in marrying the two often antagonistic roles to a degree that none of his successors have been able to equal. Unlike them, he sustained his public popularity throughout two terms and left office without damaging the integrity of the presidency.[50]

Despite the undoubted value of Greenstein's interpretation as a corrective, he may be unduly charitable to Eisenhower. 'Hidden-hand' leadership can be less flatteringly described as leadership from behind, and one may question whether it is leadership at all. It may also be questioned whether Eisenhower's obsession with preserving his personal popularity derived solely from altruistic motives. In any event, it is clear that the Roosevelt/Neustadt model of presidential power is not the only valid one. In some circumstances Eisenhower's low-key, covert brand of leadership may be more appropriate than the openly aggressive style of legislative leadership that we associate with Wilson, Roosevelt and Johnson.

In this brief discussion of legislative leadership up to and including Johnson, some account has been taken of the fact that not all Presidents have the same opportunities to exercise leadership. Circumstances in 1913, 1933 and 1963 were very favourable to leadership from the White House whereas this cannot be said of 1921, 1949 or 1953. We have also recognised that even the most able and ambitious of Presidents have only managed to dominate the

48. Thomas E. Cronin, *The State of the Presidency*, Boston, 1980, pp. 328–9.
49. *Presidential Power, op. cit., passim.*
50. Greenstein, *op. cit.*, p. 5.

legislative branch for relatively brief periods, and such success as they have enjoyed has often been greatly facilitated by the strength of their party in Congress. There has also been recognition of the fact that different eras and different circumstances require different styles of presidential leadership.

Legislative Leadership since Johnson

According to the conventional wisdom of the time, 1964 seemed to bring the development of the President's role as chief legislator to its highest peak. Lyndon Johnson was seen as the legitimate heir of the reforming liberal Democratic Presidents of the past and was well qualified to consolidate the development that they had pioneered. Lacking the intellectual quality of a Wilson, the brilliance in man-management of a Roosevelt, or the charm of a Kennedy, Johnson nevertheless brought some formidable strengths to the presidency. No President has been equipped with a better understanding of the United States Congress or exhibited more drive and determination to be its master. These personal attributes, in conjunction with the considerable political advantages of high standing in public opinion polls, a stunning electoral victory in 1964 and a massive following in Congress made Johnson virtually unstoppable, at least in the short run.

Richard Nixon brought to the White House a quite different combination of personality and experience and was elected in radically different circumstances. He had served as a member of the House and the Senate, but he had never been a true man of Congress. His most notable service in Congress had been as a member of the House Un-American Activities Committee, a body not concerned with the fashioning of legislation.[51] In 1968 Nixon defeated Hubert Humphrey by little more than 500,000 votes, less than 1 per cent of the total popular vote, and he became the first President for 120 years to take office confronted by a Congress controlled by the opposition party.

Nevertheless, Nixon was hardly less determined than Johnson to bring the American political system to heel and to be an activist in domestic policy.[52] However, activism for Nixon had a conservative thrust. It entailed a rejection of the federal paternalism of the Kennedy-Johnson years, budget cutting and a revival of the states

51. Rowland Evans and Robert Novak, *Nixon in the White House*, New York, 1972, p. 106.
52. Richard Nixon, *The Memoirs of Richard Nixon*, New York, London, 1978, p. 414.

and the cities as decision-making centres. Despite the narrowness of his election victory and the Democratic majorities in Congress, Nixon claimed that his share of the popular vote plus George Wallace's, totalling 56.8 per cent of the votes cast, 'represented a clear mandate' from the people for him to pursue conservative policies irrespective of the liberal prejudices of the media and members of Congress.[53] Accordingly and notwithstanding some early cosmetic efforts to develop a working relationship with Congress, Nixon's instinct was for confrontation rather than collaboration with the legislative branch. In similar circumstances Eisenhower had sought to exercise leadership by establishing constitutionally correct and cordial relations with congressional leaders while at the same time maintaining his personal standing in the public opinion polls.

Eisenhower's legislative liaison operation was central to his strategy, but such arrangements were accorded a much lower priority in the Nixon White House. The principal figures dealing with domestic legislative matters on Nixon's staff were H. R. Haldeman and John Ehrlichman, but neither of them had any background in decision-making in government and both singularly lacked any understanding of or sympathy for the intricacies of the legislative process. The efforts of Bryce Harlow and others nominally in charge of legislative liaison in the Nixon administration were consistently undermined by the stridently anti-Congress sentiments of aides in the President's immediate circle.[54] Furthermore the President's reclusive and introspective style, plus his reluctance to put pressure on members of Congress personally, made for less than satisfactory relations with the legislative branch.

Ralph Huitt has suggested that the relationship between President and Congress is comparable to a 'constitutional marriage of presumed equals', but that was hardly the view of Richard Nixon, who cast doubt on the legitimacy of the congressional role and was quite unwilling to treat the legislature as an equal partner.[55] Nixon asserted that his mandate took precedence over any that Congress might claim and believed that his responsibility for the overall direction of the federal government was supreme. Fortified by these assumptions, the President made a frontal assault on the power of Congress, taking upon himself an unprecedented and constitutionally unjustifiable use of the power of impoundment. Congress

53. *Ibid.*, p. 351.
54. Evans and Novak, *Nixon in the White House, op. cit.*, Ch. 5.
55. Ralph Huitt, 'White House Channels to the Hill', in Harvey C. Mansfield, Sr., *Congress against the President*, New York, 1975, p. 71.

had long accepted the legitimacy of the impoundment procedure as a means of taking account of changed circumstances and preventing waste, but Nixon claimed that his power to withhold appropriated funds was virtually unlimited, and accordingly 'He carried both the volume and the scope of impoundment far beyond the actions of any previous president.'[56]

Nixon's unprecedented use of the impoundment weapon struck at the core of legislative power. By refusing, without acceptable justification, to spend money authorised by Congress, he claimed the right to defeat the intentions of the legislative branch almost at will. Such an extravagant extension of the power of the President inevitably provoked outrage in Congress and contributed much to the chronically bad relations between the two branches that developed well before the Watergate crisis finally brought Nixon down.

Nixon faced great difficulties when he entered the White House, but the problems of his successor were even greater. Presidents seeking to lead Congress require resources, but very few resources were available to Gerald Ford. In the first place, he was bereft of a base of electoral support, having been appointed Vice-President before succeeding Nixon in August 1974. It was also Ford's misfortune to take office at a moment when, in the aftermath of Vietnam and Watergate, the prestige of the presidency was at its lowest ebb for perhaps half a century. Initially, the new President's personal standing in the opinion polls was high, but this swiftly evaporated and shortly afterwards the Republican party suffered heavy losses in the 1974 congressional elections, losing 48 seats in the House and being reduced to 37 seats in the Senate. As if all this were not enough, Ford was required to deal with a reformed and fragmented Congress in an angrily reassertive and anti-presidential mood. Given such circumstances, his modest achievements as chief legislator look rather more impressive than at first sight.

In accounting for such success as Ford enjoyed, his long experience in Congress was clearly important. Unlike Nixon, Ford was a true man of Congress, steeped in its mores and methods. Moreover, in contrast to the belligerence of Nixon, Haldeman and Ehrlichman, Ford approached Congress in a spirit of 'communication, conciliation, compromise and cooperation'.[57] Many of his legislative liaison staff were Nixon holdovers, but the President was

56. James L. Sundquist, *The Decline and Resurgence of Congress*, Washington, 1981, p. 203.
57. Thomas E. Cronin, 'A Resurgent Congress and the Imperial Presidency', *Political Science Quarterly*, vol. 95, no. 2 (Summer 1980).

Table 3.1.   PRESIDENTIAL VETOES, 1952–80

	Years served (to nearest year)	Vetoes
Eisenhower	8	181
Kennedy	3	21
Johnson	5	30
Nixon	6	43
Ford	2	66
Carter	4	31

Source: Louis Fisher, *The Politics of Shared Power*, Washington, DC, 1981, p. 26.

now a gregarious, unassuming and reassuring former legislator who met easily and freely with Senators and Representatives.

Ford's ability and willingness to interact easily and frequently with members of both parties and branches, despite strong policy differences, earned much praise for his administration's liaison with congress. His staff was generally well respected and if judged by the President's personal popularity on the Hill, or by the large numbers of vetoes sustained, it was highly effective.[58]

Ford's successful use of the veto was the most notable feature of executive-legislative relations during his presidency. As Table 3.1 shows, he made greater use of the veto than any other President since Eisenhower. While Eisenhower vetoed a lot of bills, he was in office for eight years, and of the 181 bills vetoed by Eisenhower only 100 were public bills. All but five of Ford's sixty-six vetoes were cast against public bills. Kennedy, Johnson, Nixon and Carter vetoed on average seven bills per year while Ford struck down sixty-six in two years and five months.

It is also worth noting that, despite Ford's repeated use of the veto and a heavily Democratic Congress, he was overriden on only twelve occasions.[59] On the other hand, sustaining a veto is a relatively modest achievement hardly comparable to the complexities of coalition-building required to pass bills. As one of Ford's staff members admitted, 'putting together 34 like-minded Senators or 147 Representatives isn't as difficult as it may seem. It is a hell of a lot easier than pulling a majority into place. All you have to win is one House.'[60] In general Ford demonstrated that in some situations the veto power can be a potent instrument, enabling Presidents lacking in resources to play an important, if largely negative, role in the legislative process.

58. Wayne, *op. cit.*, p. 163.
59. Edwards, *op. cit.*, p. 24.
60. Light, *op. cit.*, p. 114.

Ford's defeat in 1976 and the election of a Democratic President gave some reason for hope that executive-legislative relations would improve, but such optimism proved unwarranted. Ostensibly Carter took office well placed to realise his ambition to be an activist President. It is true that he beat Ford only narrowly, obtaining 51 per cent of the popular vote, yet at the same time the congressional elections produced Democratic majorities in both houses almost as large as those enjoyed by Johnson after the elections of 1964. However, in other respects 1976 was quite unlike 1964. The public mood was still affected by disillusionment with the imperial presidency and by memories of Vietnam and Watergate. Few Democrats in Congress owed their election to Jimmy Carter, who had run behind most of his party's candidates for the House and Senate. Moreover, by 1976 a considerable proportion of the Democrats in Congress had no experience of cooperating with a President of their own party in the White House.

By comparison with Johnson's situation, Carter faced a 'new' Congress, one which had been opened up by reform. The old lines of congressional leadership and authority had broken down, and the distribution of power was more decentralised and inchoate than it had been for many years. As Carter himself put it later:

Each legislator had to be wooed and won individually. It was every member for himself and the devil take the hindmost! Well intended reforms in the organisation of congress and of the Democratic party had undermined the power of party leaders. This situation was completely different from the time of Lyndon Johnson's presidency, when he, the Speaker of the House, and the Chairman of the House Ways and Means Committee could agree on a tax or welfare proposal and be certain that the House of Representatives would ratify their decision.[61]

In other words there were some considerable obstacles to legislative leadership when Carter became President. Nevertheless Carter was by no means entirely an innocent victim of circumstances. To a substantial degree his failure to establish a constructive relationship with Congress was of his own making.

Jimmy Carter was far removed from the Rooseveltian model of the presidency and came much closer in some respects to that of his fellow-Southerner Woodrow Wilson. For both Carter and Wilson presidential piety and a high sense of public morality produced an inflexible determination to abide by principles rather than yield

61. Jimmy Carter, *Keeping Faith*, London, 1982, p. 80. See also Samuel C. Patterson, 'The Semi-Sovereign Congress', in Anthony King (ed.), *The New American Political System*, Washington, DC, 1979.

to political expediency. Like Wilson in 1912, Carter in 1976 campaigned against 'Washington', striking out against the discredited 'old' politics associated in particular with the United States Congress. Well in advance of becoming President, he made clear his repugnance for wheeling and dealing and the politics of patronage and the pork barrel. Such talk inevitably caused resentment in Congress, but more importantly, the thinking upon which it was based severely handicapped the new President as legislative leader.

Some consideration of Carter's background is relevant to an understanding of his behaviour in office and his problems in handling the legislature. The most important part of Carter's formative experience was his training and work as an engineer. As William Pfaff has argued, engineers and scientists assume that, given the required amount of research and application of the relevant expertise, objective answers can be found to particular problems.[62] They assume further that once the answers have been found, agreement will follow provided that the channels of communication are adequate. Carter, accordingly, seemed to believe that objective answers could be found to the energy problem and the right policy developed if he personally studied the question in sufficient detail and consulted with all the relevant experts. Once the policy had been arrived at, it would be accepted by the American people and Congress, provided that Carter and his staff were competent communicators. However, scientific problem-solving and public policy-making are not the same thing, and President Carter as a policy-maker was 'a scientific man searching for certitude in an area of human experience, that of political conflict, which lacks mathematical or material certitude'.[63] Politicians do not deal in objective answers but must steer a course between often incompatible interests; they are obliged to bargain and accommodate and to settle for less-than-ideal policies.

Jimmy Carter's failure to understand or accept the rudimentary facts about the policy-making process is entertainingly but vividly conveyed by a member of Congress who envisaged the following exchanges between the Speaker, Tip O'Neill, and the President after the latter's famous 'energy is the moral equivalent of war' speech.

O'Neill: A fine speech, Mr President. Now here's a list of members you should call, you know, to keep the pressure on. We need their votes.

Carter: Tip, I outlined the problem to the people of the United States of America. It was rational, and my presentation was also rational. Now the American people are the most intelligent people in the entire world,

62. 'Carter's Science and Politics', *International Herald Tribune*, 9–10 June 1979.
63. *Ibid.*

Tip, and I am sure that when they and their Representatives think my program over, they will see that I was right.

O'Neill: Lookit, Mr President. We need you to push this bill through. This is politics we are talking here, not physics.

Carter: It is not politics, Tip, not to me. It's what is right and rational and necessary and practical and urgent that we do. . . . Say, did you like my sweater?

O'Neill (later, to his congressional colleague): That guy is hopeless. It's gonna be a long winter.[64]

Like many other incoming Presidents, Carter, at the outset, was determined to establish a good working relationship with Congress. During the transition period he met with innumerable legislative leaders and rank-and-file members.[65] At an early stage, however, things began to go badly wrong. Anti-presidential resentment began surfacing on Capitol Hill with members complaining that they were being swamped by large numbers of ill-prepared legislative proposals. Committee chairmen and party leaders objected to the lack of prior consultation on legislative matters and were outraged when the President changed his position on key issues without notifying them, particularly where they had gone out on a limb in his support. Carter's crude efforts, in early 1977, to eliminate public works water projects, dear to the hearts of some members, caused considerable anger in Congress, and congressmen were further irritated by the President's obvious contempt for the politics of patronage and his reluctance to deal even in the 'small potatoes' of invitations to the White House. Federal appointments were made without informing the relevant member of Congress, and the President took trips without informing the congressman whose district was being visited.[66]

Perhaps most important of all was the weakness of the legislative liaison office under Carter. According to Eric Davis, the organisational structure of Carter's legislative liaison operation was seriously flawed.[67] The young and inexperienced liaison staff were not involved in the formulation of policy and were not in close touch with the President. More fundamentally, Carter and his associates never appreciated the importance of coalition-building, so essential to the passage of bills.

64. Jack Beatty, 'The Life of the Party', *The New Republic*, 24 Jan. 1983.
65. Jack W. Germond, 'Congress and Carter: Who's in Charge?', *New York Times Magazine*, 30 Jan. 1977.
66. Martin Tolchin, 'An Old Pol Takes On the New President', *New York Times Magazine*, 24 July 1977; and *Congressional Quarterly Weekly Report*, 11 Oct. 1980, p. 3096.
67. Eric Davis, 'Legislative Liaison in the Carter Administration', *Political Science Quarterly*, vol. 94, no. 2 (Summer 1979).

The White House has had great difficulty in realising that congressional politics *is* coalition politics and that members of Congress will not automatically jump to the support of White House programs, even if they come from a Democratic White House and reflect the work of the best experts in the field. . . . Carter basically won the nomination without having to build a coalition. He did not have to make side payments to any of the major groupings within the Democratic Party. . . . [Carter and his staff naively believed that] since they did not have to engage in bargaining to get the nomination or to win the election, they would not have to engage in bargaining or exchange to get their programs passed on Capitol Hill.[68]

To the end, although willing to admit a few mistakes, Carter remained largely unrepentant about his methods in dealing with Congress. In his memoirs he cites *Congressional Quarterly* support scores in defence of his claim that he did 'reasonably well' in his 'overall relationship with Congress'.[69] However, this is not a view generally shared. The *Congressional Quarterly Almanac* appropriately headlines its final survey of executive-legislative relations in that period 'Carter and Congress: Strangers to the End'.[70] It would be very difficult to argue that Jimmy Carter made any positive contribution to the development of the President's role as chief legislator. It is rather the case that, notwithstanding the many difficulties he encountered, Carter demonstrated how a modern President should *not* behave if he seeks to lead Congress.

By the end of the 1970s it appeared to some that the American presidency as an institution was in serious trouble, and a variety of commentators began reflecting on the need for constitutional reform.[71] However, within a few months of Ronald Reagan's arrival in the White House such ideas became markedly less fashionable, and by the end of his first year in office he was being heralded in the press as the most effective chief legislator since Lyndon Johnson. Thus Helen Dewar wrote:

The first session of the 97th Congress ended yesterday, as it began: dominated by President Reagan and his crusade to cut taxes, strengthen the military, and reverse half a century of growth in social programs. The Republican Senate and Democratic House, although split along party lines, came together under the Reagan spell to make more history in a few months than most Congresses have made in two full years.[72]

These achievements were all the more remarkable given the

---

68. *Ibid.*
69. Carter, *op. cit.*, p. 88.
70. *Congressional Quarterly Almanac 1980*, pp. 3–9.
71. Lloyd Cutler, 'To Form a Government', *Foreign Affairs*, vol. 59, no. 1 (Fall 1980).
72. *Washington Post*, 17 Dec. 1981.

circumstances of Reagan's election. He swept in on a landslide, and his party gained a dozen seats in the Senate, thereby obtaining control of the upper chamber for the first time in twenty-six years. In the House, on the other hand, despite a loss of 33 seats, the Democrats remained firmly in control with a majority of 51. Unlike the strong legislative leaders of the past, therefore, Reagan was seriously handicapped by the opposition party's dominance of one house. In addition, the new President faced all the problems of decentralisation and individualism in the legislature that had bedevilled both Ford and Carter. All in all, stalemate between the White House and Capitol Hill seemed to be the most likely outcome of the new situation.

Apparently undaunted by these prospects, Reagan entered the White House as a conservative ideologue, convinced of an urgent need to roll back what he considered to be decades of misguided, largely Democratic government. In that sense he intended to be, like Richard Nixon, an activist but conservative chief executive. The need for changes in national economic policy had been a central theme of the Republican campaign in 1980. Reagan had argued that excessive federal expenditure was a root cause of inflation and that tax cuts were essential to revive the economy. On election the new administration continued to focus primarily on changes in economic policy. Avoiding Carter's mistake of deluging Congress with a wide range of legislative proposals, Reagan and his advisers pressed on Congress a programme of budget reductions and tax cuts, eventually scoring some major victories in this area.

In accounting for these remarkable early successes it has been argued that Reagan's landslide victory in 1980, in conjunction with the success of the Republicans in winning the Senate, gave the President, for the moment at least, control over the political agenda.

The size of Reagan's margin over Carter, and the Republican capture of the Senate, combined with the ordinary advantages a president has in influencing the framing of issues, allowed Reagan to dominate political debate on domestic policy in early 1981 and, crucial to this domination, he defined the policy choices. The crucial policy choice would lie between cutting wasteful federal spending and initiative-destroying taxes, on the one hand, thus bringing down the rate of inflation and ensuring healthy economic growth or, on the other hand, continuing the discredited 'tax and tax, spend and spend' policies of the past.[73]

Reagan's personal contribution to the new climate of opinion should

---

73. Barbara Sinclair, 'Agenda Control and Policy Success: Ronald Reagan and the 97th House', *Legislative Studies Quarterly*, vol. 10, no. 3 (Aug. 1985).

not be exaggerated. Many other factors and individuals played a part in bringing about the shift of public opinion away from some of the premises upon which domestic policy had long been based. The 1980 election, for example, was primarily a referendum on the Carter administration rather than a vote for a conservative economic policy. Nevertheless the Reagan landslide clearly contributed substantially to an altering of the terms of political debate and made it possible for the new administration temporarily to control the congressional agenda. Furthermore Reagan and his advisers manoeuvred shrewdly in Congress to ensure that changes in budgetary and taxation policy were not diluted by voting on a multitude of bills, but were focused on a few key votes.

Reagan's initial legislative triumphs were also assisted by his establishment of an effective liaison office staffed by experienced Capitol Hill insiders – in marked contrast to the Georgia amateurs of the Carter administration. The legislative liaison operation was buttressed by the President's willingness to lobby members of Congress personally and very effectively when the occasion required it. Moreover, Ronald Reagan showed few signs of the moralistic anxieties that impeded Jimmy Carter in his relations with Congress. As Governor of California, Reagan had demonstrated a readiness to compromise when it was necessary, and now as President he was not reluctant to make deals with members of Congress as a means of oiling the wheels of the policy-making process.[74] As James Baker, Reagan's first term chief of staff and head of the administration's legislative strategy group, remarked, 'Deals is a dirty word, but consensus building and pursuing the political process isn't.'[75]

Another essential ingredient of Reagan's early success in dealing with Congress was his style of leadership. In his first term Reagan's relaxed, good-humoured and modest attitude struck a sympathetic chord with public and legislators alike – who had had more than enough of intense and overbearing Presidents. Thus Allen Schick, in accounting for Reagan's budget success in 1981, reports the experiences of a Democratic congressman who supported the President. When he visited the Oval Office for an interview with the President, they did not discuss the detail of the budget.

I wasn't there more than a couple of minutes, but I didn't feel rushed and I'm not quite sure how I was shown the door. A photographer shot the usual roll of pictures; the President gave me a firm, friendly handshake. He patted me on the back and told me how much he needed and appreciated my support. He said I should call if I need help on anything. And that was it.

74. *Congressional Quarterly Weekly Report*, 24 Jan. 1981, p. 174.
75. *The Times* (London), 31 July 1981.

A meeting with Jimmy Carter in company with a number of other members of Congress had been very different.

> We had hardly got seated and Carter started lecturing us about the problems he had with one of the sections in the bill. He knew the details better than most of us, but somehow that caused more resentment than if he had left the specifics to us.[76]

Even when they disliked his policies, the American people and members of Congress have been comfortable with Reagan personally. He has been perceived as a likeable man and, in this respect at least, he evokes memories of Franklin Roosevelt, Dwight Eisenhower and John Kennedy. Aspersions have been cast on the quality of the President's intellect and there has been a lot of adverse press comment on the number of hours he spends on the job, but workaholics do not necessarily make good Presidents. Few, after all, worked harder than Nixon and Carter.

Reagan's lack of command of the detail of policy-making has sometimes provided ammunition for his enemies and caused consternation among his friends. On the face of it, lack of familiarity with the specifics of policy may be thought to be a dis-advantage in a chief legislator. The great chief legislators of the past, such as Wilson, Roosevelt and Johnson, immersed themselves in the minutiae of government. However, there is reason to believe that a President, by distancing himself from the detail, can avoid the adverse political consequences that may flow from a greater involvement in the processes of policy-making. Eisenhower, for example, protected his personal popularity by standing back from the legislative process and using such senior associates as Sherman Adams and John Foster Dulles as lightning-rods to deflect criticism. Reagan is no Eisenhower; he is much readier to involve himself in the business of cajoling and persuading members of Congress. At the same time, Reagan does this only periodically, and then it is in support of broad objectives rather than details. In the words of Stephen Wayne:

> This lack of specificity may be part of the strategy. In addition to being consistent with Reagan's personal style, it reduces his burden and, most important, his risk. Verbal blunders, poor judgement, and costly errors can be and have been blamed on subordinates. The president avoids responsibility and ridicule by not having been informed about the details. All accomplishments, of course, result from his leadership.[77]

76. Allen Schick, 'How the Budget Was Won and Lost', in Norman J. Ornstein (ed.), *President and Congress: Assessing Reagan's First Year*, Washington, DC, 1982, pp. 23–4.
77. Stephen Wayne, 'Congressional Liaison in the Reagan White House: A Preliminary Assessment of the First Year', *ibid.*, pp. 59–60.

This may explain why Reagan has come to be known in the media as the 'Teflon President', whose standing in the opinion polls remains unaffected by the reverses and mistakes of his administration.

As noted earlier, Presidents must not only be persuasive in their face-to-face dealings with legislators, but they must also effectively rally public opinion so as to bring indirect pressure to bear on the legislative process. For the modern President this requires, above all else, an ability to project a reassuring image on the television screen, and in that Ronald Reagan has clearly excelled. In his expert hands, television and radio have become invaluable weapons essential to his success in gathering support for his policies. His ability to read a script elegantly and convincingly on television has been an enormously important political resource as well as being a skill that few other Presidents have mastered. According to Fred Greenstein, 'Reagan is only the third modern president [the others being Roosevelt and Kennedy] who could be said to have exhibited a professionally adept podium manner.'[78]

Nevertheless, like every other successful chief legislator, Reagan's honeymoon with Congress was short-lived. In 1982, as his economic policies were perceived not to be working, his standing in the opinion polls slumped, and his budget was rejected by Congress. In the autumn the Republicans lost ground in the congressional elections; the President's low rating in the polls persisted; and in the *Congressional Quarterly* presidential support scores for 1982, Reagan was down 10 points on 1981.[79] For all that, although Reagan's command of Congress slipped in 1982 and despite dissatisfaction with many of his policies, expert observers continued to be impressed by his *conduct* of the presidency. Thus in January 1983, Gerald Pomper said, 'Reagan has accomplished major policy changes, which impresses me even though I oppose the direction.' Similarly, Robert Huckshorn said, 'Reagan has accomplished a great deal in both defense and in putting his economic program into place. That does not mean either will be successful.' According to Samuel C. Patterson, Reagan had 'restored a certain dignity and competence to the presidency. He knows how to be a leader.'[80]

Three years after these favourable evaluations, and despite an even larger landslide victory for Reagan in 1984, the picture is very different. As the unproductive first session of the 99th Congress drew to a close, Washington was full of recriminations regarding the

---

78. Fred I. Greenstein, *The Reagan Presidency: An Early Assessment*, Baltimore, 1983, p. 173.
79. *Congressional Quarterly Almanac*, 1982.
80. 'Mid-term Verdict on President by Political Scholars', *US News and World Report*, 24 Jan. 1983.

President's failure to provide legislative leadership. Thus the *New York Times* reported, 'Above all, Republicans and Democrats alike blame President Reagan as failing both to set a clear legislative agenda and to admit that closing the budget deficit would require new taxes and steep cuts in military spending.'[81] *Time* noted that 'By putting so much weight behind tax reform and failing to heed growing public fears about the deficit, Reagan may have forfeited his chance to exercise leadership on Capitol Hill and squandered much of the huge, if diffuse, public mandate he won only a year ago.'[82] What is the evidence for these gloomy assessments, and if they are true how do we account for the reversal? How did the miracle-worker of 1981 become an ineffective legislative leader in 1985?

President Reagan did enjoy some success in dealing with the first session of the 99th Congress. He displayed his skill in charming and cajoling members of the House and Senate into voting the funds necessary to expand the MX missile programme. He also managed to reverse an earlier congressional decision to deny an administration request for financial aid to the anti-government 'Contra' rebels in Nicaragua. However, these successes in defence and foreign policy were not duplicated on the domestic front, where the White House's strategy was found wanting in dealing with the ever-increasing deficit and the President's foremost legislative priority, tax reform. It was the deficit problem that led the President to sign the Gramm-Rudman bill into law. This legislation provides for automatic budget reductions in order to eliminate the deficit within five years. It has been widely denounced as a desperate and possibly unconstitutional measure that in the long term (assuming it survives challenges in the courts) will crudely delimit executive leadership in budgetary matters and significantly erode Congress' power of the purse. Gramm-Rudman, according to Walter Heller, is 'economically capricious, socially unfair, militarily risky, constitutionally questionable, politically irresponsible, procedurally perverse and administratively outlandish'.[83] Commentators were hardly less critical of the Reagan administration's attempts to pass a tax reform bill in 1985. In his efforts to further this cause, President Reagan allied himself with the Democratic leadership in the House, but in so doing seriously alienated members of his own party.

In accounting for the recent decline in Reagan's command of Congress, we must first of all recognise that he is the victim of forces

81. *Ibid.*, 22 Dec. 1985.
82. *Ibid.*, 23 Dec. 1985.
83. *Ibid.*

beyond his control. His most obvious disadvantage is that he is a second-term President with a consequently inevitably weakened influence in Congress. This tendency might have been partly offset if Reagan had carried large numbers of Republicans into office with him in 1984. In fact, despite his landslide in the presidential vote, the Republicans gained only fourteen seats in the House and lost two in the Senate, although they continued to control the latter.

In comparing Reagan's situation with that of other modern Presidents, the example of Eisenhower is particularly relevant. He enjoyed even greater popular support, but after a second landslide in 1956 faced a Congress with both houses controlled by the Democrats. Admittedly Eisenhower was less of a legislative activist than Reagan, but it is notable that the first year of his second term was similarly unproductive. In 1957 Congress approved only 37 per cent of Eisenhower's 206 legislative requests, his lowest score since he entered office.[84] Like Eisenhower in 1957, Reagan in 1985 was not helped by the fact that mid-term elections would soon be in prospect. Republicans in the House and Senate were worrying about their electoral fortunes and became increasingly disinclined to heed the call of party loyalty.

As was noted, discipline within the Republican party in the House was not helped by the President's manoeuvring over tax reform. In addition, in the summer of 1985 he managed to alienate the members of his own party in the Senate. As a contribution to reducing the deficit, the Senate Republican leadership took the electorally dangerous course of agreeing to a delay in social security cost-of-living adjustments, only to find that, in response to pressure from the Democratic leadership in the House, the President openly repudiated his colleagues in the Senate.

Reagan's relationship with Congress in his second term has also been bedevilled by changes of personnel. An important loss was Howard Baker, the Senate majority leader, who did not seek reelection in 1984.[85] His replacement, Robert Dole, is much less close to the Reagan administration. Presidential-congressional relations may also have suffered from changes in the administration's legislative liaison staff. At the beginning of the Reagan administration, White House lobbying was directed by experienced and skilled leaders, but there is reason to believe that the quality of that leadership has declined.[86]

---

84. *Congressional Quarterly Weekly Report*, 27 Oct. 1984, p. 2782.
85. On Baker's importance see Stephen Wayne, 'Congressional Liaison in the Reagan White House'.
86. *Congressional Quarterly Weekly Report*, 16 June 1984, pp. 1430–1.

Most important of all have been the changes that have occurred in the uppermost reaches of the White House staff. At the beginning of Reagan's second term, James Baker, who had hitherto been the President's chief of staff, switched jobs with Donald Regan, the Secretary of the Treasury. During the first term, Baker, an urbane Texan lawyer, demonstrated considerable skill in dealing with Congress on the President's behalf, but commentators have suggested that Regan, an abrasive, hard-headed businessman, is less well-qualified in terms of experience and temperament. Thus, according to Bernard Weinraub, 'Critics say Regan's relative inexperience and his brusque, commanding style have irritated key legislators, and have damaged White House relations with Congress.' A 'key White House official' is quoted as saying of Regan, 'There really is little political experience, direct and indirect, and it shows. To this day he doesn't seem to understand how politicians, and specifically members of Congress, operate.'[87] These changes of personnel are without doubt important to an understanding of President Reagan's varying relationship with Congress, yet there are also more fundamental explanations to be taken into account.

Reagan's experience confirms that the separation of powers is still alive and well in Washington and demonstrates anew the long-term tendency towards deadlock between executive and legislature. Even modern Presidents are denied the role of legislative leader as of right. Each new President is obliged to contest with Congress in his attempts to meet his responsibilities. For brief periods some modern Presidents have appeared to establish mastery over Congress and thereby to bridge the separation of powers. For a while Reagan joined this company, but, like the rest, his success has proved to be short-lived.

Notwithstanding two landslide elections, impressive opinion poll ratings and considerable personal charm, in his second term Reagan had to face a Congress which had few incentives to cooperate with him. At the best of times congressmen tend to be difficult in their dealings with the President. They are likely to be steeped in their own sense of constitutional self-importance and to be parochial in their attitudes towards most political questions. Within Congress effective collective action has always been difficult to accomplish, and Congress in the 1980s is even more individualistic than in previous eras. The erosion of party in conjunction with electoral impera-tives has led to a situation where almost every member of Con-

---

87. Bernard Weinraub, 'How Donald Regan Runs the White House', *New York Times Magazine*, 5 Jan. 1985, pp. 12 and 54.

gress is obliged to conduct a personal election campaign. Such circumstances do little to encourage members of Congress to respect the legislative ambitions of a President deep in his second term.

As a consequence, Reagan's record as chief executive will ultimately be seen, we may reasonably assume, as mixed. What, if anything, has Ronald Reagan contributed to the development of the President's role as legislative leader or, to widen the discussion, the development of the presidential office? To accept James MacGregor Burns' dictum that skill as a legislative leader is 'the classic test of greatness' in a President is to look at the office in narrow terms. We have done so in this chapter, but to do so without qualification is to weigh the discussion in favour of a particular type of President. The 'heavyweight' Presidents, according to such an analysis, are the liberal activists who successfully ram an impressive array of reform legislation through Congress. The outstanding example of this type is Franklin Roosevelt, and it is with good reason that William Leuchtenburg entitled his book *In the Shadow of FDR*.[88] As Leuchtenburg shows, the Presidents since Roosevelt have had to live and work in his shadow. Roosevelt has been the standard against which his successors have inevitably been measured.

Students of the presidency have had no less difficulty in escaping the dominance of the Roosevelt example. Richard Neustadt's *Presidential Power* is a paean of praise for Roosevelt's presidency, and that influential book has done much to set the terms of debate for the evaluation of Presidents by political scientists and historians. In recent years, however, as was noted earlier, the furthering of our understanding of Eisenhower has led to some questioning of the merits of the Roosevelt/Neustadt model of presidential power. That model, it is now recognised, may be appropriate in some periods and circumstances, but it is not necessarily the only model, and, in any case, it incorporates a liberal bias hardly suitable for those who aspire to objective understanding.

Discussions of presidential power, it would seem, need to take into account conservative Presidents such as Eisenhower and Reagan who on their own terms have been effective legislative leaders, even in the face of large majorities against them in Congress. According to this alternative model, it is a mistake for a President to allow himself to become immersed in the intricacies of the legislative process in the obsessive manner of a Lyndon Johnson. To do so is to lose sight of the fact that a President has other roles to fulfil. He

---

88. William Leuchtenburg, *In the Shadow of FDR*, Ithaca, NY, 1983.

must also, for example, be the chief of state. To exercise that
function adequately he must retain his popular support. That
support will be jeopardised if he becomes too embroiled in the
inherently divisive work of legislative politics.[89]

89. See Greenstein, *The Hidden Hand Presidency, op. cit.* See also John P. Burke,
    'Political Context and Presidential Influence', *Presidential Studies Quarterly*,
    Spring 1985.

4

THE PRESIDENT AND THE EXECUTIVE BRANCH

Robert Williams

The structure, scale and responsibilities of the executive branch have dramatically changed since 1932.[1] There has been a fivefold increase in the federal bureaucracy and a doubling in the number of independent regulatory agencies. As many executive departments have been created in the past 35 years as in the preceding 150 years. Since 1960 the federal budget has more than doubled in real terms.

This chapter examines the origins and implications of these changes and, more particularly, assesses their impact on the modern presidency. The differing experiences of the nine Presidents of the modern era will be used to test Weber's proposition that 'The power position of a fully developed bureaucracy is always great, under normal conditions overtowering'.[2] No one doubts that there have been major changes in terms of institutions and personnel, but the consequences of such changes are clouded by the assumptions and political preferences of politicians and scholars alike.

To explain properly the changes in presidential-executive relations since Franklin Roosevelt, it is essential to avoid both conceptual confusion and normative judgements based on assumptions about the desirability or otherwise of an 'imperial' presidency. We need to remember that development entails change but change does not necessarily mean development. It is possible that major quantitative changes in bureaucratic and presidential personnel have not produced qualitative changes in the President's relations with the executive branch.

Development normally carries with it some notion of purpose or objective. In this sense, we speak, for example, of child development – by which we mean to identify particular, defined stages of growth, skills and awareness. The stages constitute recognised and accepted milestones on the way to an ultimate end-state: namely

---

1. An increasing number of responsibilities are being discharged on behalf of, rather than directly by, the executive branch. See H. Seidman, *Politics, Position and Power*, 3rd edn, New York, 1980, pp. 236–40, for a catalogue of the various institutional methods of carrying out governmental purposes.
2. Max Weber, *Economy and Society*, Berkeley, 1978, p. 991.

119

Table 4.1. GROWTH OF THE FEDERAL
GOVERNMENT, 1800–1980

No. of civil servants (approx.)*	Date	Government departments	Independent regulatory agencies
3,000	1800		
50,000	1849	Interior	
	1870	Justice	
	1887		Interstate Commerce Commission
	1889	Agriculture	
200,000	1903	Commerce and Labor (1913, became separate depts.)	
	1914		Federal Trade Commission
550,000	1920		Federal Power Commission
	1927		Federal Radio Commission
600,000	1932	**Election of Franklin D. Roosevelt**	
	1933		Securities and Exchange Commission
	1934		Federal Communications Commission
	1935		National Labor Relations Board
1,400,000	1938		Civil Aeronautics Board
	1949	Defense	
2,400,000	1953	Health, Education and Welfare (HEW)	
2,400,000	1961		
	1965	Housing & Urban Development	
	1966	Transportation	
2,800,000	1971		
	1977	Energy	
	1979	Education (HEW retitled Health & Human Services)	
3,000,000	1980	**Election of Ronald Reagan**	

* For a variety of reasons, it is particularly difficult to calculate the precise numbers of federal civil servants. The above figures are rough approximations drawn from a number of sources and are intended simply as a guide to the uneven growth of the federal civil service.

becoming an adult. But political institutions are not like children, nor can their growth and change be explained by using an identical frame of reference.

To speak meaningfully about the significance of changes in presidential-executive relations since Roosevelt requires some historical perspective. To appreciate the direction and pace of change, we need to be able to place such change in a proper context. In essence, we need a synoptic view so that recent changes can be put in perspective in the larger picture. Reasons of space preclude any substantial overview, but Table 4.1 may provide some useful reference points in charting the growth of the executive branch.

Historical reference points help us understand what has remained unchanged and why change has taken one form rather than another. Table 5.1 also reminds us that 'the executive branch is a collective noun, not a unitary organisation'.[3] The President has had longer and sometimes closer relations with some departments and agencies than with others. Granted the potential multiplicity of relationships, it may be appropriate to sketch the history of some surprisingly durable and general themes in presidential-executive relations.

Historical Background

Presidential dissatisfaction with administrative tasks enjoys a venerable tradition. George Washington was moved to complain that 'these public meetings with reference to and from different Departments . . . is as much, if not more, than I am able to undergo.'[4] This complaint was made at a time when Washington administered a larger staff on his Virginia plantation than in any of the executive departments' central offices.

In 1801 there were only about 3,000 people in the federal bureaucracy, and twenty years later there were still well below 10,000. But the opening up of the West and the rapid increase in population stretched the resources of the executive departments. By 1851 the number of civil servants had reached 50,000.

Important as this numerical growth is, it is less significant for later developments than the style and character of the bureaucracy which began to emerge. By 1851 the American bureaucracy had acquired many of its distinctive and enduring characteristics. It was highly decentralised, and the vast majority of civil servants worked in field offices, especially the post offices, away from Washington. More importantly, both the recruitment of personnel for partisan reasons and the erosion of hierarchical accountability were already established, integral features of presidential-executive relations. In 1849, for example, Senator Niles could assert that the bureaux were

---

3. Richard Rose, 'The President: A Chief but not an Executive', *Presidential Studies Quarterly*, vol. 7, no. 1 (Winter 1977), p. 6.
4. Quoted in A.J. Wann, *The President as Chief Administrator*, Washington, DC, 1968, p. 3.

already 'substantially independent of the departments' which nominally directed their activities.[5]

The most notable and noticeable aspect of presidential involvement with, and influence upon, bureaucracy in this period was the development of patronage or 'spoils' as a mechanism for enlisting and rewarding political support and loyalty. This doctrine has been subject to substantial revision, but it survives as a tenuous bridge across the divides of constitutional provision. The proportion of spoils appointments increased steadily from the 1820s, but this did not appear to arouse much political opposition. The political game was to be won or lost, and patronage became the instrument of partisan revenge once the White House had been conquered. Yet it would be an exaggeration to suggest that, even at the height of the spoils system, the value of continuity and competence in administration was entirely discounted. In general, it was the post office which served as the hub of a giant wheel of patronage, appeasing the demands of political activists across the country. The Washington staffs of the major departments were much less affected by changes of administration.

Paradoxically, the expansion of the presidential role in the appointment and removal of personnel was itself a major source of frustration to successive Presidents.[6] While the spoils system came to be seen as a mainstay of the new established order, a series of pay and classification acts in the 1850s made a modest start to the long, incremental process of merit recruitment. It was President Ulysses Grant's notoriously corrupt administration which supplied the first signs of presidential leadership in the quest of bureaucratic reform. The reforms of the Grant administration were short-lived, but the endemic scandals of his second term served to elevate the spoils question to the status of a major political issue.

The consequences of a large-scale spoils system had been pointed out by Alexis de Tocqueville a generation earlier. He warned that 'of all the people in the world the most difficult to restrain and to manage are a people of office-hunters. Whatever endeavors are made by rulers, such a people can never be contented.'[7] The ultimate

5. Quoted in S.K. Bailey, 'The President and his Political Executives', *The Annals*, Sept. 1956, p. 26.
6. Presidential discretion in the distribution of patronage was very limited in the nineteenth century. The demands of congressional and party supporters were so great that it is perhaps not surprising that 'much of the initiative for reform of the spoils system was later to come from the White House'. Paul Van Riper, *History of the United States Civil Service*, Evanston, Ill., 1958, pp. 50–1.
7. Alexis de Tocqueville, *Democracy in America*, New York, 1956, p. 262.

in discontented seekers after patronage, Charles Guiteau, expressed his feelings in unambiguous fashion by assassinating President Garfield in 1881.

The assassination helped to harden public and political opinion against the spoils system and, together with the Republican losses in the election of 1882, provided the conditions necessary to secure the passage of the Pendleton Act of 1883. This legislation required non-partisanship in the selection of federal personnel and created a new Civil Service Commission. The Pendleton Act was to stand as the essential legal foundation of the federal bureaucracy until 1978. It strove to reconcile two apparently conflicting objectives by both protecting the civil service from political influence and by emphasising that the President was the ultimate source of executive power.

The Presidents of the 1880s did not regard themselves as threatened by the introduction of the merit system, nor did they or their immediate successors greatly mourn the erosion of patronage. As President Taft later complained, every presidential appointment created 'nine enemies and one ingrate'.[8] The political reality was that presidential control of patronage was more formal than substantive. In practice, patronage was controlled by members of Congress and state party organisations.

The Pendleton Act was permissive rather than mandatory. It authorised rather than required Presidents to transfer patronage posts into the merit system. Thus, successive Presidents could move as slowly or quickly as circumstances and inclination dictated. Bureaucratic reform therefore seemed to recognise and strengthen presidential authority rather than weaken it.

The development of the merit system is not without its ironies and paradoxes. The extension of the merit system was largely accomplished by re-classifying or 'blanketing-in'[9] large numbers of political appointees. The most popular and apposite occasion for re-classification occurred immediately after the news of an incumbent's electoral defeat became known. Presidents Arthur, Cleveland and Harrison all sought to transform large numbers of their patronage appointees into career officials. In these cases the merit system applied only to restrictions on removal and not to criteria for recruitment. By the turn of the century, 50 per cent of the almost 200,000 federal civil servants were classified under the merit system. It is

8. Quoted in Louis W. Koenig, *The Chief Executive*, 4th edn, New York, 1981, p. 132.
9. Posts are said to be 'blanketed-in' when they have been filled non-competitively through patronage and have later been placed under the merit system so that incumbents cannot be removed on a change of administration.

interesting to note that the merit system, which expanded largely through presidential initiative, is now often seen as a significant constraint on presidential efforts to galvanise the bureaucracy.

The growth of the merit system was paralleled by a development of potentially greater importance for presidential-executive relations: the creation of new administrative entities outside the principal departments of government. The Civil Service Commission and the Interstate Commerce Commission were early examples of agencies partially or wholly independent of the executive departments. Once the precedent had been established, opposition began to crumble and could not prevent the creation of the Federal Reserve Board in 1913 and the Federal Trade Commission in 1914. The First World War accelerated the trend and helped to overcome the remaining adherents to organisational and constitutional orthodoxy. The arguments for independence, expertise and necessity triumphed over concerns for constitutional propriety.

Thus, before the election of Franklin Roosevelt a crucial feature of contemporary American bureaucracy was already evident. The increasing fragmentation of the bureaucratic structure had begun to compound and to complicate presidential lines of communication and accountability with departments, agencies and bureaux. The hierarchical model of presidential-executive relations was significantly inaccurate before 1932.

The consistent theme of presidential statements about bureaucracy before 1932 articulated the view that the civil service was a centre of waste and extravagance. But the presidential desire for economy was matched and sometimes exceeded by a concern to exercise effective control over the new administrative agencies. In claiming that 'it is unwise from every standpoint and results only in mischief to have any executive work done save by executive bodies, under the control of the President',[10] Theodore Roosevelt spoke for both his presidential predecessors and successors.

Successive Presidents have made clear their view that independent agencies are, or should be treated as, subordinate units of the executive branch. It is probably true that Harding 'actively shunned the idea of the President's being an initiator and prime mover in governmental affairs',[11] but his resolution in presidential-executive disputes may be judged by the long struggle he waged for control of the Shipping Board and the Fleet Corporation.[12] It also appears that

10. R.E. Cushman, *The Independent Regulatory Commission*, New York, 1941, p. 681.
11. R.K. Murray, *The Politics of Normalcy*, New York, 1973, p. 22.
12. See Cushman, *op. cit.*, pp. 253—9.

both Harding and Coolidge attempted to control independent agencies by requiring signed, undated letters of resignation at the time of appointment.[13] Where the federal government was involved, Harding and Coolidge had no doubts or reservations about attempting to enforce their hierarchical interpretation of the Constitution.

Hoover viewed the spoils system as wasteful and inefficient, and this perception was a major factor in the further extension of the merit system to a pre-Second World War peak of almost 80 per cent of a bureaucracy which, by 1930, had grown to 600,000. The major personnel functions of the government were consolidated and centralised under the Civil Service Commission. The end of the spoils system seemed to be in sight.

But if congressmen had seen the well of patronage dry up, they were suspicious of executive expansion, and, in their attempts to grapple with new economic and regulatory problems, they turned with increasing frequency to the independent board, agency or bureau. The growing chaos and congestion on the airwaves, for example, brought executive proposals for a licensing bureau within the Commerce Department, but Congress predictably favoured the creation of an independent Federal Radio Commission.

Thus, despite Hoover's efforts, the steady growth and fragmentation of the federal bureaucracy continued almost inexorably. It is perhaps ironic that in view of his later record in office, Hoover's opponent in the presidential election of 1932 made much of the incumbent's inability to restrain bureaucratic expansion. Hoover's administration was condemned as one which had 'piled bureau on bureau, commission on commission'.[14] The sound of shattering panes in his successor's glasshouse must have been deafening.

This brief sketch of the history of presidential-executive relations is necessarily incomplete, but it may be useful to summarise and emphasise the key aspects which have emerged. First, it is clear that presidential control over the executive branch was shaped by a variety of forces and circumstances, and it would be inaccurate to depict the pre-Franklin Roosevelt period in static or simple terms. There was no 'Golden Age' when Presidents were masters of the federal bureaucracy and free from political, institutional and environmental opposition.

In fact, during the nineteenth century a pattern of habits,

13. M.H. Bernstein, *Regulating Business by Independent Commission*, Princeton, 1955, p. 132.
14. Quoted in William E. Leuchtenburg, *The Perils of Prosperity*, Chicago, 1958, p. 267.

conventions and expectations became established which made little allowance for an active presidential role in the direction and control of the federal bureaucracy. The competence and efficiency of public administration attracted little congressional or public interest. The problem of executive responsiveness to presidential leadership and authority exercised the minds of only a small minority of reformers. Public office was seen as a prize, as a reward for political services and loyalty, and as a means to exact partisan revenge on political opponents. Thus, presidential-executive relationships were shaped largely by electoral needs rather than by any substantial or sustained concern for coherent and coordinated policy-making.

The passage of the Pendleton Act was a significant development in facilitating presidential direction of administrative affairs, but it is important not to exaggerate its impact. To claim that the Pendleton Act 'marked the transition from the wild, unbridled spoils system of public service to the orderly, unpolitical and infinitely more efficient merit system'[15] is to stretch a valid point too far. The Act was a major step on the road to a career bureaucracy, but the exercise of the remaining elements of patronage by the President was of equal significance.

But if civil service reform served to reduce certain kinds of pressure on the President, organisational innovations such as the independent agency or bureau and the public and mixed-ownership corporations have exacerbated the problems of executive leadership. In the twentieth century Republican and Democratic Presidents alike have joined battle to ensure that the expanding and increasingly fragmented bureaucracy adhered to a common, presidentially determined line.

The full texture and complexity of presidential-executive relations was not fully explored until the election of a President resolved to exploit to the very limit the administrative resources of the government. In 1933, for the first time in American history, a vigorous attempt was made to mobilise the entire federal bureaucracy in the exclusive service of the President and in the face of a national disaster. In the age of the modern presidency the scale and the purposes of the executive branch were to be transformed.

The next section analyses the development of presidential-executive relations since 1933. It focuses on presidential perceptions of, and impact on, the executive branch and thereby illustrates the often divergent strategies and techniques employed. The final section

---

15. United States Civil Service Commission, *Biography of an Ideal: Diamond Anniversary History of the Federal Civil Service*, 13 Jan. 1958, p. 3.

draws together the threads of diverse experience and offers some general conclusions on the President's changing relationship with the executive branch of government.

From Chief Administrator to Policy Manager?

Several of Franklin Roosevelt's predecessors in the White House took a keen interest in executive administration; President Taft, in particular, was seriously concerned with questions of efficiency and economy and with financial control and accountability. But their concern was primarily with means rather than ends, and responsibility for policy and programmes largely remained with Congress. In this respect, as in so many others, the election of Franklin Roosevelt was to have a major impact on presidential relations with both Congress and the executive branch.

In one sense the statistics speak for themselves. George Washington supervised the work of nine executive agencies; Abraham Lincoln eleven; and Franklin Roosevelt sixty-three.[16] The numbers in the civil service, which remained fairly constant between 1922 and 1932 at about 600,000, reached 3,375,000 by 1945. The bureaucracy was, of course, swollen by wartime needs, but by comparison it was still more than three times larger than it had been at the end of the First World War.

Despite his campaign rhetoric, Roosevelt showed little interest in administrative economy. Rather, he was concerned to develop an effective form of management 'which would make administration more responsive to the national interest and better able to serve that interest'.[17] During the New Deal the national interest was of course largely defined by Roosevelt. Thus, the problem of managing the executive branch was one of ensuring that presidentially determined goals were pursued by administratively responsive means. Roosevelt's overriding emphasis on the responsiveness of the executive branch caused him to undermine the merit system, to disregard administrative hierarchy and to create new and different organisations to carry out the tasks of government. He was motivated by the conviction that the civil service was largely indifferent to his goals and complacent as to the gravity and urgency of the situation.

Although Roosevelt's public statements consistently supported the principle of the merit system, his first term saw a spectacular resurgence of patronage appointments. Within four years the

16. R. Polenberg, *Reorganizing Roosevelt's Government*, Cambridge, Mass., 1966, p. 25.
17. *Ibid.*, p. 7.

percentage of bureaucrats classified under the merit system had fallen from 80 per cent to 60 per cent. Thus, large numbers of those recruited into the federal service in the 1930s were enthusiastic supporters of the President's policies and were likely to be immediately responsive to White House directives. In the now established tradition of 'blanketing-in', many of Roosevelt's patronage appointments became permanent officials who survived his incumbency and later acted as guardians of the New Deal.

Roosevelt took seriously Machiavelli's dictum that 'A wise prince seeks advice continually, but when it suits him and not when it suits somebody else'.[18] He reached down and across departmental and agency hierarchies in his search for good ideas and in his concern to ensure a proper balance of presidential advice. Cabinet secretaries and senior officials were left in no doubt that Roosevelt consulted their subordinates behind their backs: thus, obstructive or secretive bureaucrats were outflanked by the President's willingness to use other than official channels.

Roosevelt's primary concern was to improve governmental performance, and he made a causal connection between this goal and the need to strengthen and extend presidential control of the executive branch. Thus, not only did he seek wider reorganisation powers and expanded institutional resources for the presidency, but he actively sought methods of overcoming or circumventing traditional bureaucratic passivity and conservatism. He was impatient with orthodox channels and conventional organisations when they had, to his mind, so evidently failed.

Given such a perspective, the emergency agency became an essential instrument in Roosevelt's unorthodox and, to some, eccentric administrative style. The fact that such agencies were frequently separate from, and independent of, the regular departments was part of their attraction. He was aware that their creation would further complicate his problem of policy coordination as well as increasing the number of people reporting directly to him. But such consequences were deemed to be the necessary price to be paid to overcome the stifling inertia of the permanent bureaucracy. Roosevelt was sensitive to the possibility that the multiplication of semi-autonomous bodies might become a political and administrative liability in the future, but he could see no other means of ensuring that his key programmes were entrusted to willing, receptive and energetic hands.

No President has ever taken such an active role in the control and

18. N. Machiavelli, *The Prince*, trans. by A. Gilbert, Durham, NC, vol. I, 1965, p. 92.

direction of administrative agencies as Roosevelt. He strove to exercise the maximum possible influence over the agencies to ensure cohesion and unity of purpose in executive activity. Frequently, there was little resistance to the President's will. In 1936, for example, a member of the Federal Communications Commission is reported as saying that the FCC had always complied with all orders and requests made of it by the President and that it had never raised any question about its obligation to do so.[19]

But on occasion Roosevelt was forced to use all his political skill and ingenuity to make individuals and organisations bend to his will. His most frequent tactic was to effect decisive changes in key personnel or in statutes. 'The judicial calm of the Interstate Commerce Commission was left undisturbed, but the most able and aggressive commissioner was created Federal Coordinator of Transportation. The US Tariff Commission was reduced to harmless condition through the passage of the Reciprocal Tariff Act.'[20] In only one area, his attempt to dismiss a member of the Federal Trade Commission, was Roosevelt thwarted, but even here his behaviour was consistent with his view of the presidency as the exclusive source of executive leadership and control.[21]

Roosevelt rebuilt the executive branch in his own image or at least to serve his own purposes. But the new agencies tended to survive beyond the crises they were created to meet, and many new agencies quickly absorbed the values and attitudes of the permanent bureaucracy. The executive branch became increasingly unwieldy and difficult for the President to coordinate or direct. For much of the Second World War the President's customary protagonists – Congress and the Supreme Court – largely withdrew from the administrative domain. But because of the fragmentation of the bureaucratic structure, the President's unchallenged supremacy was as much apparent as real. Instead, the 'battle of Washington' broke out in the form of intense conflict and rivalry between and among the proliferating executive and independent agencies and corporations.

The creation of the Office of War Mobilization (OWM) to act as a kind of super-agency with virtually unlimited authority did little to bring order to the increasing chaos in the executive branch. The performance of the OWM helped sow the modern seed of opinion which regards the executive branch as incurably balkanised and

19. Cushman, *op. cit.*, p. 682.
20. E.P. Herring, *Public Administration and the Public Interest*, New York, 1936, p. 222.
21. *Humphrey's Executor* v. *United States*, 295 US 602 (1935).

inherently unmanageable. If 'a policy coordinating agency with all the legal authority of the President behind it, without significant congressional opposition, and with no judicial interference, cannot necessarily exercise effective control over the bureaucracy as a whole',[22] the President's effectiveness as chief administrator is open to question.

Roosevelt's legacy was a giant, heterogeneous executive branch which had attempted and accomplished a greater set of tasks than any of its predecessors. But the coordination and effectiveness of government depended largely on Roosevelt's unique knowledge, skill and personality. These were qualities he was unable to bequeath to his successors.

While Truman could not inherit Roosevelt's political skills, he did inherit a presidential staff agency, the Executive Office of the President (EOP), which was established in 1939. Roosevelt had a tough legislative fight to establish the EOP, and the recommendations of the Brownlow Report were severely diluted.[23] For present purposes it is important to note that Roosevelt sought to acquire a presidential staff agency which could help manage the government. He sought to consolidate all regulatory agencies within the executive departments, and he wanted to appoint six executive assistants to expand his personal staff.

The fact that Congress denied Roosevelt important elements of the Brownlow package is perhaps less significant than the general character of the proposals. Several of Roosevelt's successors in the White House were to seek similar goals through other means. The Brownlow Report was the first of a series of presidential thrusts designed to enhance White House management capabilities. All too often, such thrusts were parried and effectively deflected by Congress.

Apart from the White House Office, the most important element within the new EOP was the Bureau of the Budget (BOB), which was transferred from the Treasury Department.[24] Within a few years of its location, the BOB was seen as a vital presidential support facility. Under Truman it moved beyond its coordinating and financial control functions, becoming involved in what Berman calls 'the

22. P. Woll, *American Bureaucracy*, New York, 1963, p. 148.
23. The formal title of the Brownlow Report is the President's Committee on Administrative Management, *Administrative Management in the Government of the United States*, Washington, DC, 1937.
24. For a detailed account of the changing role of the Bureau of the Budget, see Larry Berman, *The Office of Management and Budget and the Presidency, 1921–1979*, Princeton, NJ, 1979.

program development process'.[25] While the BOB grew in significance, two other important institutional additions were made to the EOP, the Council of Economic Advisers and the National Security Council. If Roosevelt created the EOP, Truman put flesh on the institutional skeleton.

Harry S. Truman emerged from the shelter of the Vice-Presidency into the raging storm of foreign and domestic reconstruction, a tempest exacerbated by the pressures emanating from a resurgent Congress eager to reassert its pre-New Deal authority. But Truman had no doubts as to where the responsibility lay for directing the executive branch. He viewed the presidency as 'A sacred and temporary trust, which he was determined to pass on unimpaired by the slightest loss of power or prestige'.[26]

Any successor to Roosevelt would have found him difficult to follow, but in at least one respect Truman was determined to improve on his predecessor's record. He shared the popular opinion in Washington that Roosevelt was a poor administrator, and he resolved to instil order in the management of the executive branch. What Roosevelt thought pragmatic and flexible, Truman dismissed as haphazard and chaotic. Truman's management style valued order over competition, clarity over variety. Thus, in pursuit of these aims, he strove to establish clearer lines of jurisdiction, communication and responsibility than Roosevelt had ever desired or achieved.

Government reorganisation became an early and important theme in Truman's domestic programme, and he later felt able to boast that he had accomplished more organisational reform than 'all the other Presidents put together'.[27] This judgment is shared by at least one recent student of the subject, who argues that when Eisenhower became President 'the government was probably as "inherently manageable" as it had ever been, despite the fact that it dwarfed in size Roosevelt's pre-war domain.'[28]

Although Truman perpetuated and expanded the White House staff organisation created by Roosevelt, he possessed no powerful chief of staff or cabal of aides to insulate or isolate him from the work of his administration. His preference was to control and direct the executive branch through 'his cabinet officials, not through powerful White House operatives'.[29] Truman was, above all, a

25. *Ibid.*, p. 42.
26. Dean Acheson, *Present at the Creation: My Years in the State Department*, New York, 1969, p. 415.
27. Quoted in William E. Pemberton, *Bureaucratic Politics: Executive Reorganization during the Truman Administration*, Columbia, Missouri, 1979, p. 2.
28. *Ibid.*, pp. 2–3.
29. P. Anderson, *The President's Men*, New York, 1968, p. 91.

decisive President. He evolved an advisory system whereby policies were presented to him, not for further development, but for decision.

Truman lacked the sophisticated intelligence system of Roosevelt, and he was unwilling and unable to acquire the mastery of the detail of departmental and agency activity exhibited by his predecessor. His executive style has attracted revisionist criticism which claims that 'By adopting the practice of Cabinet responsibility and delegating excessive authority to department chiefs, Truman created a structure that left him uninformed.'[30] But this allegation is not supported by the opinion of his aides or by other recent studies of the Truman presidency.[31]

Given the unprecedented pressures Truman experienced, it was perhaps inevitable that he became the first President literally unable to grasp all the complexities of the work of the executive branch. Truman was determined to ensure that he was thoroughly briefed to make the extraordinary number of 'big' decisions which only he could make. If the routine work of the executive branch was entrusted to Cabinet secretaries, departments and agencies, that was sensible, practical and unavoidable. By the time of the Truman presidency, it was clear that no President could ever be truly master of the entire executive branch of government.

The confrontations with Congress and the increasing penetration of agencies and bureaux by interest groups and congressional committees encouraged Truman to appoint non-partisan, expert commissions to make recommendations on controversial policy issues. These executive innovations found favour with many of his successors because not only did they constitute a valuable source of authoritative and apparently disinterested policy proposals, but they also gave added legitimacy to what might otherwise be seen as partisan and contentious presidential initiatives.[32] This use of *ad hoc* bodies outside the formal governmental structure was to become a striking feature of presidential-executive relations.

The 1952 presidential election could have been a turning-point in the history of the modern presidency and its relations with the execu-

30. B.J. Bernstein in J.H. Huthmacher (ed.), *The Truman Years: The Reconstruction of Post-War America*, New York, 1972, p. 107.
31. See Robert Williams, 'Harry S. Truman and the American Presidency', *Journal of American Studies*, vol. 13, no. 3 (Dec. 1979), pp. 393–408, for an assessment of Truman's perception and conduct of the presidency.
32. Truman appointed commissions to investigate civil rights, civil liberties, internal security, immigration, the unification of the armed forces and peacetime conscription. For a useful general account of such commissions, see T.R. Wolanin, *Presidential Advisory Commissions: Truman to Nixon*, Madison, Wis., 1975.

tive branch of government. In fact, it served to ratify the growth in size, function and responsibility which had been initiated by Roosevelt and consolidated by Truman. The new President, Eisenhower, was elected on a platform that promised to turn the ideological tide against the New and Fair Deals. After twenty years there was at last an opportunity for a Republican President to cut government down to size. But, as Table 4.1 demonstrates, the size of the federal service was much the same at the end of Eisenhower's second term as it was at the beginning of his first term.

The federal bureaucracy was held in low esteem by the White House in 1933 for its conservatism and resistance to change. In 1953 it was held in equally low esteem for exactly opposite reasons. Republicans viewed with deep suspicion what they saw as pervasive bureaucratic liberalism and enthusiasm for governmental intervention and regulation. In the 1930s and 1940s the executive branch 'had basked in the light of social reform and to a great extent had been both the object and agent of that reform.'[33] Any President's 'honeymoon' period with Congress is usually all too brief, but the honeymoon with the bureaucracy had lasted for two decades. Not only had the size of the federal bureaucracy increased by more than 400 per cent since 1932, but nine out of ten bureaucrats had never experienced anything other than liberal Democratic administrations.[34]

Thus Eisenhower presided over an executive branch which was largely unsympathetic to the stated objectives of his administration. The entrenchment of the merit system and the consequent decline in patronage meant that the means of effecting a change in the character and composition of the federal service were correspondingly depleted. Yet it would be a mistake to imagine that, at the highest levels, the bureaucracy remained unaffected by the change of administration.

Eisenhower introduced a new category of senior civil service post called Schedule C, which was used for positions of a confidential or policy-determining character. By September 1954, 1,098 posts had been put into Schedule C, which carried no security of tenure. While the numbers involved were not high, 'in importance of positions affected [the changes] represent the most significant cut-back of the competitive service in its history.'[35] Schedule C now included a

---

33. Van Riper, *op. cit.*, p. 474.
34. H.M. Somers, 'The Federal Bureaucracy and the Change of Administration', *American Political Science Review*, no. 1 (March 1954), pp. 131–2. This article offers a perceptive analysis of the problems of transition.
35. Task Force Report on Personnel and the Civil Service, *Hoover Commission on Personnel and the Civil Service*, Washington, DC, 1955, p. 192.

number of heads and assistant heads of bureaux; these posts had been largely career appointments in the 1940s.

By March 1954 about half of the higher civil service had been appointed to their present posts during the Eisenhower administration. Some of the posts were filled by 'outsiders', especially the assistant secretaries, but many were internal promotions. As R. N. Spann puts it, 'Politics in the American public service is as much an affair of ups-and-downs, as ins-and-outs.'[36] The irony of the Republican backlash against the bureaucracy is that 'having stamped many senior bureaux posts as "political" by putting them in Schedule C, the new Administration promptly filled the majority of them with people who were in the Federal service before they took over.'[37]

Eisenhower was not prepared to abdicate the executive branch to liberal Democrats. Personnel changes were particularly common in agencies dealing with radical new policies. At the very highest levels, outsiders were appointed 'whose careers and utterances indicate firm opposition to the programs they are to administer'.[38] Thus, the 1950s saw the first modern divide appear between presidential and bureaucratic goals. The President and his political appointees were trying to lead the country in directions in which most members of the executive branch were reluctant to go.

Unlike Roosevelt and Truman, Eisenhower believed that restraint was the key to the effective use of power. But restraint was less an accident of indolence or ill-health than a matter of deliberation and choice.[39] Eisenhower wished to restrict executive intervention, not to expand it or even maintain it. In his view, the federal government did too much, not too little or enough. The consequence, as one contemporary scholar observed, was 'that there has been a dramatic net decline in the role and leadership of the executive which has had a stunning effect on the bureaucracy'.[40]

The Eisenhower presidency certainly slowed the momentum of social reform and forced some bureaucrats on to the defensive, but it would be substantially inaccurate to claim that it significantly and permanently changed the size, role or responsibilities of the federal

---

36. R.W. Spann, 'The Eisenhower Civil Service and the Reformers', *Public Administration*, vol. 34 (Summer 1956), p. 148.
37. *Ibid.*, p. 150.
38. Somers, *op. cit.*, p. 138.
39. For a recent reappraisal of Eisenhower's qualities as President, see Fred I. Greenstein, *The Hidden Hand Presidency: Eisenhower as Leader*, New York, 1982.
40. Somers, *op. cit.*, p. 137.

government. Eisenhower was not a creature of the Republican right determined to conduct radical surgery on the body politic. The reality was that Eisenhower accepted that the vast responsibilities assumed by Roosevelt and Truman were legitimate and practically unavoidable burdens. Big government was here to stay, and, to the disappointment of the zealots, campaign rhetoric mostly remained just rhetoric.

Eisenhower was perhaps the last modern President to concede status and grant wide discretion to members of his Cabinet. He had learned from his mentor, George Marshall, the first organising principle of leadership, that 'the decision-maker must not be distracted by problems his subordinates should resolve for themselves'.[41] Consequently, he never conceived of the President as a man with his finger on every administrative pulse. More consciously and comprehensively than Truman, he believed in the importance of delegation and the value of teamwork. At his request, Cabinet members 'determined and publicly defended their internal policies and selected their own lieutenants'.[42]

The Eisenhower presidency slowed the growth of the federal government, but it proved unable and unwilling to unravel the New and Fair Deals. Eisenhower reiterated presidential claims to authority over the executive branch while acknowledging that no President could realistically deal effectively with more than a fragment of the activities for which he was nominally responsible. It was not just the scale and volume of governmental activity which defied attempts at presidential direction and management; it was also the growing linkages between executive organisations, interest groups and Congress, which were proving increasingly resistant to White House intervention. It is perhaps significant that Eisenhower ended his presidency with a solemn warning about the growing power of the 'military-industrial complex'.

The problems of executive responsiveness to White House initiative were well known by the time John Kennedy was elected in 1960. The rhetoric of the New Frontier may have promised innovation and fresh thinking, but expectation and reality proved an uncomfortable match. The nature of the problem was aptly expressed by Truman's BOB Director, Frederick Lawton, when he dryly observed that 'The spirit of adventure may flame high in many of us, but resistance to change is firmly embedded in more of us.'[43]

41. E. Richardson, *The Presidency of Dwight D. Eisenhower*, Kansas, 1979, p. 6.
42. *Ibid.*, p. 35.
43. Quoted in Pemberton, *op. cit.*, p. 17.

Thus, although Kennedy suffered neither the ideological nor party handicaps of Eisenhower, it did not take long before the new administration began to express its distrust of, and dissatisfaction with, the executive branch.

The new President was determined to ensure that his control of the executive would be as real as his predecessor's was apparent. But his presidential aides took an extreme view of the problems Kennedy faced. Arthur Schlesinger records that 'in pursuing his purposes, the President was likely to encounter almost as much resistance from the executive branch as from the others. By 1961, the tension between the permanent government and the presidential government was deep in our system.'[44] Schlesinger goes on to assert that every important mistake during the Kennedy administration 'has been the consequence of excessive deference to the permanent government'.[45] It should perhaps be remembered that, in the protection of presidential power and reputation, White House aides are often *plus royaliste que le roi.*

While demanding loyalty and responsiveness, Kennedy 'seemed to have little interest in professional management and in the managerial problems of the executive branch'.[46] The job of the President had grown so large, and the countervailing forces so powerful, that Kennedy was necessarily selective and sparing in the attention he devoted to the work of the executive departments and agencies.

Kennedy's interests and priorities lay elsewhere. As one of his Cabinet members put it, his 'absorption with politics, publicity and foreign policy allowed him little time to be concerned about the domestic departments.'[47] Rexford Tugwell, a former Roosevelt aide, is even more emphatic: 'The truth is that Kennedy did not function as an executive. He had only the most meager contacts with the secretaries of the domestic departments, largely because he had no interest in their operations.'[48]

The Kennedy administration saw a strengthening of the White House staff and a further weakening of the Cabinet and heads of departments. Kennedy preferred to deal directly with the responsible

44. Arthur M. Schlesinger, Jr., *A Thousand Days*, Boston, 1965, p. 680.
45. *Ibid.*, p. 683.
46. M.H. Bernstein, 'The President and Management Improvement', in N.C. Thomas and H.W. Baade (eds), *The Institutionalized Presidency*, Dobbs Ferry, NY, 1972, p. 86.
47. J. Edward Day, *My Appointed Round: 929 Days as Postmaster General*, New York, 1965, p. 98.
48. Quoted by Thomas E. Cronin, 'Everybody Believes in Democracy Until He Gets to the White House', in Thomas and Baade, *op. cit.*, p. 148.

aide or official, and he dismissed Cabinet meetings as a waste of time. In his quest for personal loyalty, he sometimes, as in the State Department, made appointments at the assistant and under secretary levels before selecting the Secretary of State. He hoped that, as a consequence, the loyalty of his political appointees would run more than Cabinet-deep.

He was under no illusion that the President could actually run a department, but he argued that 'at least he can be a stimulant'.[49] Thus, in the early days of his administration, Kennedy tried to increase his contact with officials, frequently by telephoning late at night to encourage, cajole or reward. His aim was to bring the presidential personality directly to bear on as many points in the administration as possible. But the pressure of priorities meant that, in practice, his approach was unsystematic and not always effective.[50]

During the Kennedy administration the pretence that the Cabinet was in any meaningful sense a collective or coordinating body was clearly and irrevocably abandoned.[51] During this period it is possible to see the beginning of a formal collapse of the distinction between the advisory role of White House staff and the operational line responsibilities of departments, agencies and bureaux. The formal, permanent institutions of the executive branch were seen to give way to the informal, personal and transient needs of individual incumbents.[52]

The difficulties Eisenhower encountered in re-directing and reducing the executive were seen to reflect more than just a Republican attempt to turn the tide of twenty years of Democratic administrations. Irrespective of party, federal departments and agencies were increasingly viewed as having fragmented lives of their own, with values and purposes distinct from those of any President. It was becoming ever more apparent that the multiple, diverse entities that make up the executive branch recognised other authorities and responded to other signals. Thus the hierarchical model of presidential-executive relationships was understood to be seriously deficient and even misleading as a description of reality.

Modern Presidents have been unwilling to condone the erosion of what they take to be their constitutional prerogatives. Thus,

---

49. *Christian Science Monitor*, 12 Jan. 1963.
50. D.S. Brown, 'The President and the Bureaus', *Public Administration Review*, Sept. 1966, p. 179.
51. For an excellent account of the role of the Cabinet, see Richard F. Fenno, *The President's Cabinet*, Cambridge, Mass., 1959.
52. A perceptive and influential account of this change is contained in Ch. 6, 'Palace Guard Government', in Thomas E. Cronin, *The State of the Presidency*, Boston, 1975.

although the hierarchical model of presidential-executive relations does not correspond with the conflicting loyalties and pressures existing within the federal government, successive Presidents have made strenuous efforts to impose their priorities and perspectives on the departments and agencies.

By the time Lyndon Johnson succeeded Kennedy, it seemed that two analytically distinct models of presidential management of the executive branch were being fused into one. The earlier model can be described, to use McGeary's term, as the 'Business Manager', whereby the President actively monitored departmental activities through hierarchically centralised control systems such as accounting, reporting and budgeting.[53] The second model, the 'Administrative Leader', saw the managerial role as a positive, creative one, concerned as much with the determination of objectives as with monitoring efficiency. In this view, the President should delegate routine work to the institutional staff agencies in the EOP to free himself to focus on the content and direction of his administration's programmes.

The fusion of these earlier models of presidential-executive relations gives rise to a synthesis of the President as 'Policy Manager', whereby the gap between political proposal and bureaucratic disposal is bridged. Essentially, the Policy Manager model merges the hierarchical control structure of the Business Manager with the policy-determining role of the Administrative Leader. The view that politics should permeate administration was gaining in acceptance, achieving its fullest expression under Richard Nixon.

It was clear that some of those working for Johnson relished and advocated the Policy Manager model of presidential direction. The attractions of policy planning originating in the White House rather than in departments and agencies were obvious and striking. If both financial control and policy initiation and coordination took place in the White House, the possibility that the President could, in a meaningful sense, actually 'run' the federal government seemed within reach.

During the Johnson presidency two new government departments were created. In addition, a new agency, the Office of Economic Opportunity, comparable in scope and purpose to some departments, was created within the EOP. But it would be a mistake to believe that Johnson possessed any sophisticated theory of organisational change. Indeed, although the beginnings of the Policy

53. Michael McGeary, 'Doctrines of Presidential Management', in Hugh Heclo and L.M. Salamon (eds), *The Illusion of Presidential Government*, Boulder, Colo., 1981, pp. 12–13.

Manager role are evident in his attitudes and the behaviour of his staff, his activity was generally piecemeal and reactive.[54]

Hence, Johnson did not follow a blueprint for presidential management of the kind supplied to Roosevelt and Truman by the Brownlow and Hoover reports. Indeed, he failed to act on the recommendation of the Heineman Task Force that he establish an Office of Program Coordination. Johnson declined to create institutional machinery capable of tackling what Heineman called 'the deeply ingrained habit of federal bureaus of operating autonomously'.[55] But according to one adviser, Johnson's omission saved the President from establishing 'a firefighting organisation that would have brought fires to our doorstep'.[56] Clearly, the emergence of the President as Policy Manager was hampered by fears of presidential overload.

Johnson shared Kennedy's bitterness at what he took to be the obstruction and recalcitrance of the permanent government. He turned, even more than Kennedy did, to his personal staff for help in directing and galvanising the executive. At the end of his presidency, Johnson 'solemnly warned the incoming Nixon administration that they should spare no effort in selecting thoroughly loyal people to man key departmental positions. It is as though Johnson believed that a significant portion of the Great Society programs had been sabotaged by indifferent federal officials.'[57] Where Eisenhower believed he encountered partisan opposition to his policies, Kennedy and Johnson claimed to have experienced passivity, departmentalism and a general lack of executive creativity and urgency.

Johnson's relationship with the executive branch, like all his political relationships, was intensely personal. The overpowering personality which had become his trademark as Senate Majority Leader was vigorously deployed in his dealings with aides and departmental heads alike. Lip-service was paid to formal structures, channels and procedures, but Johnson's approach to running the executive was always pragmatic and highly personal.

Executive personnel were given the 'bear hug treatment',[58] drawn in close to the President and overwhelmed by him. Cabinet meetings

54. See E.S. Redford and M. Blissett, *Organizing the Executive Branch: the Johnson Presidency*, Chicago, 1981.
55. Rose, *op. cit.*, p. 14.
56. *Ibid.*
57. Cronin, 'Everybody Believes in Democracy Until He Gets to the White House', *op. cit.*, p. 148.
58. H.G. Nicholas, 'The Insulation of the Presidency', in M. Beloff and V. Vale (eds), *American Political Institutions in the 1970's*, London, 1975, p. 23.

contained minimal deliberation and maximum opportunity for the President to regale and cajole his subordinates. As Nicholas observes, 'Department heads soon learnt to be chary about taking their problems to him, because the interview was swiftly turned inside out, into a presidential monologue followed by a presidential exposition of *his* problems and the imposition of a series of presidential demands or inquisitions.'[59]

Like Kennedy, Johnson felt cut off from the administrative leviathan he nominally controlled. He even imitated his predecessor's practice of calling officials without warning and often late at night. But he was unable to maintain an interest in, and knowledge of, all the activities of his administration. The Vietnam War gradually became the dominant issue of his presidency and in this matter Johnson was more comprehensively involved than any other modern President. He was immersed both in long-range strategy and short-term tactics, in peace negotiations and the selection of individual bombing targets.

As Vietnam came to dominate his policy agenda, Johnson was forced to delegate or neglect a range of presidential responsibilities. Presidential aides, especially Joe Califano, came to give orders rather than transmit requests to the departments and agencies. A partial vacuum had been created in the direction and control of important domestic departments, and the White House staff moved to fill it. In the light of later events, it is perhaps ironic that the power wielded by Califano over the departments attracted criticism from the then presidential aspirant, Richard Nixon.

The erosion of patronage and the expansion of government activities made the selection of political executives more important than ever before. But despite Johnson's warning, the Nixon administration began its appointment process inauspiciously. The approach employed has been described as BOGSAT (bunch of guys sitting around a table, saying, 'who do you know?'). Nixon's special assistant for personnel, Harry Fleming, began his task by sending letters to everyone listed in *Who's Who in America*, soliciting their recommendations for suitable candidates to fill senior positions in the executive branch and the regulatory agencies. This undiscriminating approach meant that, for example, Elvis Presley was one of those whose advice was sought, but unhappily there is no record of any of his recommendations.[60]

It is clear that Nixon's election marked the beginning of a struggle with the bureaucracy which 'was more intense, more calculated, and

59. *Ibid.*
60. See M.B. Coffey, 'A Death in the White House: The Short Life of the New Patronage', *Public Administration Review*, Sept./Oct. 1974, pp. 441–4.

far more political in design than that of any previous President'.[61] In some ways it was a re-run of the problems faced by Eisenhower (except that Nixon was less of a constitutionalist). Once again, a Republican President was taking office after a period of Democratic incumbency with the familiar legacies of swollen liberal bureaucracies and extravagant social reform programmes.

The President suspected that the federal bureaucracy was against him. Nevertheless, while allowing for the darker side of Nixon's character, it should be remembered that even the paranoid sometimes have enemies. Clearly, a sizeable proportion of senior bureaucrats, especially in the social welfare departments, were ideologically and programmatically opposed to the Nixon White House.[62] But it is also the case that several members of the Nixon administration reported no particular problems of bureaucratic responsiveness.[63]

At the outset of his administration, Nixon declared his support for Cabinet secretaries and his determination not to allow a Califano-type figure to usurp their authority. Thus he allowed department heads discretion in their choice of political executives. This almost Eisenhower-like concern for constitutional propriety and respect for formal channels was short-lived. Within a few weeks, Nixon regretted his decision and began to seek ways of restoring presidential control.

Unlike Eisenhower, Nixon never sublimated his problems with the bureaucracy because of his desire to be an activist radical President who launched new policies and killed old programmes. Nixon could not learn to live with the bureaucracy because he had an intense desire to change it. Indeed, there are good grounds for claiming that 'No president ever tried harder, against greater odds, to make the bureaucracy responsive to the White House.'[64] Nixon was strongly interested in the reorganisation and reform of the executive branch, and his appointment of Roy Ash to head a new council on the subject confirmed his managerial priorities.[65] Ash's favourite maxim,

61. R.L. Cole and D.A. Caputo, 'Presidential Control of the Senior Civil Service', *American Political Science Review*, vol. 73, no. 2 (June 1979), p. 399.
62. Joel Aberbach and Bert Rockman, 'Clashing Beliefs within the Executive Branch', *American Political Science Review*, vol. 70, no. 2 (June 1976), pp. 456—68.
63. A. James Reichley, *Conservatives in an Age of Change*, Washington, DC, 1981, pp. 236—7.
64. Robert J. Sickels, *The Presidency*, Englewood Cliffs, NJ, 1980, p. 209.
65. For a discussion of the Ash Council and its relevance to Nixon's view of presidential leadership, see Robert Williams, 'Politics and Regulatory Reform: Some Aspects of the American Experience', *Public Administration*, Spring 1979, pp. 55—69.

'Organization is policy', struck a chord with a President who was increasingly to see administration in political terms.

The President and his senior aides gave much thought to putting domestic affairs in a new direction. The fruits of these reflections were known as the New Federalism, and the proposals contained in that slogan served to intensify the conflict between the White House and the executive branch. The proposals sought to reduce federal categorical grants, consolidate departments and agencies, and eliminate bureaucratic discretion in various grant-in-aid programmes. In short, the New Federalism attacked what it saw as the vested interests of the permanent government by reducing both its power and its discretion. Such proposals inevitably exacerbated the animosity and distrust that existed between the President and the executive branch.

Nixon's response was literally 'to take over the bureaucracy'.[66] The plan was that people deemed loyal to the President were to be placed in direct charge of the major domestic programmes. This was to be achieved in two ways. First, and most important, the government would be run from the White House by establishing direct operational links between the presidential staff and the lower echelons of the bureaucracy, thus bypassing the members of the Cabinet. Secondly, a concerted effort would be made to place loyalists in key bureaucratic positions. This implied not just an increase in the number of ideological Republicans selected for political executive posts but, more significantly, the infiltration of Republican appointments to senior civil service positions.

The pressures exerted on the Civil Service Commission were considerable, and they were particularly difficult to resist because of the Commission's dual role as personnel director for the President and defender of the merit system. Some recent students of Nixon's strategy suggest that he had a definite impact in increasing the numbers of Republican supporters in merit positions. They conclude that 'the Nixon White House extended the politicization of the bureaucracy further than any previous administration.'[67]

But the development of the so-called 'counter-bureaucracy' was eventually deemed a failure even in the White House. Direct White House control meant that the presidential staff became so immersed in administration that important policy issues were pushed aside. Once the decision had been made to delve into administrative affairs, there was no clear limit, no obvious point of return.

---

66. R.P. Nathan, *The Plot that Failed: Nixon and the Administrative Presidency*, New York, p. 9.
67. Cole and Caputo, *op. cit.*, p. 410.

In practice it became clear that the senior White House staff were gradually losing touch with the work of their subordinates. The results contradict the intention in that 'Operational matters flow to the top – as central staff become engrossed in subduing outlying bureaucracies – and policy-making emerges at the bottom.'[68] Nixon's attempt to take over the bureaucracy by running it from the White House was aborted because, far from weakening the bureaucracy, the endeavour served to strengthen it.

There was no time to develop an alternative strategy because, as counter-bureaucracy was seen to fail, the Nixon administration began to turn in on itself in the face of the Watergate scandal. As his political problems mounted and his trusted advisers resigned, the President's control and influence over the domestic departments and agencies was all but non-existent. In the final days of the Nixon administration, one senior official observed, 'There is no White House any more.'[69] Thus, the President who resolved to call the tune to the bureaucracy could only watch it fiddle as the White House burned.

Gerald Ford's presidency was, almost of necessity, a kind of interregnum. As the first man ever to become President without having been elected to national executive office, he was sensitive to the fact that he had no mandate for effecting radical change, least of all in presidential-executive relations. The dark cloud of Watergate hung heavily over much of Ford's period at the White House. His pardon of Nixon did little to dispel fears that he was a creature of his predecessor, an unfortunate, if necessary, constitutional legacy of the crimes and misdemeanours of the Watergate period.

Ford assumed the presidency in especially difficult circumstances. He did not have the usual eleven-week transition period, and the delicacy of his position as Vice-President served to preclude him from planning for the succession. The Nixon White House staff were mostly discredited, and those Cabinet members not anxious to leave had consolidated the autonomy of their departments during Nixon's preoccupation with Watergate. Schlesinger, Simon and Kissinger – Secretaries of Defense, Treasury and State – enjoyed considerable independence, and it seemed unlikely that they would welcome any attempt by Ford to reassert presidential authority.

Ford's view of presidential-executive relations was apparent in his confirmation hearings for the vice-presidency. He believed that it was possible to find a middle way between Cabinet government and

68. Robert Wood, quoted in Nathan, *op. cit.*, p. 52.
69. Quoted in Stephen Hess, *Organizing the Presidency*, Washington, DC, 1976, p. 138.

White House government, between deferring to and circumventing the federal bureaucracy. In particular, he argued that 'the cabinet officers should not be beholden to some person in the White House who is appointed by the President.'[70] His presidency was, perhaps inescapably, influenced by the events which brought him to office. He held the presidency more on trust than in his own right.

The new President's instinct was to restore the constitutional balance that Nixon had upset. But he was also sensitive about his own position, and thus he was reluctant to accept Vice-President Rockefeller's views on the role and importance of the Domestic Council. The counter-bureaucracy approach was firmly rejected and described by a Ford aide as 'a ridiculous kind of structure with the Domestic Council and the OMB involved in policy and cabinet members being figureheads'.[71] The Ford transition team agreed that there should be 'greater access to the president for cabinet officers and less White House and OMB involvement in the operational details of many programs'.[72]

Ford was concerned to restore a sense of propriety and respectability to the executive branch, and he was determined that he should never be accused of the abuses of the presidential office that destroyed his predecessor. The effect, in domestic affairs, was to restore authority to departmental heads, to reduce the tensions between the White House and the bureaucracy, and generally to allow more discretion and scope to the formal mechanisms of government.

Jimmy Carter's political credentials were parochial rather than national, and hence he had never had an opportunity to develop a wide acquaintanceship with people who had served as Washington administrators.[73] His political strength was his reputation as an 'outsider' untainted by the intrigue and corruption of Washington political life. But in his relations with the executive branch, strength became weakness, cleanliness became ignorance. Carter not only lacked a direct knowledge of how Congress and the executive worked, he knew few people who did.

Carter's major claim to presidential skill was his talent as an organiser and manager. The man who had whipped the government of Georgia into shape was elected, in part, to do a similar job on the federal government. His concern to improve bureaucratic perfor-

---

70. Quoted in Sickels, *op. cit.*, p. 187.
71. *Ibid.*
72. Roger B. Porter, *Presidential Decision Making: The Economic Policy Board*, Cambridge University Press, 1980, p. 35.
73. James Sundquist, 'Jimmy Carter as Public Administrator: An Appraisal in Mid-Term', *Public Administration Review*, Jan./Feb. 1979, p. 4.

mance and responsiveness can be seen in his enthusiastic support for civil service reform and the introduction of new management techniques such as zero-based budgeting.

The passage of the Civil Service Reform Act of 1978 represented the most important reform of the federal bureaucracy since the Pendleton Act in 1883.[74] The 1978 act had two major elements. First, Carter's solution to the improper influence exercised by Nixon over the Civil Service Commission was to abolish the Commission. Its functions were divided between two new bodies, one of which was clearly identified as non-political. Thus, in 1979 the Civil Service Commission was replaced by an Office of Personnel Management and an independent Merit Systems Protection Board. The second major element of the act was the creation of a Senior Executive Service (SES). The SES embodied a new service-wide structure for selecting, developing and managing top-level federal bureaucrats. The main innovations were the loss of much of their security of tenure by SES members and the introduction of merit pay and bonuses for exceptional service. Thus the President could use 'a private sector style rewards-sanctions approach to personnel matters'.[75] Within a year, 98.5 per cent of those eligible to join SES had done so. Most senior officials probably saw the SES as 'the only game in town'.

The creation of a select élite of federal bureaucrats was by no means a new idea. The concept derives principally from a central recommendation of the second Hoover Commission in 1955. President Eisenhower, bypassing the legislative process, tried to introduce a similar scheme by executive order in 1958. Congress vented its anger by prohibiting the Civil Service Commission from using any of its funds for the programme.

There were, of course, well-established administrative reasons for the creation of the SES. The need for greater mobility and an improved structure of incentives had been widely recognised for some time. But the key to Carter's commitment to civil service reform was the same as that of his predecessors – the desire to enhance bureaucratic responsiveness to presidential leadership. After his first two years as President he realised that he had 'underestimated the inertia or the momentum of the federal bureaucracy. . . . It is difficult to change.'[76] Few students of the modern

74. For a recent discussion of the Civil Service Reform Act and its consequences, see Peter Coaldrake, 'Civil Service Reform in the USA: Promise versus Reality', *Australian Journal of Public Administration*, vol. XLI, no. 2 (June 1982), pp. 99–118.
75. *Ibid.*, p. 104.
76. *New York Times*, 23 Oct. 1977, p. 26.

presidency would have been stunned by the acuity of his insight, but Carter seemed genuinely surprised by the unresponsiveness of the bureaucracy, and he resolved to carry through his promised reforms.

In keeping with his distaste for the Nixon White House, Carter stressed the importance of the Cabinet by delegating almost entirely to his heads of departments the right to choose their deputies and assistants. Thus, in the crucial early days of his administration, Carter 'paid no systematic attention to building managerial competence in the most direct and immediately effective way – by appointing to the key managerial positions in the executive branch persons whose capacity to administer large organizations had been tried and proved'.[77]

Carter's relationship with, and control over, the permanent government was hampered by his lack of experience and by his policy of executive appointments. The appointment of his old friend Bert Lance to head the OMB meant that 'he became the first President to bring the directorship of OMB within the ambit of home-state cronyism.'[78] Appointments to second rank positions in the executive departments displayed less an indulgence of friends than a preference for outsiders. Fewer than half the appointees at deputy secretary level had previous experience in federal administration.[79]

Thus, the Carter administration was mainly a government of newcomers and amateurs. Sundquist asks: How do such people come together in effective working relationships and how do they gain control of the permanent government? At best, the answer is: slowly. The Carter administration was, *par excellence*, a 'government of strangers', and the perennial problems of executive coordination, cohesion and continuity were especially acute.

Despite Carter's early protestations of support for the members of his Cabinet, the influence of his White House staff rapidly increased. When confrontations occurred, Carter sided with his trusted aides from Georgia against the challenge of independent and vigorous Cabinet secretaries like Joe Califano.[80] It seems that the narrowness of Carter's political and organisational base made him vulnerable to, and perhaps fearful of, those whose understanding of the executive exceeded his own. When he encountered what he took to be bureaucratic unresponsiveness, the President often lacked the

77. Sundquist, *op. cit.*, p. 4.
78. *Ibid.*, p. 5.
79. *Ibid.*, p. 6.
80. For one side of the conflict, see Joseph A. Califano, *Governing America*, New York, 1981.

knowledge, resources and personnel necessary to overcome it.

Ronald Reagan sees the presidential role as a strategic one which concentrates on broad goals and is freed from day-to-day concerns. If Carter's concern with detail meant that he was eventually unable to see the wood for the trees, Reagan recognises only major forests. He shares Eisenhower's distaste for the details of policy implementation, and he is not directly concerned with organising or running the government. Reagan believes firmly in the importance of delegation. While his presidency is not isolated like Nixon's, it is clearly a sheltered one.

Despite, or perhaps because of, his initial confidence in the viability of Cabinet government, the Reagan administration is (at the time of writing) characterised by unusually close cooperation and consultation between members of the Cabinet and senior White House staff. Reagan insists that his Cabinet members should be 'good team players' and not political entrepreneurs. During his first term they were required to channel requests and suggestions through his most important aides – Edwin Meese, Mike Deaver and Jim Baker. The departure of Deaver and the shift of Meese and Baker to the Justice and Treasury departments forced an inevitable change in White House management procedures. The appointment of Donald Regan as White House chief of staff has meant that in his second term Reagan is more dependent on the judgment of one man, and the teamwork characteristic of his first term is less in evidence. Clearly, the heads of domestic departments are still expected to develop their policy proposals by means other than direct approaches and requests to the President, but now they also have to contend with an assertive and authoritative chief of staff.

To avoid the familiar war between Cabinet secretaries and the White House staff, a system of Cabinet councils has been introduced. These councils have a mixed departmental/White House membership, and they present new possibilities for strengthening presidential policy management. The councils offer a structural contribution to reducing line and staff divisions in that they build bridges between White House aides and Cabinet members and produce a stronger sense of collegiality. The unusual, even unprecedented, movement from staff positions to Cabinet secretaryships of Meese, Baker and Clark confirms that the severe institutional estrangement characteristic of some previous administrations has been at least partly overcome. The Cabinet council system has the particular advantage of helping to 'insulate political executives from the permanent departmental bureaucracies and from the congressional committees by continually convening the executives in meetings under White House auspices'.[81] The point, as Edwin Meese explained, is that 'Cabinet members all feel closer to him than they do to their departments. And he gives them a lot of opportunity to remember that.'[82] Policy development consequently takes place through departmental/White House consultation, not in departmental or agency isolation.

Reagan's preference for Cabinet councils derives not just from his concern that agency/White House policy disputes are settled at the sub-presidential level, but from his distrust of the bureaucracy. He shares his Republican predecessors' conviction that the federal government is staffed by officials who are largely unsympathetic to Republican ideals and programmes. In the Reagan administration, policy planning has been a partisan preserve with little or no place for the senior career officials. Reagan's Director of the Office of Personnel Management is on record as stating that career SES members should not be involved with policy matters, but rather should confine themselves to 'administering the government'.[83] Where Nixon thought politics should permeate the career service, Reagan has sought to purify it by reviving the classic Weberian distinction between politics and administration.

Under Reagan nearly all the important administrative positions have been filled on partisan grounds, and 'career professionals have been largely excluded from many leadership networks and responsibilities'.[84] Many heads of agencies and bureaux have been appointed who not only appear to lack much relevant experience, but who 'come to their posts as declared adversaries of their agencies in particular and the federal government in general'.[85] To Reagan loyalty is not just personal and hierarchical, but ideological and programmatic.

In practice it was often difficult to find people willing to run agencies they disapproved of in principle. Three months after his inauguration Reagan had filled none of the top seven posts in the Environmental Protection Agency, the *bête noir* of conservative Republicans. While Jimmy Carter generally sought to appoint people who had knowledge of, and sympathy with, particular forms

81. Hugh Heclo, 'One Executive Branch or Many?', in Anthony King (ed.), *Both Ends of the Avenue: The Presidency, the Executive Branch and Congress in the 1980's*, Washington, DC, 1983, p. 47.
82. *National Journal*, 3 April 1982, p. 588.
83. Coaldrake, 'Civil Service Reform in the USA', *op. cit.*, p. 110.
84. Chester A. Newland, 'The Reagan Presidency: Limited Government and Political Administration', *Public Administration Review*, Jan./Feb. 1983, p. 2.
85. Coaldrake, 'Civil Service Reform in the USA', *op. cit.*, p. 114.

of government regulation, Reagan chose people on the basis of ideological compatibility with the White House.

Reagan's basic governmental strategy has been to achieve his goals through the budget process, 'thereby tying programmatic actions to the one powerful, action-forcing process that exists on a government-wide basis'.[86] Where Nixon battled to effect major changes in the structure and delivery of social welfare programmes, the sharp edge of Reagan's budget reductions literally cut the ground from under the welfare departments and their supporting pressure groups. His budget-cutting strategy has been less successful than he hoped, but considerably more successful than many students of executive-legislative relations thought possible.

The Reagan approach possesses a disarming simplicity. The problems of comprehending and controlling an ever-expanding and ever-fragmenting bureaucratic state have been apparently resolved by radical budgetary surgery. Clearly, the Reagan technique has a directness and immediacy in its effects which encourages observers to believe that this President has reasserted presidential control over the executive branch. But Reagan's relations with the executive branch are largely shaped by the purposes of his presidency. If his successors employ similar management techniques in the pursuit of very different political goals, they cannot assume that their efforts will produce comparable results.

Conclusions

No one can seriously doubt that both the presidency and the executive branch have undergone radical change in the past fifty years. In policy and institutional terms the presidency has been transformed. Modern Presidents have assumed and accepted vast new responsibilities in domestic and foreign policy. To fulfil these responsibilities, they have equipped themselves with new institutional support facilities – the EOP and the White House Office within it – which have grown to such an extent that they may almost be termed the presidential branch of government.

There are now five times as many federal civil servants as there were when Franklin Roosevelt took office. Yet the matter is not a simple one. In the past twenty years, while federal employment has remained relatively static, there has been a massive increase in those indirectly employed in state, city, quasi-public and private organisations financed by the national government. A recent study suggests that there may be four times as many people indirectly

86. Heclo, 'One Executive Branch or Many?', *op. cit.*, p. 44.

employed by the federal government as are directly employed.[87] Growing political sensitivity about the size of the federal civil service has encouraged the contracting-out of government functions to organisations normally considered to be outside the executive branch of government. Consequently, Table 4.1 underestimates the real expansion of government activity in recent times, and it does not fully capture the accelerating fragmentation of the executive branch.

In the jargon of development studies, both the presidency and the executive branch have experienced major institutional differentiation. The consequences of this differentiation for presidential-executive relations can only be understood in the context of changes in the wider political environment. The relationship between the President and the executive is not a private one. It does not exist in a vacuum outside of, or isolated from, changes in political institutions, attitudes and behaviour.

For some years a number of important trends in American politics have been evident which, taken together, make the task of the modern President exceptionally difficult. The electorate has become more volatile; Congress has become less manageable; parties have been displaced by proliferating groups of single-issue policy activists; and the 'iron triangles' of congressional committees, interest groups and bureaucrats have become more difficult to penetrate. The centripetal force of presidential leadership is frequently more than counterbalanced by the pluralist, centrifugal forces acting elsewhere in the political system.

The sum of these changes produces what Hugh Heclo describes as policy congestion, political mobilisation and institutional estrangement.[88] According to Heclo, policy congestion arises because the President's problem is not just that the federal government has taken on more functions, but that these functions interact and overlap. The outcome is that the problems of executive coordination and priority-setting are compounded, and the President finds the task of deciding on an agenda for action increasingly difficult.

The political mobilisation of single-issue activists has lessened the President's ability to cut through policy congestion. The multiplicity of special, narrow viewpoints on issues makes the task of consensus-building even more difficult. While the President attempts to generalise and simplify, the single-issue activists fragment and complicate policy problems. Some indication of the extent of political mobilisation can be obtained from a congressional debate on natural gas pricing in 1978 which attracted 117 lobby organisations.

87. Coaldrake, 'Civil Service Reform in the USA', *op. cit.*, pp. 112–13.
88. See Heclo, 'One Executive Branch or Many?', *op. cit.*, pp. 32–40.

Institutional estrangement arises because the modern President is decreasingly perceived as having a great deal to offer Congress or the policy activists. To the extent that executive departments and agencies see the President as a liability, rather than an asset, his attempts to exercise leadership and control are likely to founder. No President since Eisenhower has served two full terms, and recent occupants of the White House have been seen as temporary, transient participants in the policy-making process. While policy activists and congressional committees strive to influence the bureaucracy, the modern President is forced to compete with more durable political forces for the attention and cooperation of the executive branch.

In assessing presidential-executive relations in the modern era, it is important not to perceive the conflicting approaches of different Presidents as conforming to, or deviating from, any arbitrary standards of propriety or orthodoxy. It is, for example, unhelpful to speak of a decline in Cabinet government since Eisenhower as if this was in some sense improper. The Cabinet has no constitutional standing in the American political system, and while the status of individual Cabinet members has varied considerably, collegial decision-making and collective responsibility are alien to the American tradition.[89] Similarly, the gradual politicising of the Bureau of the Budget (BOB) and later the Office of Management and Budget (OMB) does not constitute grounds for constitutional outrage. While one President may value neutral competence and continuity, another may prefer partisan loyalty and ideological commitment.[90]

The claim to executive leadership is one which is made by all modern Presidents. Unfortunately for them, this claim has never been fully conceded by Congress, the courts or the bureaucracy. Each President seems to feel the need to educate his institutional competitors in the righteousness of the presidential claim. To this end, a series of inquiries, task forces and commissions, from Brownlow to Ash, have been established to confirm what each President instinctively knew all the time. The recommendations of these inquiries are, in important respects, very similar, but despite

---

89. For a sceptical view of Reagan's 'new' approach, see Peter Coaldrake, 'Ronald Reagan and "Cabinet Government"': How far a Collegial Approach?', *Politics*, vol. XVI, no. 2 (Nov. 1981), pp. 276–83.

90. Different preferences, of course, produce different political and administrative difficulties; 'changing norms and relationships call into question the possibility of preserving the institution as a source of impartial continuity for the presidency.' Hugh Heclo, 'OMB and the Presidency: The Problem of Neutral Competence', *Public Interest*, vol. 38 (Winter 1975), p. 84.

the continuity and virtual unanimity of presidential advice, Congress remains unimpressed.[91] It might indeed make the President's job of executive management easier if some of the recommendations were implemented, but Congress is more often employed in defending its prerogatives than in facilitating presidential control of the executive.

Necessarily, this chapter has been concerned with broad trends in presidential-executive relations, but it is important to note that the generalisations arising from this study are subject to amendment and qualification. The executive branch contains a multiplicity of widely differing organisations, and it is often difficult to separate the rules from the exceptions. Presidents have relationships with individual Cabinet secretaries, aides and officials and with particular departments, agencies and bureaux. Organisational and personality differences, as well as constantly changing circumstances, make all generalisations tentative and provisional. The executive branch is heterogeneous, not homogeneous, fragmented rather than monolithic. It is, in Bailey's memorable phrase, a many-splintered thing.

Generalisations about, for example, political executives need to be related to time and circumstance. Writing in 1978, Greenstein asserts that political executives 'tend to have views that converge with those of the career officials in the departments – the latter having increasingly become advocates of the substantive policy directions of the programs they administer.'[92] This may well have been an accurate characterisation of the situation during the Carter presidency, but it bears little resemblance to the realities of the Reagan administration. Clearly, change and continuity are both present in the modern presidency. The problem lies in telling one from the other.

Presidential relations with, and perceptions of, the executive branch are influenced by the store of conventional wisdom about its constituent parts. In the case of the Cabinet, the presidency displays almost no capacity for institutional memory. Most modern Presidents have entered the Oval Office declaring their undying belief in Cabinet government, but, as Heclo notes, 'It is significant

91. For a sophisticated general analysis of the aims and claims of reorganising the executive branch, see Peter Szanton (ed.), *Federal Reorganization: What Have We Learned?*, Chatham, NJ, 1981. For the similarity in proposals and in presidential goals, see Robert Williams, 'Politics and Regulatory Reform', pp. 55–69.

92. Fred I. Greenstein, 'Change and Continuity in the Modern Presidency', in Anthony King (ed.), *The New American Political System*, Washington, DC, 1978, p. 73.

that no president has ever *left* office extolling the virtues of cabinet government.'[93]

Despite their ritual blind spot about the Cabinet, Presidents are quicker to identify regulatory agencies and individual Cabinet members as potential sources of obstruction. The apparent decline in the importance of Cabinet members and the rise in status of the White House staff may be partly attributed to the conventional wisdom that the former are enemies rather than allies of the President. The natural tendency, according to this view, is for Cabinet secretaries and regulatory agencies to respond to clientele pressure and act as spokesmen to, rather than representatives of, the President.

It can reasonably be argued that, in some cases, the vulnerability to political pressures lies less in the departments and agencies and rather more in the White House and Congress. The forces of clientelism acting on Cabinet secretaries appear to be stronger in the less controversial, less partisan areas of government activity. In the contentious area of agricultural policy-making, Graham Wilson found that 'Far from their Presidents having to urge them on to fulfill the Administration's programme, the problem for Eisenhower, Kennedy and Johnson was to restrain secretaries who were over-zealous.'[94] Thus, the image of successive Presidents struggling vainly to assert control over recalcitrant subordinates and rebellious bureaucratic outposts is not wholly accurate.[95]

The basic source of conflict between the President and the executive branch is to be found largely in the different perspectives and priorities which each exhibits in relation to the work of the federal government. From the President's point of view the main purpose of a number of domestic departments is to act as buffer institutions. As Richard Rose observes, 'The handshake that the President gives these Cabinet officers may be his way of saying "goodbye". A President does not want agencies dealing with issues remote from his priorities to make their problems into his problems.'[96]

Difficulties arise because departments and agencies view the situation differently from the President. As Neustadt notes, 'Agencies need decisions, delegations and support, along with bargaining arenas and a court of last resort.'[97] According to circumstance and

93. Heclo, 'One Executive Branch or Many?', *op. cit.*; p. 26.
94. Graham K. Wilson, 'Are Department Secretaries Really a President's Natural Enemies?', *British Journal of Political Science*, vol. 7 (1977), p. 28.
95. For the position in regard to presidential relations with regulatory agencies, see Robert Williams, 'Politics and the Ecology of Regulation', *Public Administration*, vol. 54 (Autumn 1976), pp. 319–31.
96. Rose, *op. cit.*, p. 11.
97. Richard E. Neustadt, 'Politicians and Bureaucrats', in David Truman (ed.), *The*

agency, the problem may be construed by the President as one of a lack of responsiveness or as one of departmental intrusion. Presidents, on occasion, reach out to galvanise departments and agencies, but in recent times they have been more likely to seek shelter behind their White House staff, who serve to prevent agency heads from determining the President's priorities and political agenda.

The characteristic bureaucratic response to presidential initiatives or directives is to delay, not to reject or defy. Bureaucrats seek ways of reconciling and accommodating the President's wishes in ways consistent with departmental priorities and values. There is, therefore, often more conflict generated about the tempo of departmental activity than about its content.

The President usually operates to a shorter time-scale than the rest of the executive branch. Four years may be a political lifetime to a President, but it is rarely a crucial period to the President's institutional competitors. Presidents rarely take the long view because 'Dates make deadlines in proportion to their certainty, events make deadlines in proportion to their heat. Singly or combined, approaching dates and rising heat start fires burning underneath the White House. Trying to stop fires is what Presidents do first.'[98]

As far as the President and his aides are concerned, everything is urgent and important and needs doing by yesterday at the latest. The President's involvement is positive proof that the White House views an issue as highly significant and requiring the earliest possible attention. The likely consequences of such a presidential perspective is that the executive branch will be condemned as sterile and unresponsive because it fails to satisfy the President's insatiable need for immediate and inexpensive solutions to complex, long-standing and intractable problems.

Presidential decisions transmitted to the executive are often only expressions of general intent without much indication of what precisely should be done, who should do it or when it should be done. The difficulty is aggravated because, in many cases, in order for a President to act at all, he may have taken a role in forging a consensus and agreeing to a relatively vague decision so that all parties can believe they have got what they wanted.[99] Problems in

Congress and America's Future, Englewood Cliffs, NJ, 1965, p. 113.
98. Richard E. Neustadt, *Presidential Power: The Politics of Leadership*, New York, 1960, p. 156.
99. See Morton H. Halperin, *Bureaucratic Politics and Foreign Policy*, Washington, DC, 1974, pp. 196–218.

implementation and compliance often arise later because the presidential consensus was purchased at the price of unsustainable ambiguity.

What is perceived in the White House as a failure to respond to policy directives may be due less to bureaucratic intransigence than to incomprehension and confusion. It is by no means unknown for departments to receive contradictory messages from different White House aides or to perceive contradictions or errors in policy directives previously agreed by the President and his staff. In either eventuality urgent, drastic action by the department concerned is unlikely. The lack of haste and seeking of clarification confirm presidential fears of bureaucratic obstruction.

Clearly, one major difficulty for the modern President is securing effective lines of communication with those who are expected to implement presidential decisions. Messages are often vague, distorted or wrongly directed. Communication problems have become more acute partly because of the increasing domestic and foreign pressures on the presidency and partly because of the scale and fragmentation of the executive branch. Issues are nearly always cross-cutting and impossible to assign to a single department or agency, and the consequent problems of coordination and communication are difficult to resolve. One White House aide likened the executive branch to the dinosaur which became extinct not just because 'it was too big and clumsy, but rather because it suffered a failure of communication. Signals were not transmitted from brain to foot, or foot to brain, rapidly or accurately enough to create a picture of reality on which the dinosaur could act.'[100]

The appointment of political executives to the highest reaches of the federal bureaucracy seems to have done little to improve coordination, communication or implementation of presidential policies. The hopes that they would serve as the President's loyal lieutenants in the bureaucracy and that they would serve as catalysts for effecting change in, and by, the bureaucracy have mostly been unfulfilled. It is still possible, however, that Reagan's political executives, recruited on ideological grounds to administer a definite and not overly-complicated programme, may prove more valuable to the President than has been the case in other administrations.

In 1977 Heclo concluded that political executives are 'transient, structurally divided, largely unknown to each other and backed by a welter of individual patrons and supporters . . . they are too plentiful and have too many diverse interests to coordinate themselves.

---

100. Cronin, 'Everybody Believes in Democracy Until He Gets to the White House', *op. cit.*, p. 163.

But they are also too few and too temporary to actually seize control and operate the government machinery.'[101] As Nixon discovered, the alternatives are not encouraging because there are strict limits as to what can be run directly from the White House. Most modern Presidents have therefore recognised that the need to create a *modus vivendi* with the permanent government is a key test of presidential leadership.

Reagan has sought to denigrate the bureaucracy and to insulate it from the policy-making process. The early political victories of his administration prompted a distinguished scholar to observe that Reagan, more than any other modern President, 'succeeded in creating a more or less unified and coherent system of political administration' during his first two years in office.[102] Thus, the 'blitz' of Congress in 1981 was controlled by Reagan's legislative strategy group with little involvement of career officials. While Reagan's early successes were impressive, they should not obscure the fact that the momentum of his programme has visibly slowed in the following years. The acid test of presidential leadership is whether early successes can be repeated and enlarged later in a presidency, and in this respect Reagan has experienced frustration and disappointment. It seems doubtful whether any administration can dispense with the resources and expertise of the bureaucracy on a long-term basis. It seems even less likely that Reagan's attempt to distinguish between policy and administration is sustainable in a political system where bureaucrats are drawn into the policy arena by political actors other than the President.

This chapter has examined the changing relationship of the President and the executive branch in the modern era. It has been possible to discern institutional and political trends which have combined to make the President's task more difficult. Yet, as the problems of presidential management have increased, so too have the institutional resources of the presidency. Just when the executive branch has appeared almost impossible to manage, Presidents who possessed clear views on how to set things in order have taken office. Contingency, circumstances and inclination have all helped shape the relationship of the President and the executive.

We have not been able to discern any inexorable, secular development of, or decline in, the President's capacity to direct the affairs of the executive branch. Clearly some changes are permanent ones. For instance, it seems unlikely that any future President could function

101. Hugh Heclo, *A Government of Strangers*, Washington, DC, 1977, p. 242.
102. Heclo, 'One Executive Branch or Many?', *op. cit.*, p. 43.

adequately without something like the White House Office or the Executive Office of the President. But each President reserves considerable discretion as to how he structures his advisory staff and how he attempts to organise and control the executive.

Thus, instead of linear development or decay, the experience of the past half-century suggests continuity, oscillation and change in almost equal measure. The four Republican Presidents all showed similar anti-bureaucratic sentiments, and each of them resolved to do something about the growth and power of the federal government. But in practice their approaches varied widely and met with differing degrees of success.

It should now be clear that Weber's hypothesis stated earlier in this chapter has, in fact, little relevance to the American experience. To test whether the power position of a fully developed bureaucracy is overtowering, you first need to locate a fully developed bureaucracy. However one seeks to characterise the modern federal bureaucracy, it can scarcely be described, in Weberian or any other terms, as fully developed. We have charted its piecemeal and uncertain development, its vulnerability to political pressure and its long-standing recognition of more than one political master. The American executive branch therefore lacks two essential and interrelated Weberian conditions. It lacks one central, legitimate, legal authority, and it also lacks any very clear sense of hierarchy.

Bureaucratic attempts to serve different political constituencies frequently result in a failure to please anyone. The American federal bureaucracy reflects the pressures exerted on it. It is at least partly true that if it 'often serves special interests and is subject to no central direction, it is because [Congress] often serves special interests and is subject to no central leadership.'[103] The disruption of Weber's key condition of hierarchy is confirmed by a study which suggests that 'contacts between civil servants and Congress are unusually intense, whereas both legislators and civil servants report less contact with departmental heads than in any other country.'[104]

Given its size, complexity, fragmentation, specialisation, multiple policy preferences and competing value systems, the executive branch offers numerous opportunities for conflict and misunderstanding with the President. Every modern President from Roosevelt to Reagan has been confronted by the reality that

103. James Q. Wilson, 'The Rise of the Bureaucratic State', in N. Glazer and I. Kristol, *The American Commonwealth 1976*, New York, 1976, p. 103.
104. J. Aberbach, Robert D. Putnam and Bert A. Rockman, *Bureaucrats and Politicians in Western Democracies*, Cambridge, Mass., 1981, p. 234–5.

departments, agencies and bureaux differ from one another in terms of their legal authority, their organisational structure and cohesiveness, and the strength and lines of their political support. The task of reconciling the bureaucracy's allegiance to its clientele, programmes, bureaux, departments, congressional committees and interest groups with the President's roles as policy-manager and chief administrator is a difficult and unending one.

The underlying trends in American politics point towards an even more uncertain and less manageable political environment for presidential-executive relations in the future. Thus, if the experience of the past fifty years suggests that presidential mastery of the executive has been elusive, incomplete and transient, the portents indicate that it will remain so.

5

THE PRESIDENT AND HIS STAFF

John Hart

Fifty years have elapsed since Franklin Roosevelt's Committee on Administrative Management, under the chairmanship of Louis Brownlow, gave birth to the Executive Office of the President. The famous passage in its report which argued that 'The President needs help'[1] was the origin of the vast staff that he has at his disposal today – a staff whose growth proceeded unchecked and largely unnoticed until the Vietnam War and the Watergate crisis began to focus attention on its pivotal role in the presidential decision-making process. The importance of the EOP is now an accepted fact. It constitutes a political force that competes for power in the pluralistic system of American government and has shown a significant propensity to upset established working relationships between the more traditional institutions in Washington. Nelson Polsby has remarked that perhaps the most interesting political development of the post-war period 'is the emergence of a presidential branch of government separate and apart from the executive branch'. It is the presidential branch, he notes, 'that sits *across* the table from the executive branch at budgetary hearings, and that imperfectly attempts to coordinate both the executive and legislative branches on its own behalf.'[2]

At the present time, the Executive Office of the President consists of nine agencies housed under its umbrella,[3] although many more units have come and gone over the years.[4] It has an annual budget running at over $100 million, a full-time staff of nearly 1,400 and is

---

1. President's Committee on Administrative Management, *Administrative Management in the Government of the United States*, Washington, DC, 1937, p. 5.
2. Nelson W. Polsby, 'Some Landmarks in Modern Presidential-Congressional Relations', in Anthony King (ed.), *Both Ends of the Avenue*, Washington, DC, 1982, p. 20.
3. These are: the White House Office, Office of Management and Budget, Council of Economic Advisers, National Security Council, Office of Policy Development (formerly Domestic Policy Staff), Council on Environmental Quality, Office of Science and Technology Policy, Office of Administration, and the Office of the United States Trade Representative.
4. For a complete list of EOP agencies see John Hart, *The Presidential Branch*, New York, App. A.

physically bursting at the seams. The old Executive Office building, next door to the White House, has long been unable to contain all the President's staff, and certain sections of the EOP are now located some distance from the Oval Office. Along with its growth in power and status, the EOP has generated a significant amount of criticism from political scientists, journalists, some former White House staffers, and Congress. Undoubtedly, the excesses and abuses of the Nixon White House staff helped to accentuate some weaknesses in the EOP, but now, more than a decade after Watergate, the criticism can no longer be regarded as simply a reaction to the Nixon experience. There is, in the literature today, a more fundamental concern about the place of the President's staff within the structure of democratic government.[5]

Much of that criticism has been directed specifically at the White House Office: the agency within the EOP that houses the President's immediate personal staff, such as his top policy advisers, political managers, speech-writers, public relations specialists, congressional liaison aides, press secretary and those responsible for his schedule. They are the key staff personnel. They work in close proximity to the President, they see him regularly, they often determine who else gets to see him and they exert more direct influence than staffers in the other units of the EOP. As the EOP has developed, so the White House Office has become the directing force and the most powerful division within it. To a great extent, the major Executive Office units now operate as satellites of the White House Office, with key political appointees directing the work of the various staffs. One consequence of this is that the often-made distinction between the institutional staff for the presidency and the President's personal staff has been somewhat eroded over the years. The focus of this chapter is the White House Office and its development from Roosevelt to Reagan. Limitations of space make it necessary to exclude consideration of the other EOP units, but I have dealt with those elsewhere.[6]

5. For a sample of recent criticism see: Stephen Hess, *Organizing the Presidency*, Washington, DC, 1976; Ben W. Heineman and Curtis A. Hessler, *Memorandum for the President: A Strategic Approach to Domestic Affairs in the 1980s*, New York, 1980; Hugh Heclo and Lester M. Salamon (eds), *The Illusion of Presidential Government*, Boulder, Colo., 1981; Arnold J. Meltsner (ed.), *Politics and the Oval Office*, San Francisco 1981; Bradley D. Nash *et al.*, *Organizing and Staffing the Presidency*, New York, 1980; and National Academy of Public Administration, *A Presidency for the 1980s*, Washington, DC, 1980.

6. See Hart, *op. cit.*, Ch. 3.

Presidential Staffing before Brownlow

Franklin Roosevelt was not the first occupant of the White House to make a plea for adequate staff assistance. One can find similar sentiments expressed by many of his predecessors. Leonard White, for example, notes that 'Jefferson frequently complained about the pressure of business and in 1806 put in one sentence a classic observation: "It is not because I do less than I might do, but that I have more to do than I can do." '[7] In 1824 John Quincy Adams, then Secretary of State, recounted in his diary how President Monroe had handed him that day two important documents which had been signed and should have been delivered some eighteen months earlier. Adams commented: 'These irregularities happen for want of system in the multiplicity of business always crowding upon the President, and, above all, from his want of an efficient private Secretary.'[8] Monroe himself asked Congress for staff assistance,[9] but none was forthcoming.

Congress had not, however, ignored the question of staff support for the President. Indeed, the matter had been debated during the very first session of the House of Representatives in 1789 – as part of a wider discussion about compensation for presidential expenses.[10] There was general agreement that the President would need secretarial help and at least twice during the debate the belief was expressed that two secretaries would not be enough to cope with the job. But the issue was not the need for staff or the desirable number of assistants; it was, rather, the propriety of specifying how the President was to spend the total sum allowed him for general expenses. It was felt by some members of the House that to do so would be an infringement of the independence of the executive. 'No part of the Constitution gives us a right to dictate to him on this head,' argued Michael Stone, the Representative from Maryland. Moreover, several members, including James Madison, took the view that congressional recognition of presidential secretaries would make them officers of the government instead of the confidential instruments of the President that they were intended to be. In the end, Congress voted a lump sum of $25,000 per annum to the

---

7. Leonard D. White, *The Jeffersonians: A Study in Administrative History 1801–1829*, New York, 1951, pp. 71–2.
8. Charles F. Adams (ed.), *Memoirs of John Quincy Adams*, vol. VI, Freeport, NY, 1969, p. 374.
9. White, *op. cit.*, p. 72.
10. See US House of Representatives, 95th Congress, 2nd Session, Committee on Post Office and Civil Service, *Presidential Staffing: A Brief Overview*, Committee Print no. 95–17, Washington, DC, 1978, p. 5, from which material for this section is drawn.

President as compensation for his services, without specifying how much was for expenses and how much for the salary element. When the distinction between 'compensation' and 'salary' became blurred, as it did very quickly, it therefore appeared that Congress had not provided for staff assistance for the President, although that was not in fact the case.

In 1833 Congress did authorise the President to nominate a secretary specifically to sign land patents on his behalf, hitherto a significant administrative burden on the President, but the post was for that purpose only, fixed for a four-year duration, and subject to the advice and consent of the Senate.[11] Not until 1857 did Congress overcome its constitutional scruples and provide additional funding to enable the President to appoint a private secretary.[12] Ten years later, in 1867, an assistant secretary, a shorthand writer and four clerks were added to the White House payroll.[13]

Although funding for presidential support staff increased slowly during the latter half of the nineteenth century, the complaints continued. The status of the private secretary was low, along with his salary, and Presidents found it difficult to obtain competent personnel for the post. Soon after his election, Garfield confided to a friend that he was more 'at a loss to find just the man for Private Secretary than for any place I shall have to fill . . . The position ought to be held in higher estimation than Secretary of State.'[14]

Grover Cleveland encountered similar problems and lamented not being able to offer his private secretary a sufficiently high salary. He wanted to be able to have something more than a private secretary and spoke of the need for an Assistant to the President, claiming that 'as the executive office is now organized it can deal with the routine affairs of Government; but if the President has any great policy in mind or on hand he has no one to help him work it out.'[15]

By the turn of the century, Congress had added a second assistant secretary to the presidential staff, bringing the total number of administrative and clerical officers to thirteen.[16] President McKinley dropped the title of private secretary and called his principal aide 'Secretary to the President', but little else changed. The salary of the Secretary in 1900 was $5,000 per annum, the same as it had been in

11. 4 Stat. 663, Ch. XCI.
12. 11 Stat. 228, Ch. 108.
13. 14 Stat. 444, Ch. 166.
14. Leonard D. White, *The Republican Era 1869–1901: A Study in Administrative History*, New York, 1958, pp. 102–3.
15. *Ibid.*, p. 103.
16. 31 Stat. 972, Ch. 830. The title of assistant secretary was dropped early in the twentieth century.

1889, and despite Cleveland's plea for policy staff in the White House, the Secretary's job was never defined as such.

The size and shape of the staff hardly changed at all during the first decade of the twentieth century, but some expansion took place in the early 1920s. By 1922 the administrative and clerical staff in the White House totalled thirty-one, although all the expansion had been at the lower end of the staff hierarchy.[17] The following year, Congress wrote a provision into the Independent Offices Appropriations Act permitting the President to borrow an unspecified number of executive branch employees 'for such temporary assistance as may be necessary',[18] thus legitimising what had become a common practice, but although this was a welcome relief to Presidents, it did not satisfy the need for more high-level assistance in the White House. Finally, in 1929, Congress agreed to increase the number of Secretaries to the President from one to three and raised the salary for that post to $10,000 per annum.[19] The addition of two senior aides allowed some division of labour and specialisation among the President's staff and thus enabled Herbert Hoover to designate one of his three secretaries, George Akerson, as Press Secretary: the first White House aide to have that title.[20]

Thus, prior to Franklin Roosevelt's inauguration, a rudimentary staff system was taking shape and displaying some of the characteristics of the contemporary White House Office. The staff was expanding in size, augmented by detailees from the departments and agencies, and had just begun to organise its workload around specialised tasks. Moreover, by the early twentieth century, Secretaries to the President were performing political duties, and one or two of them – notably Joseph Tumulty who served Woodrow Wilson and C. Bascom Slemp who served Calvin Coolidge – had been recruited primarily for their proven ability in that area. It is even possible to see parallels between the kinds of functions performed by the early presidential secretaries and those of the White House staff today. William Spragens, for example, claims that Lincoln's secretary, John Nicolay, performed a function which foreshadowed that of the modern Press Secretary. He sees

17. The relevant appropriation legislation for 1922 shows that the White House staff comprised a Secretary to the President, an executive clerk, a chief clerk, an appointments clerk, a record clerk, two stenographers, an accounting and dispersing clerk, two correspondents and twenty-one clerks. See 42 Stat. 636, Ch. 218.
18. 42 Stat. 1227, Ch. 72.
19. 45 Stat. 1230, Ch. 270.
20. William C. Spragens, 'White House Staffs 1789–1974', in Bradley D. Nash *et al.*, *Organizing and Staffing the Presidency*, New York, 1980, p. 26.

shades of Cleveland's Daniel Lamont in Sherman Adams and suggests that Joseph Tumulty did for Woodrow Wilson what the public liaison staff has done for Nixon, Ford, Carter and Reagan.[21] However, one should not take analogies like these too far. The post-New Deal presidency operates within a vastly different political context and climate of expectations. There may be parallels, but the comparison is not one of like with like. The modern presidential staff system takes off with the publication of the Brownlow Report in 1937.

The Brownlow Report

On 22 March 1936, President Roosevelt announced the appointment of a three-man committee, composed of Louis Brownlow, Charles Merriam and Luther Gulick, to study the organisation of the executive branch with the primary aim of considering the problem of administrative management. The immediate impulse for reform was, as Clinton Rossiter noted, Roosevelt's 'own candid recognition that an otherwise professional performance during his first term in the presidency was being severely hampered by the sheer multiplicity and complexity of his duties and by the want of effective assistance in their discharge'.[22]

On November 14 Brownlow and Gulick met with Roosevelt and presented him with an outline of the committee's major recommendations, most of which he approved. With the necessary changes required by the President, the final report was handed to him in January 1937. It became the basis for the Reorganization Act of 1939 and Executive Order 8248, which eventually implemented those Brownlow proposals that survived the legislative battle in Congress.

Brownlow recommended establishing the major managerial units of government, covering budgeting, planning and personnel management, in an Executive Office of the President. He also proposed an extension of the merit system in the civil service, consolidation of all government agencies – including the regulatory agencies – into a few large departments, and a major reform of the existing system of fiscal accountability. The report also advocated that the President be given up to six executive assistants, a proposal that was to become the basis of the President's enlarged personal staff in the White House Office.

21. *Ibid.*, pp. 19, 22 and 24.
22. Clinton Rossiter, 'The Constitutional Significance of the Executive Office of the President', *American Political Science Review*, vol. XLIII, no. 6 (1949), p. 1207.

The legislative passage of the Brownlow proposals was stormy and complex.[23] The reorganisation legislation got dragged down with Roosevelt's unpopular bill to pack the Supreme Court and also clashed with counter-proposals on executive reorganisation from a Senate select committee headed by Senator Byrd and backed by the Brookings Institution.[24] Although the legislation eventually passed the Senate by a narrow margin in March 1938, it was defeated in the House the following month. A much watered-down bill was finally signed into law on 3 April 1939. The proposal to enlarge the President's personal staff was one of the few features of Brownlow's report to survive the legislative process.

The report was greeted with some praise and a lot of criticism from academics, professional public administrators and politicians. The Director of the Public Administration Clearing House, Herbert Emmerich, called it 'a beacon on the road to enlightened administration',[25] whereas Edward S. Corwin thought the report was 'thoroughgoingly Jacksonian'.[26] The academic attack on Brownlow has centred principally on the committee's willingness to give Roosevelt the kind of report he wanted − a charge which Brownlow admitted and stoutly defended[27] − and on what is viewed as the committee's misguided adherence to the principles of rational organisation.[28] The political criticism at the time was more concerned with the goal of the reorganisation proposals. Roosevelt had been arguing for executive reorganisation on the grounds of managerial efficiency, as opposed to the more traditional reorganisation-for-economy argument. Furthermore, the proposals for the reform of the Civil Service Commission, the Auditor-General and the merit system were seen by many legislators as a blatant grab for power by the President and, when taken in conjunction with the Court-packing bill, led some of those legislators to believe that the American presidency was headed towards dictatorship.

The proposal to give the President additional staff assistance was

23. See Richard Polenberg, *Reorganizing Roosevelt's Government*, Cambridge, Mass., 1966.
24. On the differences between the Brookings and Brownlow proposals see B.B. Schaffer, 'Brownlow or Brookings: Approaches to the Improvement of the Machinery of Government', *New Zealand Journal of Public Administration*, vol. 24, no. 2 (1962).
25. Herbert Emmerich, *Essays on Federal Reorganization*, University, Alabama, 1950, p. 90.
26. Edward S. Corwin, *The President: Office and Powers*, 4th edn, New York, 1957, p. 96.
27. Louis Brownlow, *The President and the Presidency*, Chicago, 1949, p. 106.
28. See, for example, Schaffer, *op. cit.*

never at the centre of the criticism of Roosevelt's reorganisation bill and, apart from some journalistic cynicism, was generally accepted from the beginning. In any case, Roosevelt already had a press secretary, an appointments secretary and a secretary for political affairs prior to Brownlow and a total White House staff of thirty-seven.[29] Brownlow merely recommended an additional six, and that largely as a consequence of other reforms proposed in the report.

Irrespective of how Presidents have used their staffs since, Brownlow defined the role of the six assistants in careful and narrow administrative terms. The size of the staff was to be limited — 'a small number of executive assistants . . . probably not exceeding six', said the committee immediately following the statement that 'The President needs help'.[30] The report then went to some lengths to spell out what the aides were not to be and were not to do. 'These aides would have no power to make decisions or issue instructions in their own right,' wrote Brownlow. 'They would not be interposed between the President and the heads of his departments. They would not be assistant presidents in any sense.' Their function, according to Brownlow, was to assist the President 'in obtaining quickly and without delay all pertinent information possessed by any of the executive departments so as to guide him in making his responsible decisions; and then when decisions have been made, to assist him in seeing that every department or agency is promptly informed.'

The committee placed special emphasis on the desired personal characteristics and qualities of the new assistants. 'Their effectiveness in assisting the President will, we think, be directly proportional to their ability to discharge their functions with restraint. They would remain in the background, issue no orders, make no decisions, emit no public statements . . . They should be men in whom the President has personal confidence and whose character and attitude is such that they would not attempt to exercise power on their own account.' Brownlow then uttered the phrase he later came to regret. The presidential assistants, he said, 'should be possessed of high competence, great physical vigor and a passion for anonymity'.

Roosevelt himself contributed significantly to the cynical attitude of the press towards Brownlow's staffing proposal. Luther Gulick noted that, when the sentence describing the attributes of the staff was first read to the President, 'he burst out chuckling and laughing and read the phrase out loud a second time.'[31] When Roosevelt

29. James Roosevelt, 'Staffing My Father's Presidency: A Personal Reminiscence', *Presidential Studies Quarterly*, Winter 1982, p. 48.
30. All quotations are from p. 5 of the report.
31. Louis Brownlow, *A Passion for Anonymity*, Chicago, 1958, p. 381.

presented the report to a press conference in January 1937, he told the assembled journalists 'to sharpen your pencils and take this down. This is a purple patch, one you will never forget.' Brownlow commented later: 'The President got a laugh, as he had expected, but he also got a chorus of various audible expressions of cynical disbelief. In fact one man spoke up and said "There ain't no such animal." '[32] The press went to town with 'passion for anonymity' and the journalists even ran a contest among themselves for a poem lampooning the proposal. On one level, at least, the staffing proposal was tainted from the start.[33]

Brownlow, however, was most earnest about his design for the presidential staff. His ideas about the role of the White House staff had emerged from discussions he had had with Tom Jones, once deputy to the head of the British Cabinet secretariat, Sir Maurice Hankey. Jones had used the phrase 'passion for anonymity' to describe the attributes of Hankey and, in doing so, had recommended the British secretariat as the model for Brownlow to follow.[34] Indeed, Brownlow followed it very closely. One of his original recommendations was that Roosevelt should establish an administrative secretariat under one executive director rather than the corps of executive assistants that appeared in the final report, but the President had rejected this recommendation prior to the publication of the report because he was strongly opposed to the idea of a chief of staff in the White House.[35] Brownlow had also suggested that some of the presidential assistants should be recruited from the executive departments, do a tour of duty in the White House, and then return to their former assignments. This proposal was included in the report and was, of course, analogous to the recruitment system adopted by the Cabinet Office in Britain where positions in the secretariat are usually held on the basis of a two-year secondment from the departments.[36] The fact that Brownlow had been so impressed with the improvement in top management practices which followed the establishment of the Cabinet secretariat in Whitehall,[37] and that the presidential staff was conceived, figuratively speaking,

32. *Ibid.*, p. 397.
33. See Polenberg, *op. cit.*, p. 222.
34. See Brownlow, *The President and the Presidency*, p. 105; also *Passion for Anonymity*, p. 357. See also Barry D. Karl, *Executive Reorganization and Reform in the New Deal*, Cambridge, Mass., 1963, p. 282.
35. See Brownlow, *The President and the Presidency*, p. 106; and Polenberg, *op. cit.*, p. 20.
36. Harold Wilson, *The Governance of Britain*, London, 1976, p. 94.
37. Brownlow, *Passion for Anonymity*, p. 356.

in London, not Washington, was to have an important bearing on the subsequent history of the White House Office.

The presidential staff quickly broke loose from the tight constraints of Brownlow's framework. By 1949 Clinton Rossiter was able to claim that 'the Executive Office is no longer simply a staff that aids the President directly in the discharge of the most exacting of his major responsibilities, that of chief administrator. . . . From a purely staff service it is fast developing into an agency that also formulates and coordinates policies at the highest level.'[38] Today, senior White House staffers regularly do what Brownlow said they should not do. They are prominent figures in every presidential administration. They do make decisions, issue instructions and emit public statements. They do interpose themselves between the President and heads of departments. They do exercise power on their own account, and on occasions certain members of the White House staff have not discharged their functions with restraint. In recent years, some have clearly lacked the high competence which Brownlow thought essential and few have displayed any passion for anonymity. Brownlow's purple patch has long been a poor predictor of the reality of life in the White House.

In other respects, however, the Brownlow report has had a significant impact. Its ideas about administrative management and the managerial presidency have influenced generations of political scientists and permeated virtually all of the presidential reform commissions since. Much of the output of those commissions has been directed towards improving the managerial structure first proposed by Brownlow. As far as the White House Office is concerned, the report is far from irrelevant. Although it is not a blueprint for what exists today, the report serves as a useful basis for assessing the development of the staff system during the post-war years. The most interesting aspects of the development of the White House Office are to be found in its departures from Brownlow.

The Development of the White House Staff

In the thirty years from 1944 to 1974 the number of people employed in the White House Office increased tenfold from about 58 to approximately 560. There was a similar expansion in the number of EOP employees; at the beginning of the 1970s the staff totalled in excess of 5,000. A development of this magnitude would not have been envisaged by Brownlow, and many contemporary observers believe that staff growth has gone beyond what is desirable. Typically, textbooks on the presidency now reproduce the familiar

38. Rossiter, *op. cit.*, p. 1214.

tables or graphs detailing this staff explosion. Some authors almost let the data be self-explanatory. Others, like Thomas Cronin, encapsulate the conventional wisdom of the post-Watergate years when he writes: 'The swelling and continuous expansion of the presidency have reached such proportions that the President's ability to manage has been weakened rather than strengthened. Bigger has not been better. The effectiveness of presidential leadership has not been enhanced by a bloated White House staff.' Echoing Brownlow, he concludes: 'Today the President needs help merely to manage his help.'[39]

There are, however, a number of difficulties with the data on presidential staff growth,[40] and the best one can do is talk about trends and approximate statistics. The White House Office today is much larger than Brownlow might have envisaged, but then times have changed and those who use Brownlow as a yardstick to make statements about the present size of the White House staff are, implicitly, saying something about changing political circumstances and changing staff functions, rather than size itself. Aggregate totals of White House staffs since 1939 do not in themselves indicate a great deal about the development or the present state of the White House Office. The size of the staff is not so much the cause of the organisational problems of the modern presidency; rather it is the consequence of other political developments that have occurred since Brownlow, and it is to the causes of White House staff growth that we must now turn.

The White House staff has grown in both size and function since 1939, but we ought not to forget that this was happening before 1939 as well. Brownlow did not create the President's personal staff; rather he attempted to fix its developmental direction on a path quite different from that taken since the late nineteenth century − and he was singularly unsuccessful in doing so. The post-Brownlow White House staff continued to evolve much as the pre-Brownlow presidential staff had done, except that the post-1939 period saw a

39. Thomas E. Cronin, *The State of the Presidency*, Boston, 1975, p. 118.
40. At least three different methods of accounting are employed in the official sources. The annual Budget of the United States Government gives figures for the total number of *full-time permanent positions* in the White House and also the *full-time equivalent employment*. Neither of these includes staff detailed to the White House from other departments and agencies or part-time consultants hired by the White House. The reports which the President is obliged to submit under the terms of the White House Personnel Authorization-Employment Act of 1978 give the *cumulative number of individual employees* during each fiscal year. This figure covers all employees, regardless of length of service, and therefore includes staff turnover. The reports also list separately the number of individuals detailed to the White House Office for more than thirty days, but, because each of the detailees will spend a different length of time in the White House, the job of calculating a meaningful aggregate total is not an easy one.

significant increase in the power of the staff within the executive branch of government. That accretion of power has been consequent upon the evolving functions of the White House Office, rather than its expanding size. Similarly, the problems of the presidential staff system are, primarily, problems of what the staff does, rather than how many staff there are to do it.

The functional evolution of the White House Office is not attributable to any one factor. A number of forces have been at work to make the presidential staff what it is today. Many attempts to explain the development of the White House staff emphasise its role as a coordinator of executive branch activity – a role assumed as a direct result of the weakness of the Cabinet as a coordinating mechanism. In the mid-1950s John Steelman, President Truman's *de facto* chief of staff, noted that 'the size of the White House and Executive Office staffs and, above all, the rank of White House staff members' grows in direct relationship to the inability of the more rigid cabinet system to meet growing complexities in the management of governmental programs.'[41] Similarly, Richard Fenno maintained that the growth of the staff was 'an inevitable response to the new dimensions of governmental activity, but also in part . . . an adverse reflection on the ability of the Cabinet in coping with the difficult problems of coordination involved'.[42] Cronin makes the same point as part of his more general perspective on the evolution of the EOP.[43] The fact is that, as government has expanded during the twentieth century, so the presidential perspective and the perspectives of his heads of departments are more liable to be different. The presidential perspective on government now requires that the executive branch be coordinated by the presidential branch, and, as Pressman and Wildavsky remind us, where there is an absence of common purpose, then coordination is another term for coercion, and thus it becomes a form of power.[44]

A second important explanation is to be found in the changed and more complex nature of the constituencies to which a President must relate. All of the President's constituencies have become more demanding over the last few decades. As Richard Neustadt has recently pointed out:

41. John R. Steelman and H. DeWayne Kreager, 'The Executive Office as an Administrative Co-Ordinator', *Law and Contemporary Problems* (1956), p. 699.
42. Richard F. Fenno, *The President's Cabinet*, Cambridge, Mass., 1959, p. 142.
43. Cronin, *op. cit.*, p. 122.
44. Jeffrey L. Pressman and Aaron Wildavsky, *Implementation: How Great Expectations in Washington are Dashed in Oakland*, Berkeley, 1984, pp. 133–4.

Yet Reagan's people find, as Nixon's did and Carter's, that they call for more manpower now than fifteen years ago or than Ford chose to use in the immediate aftermath of Watergate. In part this is attributable to the media, especially TV and its developing technology. In part it is responsive to the growth of staff elsewhere, all calling for White House contact. In part it is a tribute to the president-as-clerk, with cabinet members, congressmen, mayors, governors and private leaders, also local press, now looking to his staffs to help them do a lot of things they once did on their own (or not at all).[45]

A significant proportion of White House staff activity and of the post-1939 expansion of the professional staff has occurred in precisely those areas identified by Neustadt. A number of functionally specialised units now exist within the White House Office to connect with, service and manipulate important élites in the political system. 'Outreach' is one of the principal functions of the contemporary White House staff.

White House staff have liaised with presidential constituencies since the beginning of the presidency. George Washington's private secretary, Tobias Lear, acted as a liaison between the President and his heads of departments, and Jefferson used his private secretary as a link between himself and members of Congress.[46] In the later nineteenth century the more politically astute private secretaries handled presidential relations with the press and with party leaders as an important area of their portfolio.

The earliest formal recognition of the use of the White House as a linkage to a key presidential constituency did not occur until Herbert Hoover's presidency when, having been given an additional two senior White House staff by Congress, he designated one of them to be his Press Secretary. Since then every President has had a Press Secretary in his White House Office, and the Press Secretary's staff has expanded steadily over the years. President Carter's Press Secretary, Jody Powell, had two deputy press secretaries, three associate press secretaries, one press assistant and eleven other professional staff working for him. One journalist reported that Powell had a total of forty-six employees in his office.[47] This expansion must, however, be partly set against the growth and development of the media over the last three decades. No longer is it possible for the President to meet the whole of the White House

45. Richard E. Neustadt, 'Presidential Management', in Bruce Smith and James D. Carroll (eds), *Improving the Accountability and Performance of Government*, Washington, DC, 1982, p. 93.
46. See Hart, *op. cit.*, Ch. 2.
47. Dom Bonafede, 'Powell and the Press — A New Mood in the White House,' *National Journal*, 25 June 1977.

press corps for an informal chat in his office. In 1981 about 1,700 journalists had White House press credentials.[48] Neither is it possible for the President and his Press Secretary to rely on a relatively tame and compliant media in Washington. The Vietnam War, credibility gaps, Spiro Agnew and Watergate changed all that, along with a new type of aggressive and adversarial White House correspondent who became the star of the network television news. Television, of course, made a profound difference. The size of its audience, its technical capacity to cover the President wherever he happened to be, and the fact that it conveyed an image as well as a message made the media a more demanding and more difficult clientele to handle than ever before.

President Nixon hived off some of the Press Secretary's functions when he appointed a Director of Communications to manage the wider public relations effort, and that position too has been maintained by each of his successors. Under President Reagan the Director of Communications runs a large outfit that encompasses the President's speechwriting staff, a media relations and planning unit, and an Office of Public Affairs and the Office of Public Liaison.

Liaison with Congress has also become an important staff function over the past forty years, and particularly in the post-Watergate period when Congress has become more difficult for Presidents to handle. Every President since Eisenhower has had a congressional relations staff within his White House Office, and each has made small additions to the size of the staff bequeathed by his predecessor.[49] The congressional relations staff act as the President's eyes and ears on Capitol Hill, as lobbyists, as providers of vital services to Congressmen and sometimes as policy advisers within the White House. A skilful White House Office of Congressional Relations (or Office of Legislative Affairs as it is known in the Reagan administration) can be a major asset to a President, and an incompetent one can be very costly, as President Carter was to find out.[50]

Another formal staff link to presidential constituencies, the White House Office of Public Liaison, was established by President Ford and continued by Presidents Carter and Reagan. Its function is to lobby the lobbies. It reaches out to important non-government con-

48. George C. Edwards, *The Public Presidency*, New York, 1983, p. 108.
49. Stephen J. Wayne, *The Legislative Presidency*, New York, 1978, Ch. 5.
50. Eric L. Davis, 'Legislative Liaison in the Carter Administration', *Political Science Quarterly*, vol. 95, no. 3 (1979).

stituencies, such as business, labour and ethnic, religious and women's groups, to sell the President's policies and build coalitions in support of them. The influence and status of the Office of Public Liaison has declined since its heyday in the Carter administration under Anne Wexler, and in President Reagan's second term it was subsumed within the empire of the White House Director of Communications, Patrick Buchanan. But the public liaison staff has gradually expanded its size, and its function is now well-established as an important part of White House staff work.

In the Reagan White House there has also been a noticeable development of the smaller liaison/outreach operations headed by assistants for intergovernmental relations, political affairs and cabinet relations. The Office of Intergovernmental Relations currently has twelve professional staff to liaise with governors, mayors and state and local government organisations. President Reagan established the post of Assistant for Cabinet Affairs during his first term with a staff of eight, and also an Office of Political Affairs with a staff of four. Under President Carter cabinet affairs and intergovernmental relations were handled by one unit with a staff of five and there was no Office of Political Affairs.

President Reagan's establishment of an Office of Political Affairs within the White House Office is also a reflection of the way in which the post-1968 reforms of the presidential nomination process have affected the nature and function of the White House staff. The political affairs unit is a formal recognition of the need for first-term Presidents to maintain an experienced and professional campaign organisation during that first term to cope with the demands of the new rules of the nomination game. With the choice of the party's presidential nominee now beyond the control of party leaders, and with a system so open that it positively encourages challenges to the front-runner, incumbent Presidents can no longer enjoy the luxury of automatic renomination after four years. Presidents who desire a second term in office must now give far more attention to electoral politics than ever before.

Even before the creation of an Office of Political Affairs, the White House was becoming a dumping ground for campaign specialists who were given specially created jobs to keep them occupied for four years. One doubts, for example, that the jobs and titles President Carter bestowed on White House staffers Peter Bourne (Special Assistant for Health Issues), Joseph Aragon (Ombudsman) and Greg Schneiders (Special Assistant for Special Projects) had much to do with the day-to-day work of the White House Office, but all three had played an important part in Carter's election success in 1976.

The electoral connection now looms large in the work of the presidential staff, but not only because Presidents are compelled to keep their campaign organisation intact to manage the next election. The new nomination process has made the campaign organisation a more prominent source of recruitment for the whole range of White House staff jobs than in the past because the process of choosing a party's presidential nominee tends to isolate the successful candidate from party élites and effectively restricts his options over the choice of his staff.

The reason for this is that the nomination struggle is no longer mediated in privacy by party leaders who value party unity and coalition-building in the process of selecting the nominee. Today's mediators are the mass media, which tend to encourage conflict, competition and maximum party disunity in their attempt to make the very public contest for the nomination attractive to readers and viewers. By the time a candidate has run the gauntlet of caucuses, primaries and the party convention, he has little point of contact with the party leadership and often considerable antagonism to other factions in the party built around similar candidate-centred campaigns and candidate-centred organisations. Given the difficulty of winning a party's presidential nomination, it is not surprising that party nominees choose to use the same candidate-centred campaign organisation to fight the election proper. Neither is it surprising that success in November seems to convince Presidents-elect that what is good enough to win the nomination and then win the election is also good enough to govern the country with. Presidents tend to recruit their immediate personal staff from among those they know best. By the time a candidate has won his way to the presidency, it is his campaign staff with whom he is best acquainted and who inevitably end up with White House staff jobs.

Although the practice of recruiting White House staff from the ranks of campaign aides predates the McGovern-Fraser reforms, the new nomination process has the potential to put a very different kind of campaign aide into the White House. There is little incentive for today's campaign organisers to be skilled in the arts of compromise and coalition-building since there are no party mediators to compromise with and there is no need to build coalitions to win a nomination. As Nelson Polsby has pointed out, the strategic imperative lies not in forming a broad coalition within the party, as used to be the case, 'but in mobilizing a faction by emerging first in rank-order among the numerous presidential candidates who put themselves forward'.[51] Faction-fighting requires different sorts of

51. Nelson W. Polsby, *Consequences of Party Reform*, New York, 1983, p. 129.

skills from coalition-building, yet, while the route to the White House may have changed dramatically over the last two decades, what it takes to be a successful President has not, and in government there is still every incentive to compromise and to seek supporting coalitions for presidential initiatives. White House staff recruited from today's campaign organisations may well find the transition from electioneering to governing a difficult one to make, and may also be unwilling to make it even when they are ensconced at their White House desks.

In one respect, however, the modern presidential campaign organisation shares a common characteristic with the contemporary White House Office. Both operations now require and depend upon a functionally specialised division of labour among their staff in order to cope with the nature of the task before them. Today, the typical White House staffer is much less of a jack-of-all-trades than were his predecessors forty years ago, and is now more likely to be identified with one particular area of staff work. Indeed, only the very senior presidential aides in the White House Office will have responsibilities which traverse the fairly well-defined functional divisions of the White House Office.

The need for specialisation in the White House was an inevitable consequence of several developments in American government, particularly the increased responsibilities heaped on the President in the years after the Second World War, the way successive Presidents have moved to concentrate power in the White House, and the more demanding nature of the constituencies which the President must deal with. The workload of the presidential staff is too heavy, too complex and too specialised to permit them to range too widely. One person can no longer advise on policy, draft legislation, write presidential speeches in support of the legislation, lobby on Capitol Hill and negotiate compromises to head off hostile amendments (as Thomas Corcoran did for Franklin Roosevelt).[52] There are few generalists on the White House staff today, and almost all the senior staff are known for their particular jurisdiction, be it congressional liaison, handling the media, domestic policy advice, national security management, public relations, intergovernmental affairs and so on.

Specialisation has had both positive and detrimental effects on the performance of the White House Office. On the one hand, it has, at least, enabled the presidential staff to keep pace with developments in other parts of the political system and thus enabled the presidency to respond to an increasingly complex political environment.

52. See Louis W. Koenig, *The Chief Executive*, 2nd edn, New York, 1968, p. 315.

Congress, for example, demands more sophisticated attention from the White House today than it did thirty years ago. The weakness of party leadership, the fragmentation of power, procedural reforms, the pull of constituency interests on Capitol Hill and the post-Watergate reaction to the imperial presidency have combined to make Congress harder to manage from the White House perspective. A weekly meeting between the President and the congressional leadership will no longer suffice as the method by which the White House gets what it wants from Congress. Legislators now demand individual attention on a regular basis from White House aides who must have detailed knowledge and understanding of the political circumstances in which each of those individuals operates. Consequently, *ad hoc* contacts by the White House with Congress have now given way to a much more structured and strategic approach which uses significantly more manpower, computerised records on every Congressman, a carefully organised allocation of responsibilities between the liaison staff, and coordination of the congressional liaison units in the departments and agencies. Perhaps symbolic of the new approach to Congress is the fact that White House lobbyists on Capitol Hill are now issued with paging devices to enable them to keep in touch with each other and the White House at all times.[53] What the President's congressional liaison staff do today could not be done by one general-purpose assistant whose time was divided between several responsibilities. Handling Congress today has become a specialist matter, and the same is true of the other presidential constituencies as well.

On the other hand, when staff functions are differentiated and each is defined as a specialised task managed by specialist aides, then inevitably sub-units within the White House Office tend to develop separate identities and unique perspectives on staff tasks. That in turn can lead to internal competition, empire-building and divided loyalties among the staff as a result of a close identification with the specialist constituency being served.

Distinct sub-units of the White House Office are forced to compete both for the President's attention and for influence within the various coordinating mechanisms which have been established to bring together what specialisation has forced apart. The very existence of these coordinating mechanisms, like the Legislative Strategy Group, established during President Reagan's first term of office, is testimony to the different interests and perspectives to be

53. Eric L. Davis, 'Congressional Liaison: The People and the Institutions,' in Anthony King (ed.), *Both Ends of the Avenue*, Washington, DC, 1983, p. 73.

coordinated and reconciled in the process of White House decision-making. Inclusion in key staff meetings and in the flow of important papers has become a measure of status in the White House staff hierarchy, and, conversely, exclusion can be the cause of frustration and alienation.

Specialisation has also helped to accentuate the intensely competitive atmosphere within the White House by forcing staffers to engage in activities designed to increase their influence and defend the interests and jurisdictions of their particular area of staff work. Invitations to attend high-level staff meetings are not the only symbols of power. As John Dean noted in his memoir of the Nixon White House, the size of one's office, the quality of the furnishings in it and its proximity to the President's office were vitally important signs of prestige and status. 'Movers busied themselves with the continuous shuffling of furniture from one office to another as people moved in, up, down or out. We learned to read office changes as an index of the internal bureaucratic power struggles.'[54]

Empire-building can easily become a necessary exercise for the aspiring White House staffer. It manifests itself not only in terms of office space and proximity to the President, but also in the growth of staffs and the expansion of staff functions. When Jeb Magruder, one of President Nixon's more notorious aides, commented on the phenomenal ascendancy of his colleague Charles Colson, he noted simply: 'He arrived in the White House with one secretary and by the time he left he had dozens of people reporting to him.'[55] As a measure of his own success in the Office of Communications while an assistant to Herbert Klein, Magruder comments: 'Eventually I built up Klein's office from four assistants to about twelve.'[56] In two instances Zbigniew Brzezinski expanded his staff to prevent other White House staff units invading his turf. Clearly dissatisfied with what he called 'the occasionally sputtering overall White House co-ordination with Congress', Brzezinski appointed his own congressional liaison assistant quite independently of the Office of Congressional Relations. He also appointed his own press secretary because he felt that Jody Powell, the President's Press Secretary, did not know much about foreign affairs and that Powell's office needed reinforcement.[57]

The expansion of White House staff functions is also partly,

54. John Dean, *Blind Ambition*, New York, 1976, p. 30.
55. Jeb Stuart Magruder, *An American Life: One Man's Road to Watergate*, New York, 1974, p. 71.
56. *Ibid.*, p. 101.
57. Zbigniew Brzezinski, *Power and Principle: Memoirs of the National Security Adviser*, New York, 1983, pp. 76–7.

attributable to specialised division of labour – one of the classic
characteristics of any bureaucratic structure. Yet in some respects,
as Lewis Dexter has argued, the White House Office resembles not
so much a bureaucracy, but a court whose courtiers are loyal to the
person at the top rather than a set of organisational norms and
values.[58] In a court, advancement primarily depends on pleasing the
ruler and making oneself indispensable to the person, not the organisation, but in the White House court the opportunities for most of
the courtiers to do this are constrained by the limits of the specialised
task they are given to perform. Hence court politics and bureaucratic
organisation combine to produce an almost inevitable tendency
among ambitious staffers (courtiers) to expand their specialised
tasks as far as possible.[59]

A further way in which specialisation can affect the development
of the White House Office is by its consequent tendency to tie individual staff members more closely to presidential constituencies than
would otherwise be the case if there existed a more flexible method of
distributing staff assignments. The risk is that White House staffers,
who deal with one specific constituency all day every day, will
identify so closely with that constituency that they eventually
become an advocate for its interests inside the White House. The
danger of this happening has been recognised in the past. According
to White House aide James Rowe, Franklin Roosevelt opposed the
establishment of a formal congressional liaison staff because he felt
that, as soon as his staff began to deal with congressional requests
and complaints, they would be working for congressmen as well as
for him. Roosevelt thought that if his staff then failed to respond to
the demands of legislators, they would soon lose the confidence of
their constituents and, either way, the aide's usefulness to the President would quickly diminish. In his view, the idea of a specialist
congressional liaison staff carried with it built-in obsolescence.[60] The
point was reiterated by Richard Neustadt in an advisory memorandum to President-elect John F. Kennedy on the White House
congressional liaison office. 'Go slow on staffing up Congressional
liaison,' he urged Kennedy. 'An over-organized White House liaison
operation – like the one Eisenhower built in his first term – tends
to turn Presidential staffers into chore-boys for Congressmen and

---

58. Lewis A. Dexter, 'Court Politics: Presidential Staff Relations as a Special Case
    of a General Phenomenon', *Administration and Society*, vol. 9. no. 3 (1977).
59. See, for example, the graphic description of this process given by John Dean in
    Blind Ambition, pp. 38–40.
60. Robert L. Lester, 'Developments in Presidential – Congressional Relations:
    FDR-JFK', unpubl. Ph.D. diss., University of Virginia, 1969, p. 44.

bureaucrats alike. From this the President has more to risk than gain, in my opinion.'[61]

Given the development of outreach units in the contemporary White House Office, the risk of divided loyalties among presidential staff must be a significant one. Lawrence O'Brien was frequently accused of overly representing the interests of Congress in the Kennedy White House. But the problem is not just confined to liaising with Congress. President Reagan's first Assistant for Inter-governmental Relations also seems to have become too closely identified with his constituents. According to one authoritative reporter, Richard Williamson had gone too far in defending the interests of state and local governments against a proposed round of budget cuts and lost his White House job as a result.[62]

So far, the evolution of the White House Office has been described mainly as a response to external pressures and as a consequence of inevitable bureaucratic behaviour deriving from the specialised division of labour among the staff. Ultimately, however, the White House staff is the President's personal staff and he is free to shape it as he pleases. Although not a great deal is known about how Presidents put together their White House Office, it is highly improbable that they always respond to external pressures and never initiate new directions in White House staffing. Since 1939, different Presidents have responded to similar external circumstances in different ways, and no two Presidents have organised their White House in exactly the same manner.[63] Eisenhower, for example, decided to create a formal congressional liaison staff after his two immediate predecessors conducted congressional relations without one. Kennedy managed his White House Office without a chief of staff, not wishing to have another Sherman Adams as the single top aide. During his first term of office, Ronald Reagan installed a three-man team of Meese, Baker and Deaver to do what H.R. Haldeman alone did for Richard Nixon. Some Presidents have seen a need to have economic policy coordinators on their staff and others have not. Some Presidents attach great importance to particular staff functions, while others can relegate the very same function to a low

61. John Hart, 'Staffing the Presidency: Kennedy and the Office of Congressional Relations', *Presidential Studies Quarterly*, vol. XIII, no. 1 (1983).
62. Dick Kirschten, 'New Intergovernmental Affairs Chief Charts Less Abrasive Course', *National Journal*, vol. 15, no. 41 (8 Oct. 1983).
63. There are significant differences between apparently similar operating styles. See the comparison of Roosevelt and Kennedy in Richard E. Neustadt, 'Approaches to Staffing the Presidency: Notes on FDR and JFK', *American Political Science Review*, vol. 57, no. 4 (1963).

order of priority. Some Presidents have enlarged the White House staff more than others and, depending on what set of figures one uses, one or two have actually reduced staff size during their tenure. So presidential choice must also be taken into account when considering the development of the White House Office.

Some of those choices have had a major impact on the evolution of the post-Brownlow White House staff. Eisenhower's decision to create the post of assistant for national security, for example, and, later, Kennedy's decision to fill that post with a foreign policy specialist were instrumental in establishing a foreign policy-making capacity in the White House that now routinely dominates the policy-making process. When Richard Nixon established a White House Office of Communications, ostensibly to enable him to go over the heads of what he considered to be an unsympathetic White House press corps,[64] he laid the foundation for a significantly enhanced public relations machinery in the White House and, more importantly, elevated public relations to the forefront of White House staff work. President Kennedy left a permanent mark on the way in which the modern White House deals with Congress as a result of his personal decision to reject advice from two of his advisers on how to handle congressional relations. One adviser thought there was no necessity for a formal congressional liaison staff, and the other urged caution in building-up such a staff. Neither liked what Eisenhower had done in this respect.[65] But Kennedy saw a necessity for a congressional liaison staff and, under the direction of Lawrence O'Brien, there was little reticence in developing a staff operation quite different to Eisenhower's into what was to become the model of how a President deals with Congress. The boldest of all staffing innovations, however, must be credited to President Nixon, whose decision in January 1973 to establish five senior White House aides as executive branch policy overlords to whom Cabinet secretaries would report had a profound impact on the White House Office. This episode was so important that it warrants further discussion in the following section dealing with the power of the White House staff.

Finally, when explaining the evolution of the post-Brownlow White House staff, one must consider the role of Congress — a role that has been one of almost total non-involvement. In striking contrast to the way in which Congress has actively participated in shaping the structure and functions of the Executive Office generally, the White House Office has remained immune from all

64. Michael Grossman and Martha J. Kumar, *Portraying the President*, Baltimore, 1981, p. 89.
65. Hart, 'Staffing the Presidency', pp. 102–5.

but the most perfunctory congressional oversight of its activities. Long-standing traditions of comity and courtesy between the two branches preclude the one from interfering in the other's house-keeping matters, and Congress regards the President's personal staff as such a matter. Consequently, at no stage since 1939, even in the aftermath of Watergate, has Congress done anything to restrict the President's freedom to develop his personal staff as he wishes. Indeed, by unquestioningly voting appropriations for the White House Office year after year, Congress has acquiesced in the way successive Presidents have used that freedom.

The Power of the White House Staff

There is, in the history of the pre-Brownlow White House staff, con-siderable evidence of the increasingly prominent role played by the private secretary and, from the McKinley administration onwards, the Secretary to the President. Lamont, Cortelyou, Loeb, Tumulty and Slemp did far more on behalf of the Presidents they served than their formal titles might have suggested. By any standard they were powerful political operators. But their operations were confined to political activities, and here the word 'political' is used in its more popular sense. They liaised with party leaders and party organisa-tions, handled patronage matters, managed election campaigns and manipulated the press, as far as they could, to promote the President's image. However, none of them got overtly involved in matters of policy. Generally speaking, nineteenth and twentieth-century Presidents sought policy advice elsewhere, either from members of the Cabinet or from kitchen cabinets like the one Andrew Jackson created or from individual confidants like Colonel Edward House who served unofficially as Woodrow Wilson's policy adviser.

Brownlow was concerned to check the growth in power of the White House staff and, particularly, to ensure that it did not spill over into the policy-making arena. His report and Executive Order 8248 went to great lengths to constrain the role of the new adminis-trative assistants in policy matters by specifically stating that in no event would the administrative assistants be interposed between the President and heads of departments. That, of course, turned out to be wishful thinking. It was premised on a concept of administrative management that presupposed a separation of politics and adminis-tration which could not be sustained at the highest level of American government. The post-Brownlow White House staff has continued to enhance its power in the political arena, but has also accrued signi-ficant policy-making powers as well.

The power of the contemporary White House staff derives from its political and policy functions. It advises and advocates, and does so from a privileged and most advantageous position. It coordinates, and thus attempts to control, the activities of the executive branch departments and agencies on behalf of the President, and it represents the President in all of the political and governmental arenas in which he operates. Such an accumulation of power constitutes a major departure from the Brownlow design and has been viewed critically by many post-Watergate commentators, some of whom have interpreted the power of the White House staff as an almost illegitimate development in American government. Yet for many of those critics, it was not the functions performed by the White House staff that were at issue, but rather the fact that the White House staff performed them. It became apparent to many of those trying to make sense of Watergate that the power of the presidential staff had grown at the expense of more traditional institutions of government, especially the Cabinet. The White House Office had become a force in the policy process, had interposed itself between the President and the members of the Cabinet and had usurped functions that properly belonged to the Cabinet. The growth of White House staff power was thus seen in terms of the decline of the Cabinet − a process which many thought it would be highly desirable to reverse.

Such a view was hardly surprising. The declining prestige, status and authority of Cabinet members was a very visible manifestation of the increasing power of the White House staff. It had happened gradually, with no obvious single point of origin, but by the end of President Nixon's first term the subordination of the Cabinet to the presidential staff could not be denied. Shortly after the commencement of the second term, this was quite open and official, and the nature of White House staff-Cabinet relations during the Nixon administration was central to the post-Watergate critique of the institutionalised presidency. So too was the Eisenhower experience, which was equally important in setting the context for the post-Watergate debate about the expanding power of the presidential staff.

The Cabinet derives its existence from custom, not from the Constitution or from statute law. It is a creature of the President, and Presidents are at liberty to make considerable use of it as a source of advice or they are free to neglect it completely. Andrew Jackson did the latter. Lincoln, Theodore Roosevelt and Woodrow Wilson neglected their Cabinets only a little less.[66] Other Presidents,

66. Corwin, *op. cit.*, pp. 490−1.

however, have used their Cabinets more positively, and Eisenhower was one of those. As Richard Fenno has noted: 'Probably the best example of a decision-making procedure with extensive, built-in Cabinet reliance is that of President Eisenhower.'[67] Edward Corwin went even further in asserting that 'to a far greater degree than any of his predecessors President Eisenhower has endeavoured to employ the Cabinet as an instrument of collective policy-making.'[68] Greenstein claims that the importance Eisenhower attached to Cabinet meetings is evident from their profusion (an average of thirty-four meetings a year over his two terms[69]), and certainly no President since has emulated Eisenhower in his use of the Cabinet. But what should have been regarded as just one of the various ways in which a President can use his Cabinet has come to be celebrated as a model of responsible government from which Eisenhower's successors have more or less departed. The power and prominence of the White House staff have thus become a measure of deviation from the Eisenhower 'norm'.

At the other end of the spectrum is the Nixon presidency. No President in modern times has done more to puncture the status of the Cabinet collectively or its members individually, and correspondingly to enlarge the power of the White House staff. Despite the President-elect's pre-inaugural declaration about not wanting a Cabinet of 'yes men' and about how every Cabinet member would participate in all the great issues of his administration,[70] Richard Nixon proved to be much the same as his two immediate predecessors in his disregard of the Cabinet. Both Kennedy and Johnson had opted for more flexible and informal advisory mechanisms in preference to the large and rigid formal gathering of heads of all the departments. The Cabinet was convened only thirty-one times during the Kennedy administration. Arthur Schlesinger reports that Kennedy found Cabinet meetings 'simply useless', and Theodore Sorensen claims that 'no decisions of importance were made . . . and few subjects of importance, particularly in foreign affairs, were ever seriously discussed. The Cabinet as a body was convened largely as a symbol.'[71] One member of Lyndon Johnson's White House staff thought that 'the Cabinet became a joke, it was never used for

67. Fenno, *op. cit.*, p. 41.
68. Corwin, *op. cit.*, p. 301.
69. Fred I. Greenstein, *The Hidden-Hand Presidency*, New York, 1982, p. 113.
70. Cronin, *op. cit.*, p. 177.
71. Arthur M. Schlesinger, Jr., *A Thousand Days: John F. Kennedy in the White House*, Boston, London, 1965, p. 596; Theodore Sorensen, *Kennedy*, Boston, London, 1965, p. 283.

anything near what could be called presidential listening or consultation.'[72]

The difference between Nixon and his two predecessors, however, was that while Kennedy and Johnson were not enamoured of the Cabinet as a collective entity, they did make use of the advisory talents of Cabinet members in an individual capacity. Nixon, on the other hand, moved determinedly towards a state of affairs in which heads of departments were frozen out of the White House processes of policy advice. The abnormally high turnover of Cabinet members during the Nixon years seemed calculated in part to replace politicians with organisation and management specialists whose jobs would be to manage the vast bureaucracies under them and to implement policies that had been settled by others in the White House.[73] It is interesting to note that, when announcing his new Cabinet at the beginning of his second term in January 1973, Nixon emphasised the organisational talents of his new team − 'the eleven men whom I have chosen as department heads in the new Cabinet are one of the strongest executive combinations ever put together here in Washington, in terms of management ability, personal integrity, and commitment to public service'[74] − but said nothing about their political wisdom or experience. This was a striking contrast to the fanfare which announced his first Cabinet in December 1969. Nelson Polsby has summed up Nixon's exercise in Cabinet building:

Mr Nixon increasingly appointed people with no independent public standing and no constituencies of their own. In this shift we can read a distinctive change in the fundamental political goals and strategies of the Nixon administration from early concerns with constituency building to a later preoccupation, once Mr Nixon's re-election was assured, with centralizing power in the White House.[75]

President Nixon's contribution towards the declining status of the Cabinet went beyond merely ignoring heads of departments in White House policy deliberations. He also initiated two institutional changes that significantly enhanced the power of the presidential staff. The first was the establishment of the Domestic Council in 1970.

In his memoirs John Ehrlichman notes that when the members of President Nixon's Cabinet were briefed on the Domestic Council

72. Quoted in Cronin, *op. cit.*, p. 168.
73. John Ehrlichman, *Witness to Power*, New York, 1982, pp. 110−11.
74. Public Papers of the Presidents, *Richard M. Nixon, 1973*, Washington, DC, 1974, p. 5.
75. Nelson W. Polsby, 'Presidential Cabinet Making: Lessons for the Political System', *Political Science Quarterly*, vol. 93, no. 1 (1978).

plan, one of them, George Romney, voiced an objection to what he saw as another White House staff apparatus because he feared it would only make it more difficult for Cabinet members to meet with the President on an individual basis for substantive discussions.[76] Romney's fears were correct. The real intention behind the establishment of the Domestic Council was to create a staff operation in domestic policy similar to the one Henry Kissinger had built up around the National Security Council. And just as Kissinger was dominating the national security policy-making process, so too would Ehrlichman come to dominate the domestic policy process. It was Ehrlichman and his staff who called the meetings of the Domestic Council and prepared the agenda and discussion papers for those rare occasions when the Council met. It was also Ehrlichman who conveyed the results of the Council's deliberations to the President.

The Domestic Council was also a convenient device to restrict the range of policy issues that members of the Cabinet could express their views on. It was what might be called a 'specific-issue cabinet,' confined to matters of domestic policy and with no brief to discuss foreign policy or national security issues. Moreover, the creation of the Domestic Council marked the beginning of a propensity on the part of Presidents to use such devices more and more. President Ford, for example, established the Economic Policy Board in addition to the Domestic Council, and this effectively took many economic matters away from the full Cabinet. President Reagan extended the concept of specific-issue cabinets even further. During his first term he established seven Cabinet Councils: Economic Affairs, Human Resources, Natural Resources and Environment, Food and Agriculture, Commerce and Trade, Legal Policy, and Management and Administration. This fragmented the full Cabinet as far as one possibly could.

One final point about specific-issue cabinets is that when they do function, they tend to focus on details rather than broad policy directions. This has certainly been so in the Reagan administration, where an analysis of the Cabinet council system concluded that the councils operated at a secondary level of policy-making, directing their efforts towards facilitating the implementation of policy agendas rather than policy development.[77] This kind of work is far removed from the type of activity that one might expect the full

---

76. Ehrlichman, *op. cit.*, p. 106.
77. See Chester A. Newland, 'Executive Office Policy Apparatus: Enforcing the Reagan Agenda', in Lester M. Salamon and Michael S. Lund (eds), *The Reagan Presidency and the Governing of America*, Washington, DC, 1984, pp. 153–61.

Cabinet to engage in. In specific-issue cabinets, detailed technical work managed by senior White House staff takes the place of broad political debate on future policy directions that one might associate with the textbook role of the full Cabinet.

The second important institutional development during the Nixon administration was the President's announcement on January 5 1973 of a revamped White House staff structure. This had its origin in a presidential proposal to Congress two years earlier to restructure the executive branch by abolishing the Departments of Agriculture, Labor, Commerce, Housing and Urban Development, Transportation, Interior, and Health, Education and Welfare, consolidating their functions into four new super-departments: Human Resources, Natural Resources, Community Development and Economic Affairs. Consequent upon the failure of Congress to enact the executive reorganisation plan, Nixon announced at the beginning of his second term that he would restructure the White House Office around five assistants to the President to be responsible for foreign affairs (Kissinger), economic affairs (Schultz), domestic affairs (Ehrlichman), executive management (Ash), and what was euphemistically called White House administration (Haldeman). Under these five White House Assistants (of whom Schultz and, later on, Kissinger were also heads of departments) were three Cabinet members 'elevated' to the status of White House Counsellors. Their job was to undertake responsibility for policy coordination in those areas which would have been the focus of the new super-departments had Congress enacted Nixon's plan of executive reorganisation. This brought Earl Butz (Natural Resources), Caspar Weinberger (Human Resources) and James Lynn (Community Development) into the White House policy circle, but they were to operate under the direction of John Ehrlichman. Nixon also stated that other individual department heads would report to him 'via the appropriate Assistant to the President'.[78]

There was no ambiguity in Nixon's January statement about the subservience of Cabinet members to the White House staff. Moreover, the restructuring had created a three-tiered Cabinet. Two Cabinet members had the highest status of Assistant to the President, three more were Counsellors to the President and the remainder were consigned to third-class citizenship. The Cabinet itself became redundant, even as a symbol of unity in an increasingly fragmented executive branch. Under the restructured system, unity

---

78. See John Hart, 'Executive Reorganization in the USA and the Growth of Presidential Power', *Public Administration*, vol. 52 (1974).

was symbolised through strong, centralised control from the White House.

The Nixon system soon fell apart as a casualty of Watergate. Haldeman and Ehrlichman were forced to resign their White House posts at the end of April 1973, and in order to appease criticism that the President was ignoring his Cabinet, the three Counsellors turned in their dual portfolios and returned to the rank of ordinary Cabinet members. Nevertheless, Nixon, unlike any of his predecessors, had publicly exposed the very tenuous and fragile basis underlying the President-Cabinet relationship and had given an unequivocal presidential imprimatur to a less prominent role for the Cabinet collectively and heads of departments individually as a source of policy advice.

It is not possible to quantify the extent of the longer-term damage done to the status and authority of the Cabinet and its members by the Nixon initiatives, but that damage was not erased by Nixon's premature departure from the White House. It has been claimed that President Ford did more to restore a sense of purpose to the Cabinet as a deliberative, meaningful advisory body than any post-war President except Eisenhower,[79] but Ford had much the same view about the role of Cabinet members as Nixon. 'What I wanted in my Cabinet', he said, 'were strong managers who would control the career bureaucrats . . . I would leave the details of administration to them and concentrate on determining national priorities and directions myself.'[80] There were, however, few overt signs of White House staff-Cabinet problems during Ford's brief tenure, and his presidency may well mark a short hiatus in the ascendancy of the staff. President Carter soon succeeded in re-establishing the pattern of dominance.

Despite the protestation at the beginning of his term that 'there will never be an instance while I am President when the members of the White House staff dominate or act in a superior position to the members of our Cabinet',[81] Carter's presidency illustrated the very reverse. There was a permanent and serious problem of White House staff-Cabinet conflict which has been well documented from one side of the fence by the former Secretary of HEW, Joseph Califano.[82] In April 1978 a weekend meeting of the Cabinet, the

---

79. Principally by R. Gordon Hoxie, 'Staffing the Ford and Carter Presidencies', in Bradley D. Nash *et al.*, *Organizing and Staffing the Presidency*, New York, 1980, p. 50.
80. Gerald R. Ford, *A Time to Heal*, New York, 1979, p. 131.
81. Quoted in Dom Bonafede, 'Carter White House Staff is Heavy on Functions, Light on Frills', *National Journal*, 12 Feb. 1977, p. 234.
82. Joseph A. Califano, *Governing America*, New York, 1981, pp. 402–48.

White House staff and the President did nothing to stop the situation deteriorating and when Carter discovered a 'crisis of the American spirit' during his famous retreat at Camp David in July 1979, his only tangible response was to dismiss five members of his Cabinet and to enhance the power of his top aide, Hamilton Jordan, by designating him White House chief of staff. What became known as 'the July massacre' elicited the response from one Congressman: 'Good grief! They're cutting down the biggest trees and keeping the monkeys.'[83] From that point onwards, there was no doubting the supremacy of Carter's White House staff in the policy-making process.

Apart from the feud between Secretary of State Alexander Haig and senior White House staffers early on in the Reagan administration, at the time of writing there has been little overt evidence of serious Cabinet-staff conflict since Haig's resignation. The relative absence of tension between White House staff and Cabinet members might be because loyalty to the President and ideological congruence with his programme were prime considerations in recruiting personnel for senior executive branch positions in the Reagan administration. It might also be explained by the fact that all Reagan's department heads, except the Secretary of Defense, have been effectively constrained in what they can do by the overriding importance of budgetary policy and the administration's ideological commitment to reducing domestic expenditure. A third possible explanation, however, might be simply that the expectations of members of the President's Cabinet have adjusted to the reality of centralised direction from the White House.

While post-Watergate critics observed and accepted the increasing power of the White House staff and the declining status of the Cabinet as an empirical fact and drew certain normative conclusions from it, the historical context of this development received less attention than it perhaps deserved. Rarely was it pointed out that the Cabinet's role as a deliberative body, indeed its very identity as a collectivity, was the result of an historical accident in the constitutional scheme of things. The intention of the Founding Fathers was that the Senate would be the body to perform cabinet-type functions as a dispenser of collective advice to the President.[84] As Woodrow Wilson noted at the beginning of the twentieth century: 'There can be little doubt in the mind of anyone who has carefully studied the

83. Quoted in Austin Ranney, 'The Carter Administration', in Austin Ranney (ed.), *The American Elections of 1980*, Washington, DC, 1981, p. 32.
84. Corwin, *op. cit.*, p. 82; Henry B. Learned, *The President's Cabinet*, New York, 1912, p. 85.

plans and opinions of the Constitutional Convention of 1787 that the relations of the President and Senate were intended to be very much more intimate and confidential than they have been.'[85] The accident occurred early on in the history of the presidency. When President Washington went to the Senate in August 1789 to confer over an Indian treaty, the Senators were reluctant to discuss the matter in his presence and postponed debate for two days, at which point Washington left the chamber in anger.[86] The Founding Fathers' conception 'broke down the first time it was put to the test,' notes Corwin, and thereafter Washington turned to the heads of the executive departments as an alternative source of advice and consultation.[87]

Not all of Washington's successors followed his precedent, and the fortunes of the members of the Cabinet began to decline almost as soon as the Federalist era was over. As the nineteenth century progressed, American Presidents demonstrated a greater willingness to seek advice in a more flexible way, often turning to personal acquaintances outside of the executive branch. Yet, even though the Cabinet has no constitutional basis and individual members of the Cabinet have no constitutional claim to be the sole source of policy advice to the President, the notion of the Cabinet as an advisory body managed to survive, endowed with some semi-constitutional sanctity, as a theoretically important element in the structure of executive government. That survival can be partly attributed to the absence of any credible alternative institution within the formal framework of government which might have challenged the privileged advisory position of the members of the Cabinet. So long as the Senate showed no desire to perform the privy council role that the Founding Fathers had intended it to have, the heads of departments collectively constituted the only feasible institution to fill the vacuum. But the creation of the White House Office changed the situation. Given the flexibility of the Constitution with regard to presidential advisory mechanisms, together with the preferences of most post-war Presidents about where to seek advice from, it was not too difficult for the White House staff to mount a successful

85. Woodrow Wilson, *Constitutional Government in the United States*, New York, 1908, p. 138.
86. See Henry Jones Ford, *The Rise and Growth of American Politics*, New York, 1898, pp. 77–8.
87. Corwin, *op. cit.*, p. 209; but see also Louis Fisher, *The Politics of Shared Power: Congress and the Executive*, Washington, DC, 1981, p. 8. Senate Rule 36 still makes provision for the President to meet with the Senate for consideration of executive business.

challenge to the hitherto privileged position of the Cabinet. The White House staff replaced the Cabinet in much the same way as the Cabinet had once replaced the Senate, and there is nothing constitutionally illegitimate about a President choosing to take advice from his White House staff in preference to his Cabinet. It might be unwise for a President to rely on his White House staff to the exclusion of the members of his Cabinet, but that is another question.

The constitutional structure of American government is, therefore, one important explanation for the growing power of the White House staff. By not writing into the Constitution any provision for a Cabinet, an executive council, a privy council or other type of presidential advisory mechanism, the Founding Fathers left a vacuum to be filled as circumstances and necessity dictated. When necessity eventually did dictate that the White House staff assume a more prominent position in American politics, its move to centre-stage was made easier by the absence of any fixed institutional barrier in its path. The Cabinet was no real obstacle.

It is not the case, however, that the White House staff acquired power by usurping the functions of the Cabinet. Presidents call on their staff to do things that the Cabinet, and the heads of departments individually, are ill-suited to do. As Richard Neustadt pointed out a long time ago, Presidents and Cabinet members do not share the same vantage-point in government or the same risks, and presidential choices cannot be made by anyone but the President.[88] However much Cabinet members profess loyalty to the President, they quickly become enmeshed in a network of institutional relationships, each of which commands a certain degree of allegiance from the Cabinet member if he is to operate successfully within it. Multiple allegiances inevitably result in divided loyalties, and members of the Cabinet are as much an object of the President's powers of persuasion as are all the other constituents that a President must deal with.

The White House staff, as Neustadt has emphasised, must be persuaded as well.[89] Only the President alone can see his personal stake in the choices he makes, and he begins to risk his power prospects as soon as he depends on others. Nevertheless, force of necessity obliges that Presidents depend on others to perform the numerous and demanding chores of office, and in that sense the presidency has long been too big a job for one person to handle. Presidential staff have become powerful because they are, functionally, an extension of the President himself, and because the functions they

88. Richard E. Neustadt, *Presidential Power: The Politics of Leadership*, New York, 1960, pp. 39–40.
89. *Ibid.*, p. 41.

perform place them in a strategically commanding position relative to other actors in the political process, particularly in the executive branch.

Those functions fall into three broad categories: coordinating, gatekeeping and promotion. The coordinating function relates primarily to those policy-making, budgeting and other activities within the executive branch in which the President has an interest. The object here is to bring those activities into line with the President's desires and, consequently, the White House Office becomes the arbiter of what is and what is not in accord with the President's position. As gatekeeper, the White House staff determine who and what gets access to the President, a function necessitated by the fact that the President cannot physically satisfy all of the demands that are made on his time. As the principal promoter of the President, the White House Office has responsibility for ensuring that the President and his presidency appear to his various publics in the best possible light: the objective being to create and sustain public support for the President in office and, eventually, for him as a candidate for re-election. All of these functions are control functions, giving the White House staff the final say short of the President himself.

The White House Office has acquired power because it is a functional necessity of the modern presidency. The decline of the Cabinet is merely a manifestation of that power, not the cause of it, and the impact of White House staff power extends far beyond the members of the Cabinet and other political appointees in the executive branch. Necessity and proximity to the President make staff power formidable, and in most of the recent well-publicised battles between the White House staff and other key political actors, the White House staff has emerged victorious. It is not however an absolute power, nor is the White House staff guaranteed to emerge as the dominant force in any particular power struggle in which it is engaged. The staff, like the President himself, must compete for power in a pluralistic system of government, although they do of course compete from a most advantageous position.

The power of the White House staff has also been strengthened by one very significant institutional development during the last twenty years or so − the de-institutionalisation of the Executive Office of the President. The EOP is no longer the institutional staff that it once was or that Brownlow envisaged. It is not a permanent, professional, non-partisan, expert staff serving the office of the presidency irrespective of who holds that office at any one time. The senior echelons of the Executive Office are now filled by non-career, highly partisan presidential loyalists, many of whom do not possess professional expertise in government. In 1980, for example, the top ten positions in the Office of Management and Budget went to political appointees, nine of whom were without any prior experience in the executive branch.[90]

The Executive Office of the President has been politicised, and in place of neutral competence it now provides the President with what Terry Moe has called 'responsive competence'.[91] De-institutionalisation enhances the power of the President's personal staff to control the apparatus of the presidential branch by removing the potential obstacle of a career civil service inside the EOP, possessed of expertise, experience and institutional memory. This leaves the senior White House staff as the unchallenged directors of the Executive Office. It means that EOP units are more responsive to the needs of the political leadership of the day as expressed by top presidential aides in the White House Office. This is particularly the case with the three principal divisions in the Executive Office, namely the Office of Management and Budget, the Office of Policy Development and the National Security Council, where de-institutionalisation (or politicisation) has been most apparent. In recent years each of these divisions has been run by senior White House staff or, in the case of OMB, by a political appointee close to the President.

Power and Behaviour

In giving direction to the activities of the presidential branch, the White House staff has come to be associated with a set of behavioural characteristics which, like most other aspects of presidential staffing, became a cause of concern in the aftermath of Watergate. The worst of the behavioural defects associated with the men around the President was their utter disrespect for the law of the land, which was revealed during the Nixon years when senior White House staff were involved in a range of criminal acts including breaking and entering into private premises, burglary, bugging and telephone tapping, misusing campaign funds and obstructing justice. For their sins senior White House aides like H.R. Haldeman, John Ehrlichman, John Dean and Charles Colson went to jail.

Other behavioural problems of the White House staff were of a

90. Richard Rose, 'Governments Against Sub-governments: A European Perspective on Washington', in Richard Rose and Ezra N. Suleiman (eds), *Presidents and Prime Ministers*, Washington, DC, 1980, p. 338.
91. Terry Moe, 'The Political Presidency', in John E. Chubb and Paul E. Peterson (eds), *The New Direction in American Politics*, Washington, DC, 1985, p. 239.

non-criminal nature and not confined to the Nixon administration. Perhaps the most serious of these was the alleged tendency of the staff to isolate the President from the world outside the White House. As gatekeepers, they determined which people and what information penetrated the Oval Office, and terms like 'palace guard', 'praetorian guard' and 'the Berlin Wall' (specifically applied to Nixon's three senior aides, Haldeman, Ehrlichman and Kissinger) were frequently used in the 1960s and 1970s to emphasise the power of top aides to close off access to the President.

White House staff were also frequently accused of bringing problems to the White House that did not belong there. George Reedy, one-time Press Secretary to President Lyndon Johnson, cited the number of labour disputes that Johnson was called on to resolve personally. Reedy believed that the steel strike of 1965 and the maritime strike of 1966 were not serious enough to warrant settlement in the Oval Office, but the fact that they were resolved there paved the way for presidential intervention in the 1966 airline strike which turned out to be a disastrous setback for Lyndon Johnson.[92] Such things happen because staff make judgements about what might impress the President primarily to enhance their position in the White House pecking order. If problems are solved satisfactorily, then the President benefits politically and the staff assistant responsible gains some personal credit. Reedy, on the other hand, is suggesting that there is little incentive for the White House aide engaged in such behaviour to think about the longer-term implications of his action on the President and the presidency.

Another much-criticised feature of White House staff behaviour is excessive loyalty to the President, sometimes bordering on sycophancy. It results, we are told, in an unending quest to please the boss by telling him only what he wants to hear and shielding him from the bad news he ought to hear.[93] Few White House staffers, as conventional wisdom has it, are willing to incur the wrath of the President in this way and the wise presidential assistant, George Reedy tells us, develops the facility to maintain close proximity to the President coupled with the ability to disappear at the right moment.[94]

Arrogance has also been a hallmark of White House staff behaviour. Anecdotal evidence and general impressions gained over recent years suggest that some White House aides have not accepted the power bestowed on them with sufficient humility and sensitivity

---

92. George Reedy, *The Twilight of the Presidency*, New York, 1970, p. 94.
93. Cronin, *op. cit.*, p. 139; Hess, *op. cit.*, p. 153.
94. Reedy, *op. cit.*, pp. 88–9.

towards other key actors in the political system. Sometimes they can
be openly arrogant and cause offence, as Hamilton Jordan did
during the Carter administration by rarely returning telephone calls
from Cabinet members, or when a member of President Kennedy's
congressional liaison staff was overheard on Capitol Hill asking
'Anyone have a dime? I want to buy a Congressman.'[95] At other
times, the energy, ambition, aggressiveness and loyalty of the White
House staff combine to produce an arrogance of power which more
established political figures in Washington find offensive. Indeed, a
survey conducted by Thomas Cronin showed that presidential staff
themselves perceived their own insensitivity towards departmental
officials as the single most important White House source of conflict
between the staff and executive branch departments.[96]

The most frequently mentioned manifestation of this arrogance is
the tendency for White House staffers to use the President's name to
legitimise their own actions and authority, often when there is little
justification for them doing so. A presidential assistant who can tell
someone else that the President wants something done has considerable leverage over one who might be inclined to object or argue
about it. Moreover, the expanding size of the White House staff has
also meant that a larger number of individuals than ever before are in
a position to use the words 'The President wants. . . .', and the
President has less and less control over what is being said and done in
his name.[97]

Finally, there is ambition. The White House Office can be a ruth-
lessly competitive environment in which individuals engage in an
unending struggle to increase their influence and get as close to the
Oval Office as possible. Having got there, they then engage in an
equally demanding effort to protect their privileged position, and so
the gamut of staff behaviour can range from the empire-building
activities of a John Dean, all the way to power struggles at the very
top of the staff hierarchy like those which characterised the first term
of the Reagan administration.[98]

The behavioural defects of the White House staff were well publicised during the 1970s. George Reedy set the tone for many of the
subsequent commentaries with a damning indictment of the inner

95. Abraham Holtzman, *Legislative Liaison: Executive Leadership in Congress*,
    Chicago, 1970, p. 67.
96. Cronin, *op. cit.*, p. 163.
97. Colin Seymour-Ure, *The American President: Power and Communication*,
    London, 1982, p. 78.
98. See Laurence Barrett, *Gambling with History: Reagan in the White House*, New
    York, 1984.

life of the White House in his book, *The Twilight of the Presidency*. The White House, he said, was 'an ideal cloak for intrigue, pomposity and ambition'; it 'provides camouflage for all that is petty and nasty in human beings and enables a clown or a knave to pose as Galahad and be treated with deference.'[99] He variously described it as a 'barnyard', 'a pressure cooker' and 'the perfect setting for the conspiracy of mediocrity', and urged that no one should be permitted to work there until he was at least forty years of age and had already suffered major disappointments in life (p. xiii). There may have been a little exaggeration in his analysis, as Reedy himself admits (p. xv), but the book had a significant impact on the way critics came to view the presidential staff in the Watergate and post-Watergate period. It was easy to argue that the growth of White House staff power and the behaviour that power engendered was what got the Nixon administration involved in Watergate, and it was equally easy to propose a whole set of remedies designed to reduce staff power and check its worst behavioural consequences.

While this unflattering image of the White House staff was something of a revelation in the late 1960s and early 1970s, it certainly predated the Nixon administration. Haldeman and Ehrlichman, for example, were not the first White House aides to isolate the President they worked for. As Charles Dyer Norton successfully isolated Taft, George Christian closed off access to Harding, and Lawrence Richey did much the same in the case of Herbert Hoover. There were also power struggles and intrigue in pre-Brownlow White House staffs: witness William Loeb's eagerness to step into Cortelyou's shoes or Tumulty's battles with Colonel House or the never-ending friction between the first White House staff troika of Richey, Akerson and Newton in Hoover's administration or in Louis Howe's fierce jealousy of his standing with Franklin Roosevelt.[100] Pre-Brownlow White House staffs also had their share of ambitious assistants and, if one goes back to the nineteenth century, some corrupt, dishonest and deceitful presidential aides as well. The behavioural defects of the White House staff have a long history and tradition which predate the post-war expansion in its size.

The very public exposure of the seamy side of White House staff behaviour during the Watergate crisis raised questions about the accountability of the staff, questions that had not merited much attention till then. If, as James Madison once claimed, American government was built upon the principle that 'ambition must be made to counteract ambition,' then Watergate was fairly concrete

---

99. Reedy, *op. cit.*, p. xv.
100. On pre-Brownlow White House staffs, see Hart, *The Presidential Branch*, ch. 2.

evidence that the ambition of the White House staff had not been counteracted very well. The fact that many of President Nixon's top aides went to jail for the worst of their sins, or that the President eventually took responsibility for what his staff had done in his name by forfeiting his presidency, failed to satisfy the critics. They saw a strong and unhealthy relationship between the size, the power and the behaviour of the presidential staff and called for institutional reform, not just individual punishment, to correct the situation. A great deal was written on what ought to be done, a lot less on why the White House staff had escaped the usual checks and balances of the American political system.

The Accountability of the White House Staff

For much of its history the White House Office was allowed to move to the centre-stage of American politics with few barriers in its path, and it appeared to be almost totally immune from the operation of congressional oversight. The executive branch of government is generally held accountable to Congress in a number of ways. Its most senior personnel, apart from the President and Vice-President, are subject to senatorial confirmation before their appointments become official and, having been appointed, they are then frequently required to testify before congressional committees about their activities in high office. The appropriation process affords Congress the opportunity to oversee government business, as does the capacity of Congress to conduct investigations into any area of its choice. Ultimately, of course, Congress can legislate to ensure accountability in government.

The White House Office is part of the executive branch. It is funded directly by Congress just like any other department or agency, and it does not in theory stand beyond any of these traditional methods of oversight. But in practice the White House staff escaped even the most basic scrutiny by Congress until the accumulation of staff power during the Nixon administration sparked a congressional response. Even so, that response fell far short of the potential which Congress has for bringing the White House staff into the orbit of oversight that it applies to the executive branch in general.

To its credit, Congress, through the House Post Office and Civil Service Committee, made the first serious study of the expansion of the presidential staff. The report it issued in 1972 contained no specific recommendations for change, but it did draw attention to the centralisation of power in the White House at the expense of the executive departments and also to the lack of information in

Congress with respect to presidential staffing.[101] Since then, the House Post Office and Civil Service Committee has been at the forefront of congressional attempts to strengthen oversight of the White House staff.

One direct response to the growing power of the Nixon staff was a move to make senior presidential aides subject to the Senate confirmation process. Traditionally, the advice and consent clause has not been held applicable to the President's personal staff because the relationship is considered to be a privileged one. In effect, presidential staff are treated as an extension of the President himself, but, as Louis Fisher has suggested, when presidential advisers behave as surrogates for departmental heads, the basis for that privilege must be questioned.[102] There have been several attempts in recent times to make the national security adviser subject to the confirmation process, this being a reaction to the dominance of Henry Kissinger and Zbigniew Brzezinski in the policy-making process. None of the bills progressed very far in Congress, but the Senate Foreign Relations Committee eventually held hearings on the subject after Senator Zorinsky had proposed an amendment to a State Department appropriation bill in 1980.[103] The attempt illustrated the limits to how far Congress can in practice extend the advice and consent clause to White House staff. There is no statutory position of national security adviser, and before such a post could be subject to the confirmation process, it would have to be formally established. The weight of expert evidence is against doing so,[104] and Congress has not taken the issue any further. The only way that Congress could bring senior presidential aides into the confirmation process without dictating to the President how he must organise his White House would be to legislate a blanket provision covering all White House Office employees irrespective of their assignment. This is not a likely possibility.

Congress, however, has been more frustrated by its inability to get presidential staff to testify before its committees than it has been by the problems of applying the confirmation process to the White

101. U.S. House of Representatives, 92nd Congress, 2nd Session, Committee on Post Office and Civil Service, *A Report on the Growth of the Executive Office of the President 1955–1973*, Committee Print no. 19, Washington, DC, 1972.
102. Fisher, *op. cit.*, p. 144.
103. See U.S. Senate, 96th Congress, 2nd Session, Hearings Before the Committee on Foreign Relations, *The National Security Adviser: Role and Accountability*, Washington, DC, 1980.
104. See the testimony of Richard Neustadt, I.M. Destler and Thomas Franck in *ibid.*, pp. 29–45.

House. Presidential aides who have taken over major responsibility for programmes and policies from department heads have used the doctrine of executive privilege to avoid giving testimony on matters of national importance. Henry Kissinger's refusal to go before the Senate Foreign Relations Committee while directing a controversial policy in South-East Asia was perhaps the most blatant example. The situation was exacerbated by Kissinger's high public visibility as the President's chief foreign policy adviser. It led Senator Frank Church to ask:

. . . We have to wonder whether it is appropriate for a person who is immune from congressional inquiry to act as a principal spokesman for the United States in matters of foreign policy. . . . If he can appear on 'Meet the Press', why can't he appear before the Foreign Relations Committee? Why should he be accountable to what is often called the fourth branch of government when he is not accountable to the first branch?[105]

The problem of executive privilege in respect of testimony by White House staff before congressional committees has never been satisfactorily resolved. Extensive hearings were held in both the House and Senate during the 92nd, 93rd and 94th Congresses, but no congressional action followed. Those contesting the broad claims of privilege from the White House were given scholarly support by the publication of Professor Raoul Berger's influential treatise in 1974, which argued that the doctrine had no constitutional basis at all,[106] but shortly afterwards the Supreme Court argued to the contrary in *United States* v. *Nixon* (418 US 683), although it also said that the claim of privilege was not an absolute one.

The debate about executive privilege continues, but it has also tended to obscure the very real powers possessed by Congress to compel testimony at committee hearings. The existing law makes it a misdemeanour, punishable by a fine and imprisonment, for anyone to refuse to appear as a witness if summoned by Congress and also to refuse to answer any pertinent question. There is no specific exemption for presidential staff, and generally the Supreme Court has upheld the validity of this law when its constitutionality has been challenged. It would seem that, legally, the White House staff have no claim to refuse to attend a congressional hearing. Whether or not they can refuse to answer questions on the basis of executive privilege would have to be resolved in the courts, but the effect of congressional reluctance to push the issue to the courts has made the

---

105. *The National Security Adviser: Role and Accountability*, p. 2.
106. Raoul Berger, *Executive Privilege: A Constitutional Myth*, Cambridge, Mass., 1974.

White House staff the sole arbiters of when the doctrine of executive privilege should be invoked.

Congress must, therefore, accept some responsibility for the present situation. Clearly, it would not want to deny the President any claim of privilege, but neither can it be content with a blanket claim of privilege any time it seeks to question a presidential aide. There have been opportunities when it might have been worthwhile for Congress to enforce its subpoena power but it has chosen not to do so with respect to the White House Office. For example, in 1981 Martin Anderson, who was then President Reagan's Assistant for Policy Development, refused to appear before an appropriations subcommittee considering the budget request for the Office of Policy Development. The White House claimed executive privilege, even though Anderson's predecessor in the Carter administration had appeared each year for the same purpose. But instead of testing the privilege claim, the Committee on Appropriations responded with a futile gesture by denying the budget request of nearly $3 million in its entirety.[107] In the end, almost the full request was granted to the Office of Policy Development in a continuing resolution, so the committee's protest came to nothing, and the White House got away with as broad a claim of executive privilege as one could imagine.

The appropriations process in general provides an even better illustration of the comity between Congress and the President over matters pertaining to the presidential staff. Consider, for example, the attempt of Rep. Clarence Miller of Ohio to reduce the appropriation for the fiscal year 1980 for the White House Office. The House Appropriations Committee had granted the full budget request of $18,210,000, but when the bill came to the floor of the House in July 1979 Miller moved to reduce the amount by $710,000. The proposed amendment elicited this response from Rep. Tom Steed of Oklahoma:

Mr Chairman, I rise in opposition to the amendment. Mr Chairman, this item has a very unusual and peculiar relationship to the House. This is the item where the President of the United States says, 'I need these resources to do my own personal job.' This is the President's personal staff. I do not see how anybody on Earth could vote to cut this item without their calling the President of the United States a man they do not believe because they are saying, 'I know more about what it takes to be the President of the United States than he does' . . . For the sake of the honor of this House, we ought not to meddle with this particular item.

107. See U.S. House of Representatives, 97th Congress, 1st Session, Committee on Appropriations, *Treasury, Postal Service and General Government Appropriation Bill 1982*, House Report no. 97–171 (9 July 1981), pp. 30 and 61–3.

Table 5.1.	APPROPRIATIONS FOR THE WHITE HOUSE OFFICE,
FISCAL YEARS 1971–82($)

	Budget Request	*House Committee*	*House Floor*	*Senate Committee*	*Senate Floor*	*Actual Appropriation*
1971	8,550,000	8,550,000	8,550,000	8,550,000	8,550,000	8,550,000
1972	9,342,000	9,342,000	9,342,000	9,342,000	9,342,000	9,342,000
1973	9,767,000	9,767,000	9,767,000	9,767,000	9,767,000	9,767,000
1974	9,110,000	9,110,000	9,110,000	9,110,000	9,110,000	9,110,000
1975	16,510,000	16,367,000	16,367,000	16,367,000	16,367,000	16,367,000
1976	16,946,000	16,763,000	16,763,000	16,763,000	16,763,000	16,763,000
1977	16,530,000	16,530,000	zero [a]	16,530,000	16,530,000	16,530,000
1978	17,580,000	17,580,000	zero [a]	17,580,000	17,580,000	17,580,000
1979	16,907,000	16,907,000	16,907,000	16,711,000	16,711,000	16,711,000
1980	18,210,000	18,210,000	18,210,000	18,210,000	18,210,000	18,210,000
1981	20,373,000	20,373,000	20,373,000	20,373,000	b	20,373,000[c]
1982	22,346,000	22,278,000	22,278,000	22,278,000	b	22,278,000[c]

(*a*)	The amount was stricken on the floor of the House on a point of order because no authorising language had been enacted.
(*b*)	Bill not acted upon by the Senate.
(*c*)	As provided by first continuing resolution.

Source: Figures compiled by Dr Louis Fisher of the Congressional Research Service from committee reports and appropriation bills. They do not reflect adjustments by subsequent supplemental appropriation bills or continuing resolutions.

and he concluded by saying:

I cannot recall a time in the history of this Congress that this item has ever been changed from what the President said he wanted.[108]

The amendment was defeated easily and Rep. Steed was almost correct in what he said about the refusal of Congress to tamper with the White House Office budget request. As Table 5.1 shows, in only three of the twelve years from 1971 to 1982 did the House alter the amount requested, and in eight of the twelve years neither the House nor the Senate made any reduction whatsoever to the original budget figure. Where reductions have been made, the sums involved were marginal.

In spite of the fact that some congressmen complain about the funding levels for presidential staff fairly regularly, there are also a significant number who defend what Rep. Silvio Conte has described as 'the historic tradition of comity and courtesy between the Chief Executive and the Legislative Branch and the traditional privilege which has been granted to the President's personal staff'.[109] It

108. *Congressional Record*, 16 July 1979, p. H5967.
109. Committee on Appropriations, *Treasury, Postal Service and General Government Appropriation Bill 1982*, p. 61.

appears that the 'comity' and 'courtesy' of which Conte speaks and the 'honour' described by Steed precludes the appropriation process from being an effective method of congressional oversight of the White House staff.

The most serious congressional effort to exercise oversight of the presidential staff in recent years was promoted by the House Post Office and Civil Service Committee and culminated in the passage of the White House Personnel Authorisation-Employment Act (Public Law 95 – 570) signed by President Carter in November 1978. One of the principal features of the Act was a telling comment on the casual manner in which Congress had regarded the expansion of the presidential staff system. Since 1948 Congress had routinely appropriated money for more and more presidential staff without any authorisation for the additional personnel – a practice contrary to House Rule XXI which prohibits appropriations for any unauthorised expenditures. Until the passage of the 1978 legislation, there was authorisation for only fourteen administrative assistants in the White House Office.[110] The Act also established limits on the numbers of executive-level and supergrade-level personnel that could be employed on the President's staff at any one time, although those limits were considerably in excess of the numbers actually employed in those categories at the time, which in fact gave the President an opportunity to double the number of top-level aides.[111] Moreover, an attempt to fix a ceiling on White House staff numbers was defeated in committee, and the final version of the bill authorised the President to employ as many assistants below the GS-16 level as he deemed to be necessary.

One other provision of the Act deserves mention. It requires the President to make an annual report to Congress on the total number of staff employed in the White House Office during each fiscal year, including detailees and part-time consultants. (The reporting requirement also applies to the Office of the Vice-President, Office of Policy Development, Office of Administration and the staff assigned to the Executive Residence). The reports have been of some value in that they provide the most realistic indication of the size of the White House staff given in official statistics, but the data are not

110. U.S. House of Representatives, 95th Congress, 1st Session, Hearings before the Subcommittee on Employee Ethics and Utilization of the Committee on Post Office and Civil Service, *Authorization for the White House Staff*, Washington, DC, 1977, p. 1.
111. The Act limits Presidents to fifty employees at the executive level and fifty at the supergrade level (GS 16–18). During a debate on the bill it was pointed out by Rep. Bauman that there were only fifty-two personnel at these levels at the time the bill was being considered. *Congressional Record* (4 April 1978), p. 8635.

as complete as they might be. They do not distinguish between professional and clerical staff, their reporting categories are too broad, they say nothing about who is doing what job in the White House and, because the aggregate figures include staff turnover, they tend to overstate the true size of the staff. In a fiscal year during which the presidency changes hands, the reports can become meaningless. At the time of writing there is renewed pressure from within the House Post Office and Civil Service Committee to get the White House to agree to a more acceptable reporting format.

The impact of the 1978 legislation has been slight, and on one level it can be seen as little more than a congressional housekeeping measure which has restored the importance of an authorising committee in relation to an appropriations committee. Several amendments weakened the bill significantly during its passage through Congress, and the only detectable effect it has had on the organisation of the White House staff has been to encourage Presidents to boost the number of senior aides — not quite the intent behind the motives of the reformers. The personnel reports issued by the White House have generated no publicity and aroused little interest on Capitol Hill. This was perhaps surprising considering that the first two reports indicated a substantial discrepancy between President Carter's widely publicised claim to have reduced the White House staff by one-third and the actual figures reported by his own Special Assistant for Administration.[112]

The weakness of congressional scrutiny in this area has continued to frustrate one or two legislators, but Congress as a whole shows little interest in moving to strengthen the accountability of the White House staff, especially now that the Watergate era has passed. Yet it must also be pointed out that the White House staff have remained relatively immune from congressional scrutiny, not necessarily because traditional techniques of oversight have no teeth, but rather because the President's staff are treated as a special case. The underlying set of beliefs and values about the relationship between Congress and the President, encapsulated in the terms 'comity' and 'courtesy', are a powerful deterrent to those seeking to apply the same standards to the White House staff as are applied to the departments and agencies. Cynics may argue that it has a lot more to do with the unwillingness of Congress to draw attention to its own staffing practices, and there is a grain of truth in this, but the con-

112. President Carter frequently boasted about his achievement in reducing the White House staff to 351, but his reports to Congress under the terms of the 1978 Act show considerably higher numbers of full-time staff. The cumulative total (one that includes staff turnover) was 478 in fiscal year 1979 and 489 in fiscal year 1980.

gressional tradition of hands-off-the-President long predates the staff explosion on Capitol Hill. The attitudes displayed by many Congressmen today, even in the aftermath of Watergate, are little different from those expressed in the very first Congress by Madison and others when they spent so long discussing the propriety of interfering with the President's expense account.

Presidential Staff and the Structure of Government

The development of the White House Office has been organic, remarkably rapid and consequent upon profound changes in the wider framework of American politics. It is now a structurally complex, functionally sophisticated and politically powerful unit operating at the very heart of the governmental process and has clearly expanded the President's capacity for leadership. In three critical areas – control of the executive branch, political outreach and policy advice – the presidential staff have enabled the President to do things he would otherwise be unable to do on his own. Without such assistance the modern presidency would be a perilously weak institution. Few would want to deny that the White House staff have a necessary and legitimate role in the structure of government.

Yet the staff occupy an ambivalent position within that structure. Constitutionally, they are regarded as merely an extension of the President with no separate identity of their own. They do the President's bidding as though the President were doing it himself and, unlike some other divisions of the executive branch, they have no statutory or constitutional obligations to any other branch of government beyond those specifically laid upon the President. Ultimately, the President himself is answerable for the activities of his staff. This literal view of the place of the presidential staff in the structure of American government finds its clearest expression in the doctrine of executive privilege, a practical manifestation in the immunity the staff enjoy from the usual application of congressional oversight, and a vindication in Watergate where President Nixon's resignation in a large part had something to do with what others did on his behalf.

On the other hand, the White House staff also have a life of their own. Senior members become well-known public figures and are never merely automata responding to every presidential direction without question. They may sometimes disregard instructions when their judgement of what is in the best interests of the President conflicts with his, and they certainly exercise a degree of discretion in the way they execute their functions. Many of the more recent criticisms of the presidential staff reflect their separate identity. For example, they are often accused of bringing problems into the White House that do not properly belong there – an indication of the independent initiative residing with the staff – and of isolating the President from the outside world, a testimony to their gatekeeping powers. And, notwithstanding their vantage-point and proximity to the President, in the end presidential aides must compete for the attention of the President along with other influential élites in Washington.

Since Watergate, political scientists have begun to focus on the behavioural weaknesses and, to a lesser extent, the structural defects of the White House staff. Analytically, at least, the staff are treated as something more than an extension of the President, taking on the appearance of almost a separate political institution. Most of what has been written has reinforced Richard Neustadt's warning that staff are no guarantee of leadership and have the propensity to make things worse rather than better for the President.[113] Watergate is, of course, the most obvious case, but others come to mind. It is quite conceivable, for example, that President Carter might have been better off without an assistant for congressional relations, given that the role both magnified and exacerbated his own personal failings in this area.

The structural weaknesses are equally important. The system which has evolved since 1939 lacks institutional continuity and institutional memory simply because there is usually no senior staff residue when one President hands over to another. The best that one can hope for, it seems, is the brief and hurried discussions that now take place between the outgoing and incoming staff during the hectic period of the transition. The White House Office also lacks expertise in government. The pattern of recruitment over the last twenty years, which draws heavily upon campaign specialists, does not equip the presidential staff to deal with many of the problems they face in office. In most recent administrations White House staff have had to learn on the job and, while some have learned faster and better than others, the lack of expertise at the outset can have a damaging effect on the President himself. A third significant weakness is the more or less adversarial relationship that has developed between the White House staff and the career bureaucrats in the departments and agencies.[114] Competition, rather than cooperation, seems to be the normal state of things, and there is little incentive on either side to assist or protect the other when necessary. In that sense, the injection of the White House staff into the policy-making

113. Neustadt, *Presidential Power*, p. 39.
114. Cronin, *op. cit.*, Ch. 6.

process has further fragmented the structure of American government.

Despite the behavioural and structural defects, Presidents, for reasons already indicated, are unlikely to respond to pleas to reduce White House staff size and influence, nor are they likely to initiate a more open and accountable staff system when Congress shows no interest in doing so. The future of the White House staff, like their past, will be shaped by changing political circumstances and the desires of those occupying the White House. The problem of reforming the White House staff arises out of their ambivalent position in the structure of constitutional government. The literal view of the role of the staff does not correspond too closely to the way they operate in practice, but, at the same time, their constitutional anonymity protects them from major reform or at least reform in the direction which post-Watergate reformists are pointing.

6

THE PRESIDENT AND FOREIGN RELATIONS

Phil Williams

Superficially the foreign policy problems which faced Ronald Reagan immediately after his inauguration as President were not very different from the agenda which confronted Franklin Roosevelt in 1933.[1] What priority should be given to arms control and disarmament? How could the new administration most fruitfully promote international economic cooperation? To what extent should the United States intervene in Latin American affairs? Such questions loomed large for both Presidents. Yet the similarities should not be exaggerated: despite apparent continuities in United States foreign policy since the early 1930s, it is the forces of change which are most striking.

One feature that would almost certainly have astounded Roosevelt is the sheer scale, extent and apparent permanence of American involvement overseas. Senator Robert Taft, when accused of moving in on foreign policy, retorted that foreign policy had moved in on him. American Presidents from Roosevelt onwards could make the same claim – and with far greater validity. Foreign policy and national security, which in Roosevelt's first term had a relatively low salience, have now become a pre-eminent part of the President's activities and concerns, and according to some estimates consume between half and two-thirds of his time.[2] The modern presidency is perhaps above all else a foreign policy presidency.

This transformation, of course, reflects the changed status of the United States in international affairs. American Presidents have had a world leadership role thrust upon them. Some have welcomed it, others accepted it only reluctantly, but all have found it inescapable. A hemispheric foreign policy – or what Charles Beard termed 'American continentalism'[3] – has been replaced by a policy of

---

1. A very detailed historical account of Roosevelt's foreign policy can be found in R. Dallek, *Franklin D. Roosevelt and American Foreign Policy*, New York, 1979.
2. See T. Cronin, *The State of the Presidency*, Boston, 1975, p. 13.
3. Quoted in W.G. Carleton, *The Revolution in American Foreign Policy: Its Global Range*, New York, 1967.

global range. Substantial commercial involvement overseas, which has always been part of the American tradition, is now accompanied by extensive military involvement. A moralistic approach to world affairs, while still visible, now tends to be combined with a shrewd appreciation of *realpolitik*. A distaste for international organisations – while still evident, especially in the stance of the Reagan administration – has given way to participation in 'entangling alliances'. A penchant for unilateralism, although apparent in much of the Reagan administration's foreign policy, coexists with notions of collective security that can be traced back to the 1940s.

There was something inevitable about this transformation in American foreign relations, reflecting as it did long-term geopolitical trends which eroded the 'surplus of security' the United States had enjoyed in the nineteenth century. The process was accelerated and accentuated by internal developments. Indeed, it is not necessary to accept radical interpretations of American foreign policy to acknowledge that industrialisation, with its compelling demands for markets and raw materials, made it impossible for the United States to remain indifferent to events in Asia and Europe. Economic power and diplomatic insulation are uncomfortable partners at the best of times; with the rise of Germany and Japan such a combination became impossible as the United States was propelled into entanglement, confrontation and hostilities. The results were dramatic. 'From 1941 to 1945 the United States fought a global war, led the mightiest alliance in history, became deeply and irrevocably involved in all parts of the earth, and made the pivotal decisions that affected the future everywhere.'[4]

Nor did the final victory over the Axis powers offer anything more than a temporary respite. The Second World War revealed, encouraged and catalysed several trends which did much to shape the post-war role and policies of the United States. The collapse of the balance of power in Europe, the emergence of a bipolar international system in which the two great powers shared a profound ideological antipathy towards one another, the development of nuclear weapons and the decolonisation process all had far-reaching implications for American foreign policy and with it the role of the presidency. The immediate post-war aspirations for a return to 'normalcy' reluctantly but inexorably gave way to an acceptance of both America's superpower status and the intractability of the Soviet-American relationship, with its battlegrounds in Europe and elsewhere. Although the dangers of escalation put a premium on the avoidance of direct hostilities between the two states,

4. *Ibid*, p. 35.

decolonisation, with its attendant instabilities, provided various temptations to conflict and encouraged extensive involvement by the superpowers in the Third World.

The novelty of all this, of course, should not be exaggerated. Expansion in the Pacific had been a feature of United States policy in the nineteenth century, while isolationism had never meant non-involvement in the affairs of Latin America. Indeed, it is in the Western hemisphere that the continuity in United States policy is most remarkable: the two strands which have been most evident in the post-war period have long pedigrees.[5] The moderate or conciliatory approach found in John Kennedy's 'Alliance for Progress', Jimmy Carter's emphasis on human rights, and the Panama Canal Treaty follows the 'Good Neighbour' tradition established most explicitly by Franklin Roosevelt. The second, and more pervasive, thread – United States dominance and periodic intervention – has an even longer history. As one analyst has noted, 'From the time of President Monroe's message of 1823 onwards, US leaders . . . claimed fear of extra-continental intervention as justification of their own interventions', and 'affirmed that they were acting to forestall the machinations of non-American forces.'[6] The onset of the cold war accentuated this tendency as Latin America was increasingly viewed in Washington as 'a staging ground in an epic and global East-West conflict' as well as 'a place where United States economic interests dictated that radicalism be contained'.[7] United States military intervention in Guatemala, Cuba and the Dominican Republic, and the overthrow of the Allende government in Chile, were all manifestations of this hard-line stance. So, too, is the Reagan administration's stance towards Nicaragua. The Sandinista regime is seen as a proxy of Cuba, which in turn is seen as a proxy of the Soviet Union. Almost by definition, the opponents of President Daniel Ortega, the 'Contras', are seen by the administration as allies in ridding the hemisphere of non-American forces.

If fears about the spread of communism have influenced the American approach to its southern neighbours, it has also had substantial impact elsewhere – contributing to the direct military involvement in both Korea and Indochina. The reaction to the

5. See I. Katznelson and K. Prewitt, 'Constitutionalism, Class, and the Limits of Choice in US Foreign Policy', in R. Fagen (ed.), *Capitalism and the State in US-Latin American Relations*, Stanford, 1979, p. 250.
6. G. Connell-Smith, *The United States and Latin America*, New York, London, 1974, p. 145.
7. M.T. Klare and C. Arnson, 'Exporting Repression: US Support for Authoritarianism in Latin America', in Fagen, *op. cit.*, pp. 158–9.

Vietnam War did lead to some retrenchment in the 1970s; nevertheless the United States still retains an impressive global network of
bases and military installations.[8] Indeed, the 1970s saw not only the
American military disengagement in South-East Asia, but also
growing interest in Africa. This was prompted by Soviet and Cuban
activities in Angola and the Horn of Africa and by the emergence of
a black caucus in Congress concerned with African developments.
The Soviet intervention in Afghanistan had a similar effect. Coming
soon after the fall of the Shah of Iran, who had acted as
Washington's surrogate policeman in the Persian Gulf, the Soviet
action aroused unprecedented anxiety about Soviet penetration into
the Gulf and the Middle East. It provoked the United States into
developing a Rapid Deployment Force which, for all its conceptual
and organisational shortcomings, symbolises the American position
as a global power.

With these changes in the American position in the world have
come equally dramatic changes in the presidential role in foreign
policy and national security. Presidential responsibility in these
fields, of course, derives from the Constitution with its grants of
power which made the President both chief diplomat and
Commander-in-Chief of the armed forces. In addition, the 'silences
of the Constitution' joined with practical considerations, practice
and precedent in ways which allowed the President to augment his
power, largely at the expense of Congress.[9] During the interwar
period, however, a semblance of balance was restored, and Franklin
Roosevelt, in his first two terms, was severely circumscribed by congressional desires to avoid being dragged into a European war.
Neutrality legislation was the most obvious and most formal
restraint; but it was not the only one. At several junctures the anticipated reaction of Congress to possible diplomatic initiatives
inhibited a President who was loath either to expend his power
prematurely or to challenge Congress in ways which might spill over
and reduce its support for New Deal legislation.[10] The consequence,
as Arthur Schlesinger has pointed out, was that 'Congress . . .
proceeded to assert itself on all issues of external relations that might
involve the nation in war. It pursued this course with astonishing

8. For details see *United States Foreign Policy Objectives and Overseas Military
Installations*, Washington, DC, 1979. This was prepared for the Committee on
Foreign Relations, United States Senate, by the Foreign Affairs and National
Defense Division, Congressional Research Service, Library of Congress.
9. See Arthur M. Schlesinger, Jr., *The Imperial Presidency*, Boston, 1973, esp.
Ch. 1.
10. Dallek, *op. cit.*, p. 153.

success in face of the fact that the domestic crisis of depression was producing an unprecedented delegation of powers to a new President and that the President himself not only was masterful in the use of these powers but enjoyed exceptional public confidence.'[11]

This divergence between the domestic presidency and the foreign policy presidency was only temporary. Just as the crisis at home had elevated the presidency to new heights of leadership in domestic affairs, the international crisis was to have the same impact on the presidential role in foreign affairs. The Second World War – like previous wars – 'nourished the Presidency'.[12] This time, however, the emergency did not end with the cessation of hostilities. 'The Cold War made emergency a permanent condition.'[13] It also made the wartime presidency a peacetime institution. This was not immediately apparent at the end of the war. But with the passage of legislation establishing a much more formalised and elaborate organisational structure for national security decision-making, the broad outlines of the foreign-policy presidency were laid down. Indeed, it is little exaggeration to suggest that on matters of foreign policy and defence the key year in the evolution of the modern presidency was 1947 rather than 1932. The period since the Truman Doctrine and the National Security Act has a cohesion and unity which differentiate it very clearly from the previous fifteen years. Although the presidency has had its ups and downs in the last forty years, the competition with the Soviet Union has given it a very distinctive character.

Most of the period since 1945 has, in fact, been marked by the pre-eminence of the presidency in the foreign policy-making process. It has also been characterised by the fact that the incumbents have been confronted with problems, responsibilities and burdens far in excess of anything known to their predecessors. Indeed, it is possible to discern several key roles which every post-war President, to a greater or lesser degree, has had to fulfil. Although there is inevitably some overlap between them, for analytical purposes they can be summarised under three headings: the President as 'cold warrior', the President as peacekeeper and the President as ultimate decision-maker. Such a categorisation does not convey the full flavour of the remarkably broad agenda confronting the President in his dealings with other states. For example, the summits of the late 1970s and 1980s, in which the President met with the heads of government of the other leading industrialised countries to discuss problems of eco-

11. Schlesinger, *op. cit.*, p. 95.
12. *Ibiḍ.*, p. 122.
13. M. Mandelbaum, *The Nuclear Revolution: International Politics before and after Hiroshima*, Cambridge University Press, 1981, p. 186.

nomic management in a period of inflation and recession, do not fall naturally into the scheme. However, this omission is perhaps not too debilitating: foreign economic policy has long been a concern of Presidents and will loom increasingly large in the future. But for most of the post-war period it has been overshadowed by the problems of peace and security. In dealing with these problems the chief executive has, of course, been subjected to all sorts of pressures and demands, which have often had a detrimental effect on his conduct of foreign policy. After we have examined the President's roles and responsibilities an attempt will be made to identify the major impediments in relation to his capacity to deal rationally and effectively with international problems, challenges and issues.

The President as 'Cold Warrior'

The description of the President as a 'cold warrior' encapsulates a series of widely differing problems and responsibilities which extend from his role as alliance leader to the task of managing national strategy. Furthermore, successive Presidents have been faced with the problem of defining or redefining the national interest of the United States and of identifying the major challenges or threats to American security. In this process, however, Presidents have tended, either consciously or unconsciously, to regard the national interest and their own political interests as synonymous – even when, it can be argued, they diverged very considerably. Thomas Halper has argued very persuasively that on several occasions Presidents have defined situations as crises not because they involved a threat to national security as such, but because they challenged national and, more especially, presidential appearances of strength, resolve and determination.[14] One need only take this idea a little further to suggest that during the post-war period the presidency has become the prime embodiment of a kind of national *machismo*. This notion of *machismo* is central to our understanding of United States foreign policy in the post-war period. The difficulty with it is that the concern with projecting an image of toughness has highly diverse roots which range from culture and personality through strategic considerations to political calculations.

In part *machismo* can be seen as stemming from a distinctive American culture. In a society founded on competitive individualism and brought up on the frontier ethic and the myth of the 'Old

14. T. Halper, *Foreign Policy Crises: Appearance and Reality in Decision-Making*, Columbus, Ohio, 1971.

West', the chief executive could hardly be unaffected by, or oblivious to, *machismo*. If this is something which influences all Presidents, however, it does so to different degrees, depending on individual personality and background. None of the post-war Presidents, for example, could match Theodore Roosevelt for the sheer exuberance with which he wielded power and courted danger. It is arguable though that since the Second World War *machismo* has, in a sense, become more institutionalised and more a quality of the presidency and not just of individual incumbents.

There was something inevitable about this process. Part of the reason was the 'lesson' of the interwar years or what is sometimes termed the 'Munich syndrome' which destroyed the legitimacy of actions designed to appease or conciliate adversaries.[15] Even more important was the nature of the cold war which seemed to put a premium on toughness. The cold war was a conflict in which each superpower wanted to avoid hostilities with the other, but in which it was widely acknowledged – in the United States at least – that weakness, indecision and vacillation could only encourage aggression. The early experiences of the Truman administration certainly seemed to point to this conclusion. Firmness paid dividends both in countering Soviet pressure on Iran and Turkey and defeating the Communist insurrection in Greece. Furthermore, as American commitments expanded, there was an immediate – albeit probably unwarranted – assumption that they were interdependent: any hint of weakness under threat in one area might be interpreted as a sign of weakness elsewhere, thereby encouraging further adventurism by the Soviet Union or its allies. The result was that areas and issues which had little intrinsic importance and no strategic significance for the United States were nevertheless imbued with great symbolic importance. West Berlin was the most obvious example, but both South Korea and South Vietnam were part of the same pattern. Another consequence was that compromises were made more difficult and attempts to relinquish untenable or anomalous positions ruled out as abject surrender. Oversimplified analogies with falling dominoes, which seem to have been present at least in embryonic form as early as 1946, only intensified the process, as did the belief that the cold war was a zero-sum game in which setbacks or losses for the United States were immediately and very simply translated into corresponding gains for the Soviet bloc.

If the Cold War encouraged presidential preoccupation with

15. The importance of this analogy is brought out in E.R. May, *The 'Lessons' of the Past*, Oxford University Press, 1973.

images of strength, American domestic politics transformed this into an obsession. Once again, the pattern was established during the Truman era. Despite the support of Senator Vandenberg and the triumphs of 'bipartisanship', President Truman was constantly reminded of the 'sell-out' at Yalta and Potsdam. The furore over the 'loss of China' to the Communists — even though China had never been America's to lose — and the boost this gave to McCarthyism reinforced the lesson in a particularly dramatic and unpleasant manner. Indeed, projecting an image of strength and resolve in dealing with the Soviet Union and the Chinese People's Republic was no longer desirable solely for diplomatic or strategic reasons; it had also become almost a prerequisite of the President's effectiveness on the domestic scene. To some extent this may have been a self-inflicted problem in that the Truman administration's 'overselling' of the threat in the late 1940s — although an understandable and perhaps unavoidable tactic to overcome residual isolationism — created fears and anxieties which could be exploited by a powerful and ruthless demagogue such as McCarthy.[16] Nevertheless, its repercussions were to prove far-reaching.

As well as stemming from these cultural and political factors, presidential *machismo* can also be understood as a rational response to the Soviet challenge. The calculation that presidential weakness would encourage aggression, while overly simplistic, is nevertheless understandable, given the nature of the cold war and the 'inherent bad faith' model of the Soviet Union which seems to have been held by American decision-makers.

The difficulty, of course, lies in the attempt to disentangle each of these elements in the approach of post-war Presidents to foreign policy. Yet it is essential that the effort be made. After all, presidential concern with communicating strength and resolve has on several occasions led to increases in the defence budget beyond those initially planned; it has encouraged American military intervention in both Latin America and Asia; and it has frozen American policies into more rigid patterns than may have been necessary. It is all the more important, therefore, to ask whether such consequences have stemmed primarily from strategic concerns, political considerations or personal needs.

In the case of President Truman, *machismo* seems to have been a product of strategic calculation, albeit strongly reinforced by domestic pressures and criticisms. Hence, although Truman's

---

16. R. Freeland, *The Truman Doctrine and the Origins of McCarthyism*, New York, 1975.

decision to intervene in Korea probably owed less to domestic considerations than to the desire to demonstrate to the Soviet Union that
aggression would not succeed and to reassure the European allies
that the United States could be depended upon, the President and his
advisers were certainly not insensitive to the political dangers of
inaction or oblivious to the benefits (at least in the short run) of a
decisive and firm response to the North Korean attack.[17]

If Truman did much to establish the pattern for most post-war
Presidents in his handling of foreign policy, his immediate successor
did not conform to that pattern. Indeed, of all post-war Presidents,
Eisenhower seems to have been the incumbent least concerned about
projecting an image of strength. There are several possible reasons
for this. His military background was probably one factor. The early
success in ending the Korean War, through threats to enlarge it, was
another. Having displayed his determination to considerable effect
and thereby established his credentials as a 'cold warrior' early in
the life of his administration, there was less need for repeat
performances – for either the domestic or the international
audience. Insofar as the need remained, it was met by the Secretary
of State, John Foster Dulles. Indeed, it was Dulles rather then Eisenhower who in many ways set the tone of the administration's foreign
policy with his pronouncements about massive retaliation and brink-
manship. *Machismo* was not absent from the Eisenhower administration, but until the death of Dulles it was embodied in the Secretary
of State rather than the President.

In the Kennedy administration the President did not have a Secretary of State who was in any way comparable to Dulles. A further
difference was that unlike Eisenhower, whose initial actions had
been very successful, Kennedy began badly. The Bay of Pigs
episode, in particular, considerably damaged his prestige. The
decision to attempt to overthrow Castro was partly a result of
'bureaucratic momentum' in that the planning process had started
during the previous administration, but it also owed much to
Kennedy's desire to live up to the campaign rhetoric in which he had
condemned the Republicans for allowing a Communist state to be
established in the Western Hemisphere. At the same time the President's unwillingness to allow direct formal participation by United
States forces, and especially air power, created 'a major gap between
means and ends'.[18] Although the intervention revealed the new
President's concern with consolidating his credentials as a 'cold

17. See G. Paige, *The Korean Decision*, New York, 1968.
18. Z. Brzezinski and S.P. Huntington, *Political Power USA/USSR*, New York,
    1965, p. 381.

warrior', the fact that it was not followed through left considerable doubt about his toughness.

The Vienna Summit and the Berlin crisis of 1961 in which the President, while standing firm on the status of West Berlin, accepted the division of the city, did nothing to redeem his reputation. Indeed, it is conceivable that miscalculation of Kennedy's resolve may have been a major factor in Khrushchev's decision to install medium-range ballistic missiles in Cuba in 1962. Furthermore, the President's firm response can be understood partly as an attempt to re-establish his credibility in a way which would deter Khrushchev from any further adventurism such as might be directed, for example, at West Berlin. In his handling of the Cuban missile crisis, therefore, Kennedy was concerned not only with the immediate problem, but in managing the confrontation in such a way as to inhibit future challenges. His approach seems to have been remarkably similar to Truman's when faced with the North Korean invasion of South Korea in 1950: both Presidents seem to have felt that a failure to act decisively could only encourage further aggression and lead to general war in the future. Another similarity was the way in which domestic factors reinforced strategic considerations. One failure over Cuba was hardly tolerable for the Kennedy administration; a second would almost certainly have undermined its effectiveness in domestic as well as foreign policy.[19]

It is perhaps not surprising, therefore, that concerns over Cuba spilled over and influenced the Johnson administration's approach to Latin America. Indeed, there is considerable evidence that United States intervention in the Dominican Republic in 1965 was prompted in large part by the determination to prevent the establishment of a second Cuba in the western hemisphere, which, Johnson apparently felt, would lead to 'bad politics' at home.[20] The same desire to avoid anything which might impair or disrupt his 'Great Society' pro-gramme seems to have been a major influence in Johnson's decisions to escalate the Vietnam War. As he later told his biographer, 'I knew that if we let Communist aggression succeed in taking over South Vietnam, there would follow in this country . . . a mean and destructive debate − that would shatter my Presidency, kill my Adminis-tration and damage our democracy.'[21] For Johnson the domestic consequences of the 'loss of China' provided an alarming precedent

19. This point is discussed more fully in G. Allison, *Essence of Decision*, Boston, 1971.
20. See P. Geyelin, *Lyndon B. Johnson and the World*, London, 1966, pp. 231−58, esp. p. 254.
21. D. Kearns, *Lyndon Johnson and the American Dream*, New York, 1976, p. 264.

which underlined his determination not to be the President who lost Indochina. It was his tragedy that the escalation of the war not only created the divisions and dissent which it had been intended to avoid, but dislocated and disrupted the progressive social welfare programmes which the President valued so highly.

For Lyndon Johnson, therefore, maintaining the presidential image of strength seems to have been important primarily for domestic political reasons. His concern was symptomatic of liberal anxieties in dealing with what was seen as fundamentally a conservative nation and in particular a Congress in which key committees were controlled by conservatives. As Gelb and Betts put it, 'liberals were always running scared when it came to national security.'[22]

Richard Nixon, of course, did not face this kind of problem. Indeed, he was sufficiently secure in his reputation as a 'cold warrior' to act as the major architect of both Soviet-American and Sino-American *détente*. Some commentators have suggested that he was able to embark on such ventures precisely because he was the first President who did not have Richard Nixon to worry about. Yet Nixon too was concerned with projecting an image of resolve, and seems to have had almost a pathological desire to prove himself a formidable and tough President. His passion for the film *Patton − Lust for Glory*, his view of life as a succession of crises and struggles, and a series of public statements and private comments all suggest that he was motivated far more by personal need than by the kinds of political concern that had driven his predecessor. This would help to explain actions, such as the invasion of Cambodia in 1970 and the mining of Haiphong harbour in 1972, for which it is difficult to find a convincing strategic rationale. Indeed, Nixon's public justification of the Cambodian decision displays clearly his obsession with toughness. In a statement that was reminiscent of the most extreme cold war rhetoric, the President argued that it was not American power but America's will and character that were being tested. As he said:

If, when the chips are down, the world's most powerful nation, the United States of America, acts like a pitiful, helpless giant, the forces of totalitarianism and anarchy will threaten free nations and free institutions throughout the world . . . If we fail to meet this challenge, all other nations will be on notice that despite its overwhelming power the United States, when a real crisis comes, will be found wanting.[23]

22. L.H. Gelb and R.K. Betts, *The Irony of Vietnam*, Washington, DC, 1979, p. 225.
23. Quoted in W. Shawcross, *Sideshow*, New York, 1979, p. 147.

Nor is it coincidental that part of this excerpt from the speech was singled out by the President for inclusion in his memoirs.[24]

Yet it is far from clear that the 'chips' *were* down or that America's 'will and character' were being probed and tested. It seems feasible to argue, in fact, that privately the President saw the decision primarily as an opportunity to display *his* will and character – to demonstrate to his domestic as well as his international opponents that he was willing to 'bite the bullet'.[25] As one analyst has commented: 'Whatever else he thought of Cambodia, Nixon also saw it as a chance of restoring his slighted authority – "Those Senators think they can push me around, but I'll show them who's tough", he warned Kissinger after one Congressional appeal for caution.'[26] There was little new in all this: Richard Nixon was not behaving in a manner that was completely different from other post-war Presidents. Nevertheless, it is ironic that a tendency that was inherent in the cold war presidency and encouraged by domestic politics was elevated into a governing principle of foreign policy by an incumbent who did much to ease cold war tensions and who was relatively impervious to the political constraints faced by some of his predecessors. Richard Nixon was not unique in his *machismo*, but he may have been unique in that it stemmed more from personal than either political or strategic needs.

There is an added irony in that both during and after Watergate, Henry Kissinger became anxious about demonstrating to the Soviet Union that the United States could still act decisively in foreign policy. Indeed, Kissinger displayed all the concerns with establishing and maintaining credibility that had been evident under Nixon and most of his predecessors during the post-war period. This tendency was evident in the Middle East war of 1973. When the Soviet Union threatened to intervene directly in the region to save the Egyptian Third Army, its preparatory actions and its messages were designed primarily to force the United States into exerting greater restraint on Israel and ensuring that the United Nations cease-fire was observed. Kissinger, while recognising that he had been somewhat insensitive to Soviet interests, nevertheless felt the United States had to respond decisively in order to make clear to Moscow that it should not try to take advantage of the domestic crisis. As a result, American strategic and conventional forces worldwide were placed on a 'Defcon 3' alert. Although Kissinger also ensured that the Israeli

24. R. Nixon, *The Memoirs of Richard Nixon*, New York, 1978, p. 452.
25. See Shawcross, *op. cit.*, p. 144.
26. *Ibid*, pp. 134–5.

grip on the Third Army was relaxed, thereby acknowledging the legitimacy of Soviet concerns, the alert was widely criticised as an overreaction.

In spite of this, Kissinger retained his concern with credibility. This was evident in the *Mayaguez* incident in 1975 which revealed the strength of the urge to restore American prestige in the aftermath of the fall of Vietnam. The same year, Kissinger entered a competitive game with Moscow in Angola, not because the United States had major interests at stake but because he wanted to ensure that the Soviet leadership did not conclude that it could intervene in the Third World with impunity. Congress did not share his concern with credibility, however, and in December 1975 cut off the funding for further covert intervention. Although President Ford resisted the imposition of restraint by Congress, both he and his successor Jimmy Carter were much more circumspect in the use of American power than their immediate predecessors.

Carter in particular was strongly opposed to American intervention abroad. It is noteworthy that, apart from the ill-fated attempt to rescue the hostages in Iran, Carter managed to avoid the military entanglements which had been so prevalent a feature of American foreign policy since 1945. Despite this, both Ford and Carter were propelled into adopting a harder line towards the Soviet Union than they regarded as either necessary or desirable. As a result of Ronald Reagan's challenge for the Republican nomination in 1976, Ford was compelled to ban the word '*détente*' from his political vocabulary. Similarly the challenge from Reagan in the presidential campaign of 1980 seems to have been a major factor in Carter's adoption of a tougher stance in foreign policy. Afghanistan provided the occasion for the Carter 'conversion', and he seems genuinely to have felt a sense of betrayal similar to Kennedy's reaction at the discovery of Soviet missiles in Cuba. However, even before the Soviet intervention in Afghanistan, there were indications that domestic pressures, particularly from a more 'hawkish' Senate, were inexorably pushing the President in this direction. Indeed, there are striking parallels between the Carter administration's concern with military preparedness in its last eighteen months and that evident towards the end of the Eisenhower administration twenty years earlier. Democratic Presidents may have felt particularly vulnerable to domestic criticism regarding the level of provision for defence, but Republicans have certainly not been immune to this.

In Carter's case, however, the impression of weakness was not dissipated by a hardline stance towards the Soviet Union. Not only was the Carter administration accused of doing too little too late, but any political advantage it might have obtained was more than offset by the President's failure to secure the release of the American hostages in Iran through blandishments, coercion or the use of force. The impasse was widely regarded as a national humiliation. The resulting criticism was levelled not only at Carter's policies, which were widely deemed to have deprived the United States of the power necessary to deal with such challenges, but also the President's personality: a President who did not convey an image of toughness seemed particularly unsuitable at a time when the United States was facing what many regarded as unprecedented challenges to its security and prestige. The election of Reagan as President was testimony to this. Indeed, Reagan reflected the public desire for a hardline stance towards the Soviet Union and other enemies of the United States, even more than he created it. It appears that *machismo* is as significant a quality of American Presidents in the 1980s as it was ten or twenty years earlier.

Reagan's performance in office bears this out. Although the use of force has been constrained by a residual 'Vietnam syndrome', Reagan has fitted the mould of most post-war Presidents in his concern with toughness. Indeed, the President has responded to what might be termed the 'Iran syndrome' − the impulse that the United States should never be subject to humiliation as it was in the hostage crisis. The result has been that although the use of force in Lebanon was unsuccessful − and the President as a result of congressional pressure was forced to withdraw or 'redeploy' the American marines − there have been other uses of military force designed to demonstrate that the United States is prepared to uphold its interests by whatever means necessary. The intervention in Grenada, for example, was short, sharp and decisive. The Reagan response to state-sponsored terrorism has the same elements of symbolism and can be understood as an attempt to underline American will and credibility and to restore American pride after a decade in which the United States appeared to be on the retreat. In this connection, Colonel Gaddafi of Libya has been an important target of convenience.

While the hardline approach has been popular at home, it has won less approval from America's allies, especially those in Western Europe. Such differences have been all the more serious because the President's role as 'cold warrior' encompasses that of alliance leader. Since the late 1940s Presidents have been concerned not only with the security of the homeland, but also with the security of states in Europe and Asia. As Koenig has put it, 'the contemporary President is heavily engaged as a builder and custodian of alliances, a responsibility his forebears never had to face.'[27]

---

27. L.W. Koenig, *The Chief Executive*, 4th edn, New York, 1981, p. 254.

The resulting task of alliance management is a formidable one, particularly in relation to NATO, which, because of its size and diversity and the differing attitudes and interests of its governments, has frequently been in a state of considerable tension. Maintaining Atlantic relations in good repair has not been easy. On the one hand the United States has been slow to adjust its attitudes and policies as the Western Europeans moved from a position of almost total dependence on Washington in the aftermath of the Second World War to become more prosperous and more assertive. On the other hand there has been a European tendency simultaneously to demand American protection but to bridle at American dominance, to want consultation but to reject responsibility-sharing, and to object to anything which smacks of superpower collusion on the one hand and superpower collision on the other. Furthermore, successive administrations in Washington have been faced with the problem of designing strategies for the alliance which reconcile divergent interests rooted in differing geopolitical perspectives. President Kennedy's strategy of flexible response failed completely to do this, at least initially, and aroused considerable antipathy before being accepted in a modified form more palatable to the Europeans as official NATO doctrine.

In the last analysis, though, the critical issues in alliance relations are less doctrinal than political, less a question of strategy and more a question of confidence. Whatever else may be said about the American nuclear guarantee to Western Europe, it is the President who is its ultimate repository: in the unlikely event of Soviet aggression against Western Europe, it is he who would have to decide whether to respond by authorising the use of nuclear weapons. It is hardly surprising, therefore, that confidence in the President is a prerequisite for maintaining cohesion and harmony in NATO. For example, Atlantic relations became severely strained during Jimmy Carter's presidency as the Europeans were increasingly disillusioned with the quality of his leadership. Yet Carter had started well enough. It was his initiatives which led to the NATO summit meetings in 1977 and 1978 – meetings which galvanised the alliance into embarking on a long-term defence programme and agreeing in principle to a real increase of three per cent per annum in defence budgets. Gradually, however, the Europeans became unhappy about a President whose style was all too easily construed as vacillating and weak. Inconsistency in the administration's policy towards the Soviet Union and the President's mishandling of the neutron bomb decision provoked early doubts about Carter's capacity to manage foreign affairs, but it was the general impression of ineptitude and political expediency in Carter's response to Afghanistan which really alienated many of the allies and helped to create a serious rift in Atlantic relations. Still too 'doveish' for many Americans, President Carter, after Afghanistan, became too 'hawkish' for many Europeans.

During his first two years in office President Reagan provoked even greater disquiet in Western Europe. The President's ill-chosen remarks about limited nuclear war in Europe, combined with trans-Atlantic arguments about the nature of the threat and most appropriate response to it, engendered a pervasive sense of crisis within NATO. Although the alliance proved extremely resilient in the face of such difficulties, the Reagan presidency has not been very successful in terms of alliance management. The President's Strategic Defence Initiative was announced without any prior consultation with the Europeans and will almost certainly be a continuing source of tension in Atlantic relations. What are called 'out of area' issues also have a continuing potential for conflict, with European concerns that the United States is excessively belligerent mirrored by American worries that the Europeans are excessively timid. Perhaps the most important differences, however, are those relating to the fundamental questions of security and the relationship with the Soviet Union. Increasingly the Europeans appear to be groping towards a conception of security in which alliance defence efforts are supplemented by collaborative arrangements with Moscow. The Reagan administration, in contrast, has reverted to a zero-sum approach in which the emphasis is on American strength, and collaboration has little part. This approach and the restoration of American self-confidence have won the President many plaudits in the United States itself, even though many of Reagan's actions have received a critical reception in Western Europe.

This highlights the problem of accommodating domestic pressures on the one side and demands of allies on the other. Yet this is merely one aspect of a dilemma familiar to previous Presidents — how to satisfy multiple constituencies with differing expectations and anxieties. It is interesting in this connection that Carter's preoccupation with revitalising NATO, when coupled with his decision (later reversed) to withdraw United States ground forces from South Korea, created anxieties in Japan that the United States might cease to be an Asian power. Although such fears were eventually placated, they demonstrate how difficult and onerous the President's task is. Choices obviously have to be made about how best to apportion the President's time, energy, prestige and commitment. The problem is that these choices often have unintended and unforeseen consequences. As a result presidential management of foreign policy is often reduced to a series of balancing acts demanding delicate trade-offs between ostensibly separate issues and areas. It is not surprising then that the President's actions as a 'cold warrior' have to be balanced by his responsibilities as a peace-keeper. Indeed, the two roles are closely related in that effective conduct of the cold war has demanded a recognition that the super-powers are partners in the task of 'disaster avoidance' as well as being adversaries. The implications of this must now be examined.

The President as Peacekeeper

It is one of the ironies of Soviet-American relations that it is during the confrontations resulting from their conflicting interests that the common interests of the two superpowers become most pro-nounced. Accordingly, the management and resolution of crises has been a sporadic but essential task of all cold war Presidents. Crisis decision-making, in most cases, has been characterised by the sus-tained personal involvement of the President. Acting in his role as 'ultimate decision-maker' and fusing his responsibilities as chief diplomat and Commander-in-Chief, the President, surrounded by a small group of advisers, has kept firm control over decisions and actions liable to precipitate superpower hostilities. The pattern was clearly discernible in the Berlin crisis of 1948. 'As the concern to avoid an increase in tension and inadvertent military escalation became more pronounced, the U.S. decision-making structure became more clearly pyramidal with the President at the apex.'[28] This was perhaps only to be expected, given Truman's style of presi-dential leadership. Yet the pattern was continued under his succes-sor, who generally played a more passive role in foreign policy-making. Although Eisenhower was content to leave much of the day-to-day policy to Secretary of State Dulles, the President became much more assertive during crises involving the risk of war with Moscow or Peking. In both the Indochina crisis of 1954 and the con-frontation over Quemoy, it was Eisenhower who was not only the voice of restraint in a divided administration, but was also the deci-sive voice. This prompted one of Dulles's biographers to contrast the President's 'remarkable and largely benign detachment from much that went on inside his administration' with 'his determined control of essentials, especially those bearing on the issue of war and peace'.[29]

28. See the chapter on the Berlin crisis by A. Shlaim and J. Lodge in M. Brecher (ed.), *Studies in Crisis Behaviour*, New Brunswick, NJ, 1979.
29. T. Hoopes, *The Devil and John Foster Dulles*, Boston, 1973, p. 280.

Firm presidential control of crisis decision-making was also evident in the Kennedy administration. It is arguable in fact that Kennedy took this to greater lengths than any of his predecessors or successors. As the Berlin confrontation developed through 1961, for example, he immersed himself so much in the details of the problem that he became known throughout the foreign affairs bureaucracy, somewhat reproachfully, as the 'Berlin desk officer'.[30] The same pattern was evident in the Cuban missile crisis the following year. Although Kennedy deliberately absented himself from some of the discussions in order to facilitate fuller and more aggressive consideration of the alternatives, it was he who finally decided to initiate a naval blockade and to reject (at least initially) the air strike option. Although presidential *machismo* had some impact, it was tempered by an acute sensitivity to the risks involved in superpower crises. This concern with minimising risk prompted the President to go beyond the decision-formulation stage and exercise careful and continual oversight of policy implementation. Just as Truman in 1948 limited the discretion of the officials in Berlin, so Kennedy, together with his Secretary of Defense Robert McNamara, gave detailed instructions to the Navy as to how the blockade was to be implemented. Although the President was not fully aware of the vigour with which the Navy would carry out anti-submarine operations when he authorised protective measures, this was a lapse in an otherwise impressive record of careful oversight. Indeed Kennedy, like Truman in 1948, was anxious not to cross the line between coercion and violence, and was intent on impressing this on subordinates. Tensions in civil-military relations and between the immediate theatre of operations and Washington were the inevitable result.[31]

Such tensions are a price that Presidents have been willing to pay in their attempt to coerce the Soviet Union without backing it into a corner. Indeed, the more intense the confrontation, the greater the sensitivity to the opponent's position. As part of this process, there has sometimes been a subtle transformation in presidential perceptions of the enemy. In crises the President has tended to think of his adversary in a less abstract and rather more personal way by recognising that his counterpart in the Kremlin is the one person who shares the same destructive power and responsibility as himself, acknowledging that he too may have problems with subordinates and advisers who want a less cautious and more assertive approach. This

30. H.M. Catudal, *Kennedy and the Berlin Wall Crisis*, Berlin, 1980, pp. 35, 150–1.
31. For a fuller discussion of many of the points raised in this and the following paragraphs see P. Williams, *Crisis Management*, London, 1976.

certainly seems to have been the case in 1962 when, as Robert
Kennedy described it, 'President Kennedy spent more time trying to
determine the effect of a particular course of action on Khrushchev
or the Russians than on any other phase of what he was doing.'[32]

This attempt to achieve a degree of empathy with the adversary
was facilitated by the communications process. Indeed, it is a feature
of all superpower crises that sustained attempts have been made to
maintain communications in an effort to minimise mistakes and mis-
calculations and to ensure that events did not get out of control.[33]
Public statements and private messages using both formal and
informal channels have been supplemented by symbolic actions
designed largely as exercises in tacit communication. This was
certainly the case in October 1962. Nevertheless, ambiguities and
difficulties remained, and it is not coincidental that in the aftermath
of the missile crisis the superpowers established a more direct, more
reliable and much more rapid communications link. The installation
of the 'hot line' was a recognition that existing crisis management
techniques and instruments should be augmented. Its use has symbolised the desire of Washington and Moscow to establish a relationship based less on crisis management − with its inevitable hazards
and improvisations − and more on crisis prevention. This was
certainly the case in 1967 when President Johnson used the 'hot line'
to reassure the Soviet leaders that American naval and air movements in the Mediterranean were not a prelude to American intervention in the hostilities between Israel and its Arab neighbours.

However, like all other communication channels, the 'hot line'
can be used to threaten as well as reassure. During the Middle East
war of 1973 there was an abrasive series of messages between the
Soviet and American governments, although it seems that
Dobrynin, the Soviet Ambassador to the United States, was the
major conduit and that the 'hot line' was not used extensively. It is
noteworthy too that the direct messages were supplemented by
actions designed to underline concern over the course of events and
to establish each side's determination to do something about it if
necessary. In the event both the Soviet preparations for intervention
and the American alert of conventional and nuclear forces were a
prelude to accommodation rather than to escalation. Soviet actions
in particular may also have been a precondition for the ending of
hostilities. Until the extent of Soviet concerns was made apparent,

32. R.F. Kennedy, *Thirteen Days*, New York, London, 1969, pp. 121–2. See also
    Allison, *op. cit.*
33. See Williams, *op. cit.*, and G.H. Snyder and P. Diesing, *Conflict among Nations*,
    Princeton, NJ, 1977, for a fuller analysis.

the decision-makers in Washington did not exert sufficient pressure on Israel to ensure that it observed the initial cease-fire agreement. Even Brezhnev's messages, which were variously described as 'tough', 'brutal' and 'leaving little to the imagination', might not have had the desired effect without the urgency given them by the preparations for intervention. Although the 'hot line' together with more traditional diplomatic channels may *ease* communication during periods of superpower tension, therefore, tacit communication through carefully chosen symbolic actions may still be necessary.

Thus although the 'hot line' is not a panacea, it nevertheless highlights the desire of American Presidents and their Soviet counterparts to establish some understanding about the limits of permissible behaviour, and it is noteworthy that despite the downturn in superpower relations since the late 1970s, there has been an agreement on modernising and upgrading the 'hot line'. A similar desire to arrive at a *modus vivendi* has provided the rationale for East-West summitry. The history of American involvement in summitry is an interesting one. Having not been used extensively prior to the Second World War, it became a major feature of the wartime collaboration between the United States, Britain and the Soviet Union, with meetings at Casablanca, Quebec, Tehran, Yalta and Potsdam.

With the deterioration in Soviet-American relations after 1945 and the domestic controversy over the 'sell-out' at Yalta, summitry fell into some disrepute and was ruled out as a feasible option. President Eisenhower, however, not only reinstated the idea but turned it 'into a major technique of diplomacy during his Administration'.[34] One of the most notable exercises in summitry was the Geneva conference of 1955 which produced at least a temporary improvement in the superpower relationship. Much of the credit for this was due to the President himself, who emerged with his reputation enhanced as a 'man of peace'. 'In every encounter he projected an earnest and pacific intent, a serious yearning for conciliation, a readiness to grant the other side a rectitude no less than his own,'[35] thereby helping to dispel the rather belligerent image which his administration, largely through the posturing of Dulles, had acquired. Nevertheless, the predominant view of the Eisenhower-Khrushchev summit meetings is that, in spite of the good intentions, they yielded little tangible benefit; any improvements in superpower relations, if not wholly cosmetic, were transitory at best. In this view

34. M.D. Irish and E. Frank, *United States Foreign Policy: Context, Conduct, Content*, New York, 1973, p. 339.
35. Hoopes, *op. cit.*, p. 297.

the U-2 episode which disrupted the Paris summit in 1960 provided an appropriate epitaph for what were exercises in style rather than substance.[36] There is something to this line of argument. The summit meetings of the 1950s created far greater expectations than they could fulfil, and the Vienna encounter between Kennedy and Khrushchev in 1961 seems to have contributed to the Soviet leader's miscalculation of Kennedy's will and determination.[37] To conclude, however, that presidential diplomacy of this kind was futile would be to go too far. At a time of apparently unremitting hostility between the superpowers, the gradual emergence of a dialogue was a significant step forward.

Indeed, it is no accident that the *détente* of the early 1970s coincided with a series of summits between Nixon and Brezhnev. Nixon's visit to Moscow in 1972, for example, not only produced the first SALT agreement but also a variety of ancillary measures, the most important of which, the Agreement on the Basic Principles of Relations, was an explicit (if in retrospect only partially successful) attempt to codify the 'rules' of superpower conduct. This underlines a vital difference between the summitry of the 1950s and that of the 1970s: during both the Nixon and Carter presidencies, summitry represented not the beginning of a general process of accommodation, but the conclusion of specific negotiations. Gone were the empty agendas and the discussions of generalities. In their stead were highly detailed and carefully worked out compromises, often on very technical issues. The meetings between the heads of government were not purely ceremonial in that they were used, when necessary, to work out final agreements on particularly intractable issues. For the most part, however, they merely set the seal on calculations, decisions and trade-offs which had already been made.

This is not to suggest that there was no presidential involvement in the negotiations preceding the summits. Presidential preferences provided broad guidance for the discussions, and at critical junctures Presidents intervened in the negotiations themselves. This was certainly the case during the Carter administration. When Carter went to Vienna in June 1979 for the summit with Brezhnev which was to result in the SALT II agreement, he was completely familiar with the terms of what was a long and complex document. As one close observer noted,

He had been living and struggling with it for two and half years. He had participated in many of the deliberations and made many of the decisions that

---

36. L.W. Koenig, *The Chief Executive*, 2nd edn, New York, 1968, p. 230.
37. A good account of the Vienna summit can be found in Catudal, *op. cit.*

determined its evolution and its present construct. He had intervened to resolve many of the inter-agency squabbles within the US government over the formulation of various provisions. At key moments along the way, he had personally negotiated with Brezhnev's emissaries in Washington. He knew intimately the baffling terminology, the hierarchy of numbers, the convolutions of legalese, the artful and arcane definitions and disclaimers. He could cite chapter and verse of any of the nineteen articles of the treaty, any of the four articles of the protocol and many of the scores of agreed statements and common understandings.[38]

For Reagan, the issues involved in SALT II were much simpler. He made clear during the 1980 election campaign that he regarded SALT II as 'fatally flawed'. Despite his hardline approach, however, Reagan has also engaged in summitry. Yet his meeting with Gorbachev in 1985 was in many ways a reversion to the 1950s. Although the two leaders agreed to explore the possibility of establishing nuclear risk reduction centres in Washington and Moscow, for the most part the summit was symbolic rather than substantive. It gave a slight boost to Soviet-American negotiations on arms control, but the differences between the two sides remained significant, especially over Reagan's Strategic Defence Initiative.

The fact that the Reagan administration is negotiating with Moscow on arms control is not really surprising. Presidential interest and activity in arms limitation goes back at least to Roosevelt and the Washington naval agreement. Furthermore, every President since 1945, as part of his peace-keeping role, has taken up arms control negotiations with the Soviet Union: the Truman administration had its Baruch Plan, Eisenhower the Open Skies proposal, Kennedy signed the Test Ban Treaty, while Lyndon Johnson helped to engineer the Non-Proliferation Treaty.[39] For Nixon, Ford and Carter, managing the SALT process was one of the most important tasks they faced. Although achievements have not always matched aspirations, the commitment to negotiations is one that no President has been able to avoid. There has been much criticism of particular agreements, especially SALT II, but the principle of arms control itself has not been challenged directly.

Even President Reagan has conformed to this pattern: strategic arms limitation talks have been replaced by strategic arms reduction talks (START) while the administration has also opened negotiations on limiting intermediate nuclear forces in Europe and agreed to discussions on limiting space weaponry. For all this, Reagan's commitment to arms control in practice remains uncertain. There is

38. S. Talbott, *Endgame: The Inside Story of SALT II*, New York, 1979, p. 3.
39. Mandelbaum, *op. cit.*, pp. 190–4.

a recognition that negotiation is a necessary legitimising device for continued force modernisation. Participation in negotiations, however, is not the same as seeking agreement, and it is far from clear that the Reagan administration wants an agreement. Indeed, the President seems to attach more importance to the Strategic Defence Initiative than to arms control. It is possible of course that statements that SDI is not negotiable, and the announcement that because of continued Soviet violations the United States will no longer tacitly observe the SALT II limits, are simply designed to put pressure on the Soviet Union to make further concessions. The ultimate logic of SDI, however, is abandonment of the ABM treaty of 1972, and it seems that unless there is a change of direction, the arms race will not be effectively regulated or constrained. This is not to claim that negotiations will cease. Indeed, there is a sense in which the cold war presidency has also become an arms control presidency. Although this has been primarily a cosmetic matter under Reagan, the emergence of the nuclear freeze movement in the early 1980s showed that the cosmetics cannot be ignored.

The Strategic Defence Initiative of March 1983, which was very much a top-down decision, not only revealed Reagan's approach to security issues, but also showed how even a President who has little mastery of detail and is highly dependent on subordinates can set the general direction of American foreign and security policy. Presidents, to a greater or lesser degree, depending on inclination and style, can also do much to determine day-to-day actions and reactions. It is to the organisational framework within which Presidents have done this that we now turn.

The President as Chief Decision-Maker

The broad range of responsibilities undertaken by the contemporary President in both domestic and foreign policy has placed enormous demands on the incumbent's time and energy. One consequence of this has been a substantial increase in the White House staff, a process which began with the Executive Reorganisation Act of 1939. The Act was designed, on the one hand, to provide better information and advice for the chief executive and, on the other, to monitor the performance of the bureaucracy and thereby ensure fuller compliance with White House preferences. The process was extended into foreign policy-making by the National Security Act of 1947.[40]

40. This discussion of the NSC system rests heavily on Senator Henry Jackson (ed.), *The National Security Council*, New York, 1965; K.C. Clark and L.J. Legere (eds), *The President and the Management of National Security*, New York,

As well as creating the Central Intelligence Agency and a unified Department of Defence, the Act established the National Security Council. The NSC was to consist of the President, the Vice-President, the Secretary of State, the Secretary of Defense and the secretaries and under-secretaries of other executive and military departments. Modelled on the British Committee of Imperial Defence, the NSC also grew out of American experience in the Second World War and was the direct successor to the State-Navy-War Coordinating Committee which had overseen policy during the later stages of hostilities. Seen as a way of institutionalising information and advice for the President and providing a forum for coordinating domestic, foreign and military policies, the NSC was intended to constrain the President by formalising his links with executive departments and their heads.

The consequences, however, have been very different from the intentions. Rather than constraining the President, the NSC has provided a means whereby Presidents have, by and large, expanded their control and influence over foreign policy. Indeed the organisational framework established in 1947 was highly flexible, and in practice it has been 'at the mercy of particular Presidents to be used, developed or ignored as they prefer'.[41] Accordingly, its evolution has been determined primarily by the different preferences or practices of successive Presidents. As Destler has said,

The Council has affected advice to Presidents in three major ways. It has been used as an advisory forum of senior officials reviewing foreign policy issues for the President, usually in his presence. It has provided a focal point for the development of formal policy planning and decision processes. It has provided the umbrella for the emergence of a Presidential foreign policy staff. Its founders mainly conceived it as the first; the last is what it has most importantly become.[42]

President Truman treated the NSC with considerable caution. This was largely because of a concern over presidential prerogatives and an awareness that his actions might be construed as precedents and used to hamper his successors. He emphasised that the NSC's role was advisory rather than authoritative and that even this circumscribed role was a matter for presidential discretion. Although the NSC met more frequently after the outbreak of the Korean War

---

1969; and I.M. Destler, *Presidents, Bureaucrats and Foreign Policy*, Princeton, NJ, 1974, together with several articles by Destler.

41. I.M. Destler, 'National Security Advice to US Presidents: Some Lessons from Thirty Years', *World Politics*, Jan. 1977, p. 160.

42. *Ibid.*, p. 146.

in June 1950, Truman still relied primarily upon individual Cabinet officers, especially the Secretary of State, Dean Acheson, to take much of the initiative in foreign policy.

Acheson's successor as Secretary of State, John Foster Dulles, was an equally important figure, dominating many aspects of the Eisenhower administration's foreign policy. Nevertheless, it was during the Eisenhower era that the NSC advisory system was institutionalised. A Planning Board was established to achieve consensus among competing views and advocates. Agreed papers were then forwarded to the National Security Council and the President for consideration. Finally, an Operations Coordinating Board (OCB) was created to ensure effective implementation of the resulting decisions. Although this process reflected Eisenhower's penchant for clear divisions of responsibility, it was severely criticised as being excessively rigid, for acting mainly as a 'paper mill' and for concealing important differences of opinion from the President.[43]

Such criticisms were reflected in Kennedy's approach to the NSC and, in particular, in his decision to abolish both the Planning Board and the OCB. More vigorous than his predecessor and wanting a much more active part in the foreign policy-making process, Kennedy worked outside the NSC system. At the same time, he looked to the NSC staff to act as his 'eyes and ears' within the bureaucracy in an attempt to acquire new information and ideas. The head of the staff too became much more important under Kennedy. The post of Special Assistant for National Security had been created in 1953, but took on novel significance with Kennedy's choice of McGeorge Bundy to fill it. Furthermore, the increased importance of the staff and the President's sustained interest in foreign policy were symbolised by the establishment of the White House Situation Room, which was designed to facilitate quick, decisive and well-informed responses to major international events.[44]

Under Lyndon Johnson the *formal* role of the National Security Council was equally circumscribed, largely because the President relied instead on the 'Tuesday lunch', where he met informally with a small number of select foreign policy advisers. The Special Assistant, however, remained an important figure. Although Johnson put more faith in Secretary of State Dean Rusk than Kennedy had done, Walt Rostow, who eventually replaced Bundy as Special Assistant, gradually emerged as a pivotal figure in the administration's policy, especially towards Vietnam. Not only did Rostow

43. See, for example, Jackson, *op. cit.*, pp. 30–42.
44. I.M. Destler, 'National Security Advice to US Presidents', *op. cit.*, p. 157.

control the flow of information to the President, but by trying to shield him from assessments critical of the Vietnam involvement and by constantly reassuring him that escalation was unavoidable, he contributed significantly to the rigidity of the American stance. In the process, as one commentator has observed, Rostow transformed the role of National Security Adviser from that of an avowedly neutral manager and coordinator to that of a fervent and aggressive advocate.[45]

This trend was to be taken even further in the Nixon administration. Although Nixon was extremely critical of Johnson's failure to work through the National Security Council, he gradually adopted a similar pattern. By 1973 the NSC as an advisory body and a forum for high-level discussion had fallen into 'unprecedented disuse'.[46] Alongside the relegation of the Council had gone the further elevation of the Assistant for National Security ('Special' was dropped in 1969). This was partly because of Nixon's desire to centralise foreign policy decision-making in the White House and partly because of the personal qualities of Rostow's successor, Henry Kissinger.

As Alexander George has noted, 'Kissinger created a structure of NSC-centered interdepartmental committees that was designed to strengthen the intellectual and bureaucratic resources of the White House and to weaken the autonomy in foreign policy-making of the departments and agencies.'[47] By using these committees and an expanded NSC staff, Kissinger succeeded in extending both his and the President's control over foreign policy. Indeed, he not only became an advocate of particular policies, but also, on some issues at least, was the key decision-maker. In addition, he acted as special envoy and personal negotiator for the President. Together the two men adopted a style that combined meticulous and highly secret diplomatic preparation with a flair for flamboyant and dramatic public presentation of the results. Although Kissinger has distanced himself from the excesses of the Nixon White House, the key to his position, at least initially, was his close relationship with the President. In fact it was this which enabled him to assume the role of Secretary of State and totally eclipse William Rogers, who was nominally in charge of American diplomacy.

Kissinger's eventual appointment as Secretary of State, therefore, was little more than an acknowledgement of the realities, as opposed to the formalities, of the foreign policy-making process.

45. I.M. Destler, 'National Security Management: What Presidents Have Wrought', *Political Science Quarterly*, Winter 1980–1, pp. 577–80.
46. I.M. Destler, 'National Security Advice to US Presidents', *op. cit.*, p. 149.
47. A.L. George, *Presidential Decisionmaking in Foreign Policy: The Effective Use of Information and Advice*, Boulder, Colo., 1980, p. 177.

Nevertheless, the change allowed Kissinger to remain relatively aloof
from a White House increasingly embroiled in Watergate. Nor is it
coincidental that with Kissinger's move to State the locus of
decision-making shifted from 1600 Pennsylvania Avenue to Foggy
Bottom. So long as Kissinger retained the two posts – National
Security Adviser and Secretary of State – the change was not particularly dramatic or obvious, but it was intensified when President
Ford appointed Brent Scowcroft to replace Kissinger as the Assistant
for National Security. Nevertheless, Kissinger's experience in this
office had done much to establish it as a potential rival to the Secretary of State.

President Carter was determined to avoid such an occurrence. In
his campaign for the presidency he echoed many of the then current
criticisms of the Republican administration's handling of foreign
policy-making. The system which had evolved under Nixon, Ford
and Kissinger was widely seen as too narrow and exclusive, too
highly centralised and too secretive. Furthermore, by taking on so
many tasks, Kissinger, like Rostow, had compromised and perhaps
even neglected his role as coordinator and manager of the policy-
making process. What made this all the more damaging was that the
centralisation engineered by Nixon and Kissinger had resulted in a
serious overload in the White House – a problem which made the
coordination and management functions particularly important.[48]

The experiences of the Carter presidency, however, tended to
evoke a nostalgia for at least some aspects of this system. Centralisation was replaced by divergent and inconsistent approaches, decisiveness by vacillation and hesitancy, and a coherent, if flawed,
strategic design by a 'total addiction to erratic tactics'.[49] Part of the
problem was structural: the gradual emergence of the National
Security Adviser into a policy-making as opposed to simply a managerial role had inexorably set him on a collision course with the
Secretary of State. As long as one or the other achieved a position of
dominance, this was not too damaging. Under Carter, however, this
did not occur until towards the end of his administration, with the
result that the tension and competitiveness between the two officials
became severely debilitating. The National Security Adviser,
Zbigniew Brzezinski, was regarded by Carter not only as a policy
coordinator and manager but also as a 'policy thinker' who would
generate new ideas (but whose role would be much more circumscribed than that of Kissinger). Difficulties arose because
Brzezinksi's thinking on foreign policy, especially that towards the

48. For a discussion of the overload problem, see *ibid.*, p. 183.
49. S. Hoffman, 'Requiem', *Foreign Policy*, Spring 1981, p. 9.

Soviet Union, was totally at odds with the approach advocated by the Secretary of State, Cyrus Vance.

Had Carter given full support to either Brzezinski or Vance, the damage caused by their differences could have been minimised. As it was, however, the President – at least until the Soviet invasion of Afghanistan – seemed to oscillate between the conciliatory approach of his Secretary of State and the hardline stance of his National Security Adviser. The result was a period of uncertainty for America's allies and adversaries alike. Indeed, the position of National Security Adviser was in danger of becoming a liability rather than an asset. Initially conceived as a coordinator, the Assistant had gone beyond this in ways which actually increased the problems of coordination.

Under the Reagan administration there seems to have been a reversion to the earlier conception of the National Security Adviser as a neutral manager rather than a major protagonist in working out the substance of foreign policy. This was both reflected in and accentuated by the nature of the occupants of the post and the extremely rapid turnover. The first, Richard Allen, was not particularly assertive, while his successor, William Clark, had little experience in diplomatic or security issues, but had a good reputation as someone who could synthesise and coordinate views for the President. Much more impressive was Reagan's third National Security Adviser, Robert McFarlane, who was not only an effective manager but took steps to improve the quality of the NSC staff which initially had been filled with ideologues. However, in December 1985 McFarlane resigned, partly because the new White House Chief of Staff, Donald Regan, had made his task increasingly difficult and partly because of continued feuding between the top officials concerned with national security. McFarlane was succeeded by John Poindexter.

Despite the relatively low profile of successive National Security Advisers in the Reagan administration, jurisdictional disputes have certainly not been absent. On the contrary, they have frequently been as intense and as public as in the Carter years. Part of the reason for the departure of Reagan's first Secretary of State, Alexander Haig, was that he had not obtained the power and the exclusive responsibility in foreign policy that he wanted. Although Haig did not have to contend with a powerful National Security Adviser, he had to deal with a formidable Secretary of Defense, Caspar Weinberger, at a time when diplomatic and military issues were becoming increasingly intertwined. Considerable antipathy also developed between Haig and the leading members of the White House staff – Edwin Meese, James Baker and Michael Deaver. Like

Weinberger and indeed Clark, all three aides were much closer to the President than was Haig. The decision to give Vice-President George Bush responsibility for crisis management was indicative of the tensions between the Secretary of State and the White House. It also intensified those tensions. Thus the resignation of Haig, following disputes over policy on the gas pipeline deal between Western Europe and the Soviet Union, was not unexpected.

Haig's successor, George Shultz, had a warmer personal relationship with the President and was more conciliatory towards the White House staff. Nevertheless, the disputes have continued, albeit in less dramatic form than when Haig was Secretary of State. There have been two fundamental issues on which Weinberger and Shultz have disagreed. The first is East-West relations, where Shultz is relatively conciliatory and Weinberger much more hardline. In the two years after Reagan's reelection there was a continuing battle for the 'soul' of the administration, especially in its policy towards Moscow. Although this conflict was not fully resolved, the hardliners managed to ensure that the Reagan-Gorbachev summit was not the precursor to a new accommodation. The second divisive issue concerns the use of force. On this Shultz has tended to be more enthusiastic and Weinberger much more reticent. In November 1984 the Secretary of Defense outlined the conditions which he believed had to be present before the United States should use military force, and these conditions were inevitably dubbed the Weinberger Doctrine. His caution has also been evident in the deliberations over the American response to terrorism. On the terrorism issue, the harder line of Shultz has generally prevailed. In the final analysis, of course, the outcome of these battles depends on the preferences of the President. Yet no clear victor has emerged from the Weinberger-Shultz battles. Both have had victories and both have suffered defeats, and it may be that this reflects not only Reagan's substantive preferences on the individual issues but his general desire to maintain a balance between his senior advisers.

If this is the case, then it underlines once again the importance of presidential preferences and style. Indeed, when there has been a dominant figure in foreign policy-making that figure has generally had the total trust of the President. This was the case in the Truman administration. Secretary of State Acheson was the key figure in foreign policy-making because he had the confidence of the President. The same was true of Secretary of State Dulles in the Eisenhower years, while Kissinger's rise to pre-eminence as National Security Adviser owed a great deal to his ability and willingness to cultivate President Nixon.

What general observations can be made about the experience of the National Security Council since its creation? The first is that Presidents have been able to use the organisational framework established by the 1947 Act to strengthen their own positions in the policy-making process. This was particularly true for Kennedy, Johnson and Nixon and was reflected in the growth in size of the NSC staff. A staff which consisted of about twelve members under Bundy and eighteen under Rostow increased to fifty under Kissinger, after which it was reduced slightly in size under Scowcroft and went down to about thirty-five members under Brzezinski. A second and closely related comment is that each President has used the NSC in ways which reflected his own personal preferences and decision-making style. Thus the evolution of the NSC has not been linear but has depended instead on the particular approach of each incumbent.

The results of this have not been entirely satisfactory. It is a truism to state that organisational arrangements are not neutral, in the sense that the prevailing patterns of communication, information and advice may enhance the influence of certain agencies, groups and individuals within the bureaucracy at the expense of other departments, groups and individuals. In the United States it is the President who, more than anyone else, determines the precise form these organisational arrangements take, at least at the higher levels. In a comprehensive study of presidential decision-making in foreign policy, Alexander George has suggested that 'the operation of organisational, procedural and staff arrangements in support of presidential decision-making serves to structure and discipline a president's choices.'[50] But it is equally plausible that instead of compensating for the personal preferences, idiosyncrasies and possible weaknesses of each President, the system will tend to accentuate them.

Eisenhower's reluctance to pursue a highly active foreign policy was mirrored in the development and use of the NSC, with its slow and laborious process of consensus-building. Kennedy's much more active and energetic, but highly random, approach was reflected in his informality, his forays into the bureaucracy and his disregard for the traditional patterns and procedures. This approach tended to have a very unsettling effect on officials accustomed to working through regularised channels. Under Johnson the reliance on a small informal group of like-minded advisers rather than on formal NSC meetings seems to have reinforced the rigidity of the President's approach to Vietnam. This trend towards the self-imposed isolation of the presidency was taken even further under Nixon, when

50. George, *op. cit.*, p. 4.

decisions such as that to invade Cambodia were made with minimal consultation. Neither Johnson nor Nixon was tolerant of dissent, and the increasing exclusiveness of decision-making in relation to foreign policy helped to filter out criticisms and suppress alternatives. The Carter system did not suffer from these problems, but worked in ways which intensified the President's indecisiveness, while the Reagan approach, at least initially, seemed to put more emphasis on advisers the President found congenial than on knowledge and expertise.

In order to overcome or eliminate such defects, several analysts have suggested the need for decision-making arrangements which promote 'multiple advocacy' or 'vigilant appraisal' and thereby not only prevent the premature exclusion of certain options but also ease the pressure to conform to group norms and attitudes.[51] These prescriptions extol the virtues of a kind of intellectual as well as organisational pluralism which, it is argued, encourages vigorous probing of issues, critical examination of alternatives and a thorough appraisal of the possible consequences of any decision or action. There is much to recommend such practices, and they seem particularly relevant to decision-making in crises when an awareness of the risks involved encourages a more rigorously analytical approach. In many non-crisis situations, however, the prescriptions ultimately run up against the very problem which made them necessary in the first place − the imposition of presidential preferences and personality on the decision-making process. After all, multiple and conflicting advice is always available to the President *if he wants it*. The difficulty has been that Presidents have not always wanted it. Dissenting arguments on American policy in Vietnam, for example, were carefully articulated both inside and outside the Johnson administration. Former colleagues of the President in the Senate, such as the Majority Leader, Mike Mansfield, and the Chairman of the Foreign Relations Committee, William Fulbright, provided highly perceptive analyses of the Vietnam involvement which, in the President's view, suffered from one major defect − they were critical of his policy. There are many other examples which suggest that advice is unlikely to be heeded if it runs counter to the established policies, preferences and prejudices of the President.

All this is not to argue that Presidents should be completely open-minded or equally responsive to all advice. That would prove as

51. See I. L. Janis, *Victims of Groupthink*, Boston, 1972, for a discussion of vigilant appraisal. See also A. L. George, 'The Case for Multiple Advocacy in Making Foreign Policy', *American Political Science Review*, Sept. 1979, and George, *Presidential Decisionmaking in Foreign Policy*, *op. cit.*

debilitating and damaging as rigidity and closed-mindedness. Indeed, it has to be acknowledged that presidential decision-making in foreign policy, like presidential diplomacy, consists of a series of balancing acts. The need for speed and decisiveness, for example, has to be balanced against the need for full and frank discussion. Receptiveness to new information and unpalatable advice has to be set against the need to operate on the basis of reasonably stable assumptions and expectations. The above analysis suggests that successive Presidents have often failed to get the balance right, with the result that decision-making has been less effective than might have been hoped. To some extent this has been the fault of particular Presidents, some of whom have gone too far in the opposite direction in an effort to avoid the most obvious mistakes of their immediate predecessors. Perhaps equally important are certain problems which are inherent in the presidency and its place in the American political system and which make it difficult for any incumbent to cope effectively with the challenges and problems associated with America's world role. It is to these problems that we now turn.

The Problems of the Presidency

During the cold war years there was a tendency on the part of many commentators to regard a strong presidency as the key to America's salvation. Closer analysis of the experience of the last thirty years or so, however, suggests that such an assessment was both premature and optimistic. Indeed, it is possible to argue that the presidency, far from being a *solution* to the problems of American foreign policy-making, is a major source of the difficulties.

One of the reasons for this is that there is no obvious and well-proven apprenticeship system for the presidency. The vice-presidency is perhaps the nearest thing to it, but even this has many short-comings, not the least of which is the nature of the apprentices themselves. Vice-presidential candidates are generally chosen on grounds of political expediency and likely partisan advantage rather than any assessment of their statesmanship. In this light it is not surprising that the elevation of Lyndon Johnson to the presidency was the prelude to a series of disastrous and ill-considered moves in foreign affairs. On the other hand, the Johnson experience is not the only possible model. Harry Truman clearly demonstrated that a Vice-President *can* become a highly competent and efficient foreign policy decision-maker. Nevertheless, Johnson's dismal record in foreign policy serves as a warning that the position of Vice-President is not necessarily an adequate or effective preparation for the responsibilities of the presidency.

A similar point could be made about service in the Senate, where much will depend on an individual's committee assignments. Even so, experience on Capitol Hill provides much more exposure to the broad range of national and international issues likely to face a President than does experience as a governor. Indeed, it can be argued that while none of the proving grounds for the presidency is entirely satisfactory, the gubernatorial is the least appropriate, a conclusion made all the more disquieting by the recent trend in which a period as governor has been a preliminary to a successful challenge for the presidency. Neither Jimmy Carter, who had been Governor of Georgia, nor Ronald Reagan, a former Governor of California, came to Washington with any experience of foreign policy, and Carter's ineptitude in this area has been matched by that of his successor, especially in dealings with the European allies. Of all Presidents since Roosevelt, only Eisenhower, with his wide-ranging experience in national and international security affairs, was reasonably well equipped to take charge of United States foreign policy.

Another problem of presidential foreign policy can perhaps best be described as that of early learning. Although the White House is, in Roger Hilsman's words, 'no place for on-the-job training',[52] there seems to be little alternative to learning the trade at first hand. The difficulty is that this can be a highly painful process leading to costly mistakes. This is all the more likely because of the lack of institutional memory in American government. However helpful the outgoing presidential team attempts to be, it can still take a new President and his advisers twelve to eighteen months to establish clear patterns and procedures and to acquire a reasonable grasp of the issues. Indeed, some administrations never succeed in coming to terms with the complexity of the problems confronting them. The Reagan administration, after six years in office, still had an anti-Soviet fixation rather than a coherent and well-rounded foreign policy. Yet the administration at least avoided major fiascos. Some of its predecessors were less fortunate. It is no accident, for example, that the Bay of Pigs occurred during Kennedy's first four months in office, that the decision-making group was 'almost entirely new to the exercise of power' and that its members had 'limited foreign and military experience'.[53] Similarly Carter's initial and wholly unrealistic proposal for 'deep cuts' in SALT II was made very early in his administration.

Although Kennedy and Carter learned a great deal from such mistakes, there is little room for complacency, especially with the trend

52. In a paper presented to the Dept. of Politics, University of Southampton, England, March 1979.
53. Brzezinski and Huntington, *op. cit.*, p. 386.

towards more rapid presidential turnover. With Roosevelt, Truman and Eisenhower, the presidency appeared to be a force for continuity and stability. In the 1960s and 1970s it began to look very different. It is ironic that so much scholarly attention has been devoted to the issue of political succession in the Soviet Union when it is actually a much more salient problem in the United States: after all, Brezhnev had to deal with five different occupants of the White House. Although the tradition of bipartisanship and the reelection of Ronald Reagan have done something to mitigate the worst effects of what might be termed institutionalised succession crises, the task of maintaining coherence and continuity during periods of political transition remains formidable.

It is made even more so by the increased length of the possible transition periods. The President spends eighteen months or so of his first term learning his job and the last year or eighteen months attempting to extend it. The lengthy primary campaigns make it difficult if not impossible for the President to remain above the battle. Foreign relations are often one of the first casualties as Presidents either trim their sails to what they see as the prevailing electoral winds or become so preoccupied with campaigning that United States foreign policy is allowed to drift without clear direction.

A less obvious but not unrelated consequence of the four-year term is that it gives the President an essentially short-term perspective. To some extent, of course, this is inherent in foreign policy, which is composed of a wide range of day-to-day issues, unconnected initiatives and *ad hoc* responses. As Dean Acheson noted, the 'thundering present' dominates the attention of foreign policymakers. Presidents in particular have to hop from crisis to crisis and issue to issue with little opportunity for reflection on, let alone planning for, the long term. The four-year election cycle compounds the problem as it demands that Presidents focus on short-term challenges, the successful management of which might have useful electoral benefits. This is not unique to the United States, but what makes it more disquieting in this case is the importance of America in the world arena and the fact that an increasing number of issues such as nuclear proliferation, poverty in the Third World and diminishing energy resources demand a long-range perspective.

In the light of all this, the idea of a six-year term and a one-term President is very attractive. This proposal is not without its drawbacks, however. It would neither overcome the difficulty of early learning nor make the President a non-partisan figure. Most important of all, it immediately runs up against arguments about presidential accountability.

There is no easy way of reconciling the demands of efficiency with those of accountability. This is equally true with respect to presidential-congressional relations. Indeed, the difficulties of formulating foreign policy in a system of shared powers were side-stepped for part of the post-war period by a congressional abdica-tion of its foreign policy role. After a period of close, albeit unequal, cooperation on foreign policy from 1945 to 1950, Congress, and especially the Senate, became much more assertive, challenging the President in 1951 over the troops to Europe decision and in 1954 over executive agreements. In both instances the presidency emerged unscathed, and Congress was content to play a subordinate role in foreign policy-making until the excesses of the Vietnam involvement prompted another and more successful revolution. From the mid-1950s to the mid-1960s Congress gave up its constitutionally mandated role in foreign policy on the grounds that an unfettered executive could more effectively deal with an adversary who had none of the disadvantages of democracy. Senator Fulbright, who would later emerge as a champion of congressional rights and responsibilities in foreign policy, suggested as late as 1961 that the President had been severely hampered by too niggardly a grant of authority.[54]

The imperial presidency, however, was not solely a product of congressional abdication. It was also a result of Presidents extending their own authority and power. In the 'Great Debate' of 1951, for example, Truman made assertions about his authority to deploy American troops overseas which were as inflated as any of the claims made by Johnson and Nixon in the 1960s and 1970s.[55] Eisenhower, in contrast, displayed considerable caution and restraint in his dealings with Congress. His successors were less inhibited. The Tonkin Gulf Resolution of 1964 was of major importance in this connection, partly because it was approved overwhelmingly on the basis of the executive's falsified account of events, but also because it was then treated by the Johnson administration as the equivalent of a congressional declaration of war which permitted the President to escalate American involvement in Vietnam more or less at will. It was this escalation, together with the almost simultaneous relaxation of Soviet-American tensions, which began the breakdown of the foreign policy consensus and the resurgence of Congress. These processes were not only encouraged by Nixon's actions in Cambodia

54. See K. Tweraser, *Changing Patterns of Political Beliefs: The Foreign Policy Operational Codes of J. William Fulbright 1943–1963*, Beverly Hills, 1974, p. 24 and pp. 50–4.
55. This episode is dealt with at length in P. Williams, *The Senate and US Troops in Europe*, London, 1985.

and his impoundment practices, but were also facilitated by his involvement with Watergate.

As a result, the 1970s saw not only a revival of the congressional role in foreign affairs but also an attempt by Congress to pass legislation which would enable it to co-determine many aspects of foreign policy.[56] The War Powers Act was only the most obvious manifestation of this new congressional activism which led some observers to talk about 'foreign policy by Congress' and others to conclude that the imperial presidency had been replaced by an imperilled presidency.[57]

This was certainly the prevailing orthodoxy during the Carter era, when it appeared that the weakening of the presidency *vis-à-vis* Congress was intensified by a weak incumbent. Yet it can be argued that, as a result both of intent and inadvertence, Carter strengthened the presidency. His image as a weak President and the consequent difficulties of providing coherence to American foreign policy helped to legitimise once again the idea of a strong, albeit not unconstrained, presidency. Ironically, the image of weakness was not wholly deserved — at least as far as executive-congressional relations were concerned. Carter had several notable successes in his dealings with Congress. Senate consent to ratification of the Panama Canal treaties, despite an unprecedented lobbying campaign by hostile pressure groups, was a major achievement, even if tarnished slightly by the President's visible engagement in horse-trading. Furthermore, Carter's decision to withdraw diplomatic recognition from Taiwan, although challenged by members of Congress, was upheld by the Supreme Court. Nevertheless, by 1980 the United States was ripe for a President who conveyed a stronger image and who seemed better able to manage Congress.

President Reagan, coming to the White House with overwhelming public support, was extremely effective in mobilising congressional opinion behind his policies during his first administration. The most notable example of Reagan's persuasiveness on foreign policy matters was the sale of AWACS to Saudi Arabia. This deal won Senate approval in the face of strenuous objections from the Jewish lobby and the serious doubts of many senators. Yet even Reagan has had to face many problems. Congress agreed to fund production of only half the number of MX missiles the President wanted and proved unwilling to continue funding the levels of defence spending desired by the administration. In addition there have been continued

56. T. Franck and E. Weisband, *Foreign Policy by Congress*, New York, 1979.
57. See *ibid.*, and R. Hass, *Congressional Power: Implications for American Security Policy*, Adelphi Paper 153, London, 1979, p. 1.

difficulties in obtaining approval for arms sales to moderate Arab states such as Jordan, while in 1985, under congressional pressure, Reagan was forced into a tougher line on South Africa.

Such developments should not be surprising. The experience of the cold war years has instilled into Congress both an unwillingness to grant Presidents too much discretion and a determination to assert its own preferences, even when these differ from those of the White House. Once again the difficulty lies in striking the appropriate balance. The events of the 1960s and early 1970s underscored the dangers of an unrestrained presidency. On the other hand, the controversy over the SALT II treaty in 1979 highlighted the difficulties of conducting a rational and coherent foreign policy when the President's wishes are thwarted by an assertive and irreconcilable Senate.

A middle way has to be found therefore between the irresponsibility of untrammelled power and the dangers of stalemate or abrupt reversals of policy. The dilemma is how to keep the President responsive to Congress without constantly placing him in a position where both he and his policies might be repudiated. It is the perennial problem of the American political system, and it is given greater urgency by America's role and responsibilities in the current international system. A twentieth-century superpower and an eighteenth-century constitution are not ideal partners. This is not to suggest that the presidency has been a stagnant, unchanging institution. On the contrary, it has displayed an impressive capacity for growth and adaptability, albeit not always with positive consequences. This makes it all the more necessary to attempt an overall appraisal of the evolution of the foreign policy presidency since 1933.

Conclusions

The presidency today is a highly complex and chameleon-like institution which has been shaped both by the demands of the international system and by the personal qualities and characteristics of individual incumbents. Although the Roosevelt era foreshadowed many of the traits that are now seen as an integral part of the modern presidency, the key developments were those which took place in the late 1940s. The post-war period has a certain distinctiveness, and it is not fortuitous that many of the institutional arrangements, procedures, practices and – perhaps most important of all – attitudes which emerged during the Truman administration are still visible. Within this broad framework, of course, each incumbent has imposed his own unique style on United States foreign policy, whether it be in the area of diplomacy, crisis management or military intervention.

Even allowing for the variations between individuals, however, it is hard to avoid the conclusion that the presidency has in some ways become a dangerous institution. The inhumanities perpetrated on Vietnam, for example, had their roots in an approach to the world which seemed to be embedded in the office itself. On the other side of the ledger is the prudent and careful handling of superpower confrontations, the initiation of summitry and the promotion of arms control, all of which suggest that the presidency is capable of considerable achievement as well as great harm. Presidential decision-making exhibits schizophrenic qualities, having produced eminently wise and extremely foolish policies.

What makes this particularly disturbing is that the world of the 1980s and 1990s is one in which the United States is far less dominant than it was in the 1940s and 1950s. Thus future challenges will come in a period when American power relative to that of other states has declined. Henry Kissinger acknowledged this in 1974 when he stated that the United States increasingly had to conduct foreign policy 'the way other nations have had to conduct it throughout their history' because Washington no longer had the 'overwhelming margins of safety and . . . resources' it had enjoyed for most of the post-war period.[58] Jimmy Carter seemed to exemplify American policy in the age of limits. Yet Reagan, at least in terms of public perceptions, has transcended these limits and restored a sense of confidence and dynamism to the United States that was lost with the assassination of John Kennedy and the Vietnam involvement. The contrast with Carter, who recognised the limitations of operating amid complexity, is enormous. In the long term, though, Carter's approach may be a more appropriate model than Reagan's. It is not clear that the revival of American leadership and the resurgence of American power is sustainable beyond the Reagan presidency. Consequently, the United States will once again have to come to terms with the limitations of power and influence. This will be an uncomfortable process. Future Presidents will almost certainly find that surplus military or economic capabilities will no longer be available to compensate for a dearth of statesmanship. In the final analysis, therefore, the American capacity to handle the problems of security and to contribute to peace and prosperity will depend on the ability of these Presidents to transcend the difficulties and limitations that are inherent in their office. Like Dr Johnson on the subject of marriage, it is perhaps necessary to believe in the ultimate triumph of hope over experience.

58. Quoted in G. Connell-Smith, *op. cit.*, p. xvii.

7

THE TRADITIONAL AND MODERN PRESIDENCIES

Malcolm Shaw

In the introductory chapter it was noted that the intention in this book is to look at change in the presidency from two perspectives: the changes before and after 1933 and the changes since 1933. The authors of the chapters on specialised aspects of presidential development have stressed the changes since 1933 while also giving some attention to the pre- and post-1933 dichotomy. In this chapter the intention is to reverse these priorities; accordingly, I devote a great deal of attention to identifying differences between the presidencies before and after 1933, and in the course of this analysis I use the categories identified by Fred Greenstein – the 'traditional presidency' and the 'modern presidency'.[1] Where appropriate, I also deal with changes that have occurred during the era of the modern presidency, particularly when they shed light on this dichotomy.

In endeavouring to accomplish the foregoing, my basic data consist of the analyses in the preceding chapters. At the same time, in using this material, I have placed the segmented analyses in the broader focus which is possible when one has an overview of all the segments. In doing so, I have found it convenient to retain the division into specialised topics to which the other authors have addressed themselves, while introducing further perspectives obtained from other sources. In the final section, I attempt to determine the viability of the concept of the modern presidency.

The Constitutional Factor

It is clear that the change from the traditional to the modern presidency cannot be attributed to changes in the formal ground rules. During the modern era, six amendments to the Constitution have

---

1. These categories are used in Fred I. Greenstein, 'Change and Continuity in the Modern Presidency', in Anthony King (ed.), *The New American Political System*, Washington, DC, 1978, pp. 45–85; and Fred I. Greenstein, Larry Berman and Alvin S. Felzenberg, *Evolution of the Modern Presidency: A Bibliographical Survey*, Washington, DC, 1977, pp. i–ix.

come into effect, and five of them concern the presidency. However, none is sufficiently major that a causal link with the development of the modern presidency arises. The amendments limit presidential terms to two, change the day on which the terms begin, enable residents of the District of Columbia to vote for President, prohibit poll taxes in federal elections, specify procedures related to presidential disability, and lower the voting age to eighteen. Taken together, these amendments have far less significance for the presidency than, say, the amendment which in 1913 authorised the federal government to tax incomes. Burns has characterised the income tax amendment as a key factor in making executive expansion possible.[2]

There have been momentous changes in the nature of the presidency since 1933. Greenstein says that even a President serving in the 1920s would have difficulty making sense of the modern presidency, whereas in the case of Congress Patterson has suggested that it continues to function in ways reminiscent of the pre-Civil War period.[3] But it has to be said that this metamorphosis has occurred in the absence of any but relatively minor changes in the language of the Constitution. The development of the modern presidency has been accommodated within the broad requirements of the eighteenth-century document. This has been possible, as is frequently noted, because of the generality and economy of language of the Constitution. As Richard Hodder-Williams says in his chapter, 'The Constitution as interpreted by the Supreme Court . . . has been flexible enough to permit such changes.' Thus the economic and social reforms of the New Deal, the corresponding enlargement of the executive branch, the creation of the Executive Office of the President, world war, cold war, superpower politics, the Great Society reforms, the Vietnam War, Watergate and the resignation of a President have all occurred within the existing constitutional framework. It seems clear that after more than a century and a half of living with the office, Americans are not willing to entertain major changes in the formal position of the President within the constitutional system. Rather, Americans 'have always considered a change in personnel as the quickest, surest, and easiest solution to presidential abuse or incompetence.'[4]

At the same time, the looseness of the framework has necessitated numerous delineations of specific issues; these delineations have occurred within the context of presidential-congressional relations

2. James M. Burns, *Presidential Government*, Boston, 1965, pp. 68–9.
3. Greenstein, 'Change and Continuity in the Modern Presidency', p. 82.
4. Bruce Buchanan, *The Presidential Experience*, Englewood Cliffs, NJ, 1978, p. 122.

and judicial rulings. In relation to domestic affairs, where the President has less leeway than in foreign affairs, Hodder-Williams discusses the New Deal programme, the legislative veto, dismissals of executive personnel by the President, the impoundment of funds, and executive privilege. In relation to foreign affairs, the President's general primacy over Congress in this policy area, executive agreements, the commitment of troops to action overseas, declarations of war and issues that arose during the war in Vietnam are discussed.

In these and other issue areas the Constitution has not usually stemmed the accrual of presidential authority. This was so in the traditional as well as the modern period, and in that sense the development of the presidency has been linear. Yet an oscillatory tendency has also been strong, particularly during the traditional era, which saw a succession of what are now considered to be 'weak' Presidents interspersed with such 'strong' Presidents as Jackson, Polk, Lincoln, Cleveland, Theodore Roosevelt and Wilson. Prior to 1933, constitutional language was generally permitted to bend to the needs of the chief executive, with the acquiescence variously of Court, Congress and people.

From the Washington to Hoover administrations the majority of American Presidents allowed congressional leaders to carry the day. From time to time, however, the public's expectations of the President and the President's own claims expanded current notions of what the President was legally entitled to do . . . Moreover, a legal rationale for presidential activism . . . accumulated, often with the benediction of the Supreme Court.[5]

After the enhancement of presidential authority beginning with the New Deal, the Constitution continued to provide a flexible framework. According to Hodder-Williams, 'the reality is simply that there has been a steady and widely accepted expansion of presidential authority and Supreme Court connivance in this expansion.' At the same time, there is no inevitability in the tendency of the Court to interpret presidential powers in such a way that the President's actions are endorsed. Hodder-Williams notes that the Constitution retains an ability to *limit* the exercise of political power, as was originally intended.

The prime example of the imposition of constitutional restraint during the modern era relates to the Watergate scandals. The criminality of Watergate, involving as it did a long list of indictable offences committed by the President and leading members of his administration, resulted in a situation where it was clear that unless Nixon resigned he would be impeached, convicted and removed

5. Greenstein, Berman and Felzenberg, *op. cit.*, p. ii.

from office. In accordance with a constitutional procedure which had been employed only once before against a President, three articles of impeachment were voted by the Judiciary Committee of the House of Representatives. After leaving the White House, Nixon told a television audience: 'When the President does it, that means it is not illegal.'[6] The cast of mind revealed by that statement had caused a challenge to constitutional government which, in the end, was effectively met.

Constitutional restraint was also applied to specific acts during the Nixon presidency. Nixon's massive impoundments of appropriated funds, amounting to some $25 billion between 1971 and 1973, were met with repeated court rulings striking down specific impoundments. In addition, the Supreme Court struck down Nixon's expansive views on the use of executive privilege. It is worth noting that Nixon is not the only modern President to be curbed by constitutional requirements as interpreted by the Supreme Court. Rulings of major importance were also directed against policies pursued by Franklin Roosevelt and Harry Truman.

Notwithstanding these examples of constraint, the Constitution has accommodated a transition from a dominant belief that political authority ought to be located primarily in the legislature, with the House of Representatives as the people's institution, to a subsequent belief that the executive ought to have a stronger directive role, with the President serving as the people's spokesman. This change in orientation surfaced intermittently before 1933 and permanently after that year.

While, as Pritchett has said, the Watergate scandals provoked an unprecedented reconsideration of presidential powers,[7] the strength of the post-1933 trend is such that this reappraisal did not alter the basic character of the modern presidency, once the immediate loss of faith dissipated itself during the Ford and Carter incumbencies.[8] Neither did the trauma of Vietnam deflect the presidency in any fundamental way from its assertive role in the modern era. Vietnam saw the political extinction of a President during the primaries of 1968, as Watergate would do more emphatically six years later, but the institution survived intact.

6. *New York Times,* 19 May 1977.
7. C. Herman Pritchett, 'The President's Constitutional Position', in Thomas E. Cronin and Rexford G. Tugwell (eds), *The Presidency Reappraised*, 2nd edn, New York, 1977, p. 14.
8. This is not the only example of a reaction following a strong incumbency. A backlash effect can also be said to have adversely affected Jefferson's successor (Madison), Lincoln's successor (Andrew Johnson) and Franklin Roosevelt's successor (Truman). This reaction may manifest itself not only in Congress but also in the bureaucracy, the press and the public.

Nevertheless, there have been cross-pressures. As Hodder-Williams points out: 'The rise of the United States to the status of a superpower and the changed nature of war and international relations has clearly strained the constitutional fabric.' This tension was manifest when the Constitution was initially seen by the Supreme Court to preclude major New Deal measures. However, the Court's subsequent retreat ('the switch in time that saved nine') meant that after losing the battle, Roosevelt won the war with the Court.

It has to be concluded that the requirements of the Constitution have not made the modern presidency what it is. Indeed, on many important questions the Constitution is silent or inconclusive. For example, the controversy over the greatly increased presidential use of executive agreements in international dealings has been fought out by the President and Congress in the absence of constitutional guidance. The constitutionality of such agreements has not been challenged in the courts in such a way that the Supreme Court has been obliged to make an authoritative judgment on the matter. The same applies to the President's use of his war powers. Of course, a President may use the Constitution to advance his policy preferences, as with civil rights, but this illustrates the main point in that the initiative in such an instance is normally with the administration.

The real terrain is political. As Hodder-Williams puts it, 'Because the Constitution and its interpreters, the nine justices of the Supreme Court, do not generally play a major role in defining the bounds of presidential power, the interplay of political forces does.' In the remaining sections of this chapter I shall be looking at the non-judicial actors in American politics whose exercise of skills, in the context of social circumstances, has largely determined the reach of presidential power.

President and Party

What has happened to the President's relations with his political party is a complex matter. When one tries to say something general about this, there are numerous variables, as John Lees makes clear in his chapter. Factors which have to be considered in order to obtain a reasonably full picture of the nature of the party connection include the following: the traditional/modern dichotomy, personal inclination, political situation, social developments, electoral arrangements, the White House staff and the party in the country.

First, there is the division between the traditional and modern eras. In this connection the idea of a dichotomy is less persuasive than it is in relation to some of the other main considerations with which this book deals. Specifically, it cannot be said that a marked change in the President's relations with his party dates from New Deal days; such changes as have occurred mainly arose later. Lees considers 1960 to be a significant transitional year. 'The election in 1960 of Democrat John Kennedy', he says, 'marked the beginning of a period in which the disincentives of overt party leadership by Presidents became greater.' This statement highlights the key change in the presidential-party relationship in the modern era – namely, a loosening of the President's tie to the party that he in some degree leads.

Examining this relationship illustrates the difficulties that can arise when attempting to isolate the last fifty or so years in the 200-year history of an institution – the problem being that it is difficult to discern discrete periods. During the traditional era, a few Presidents, such as Jefferson, Jackson and Wilson, were forceful party leaders, guiding their parties in Congress in accordance with what Burns has called the Jeffersonian model[9] and others have called party government. However, these examples were untypical. Nearly all of the traditional Presidents were weaker within the political system than the modern Presidents have been. At the same time, the traditional Presidents tended to coexist with party leaders who were stronger politically than their modern counterparts. Franklin Roosevelt operated within the framework of traditional party norms, but his Hamiltonian[10] presidency was instrumental in reorienting future White House-party relations.

Secondly, there is the matter of personal inclination. Some Presidents choose to involve themselves more fully than others in party matters. This may mean involvement with the congressional party, with the national chairman and national committee members, with party candidates in elections and with the state and local parties. Lees suggests a wide variation in disposition as regards the first three of the modern Presidents: 'Roosevelt was an active party leader in almost all respects, yet not a totally successful one. Truman was an aggressive partisan but an ineffectual party leader. Eisenhower was publicly a non-partisan leader who did much covertly to help strengthen and unify his party in government and in the country.'

The inclination to follow the partisan or non-partisan route in relation to one or more of the dimensions of party activity may be temperamental. Equally, it may depend on one's experience. If, as

9. Burns, *Presidential Government*, pp. 28–31.
10. *Ibid.*

with Johnson and Ford, one has been a party leader in Congress, that experience cannot help but colour one's outlook. If, by contrast, one has been elected governor and President through a non-party strategy, as with Carter, that approach is also likely to have an impact on behaviour.

Thirdly, the President's partisanship and involvement in party affairs are strongly influenced by the prevailing political situation, which may change significantly during an incumbency. It is crucial to a President's success that he makes a shrewd assessment of what the existing political circumstances require in party terms. Lees suggests that Kennedy and Ford were more partisan and played a stronger party leadership role than circumstances made desirable, while Johnson and Carter tended to less partisanship than might have been advisable.

A situation which normally calls for muted partisanship or 'bipartisanship' is the one that exists when American armed forces are used − or considered for use − overseas. All nine modern Presidents have directed military activities overseas, ranging from involvement in world war, to shows of force, to hostage rescue attempts. During such crises the tendency for politicians and electors, irrespective of party, is to defer to the President. Since 1941 these occasions have provided chief executives with frequent occasions when partisan behaviour would be ill-advised, and they contrast sharply with the political situations which tended to constitute the presidential agenda during the traditional era.

Other situations which have a bearing on whether the exercise of party leadership by the President is advantageous can be mentioned: foreign or domestic policy is an obvious example. In terms of domestic policy, some issues produce different vibrations − in party terms − than others. The extent of the President's support in the country, as indicated by election results or opinion polls, is relevant. So, too, is the party composition of Congress. Does the President have a party majority, or an 'ideological' majority, or neither?

Fourthly, there have been certain developments in American society since 1933 which have affected the nature of the President's involvement in party politics. The more significant of these can be said to include the attitudes that citizens have adopted towards political parties, changes in the way public opinion is measured and changes in the methods of communication.

A widely discussed and measured phenomenon has been the retreat by Americans from a willingness to identify with a political party. There has been a steady increase in the proportion of electors who consider themselves to be independents. The change has not meant a movement between parties so much as a refusal to acknowledge a party allegiance at all. As a consequence, the number of both Democratic and Republican identifiers has declined. Surveys since 1950 show an increase in the independent sector from about one-fourth of the voting population to about one-third, although the factor of intensity can make measurement difficult.

Traditionally, the independents were supposed to be mainly uninterested in politics, but the new-style independents include, in greater proportions than before, citizens who are vitally interested, highly educated and issue-oriented. Whether in office or as candidates, Presidents cannot ignore this weakening of party ties, and a changed perspective on the utility of trying to be a party leader has resulted. When considering the decrease in partisanship, one cannot help but link the tendency with the general feeling that prevailed among those who created the constitutional system in 1787. The Founding Fathers were predominantly anti-party, and therefore current trends can be seen as constituting a belated fulfilment of their preferences.

New organisations have been formed, or existing ones have adapted themselves, to perform functions which were once the province of political parties. Such efforts may supplant parties in relation to particular activities, or they may supplement parties, or they may introduce new techniques into the political process. For example, newspaper and television journalists now form the link between candidates and voters that party professionals once provided. The media discover, assess and endorse candidates, exposing their strengths and vulnerabilities to the public.

Notwithstanding such encroachments, there must still be organisation if political goals are to be achieved. An example of a new type of political organisation is the non-party citizen group which participates in the conduct of presidential election campaigns. While the earliest major manifestation of this kind of effort surfaced in 1952, the best known was the notorious Committee for the Reelection of the President, whose efforts on behalf of Nixon in 1972 included the break-in at the Democratic national headquarters. The use of advertising agencies and consultants has become commonplace during the era of the modern presidency, providing a contrast with the traditional era.

Modern social differentiation has produced political advisers who are experts on opinion polls, the media, the use of computers and direct mailings. Joseph Napolitan, a media consultant, acknowledged the non-party character of many of these efforts when he explained that he is concerned with 'the art of communicating a candidate's message directly to the voter without filtering it through the party organization'.[11] Jimmy Carter indicated the importance of such assistance when he sent a note to one of his chief advisers, Gerald Rafshoon, after the 1976 election, saying facetiously, 'I'll always be grateful that I was able to contribute in a small way to the victory of the Rafshoon agency.'[12]

A key element in the new differentiation is the organisation which conducts public opinion polls. Its activities can be associated with the modern era, an important landmark being the establishment of the Gallup Poll in 1935. Much has been written about the effects of polling on candidates, office-holders and electors, but for present purposes the phenomenon provides a further example of a task carried out by private organisations which was previously executed by political parties. Traditionally, political opinion was assessed by party canvassers and aggregated by party managers whose conclusions, supplemented by straw polls reported in newspapers, were not dissimilar from those reached by modern polling organisations. The difficulty in claiming a traditional-modern dichotomy is illustrated by this example, although polling has obviously become more elaborate and systematic in the later period.

Media advisers began providing a further dimension of non-party assistance after television became important in the early 1950s. We have since been assured that 'media politics' is crucial to the success of Presidents, whether as incumbent or candidate. John Lees' 'autocue partisan' – Ronald Reagan – is frequently offered as evidence of this inasmuch as his considerable popularity with the electorate is linked with his acknowledged preeminence as a television performer. He is, after all, the only professional actor to be elected President. Late in his second term when Presidents normally find their popularity sagging, Reagan was recording approval ratings in excess of those recorded at a comparable stage by Roosevelt and Eisenhower. In March 1986 a national survey showed 62 per cent approving of the way in which Reagan was handling his job as President. A month later, after the American bombing raid on Libya, Reagan's approval rating went up to 67 per cent, with only 21 per cent expressing disapproval of his performance as President.[13] In the same month an American television news editor said he had stopped pointing out mistakes in Reagan's speeches, because to do so might be unpopular.[14]

11. Joseph Napolitan, *The Election Game and How to Win It*, New York, 1972, p. 65.
12. Richard M. Pious, *The American Presidency*, New York, 1979, pp. 89–90.
13. *Newsweek*, 28 April 1986, p. 14.
14. John Mortimer, 'My Voyage Round Reagan's America', *The Spectator* (London), 26 April 1986, p. 11.

Fifthly, the President's relations with his party have been affected by formal changes in the conduct of elections. The central development has been the proliferation of presidential primaries. It cannot be said that there has been a linear increase in such primaries as there was a dip in their use between the two world wars. After the Second World War, however, the proportion of the electorate living in states where presidential primaries are held increased steadily. The last candidate for President to be nominated by a strategy of obtaining the support of key people in his party while avoiding the primaries was Hubert Humphrey, the Democratic nominee in 1968. In that year seventeen states held primaries to choose about one-third of the delegates to the national conventions of the major parties. In 1976, 1980 and 1984 two-thirds to three-fourths of the delegates were chosen in this way.

The main point here is that there has been a shift away from the choice of presidential nominees by party leaders to choice by the electorate. Prior to the First World War it was largely a matter for party leaders. Subsequently, the choice involved a mixture of élite and popular approval. During the era of the modern presidency such party leaders as are still visible have increasingly been shut out. This change provides another illustration of the diminished reliance which Presidents have on their parties, whether as outsiders hoping for election to a first term or as incumbents making plans for a re-election campaign.

The 'democratisation' of candidate selection has meant a decline in the importance of national conventions. An important decisional arena where party leaders held sway in the traditional era, the national convention, has since become a ratifying body where primary outcomes are endorsed. Since 1933 the Democrats have had only one convention (1952) where there was more than one ballot for the presidential nomination, and the Republicans have had only two (1940 and 1948). It is significant that the disappearance of the contested convention coincided with the emergence of television. A recent indication of their decline is the fact that in 1984 the Democratic and Republican conventions became the first in the television era not to have 'gavel to gavel' coverage by the national networks.

Sixthly, the President's relations with his party have been strongly affected by the development of presidential staffing. Lees suggests that 'perhaps the most important change since the 1930s which has affected relations between Presidents and their party is the development of the White House Office.' Chronologically, the intervention of staff into what used to be the preserve of the parties begins when a group of organisation men, with little or no experience of party work, pin their futures on a presidential hopeful. Their identification of him as someone who could make it to the White House usurps the traditional role of party leaders who used to be the kingmakers. If they have backed the right horse, the non-party organisation men are rewarded in due course with important posts in the White House and become the President's principal political advisers. In this, they upstage those in leadership positions in the President's party. An extreme example of this occurred when members of the White House staff would not permit the Republican National Chairman, Senator Robert Dole, despite repeated efforts, to see Nixon at any time during the President's campaign for reelection in 1972.[15]

This exercise, involving President, staff and party in the candidate and incumbent contexts, results in a variety of styles of operation. Presidents are aware that there remains a significant element of interdependence between presidential and party performance. In endeavouring to allow for this, dangers can arise from a too heavy-handed staff-oriented strategy, as seen in the Nixon and Carter examples, while those Presidents who have attempted too party-oriented an approach, for example by intervening in mid-term primaries, have highlighted the dangers of assertive party leadership. It is not surprising that, as Lees has noted, 'the period has been marked by tension between the White House staff and those more closely linked with the party.'

Lastly, there is the matter of the President's relations with the nationwide party organisation. This means the national committee and its chairman and the state and local organisations. Traditional Presidents tended to share influence with leaders in their party serving in Congress, the Cabinet, state and local government, and party offices at all levels. The National Chairman operated somewhat independently of the White House. To become President, an aspirant had to win the support of an important cross-section of the party establishment. Jim Farley, the Democratic National Chairman in the 1930s, broke with Roosevelt over the third term issue and later recalled that after the break 'I was no longer called to the White House for morning bedside conferences. My phone no longer brought the familiar voice.'[16]

More recent national chairmen tend neither to have the authority that would enable them to oppose the President on a fundamental issue nor to enjoy the intimate political relationship that Farley had with Roosevelt before 1940. Since the New Deal, the President has acquired a clear-cut ascendancy over the National Chairman and his committee. As the authority of the President has increased, the

15. Theodore H. White, *The Making of the President, 1972*, New York, 1973, p. 49.
16. James Farley, *Jim Farley's Story*, New York, 1948, p. 68.

standing and personnel of parties at all levels has diminished. This is reflected in the disposition of Presidents to work with consultants who operate outside the party framework. These operators may use the party mechanism as one of the various avenues they use in their efforts to enable their 'client' to prevail politically. If the National Chairman wishes to see the President, he can watch him on television, as Dole was invited to do. One authority suggests that the way Presidents usually operate is to appoint a nonentity to the national chairmanship, downgrade the job and humiliate the incumbent.[17] But the matter is not simple. Some modern Presidents, such as Kennedy and Ford, chose to intervene prominently in the affairs of their party organisations.

It has been argued that the distancing of the modern President from his party has diminished the presidency while introducing problems related to the conduct of responsible government.[18] The Nixon presidency provides an obvious example of how things can go wrong in the era of the non-party organisation men. The dangers are implicit in advice given to Carter by his pollster, Patrick Cadell. Urging Carter to rely on media politics in running the government, Cadell remarked: 'Too many good people have been beaten because they tried to substitute substance for style.'[19]

President and Congress

There have been major changes in the relationship between the modern Presidents and Congress as compared with the corresponding relationship prior to the New Deal. A vital aspect of this change has been the post-1933 expectation – presidential, congressional and public – that the President will take the initiative in determining the issues with which Congress deals. As Huntington has said, 'The President now determines the legislative agenda of Congress almost as thoroughly as the British Cabinet sets the legislative agenda of Parliament.'[20] This does not mean that Congress necessarily feels obliged to comply with the policy preferences of the President when it resolves the issues he has identified. At the same time, identifying the tune cannot help but give the President some leverage in calling it.

17. Pious, *The American Presidency*, p. 126.
18. Louis W. Koenig, *The Chief Executive*, 4th edn, New York, 1981, pp. 2–5.
19. *New York Times*, 4 May 1977.
20. Samuel Huntington, 'Congressional Responses to the Twentieth Century', in David B. Truman (ed.), *The Congress and America's Future*, Englewood Cliffs, NJ, 1973, p. 23.

Before 1933, with notable exceptions, Presidents tended to be much less conspicuously involved in the legislative process. The prevailing viewpoint was what has been called the literalist or Madisonian or Whig view of the proper role of the President in his relations with Congress: Congress formulated public polioy while the President, whatever his party, enforced the laws initiated and approved by Congress. This modest role for Presidents was seen to be in keeping with the letter and spirit of the Constitution.

An illustration of the above is found in the traditional and modern practices concerning the submission of presidential messages and bills to Congress. In his chapter David Mervin quotes Bryce on the tendency of congressmen in the nineteenth century to give only perfunctory attention to communications from the President. For example, when Lincoln sent a draft bill with a message, Congress responded angrily. Since 1933, by contrast, initiatives from the White House have been viewed as crucial inputs into the congressional process. It was commonplace for Franklin Roosevelt to submit draft bills – as it has been for all subsequent Presidents.

Another example of the change in presidential-congressional relations relates to control of the bureaucracy. During the traditional era Congress directed the executive branch to a greater extent than is feasible in the modern era. Writing in 1885, admittedly during the nadir of presidential influence, Woodrow Wilson said in relation to the executive departments:

The Secretaries . . . find themselves bound in all things larger than routine details by laws . . . which they have no legitimate means of modifying . . . The Secretaries . . . look toward a strict obedience to Congress. Congress made them and can unmake them. It is to Congress that they must render account for the conduct of administration.[21]

While congressional intervention in executive operations has been conspicuous during the modern era as well, as a matter of degree post-1933 intervention has been less strident. This matter is complex, however, because a meaningful longitudinal comparison should take into account the much enlarged scope of central administration and the public sector, the modest provision of presidential staffing before 1939 and the shift in presidential priorities from domestic to foreign affairs.

Notwithstanding such considerations, during the traditional era members of Congress and party leaders played a more prominent role than subsequently in the matter of appointments. Cabinet

21. Woodrow Wilson, *Congressional Government*, New York, 1956, pp. 174–5.

members were often foisted upon the President.in the course of bargaining at national party conventions.

The nineteenth century established the tradition that staffing the administration − from top to bottom − was a complex process in which party leaders, congressional leaders and representatives of interest groups bargained for their protégés; appointees would therefore be expected to function within the administration in accordance with the wishes of . . . [their] constituencies.[22]

Once in office, pre-modern heads of departments would deal directly with Congress on legislation and appropriations while bypassing the President. This occurred in the absence of the central clearance by a presidential staff which was later to become a standard procedure.

In view of the above, it is not surprising that prior to 1933 the great domestic issues tended to be resolved by Congress. As Pious has said, issues such as slavery, sectionalism, banking, the tariff, taxation, reconstruction and the control of manufacturing and commerce were dealt with principally by Congress; they were sometimes influenced by, but almost never controlled by, the executive branch. The compromises of 1820, 1850 and 1854 − designed to hold the Union together − were hammered out entirely by congressional leaders. Efforts by some traditional Presidents to move towards national regulation of the economy in the public interest failed conspicuously.[23]

The use of the veto is an interesting variable. In this, there is a far from clear-cut difference between the two eras. While traditional Presidents tended to be diffident about encroaching on Congress' constitutional domain, the use of the veto is a presidential entitlement. It is therefore not surprising that the veto has been called the President's most important power in influencing domestic affairs prior to 1933.[24] However, the traditional period lacks cohesion in this matter (as does the modern period). Before Cleveland became President, only Andrew Johnson and Grant had cast more than a dozen vetoes. But after Cleveland showed the way by casting 584 vetoes, his successors up to 1933 used the veto more frequently than the Presidents who served before Cleveland. From 1900 to 1933, as Mervin has noted, Presidents vetoed about nine bills per year.

22. Richard M. Pious, 'The Evolution of the Presidency, 1789−1932', *Current History*, vol. 66 (June 1974), p. 243.
23. *Ibid.*, p. 244.
24. *Ibid.* In the nineteenth century Presidents would influence policy outcomes by negotiating with congressional leaders on the terms which would enable them to sign rather than veto bills.

Turning to the modern era, its first three Presidents were the most frequent naysayers in presidential history if we omit Cleveland. Roosevelt cast 635 vetoes, Truman 250 and Eisenhower 181. Together, these three Presidents were responsible for 44 per cent of all vetoes cast since 1789 if we omit Reagan's. After Eisenhower left office, vetoing became less fashionable. Kennedy, Johnson, Nixon, Carter and (as of August 1986) Reagan vetoed about seven bills per year, a rate surpassed by the pre-New Deal Presidents in this century. But the pattern after 1960 is not consistent since Ford cast 66 vetoes during his short incumbency. Generalisations that can be made in the matter of vetoing bills are that there has been a stronger disposition to do so during the modern era, particularly the early part of it, and the heavy vetoers have tended to serve consecutively.[25]

Perhaps the most crucial differences between presidential-congressional relations in the traditional and modern eras arise from attitudes held by ordinary people towards the two branches of government. Broadly speaking, as has been mentioned, Congress – in particular the House of Representatives – was seen as the popular branch during the traditional era while the President's links with the people during those decades tended to be tenuous. While presidential-congressional relations have had their linear and oscillatory aspects, a dichotomy is sufficiently real to merit further explanation.

In this regard it has been estimated that the popular vote obtained by winning candidates for President did not amount to more than 10 per cent of the 'free' population until as late as the 1920s.[26] According to this analysis, even the 'strong' traditional Presidents gained support below that level in the constricted electorate of the time. Thus Jackson received 5.8 per cent of the vote of the 'free' population in 1832, Lincoln received 6.8 per cent in 1860, Cleveland received 8.8 per cent in 1884, Theodore Roosevelt received 9.3 per cent in 1904 and Wilson received 8.9 per cent in 1916. Nominated by party professionals in the absence of primaries and modern communications technology, candidates elected on this basis could not be said to have won as à result of a mass popular mobilisation. Because Presidents were not generally seen as leaders of popular opinion or as effective party leaders, congressmen felt able to ignore administration requests and act unilaterally.

In 1933 all this changed. Roosevelt was elected on a wave of

25. The most vetoes in the nineteenth century were cast by Johnson and Grant, who served consecutively, and by Cleveland, Harrison and McKinley, who also served consecutively. In the twentieth century the adjacent incumbencies of Roosevelt, Truman and Eisenhower produced the highest totals.
26. Pious, 'The Evolution of the Presidency', pp. 241–2.

expectation that he would act decisively in relation to the Great Depression. The people and Congress awaited his initiatives, with Congress ready to enact almost any legislation proposed by the White House. The President was the focus of the nation's aspirations, and he was perceived as entitled to act in accordance with a direct popular mandate. During the 100 days, as a commentator subsequently put it, 'The federal government, for the first time on such a scale, addressed itself to the major social and economic ills facing the country'.[27] The era of the modern presidency had begun. From that time on, the President was America's chief legislator.

For analytical purposes it has been convenient to compare relations between the President and Congress in the two eras in categoric terms, but this analysis needs to be refined. While the aforementioned configurations may be valid in a general sense, particular 'traditional' Presidents adopted a modern approach in their relations with Congress. At the same time, each such interlude had distinctive characteristics. Jefferson presided over majoritarian party government. He worked as party leader with his followers in the Republican caucus in the House of Representatives. Having moulded a new party, he used it to dominate Congress. Jackson, too, was a strong congressional leader, but with a difference. While Jefferson engaged in cosy collaboration, Jackson was more combative in his insistence that the presidency was an instrument of popular power. In this he challenged the assumption that Congress had a monopoly in representing the people. Lincoln had another approach. In a series of extraordinary actions, including spending money without congressional appropriation, he acted unilaterally, asking Congress to give its approval after the event. He successfully asserted emergency prerogatives as a leader in wartime, maintaining that he had done nothing beyond the constitutional competence of Congress.

In this century two pre-1933 Presidents — Theodore Roosevelt and Woodrow Wilson — used post-1933 styles in their relations with Congress. Making the juxtaposition of time and style explicit, Rossiter calls Theodore Roosevelt 'our first modern President' while acknowledging that Franklin Roosevelt 'created the modern presidency'.[28] A significant aspect of the legislative achievements of the first Roosevelt, as Mervin points out, is that he successfully intervened in all stages of the legislative process during a non-crisis

---

27. George H. Skau, 'Franklin D. Roosevelt and the Expansion of Presidential Power', *Current History*, vol. 66 (June 1974), p. 247.
28. Clinton Rossiter, *The American Presidency*, London, 1957, pp. 75, 111.

period. This presaged the expectation after 1933 that all Presidents would press their programmes in Congress all the time. Theodore Roosevelt has been characterised as the first President since Jefferson to initiate a broad programme of major legislation from the executive branch. Relying on direct appeals to the people, he 'put the Presidency on the front page of every newspaper in America, and there it has remained ever since'.[29] Wilson was similarly assertive in leading Congress. His position was like Lincoln's in that a situation of crisis was combined with public receptivity to strong leadership and the inclination and skills on the part of the President to provide it. Wilson was a successful leader of his congressional party during most of his incumbency. An important landmark was his success in obtaining congressional approval for his exercise of 'almost totalitarian control of the American economy' in wartime.[30]

It is clear that the history of presidential-congressional relations exhibits linear, oscillatory and dichotomous tendencies. The relationship is linear in that it culminated in a norm of presidential assertiveness after 1933 as the United States became a complex industrial society with an enlarged central government. The relationship is oscillatory in that during the first 150 years there were interludes of forceful leadership of Congress in a sea of weak 'leadership'. There have also been oscillations within the context of the new norm after 1933. The relationship is dichotomous in that, with exceptions, the President did not lead Congress prior to 1933 whereas after that year he became the chief legislator. 'From the 1930s onward', as Greenstein has said, 'Presidents have had to be leaders whether they chose to be or not.'[31]

The oscillations have occurred for a variety of reasons. It may be useful to identify five of them:

1. Crises such as war, international tension and economic upheaval are often associated with strong leadership of Congress from the White House. But there may be interesting variations on this theme as Greenstein points out when discussing the pre-New Deal Presidents:

Presidential leadership tended to occur during crises or when the incumbent President was motivated to be a strong leader. Sometimes these factors coincided, as with Woodrow Wilson's leadership in World War I and Abraham Lincoln's in the Civil War. Sometimes a crisis failed to produce leadership (Buchanan), or a leader produced a crisis (Polk), or, in the presence of rela-

---

29. *Ibid.*, p. 76.
30. Marcus Cunliffe, *American Presidents and the Presidency*, London, 1969, p. 209.
31. Greenstein, Berman and Felzenberg, *op. cit.*, p. iii.

tively moderate external stimuli, an activist President was more assertive than other Presidents of his era (Cleveland and Theodore Roosevelt).[32]

2. The separation of powers invites a struggle for ascendancy. The result has been that short-term factors have produced an alternation of congressional and presidential ascendancy during the past 200 years. This oscillation has occurred during both the traditional and modern eras, but under a different framework of expectations during the latter period.

3. Closely related to the above is what might be called the cyclical imperative. If one side prevails for a time, a new balance must be struck:

The American system has built-in regulators that assure impermanence in the President's power circumstances . . . For a time it [Congress] can acquiesce to the President's initiatives, but sooner or later it must contest and reject them . . . Similarly, the public mood . . . is controlled by a limited span of attention. The presidential summons to join in noble purpose can be sounded just so often.[33]

This imperative applies *during* an incumbency as well as between incumbencies. Mervin makes a useful analysis of the heights and depths reached by Wilson, Roosevelt and Johnson in their dealings with Congress during the earlier and later phases of their administrations.

4. The President's skills as a legislative leader are of course pertinent. These were possessed in impressive measure by the strong traditional Presidents who have been mentioned. In the modern era Roosevelt and Johnson were especially endowed in this respect, while Carter was not.

5. The previous experience of the President can be relevant, but the evidence is not clear-cut. In accounting for the success of the two Roosevelts and Wilson as leaders of Congress, Rossiter stresses their common experience as governors who had led their state legislatures.[34] Yet the example of Carter confounds this explanation. Moreover, the vagaries of Truman, Kennedy, Johnson, Nixon and Ford suggest that prior congressional experience is also an imperfect indicator.

It is instructive to look at presidential-congressional relations at points a century apart. In 1865 Congress reacted with more than a little pique to Lincoln's robust exercise of power. Congress

32. *Ibid.*
33. Koenig, *op. cit.*, p. 6.
34. Rossiter, *op. cit.*, p. 83.

humiliated his successor and ushered in a period best summarised by the title of Woodrow Wilson's book — *Congressional Government*. In 1974 Congress was incensed for different reasons by Nixon's behaviour. Congress adopted a uniquely far-reaching series of reforms intended to reclaim power it had lost to the presidency, and some said the end-result would be a diminished presidency. This prediction seemed to be borne out when public appearances by Ford did not produce the kind of reverential deference that had been generated among crowds by past chief executives, and Ford also lost contests over policy with Congress that Presidents usually win.[35] Carter, too, felt the chill. Writing in 1978, one observer said: 'The psychological bond between the people and the presidency, . . . weakened by Watergate, has yet to be restored to previous levels of strength.'[36] Nevertheless, there clearly has been no reversion to congressional government. The modern presidency lives on.

The time has come to identify a concrete change. The institutionalisation of the presidency after 1939 entailed important changes in the President's way of dealing with Congress. Specifically, the modern era has seen the establishment of a congressional liaison office in the White House as part of the Executive Office of the President. As with various other developments, there was a delay in this. Franklin Roosevelt dealt with Congress much as Theodore Roosevelt and Wilson had done. He had no liaison unit, but he used particular aides as emissaries and involved himself personally. Differentiation began under Truman, who set up a small unit for legislative liaison, but the formal establishment of a congressional liaison office in the White House is associated with Eisenhower. This component of the White House Office has existed in all subsequent administrations, with varying degrees of success in dealing with Congress and in maintaining access to the Oval Office.

In addition to this enhancement of the President's capacity for dealing with members of Congress, his capacity for dealing with the products of the congressional process was also enlarged. The latter was achieved through an extension under Roosevelt of the work of the Bureau of the Budget. Created in 1921, the BOB was originally intended to produce efficiency and economy through the preparation of a unified federal budget. But the latent possibilities were not realised until Roosevelt added central clearance of legislation to the BOB's coordinating activities in budgeting. Indeed, the BOB's concerns were extended to bills at all stages — proposed, pending and enrolled:

35. Philip Shabecoff, 'Appraising Presidential Power: The Ford Presidency', in Cronin and Tugwell, *op. cit.*, p. 25.
36. Buchanan, *op. cit.*, p. 92.

As in most other matters, profound changes took place with the advent of the Roosevelt administration. A newly strengthened [Budget] bureau was given the mandate to clear all agency proposals for legislation or testimony before Congress to make sure such action was in line with the President's wishes . . . With Truman the bureau was made even more powerful.[37]

Later the élite unit of civil servants in the BOB lost influence to others in the President's staffing apparatus, but central clearance of legislation continued. Under Nixon the name of the bureau was changed to the Office of Management and Budget, and significantly its head was given an office in the White House separate from his staff. The point is that today the possibility of presidential evaluation of legislation is much enhanced as a consequence of innovations in the 1930s. Yet we must always guard against claiming too much, for there was centralised budgeting when Alexander Hamilton was Secretary of the Treasury, a practice which lapsed under his successor in 1795.

In general the President's capacity to deal effectively with Congress has been enhanced by changes dating from the New Deal. These include the establishment of the White House liaison office, the extension of the activities of the BOB/OMB, the development of other components of the Executive Office of the President, and the enlargement and differentiation of the bureaucracy. Congress did not take these 'threats' lying down. The institutionalisation of the presidency has been accompanied by the institutionalisation of Congress. Included in the latter have been increases in the staffing of individual members, committees and Congress as a whole; differentiation in the form of a multiplication and strengthening of subcommittees; and an increase in the influence of individual members through changes in the rules of the two chambers. Not surprisingly, a number of important reforms came into effect in 1975, the year after Nixon's resignation.[38] Greenstein has remarked on this co-equal development: 'The human and organizational resources available to the President have grown to where they are approximately equivalent in personnel and staff support to the modern Congress, with its 535 members and several thousand staff and clerical aides.'[39]

As for the President's relations with his congressional party, numerous scenarios apply, depending on skill, personality and situation. It is instructive to consider the two occasions when

37. William F. Mullen, *Presidential Power and Politics*, New York, 1976, p. 56.
38. See Malcolm Shaw, 'Congress in the 1970s: A Decade of Reform', *Parliamentary Affairs*, Summer 1981, pp. 272–90.
39. Greenstein, Berman and Felzenberg, *op. cit.*, p. iii.

modern Presidents found Congress especially receptive to their leadership — during Roosevelt's first term and in 1965 and 1966. On both occasions Democratic Presidents enjoyed very large Democratic majorities in the House and Senate. However, both Roosevelt and Johnson, while carrying their parties with them, were not particularly partisan in their approaches. Indeed, when Roosevelt became more partisan during his second term, his relations with Congress deteriorated, and Johnson (the Vietnam War notwithstanding) was one of the most consensual political leaders in American history. Truman and Kennedy, on the other hand, were more partisan, but less effective than Roosevelt and Johnson in dealing with Congress. These examples illustrate that strong partisanship is only rarely an effective presidential posture, even less so for the modern Republican Presidents than for the Democrats. Indeed, it is a less feasible option than it used to be, with Congress more assertive, more decentralised and more electorally independent of the President. It was easier for Speaker Rayburn to 'deliver' for the President than it has generally been for subsequent party leaders in Congress.[40]

The Chief Executive

One of the most significant and conspicuous changes that accompanied the onset of the modern presidency was the enlargement of the executive branch and thus of the President's responsibilities as chief executive. This enlargement has several aspects. First, the executive has been enlarged numerically. Secondly, the executive has been enlarged in terms of its responsibilities. Thirdly, the executive has been enlarged in terms of its modes of operation.

On the matter of numbers, it is made clear by Robert Williams that, while the number of federal civil servants has increased steadily during the past 200 years, the increase that took place during the New Deal years was extraordinary. The federal civil service increased from 600,000 in 1932 to 1,400,000 in 1938, an increase that continued under Roosevelt's successors until by the 1980s there had been a five fold increase since 1932 to about 3,000,000. The enhanced scale of operation of the federal executive during the past fifty years has confronted Americans with a fundamentally new

40. The incidence of Presidents serving while one or both houses of Congress have non-presidential party majorities has not increased in the modern era. Nineteen Presidents have served with both houses of Congress controlled by their own party while twenty have served with one or both houses in the control of the non-presidential party. Fifteen of the latter were pre-1933 and five were post-1933.

governing situation compared with the era of the traditional President. The change is even more dramatic if one includes military personnel in the picture. The existence in the peacetime years of the 1980s of some 2,000,000 American servicemen would have astonished Americans in the traditional era, or even in the 1930s, as would the $320 billion defence budget for 1987 submitted to Congress by the Reagan administration. In 1939 the United States armed forces numbered some 300,000 men.

As Robert Williams points out, however, the number of federal civil servants has remained relatively stable in recent years. Instead there has been a massive increase in those employed in state, city, quasi-public and private organisations who are financed by the national government. Williams refers to evidence that there may be four times as many people indirectly employed by the federal government as are directly employed. This suggests that capacity can continue to grow while political sensitivity about size can be accommodated, enlargement taking the form of 'contracting out'. Thus, as Williams suggests, counting the number of federal civil servants underestimates the real expansion of government activity in recent times. Yet the conservative Presidents who have served since 1968 can be seen to be holding the line against 'bloated bureaucracy'.

As for the enlargement of the President's responsibilities, this arose from changes in public policy that in turn produced the enlarged executive. The circumstances which precipitated this were explored in chapter 1. It was suggested that by 1933 the United States had reached the stage of 'integration' in its national development. As a consequence, demands for national solutions to problems became more prevalent, leading to the adoption of policies which required a larger and more complex public service. As its leader, the President acquired more responsibilities.

Various circumstances in the 1930s can be identified as supporting and precipitating factors. Among them were the existence of a severe economic crisis, the election of a President with unique political skills and a strong popular mandate, the inadequacy of the state governments to cope with the situation facing the country, the experience of a doubling of civilian employment in the federal government during the First World War and the economic and social regulation that accompanied it, and a decline in the commitment to a laissez-faire attitude towards government.

Taken together, this led to a perception of the President as holding the ring in a much enlarged executive with much enlarged concerns:

The new sense of a need for social security, for protection from unemployment and from the grave hazards created by economic crises, gave Franklin

D. Roosevelt an overwhelming majority in 1932. The laissez-faire individualism that had dominated public opinion received a severe shock from which it has never recovered. The concept of the welfare state . . . gained an important following.[41]

The President's economic responsibilities were set out in the Employment Act of 1946, which requires the federal government to promote full employment, high production and stable purchasing power. Broadly, the President is expected to keep unemployment and inflation down. Such obligations contrast sharply with the pre-New Deal outlook. 'Hoover's reluctance to intervene in the economy . . . signaled the end of an era of chief executives whose conception of the office avoided the direct involvement of the president in furthering the economic welfare of the people.'[42] The four Republican Presidents of the modern era have tended to show less enthusiasm for some of their enlarged responsibilities than the five Democratic Presidents, but generally the new pattern has persisted irrespective of party.[43]

On the matter of expanded modes of operation, this refers to the development of an executive branch of a more administratively diverse nature than existed previously. The most obvious example of such diversification was the creation of the Executive Office of the President in 1939, a matter to which the next section of this chapter is devoted. The independent regulatory agencies provide another example. Some of these existed prior to 1933, but others were created during the modern era. The attempts by Congress to remove the regulatory agencies from presidential control have not contributed to coherent direction. In addition, new departments and agencies have come into existence during the modern era, complete with autonomous bureaux, and they have contributed to the diversity. So, too, have entities variously called 'issue networks', 'subgovernments' and 'iron triangles'. They carve out sectors of policy-making and are, Heclo advises us, increasing in scale, political significance and remoteness from the President.[44] Finally, there are emergency

41. Robert M. MacIver, 'Two Centuries of Political Change', in David Spitz (ed.), *Politics and Society*, New York, 1969, p. 381.
42. Mullen, *op. cit.*, p. 35.
43. When Eisenhower became the first Republican President after twenty years of the New and Fair Deals, he failed to reduce public expenditure below its level in Truman's final year. In fact the federal government's gross expenditure increased from $99.8 billion in 1952 to $151.3 billion in 1960. F.C. Mosher and O. Poland, *The Costs of American Government*, New York, 1964, p. 155.
44. Hugh Heclo, 'Issue Networks and the Executive Establishment', in Anthony King (ed.), *The New American Political System*, Washington, DC, 1978.

agencies, presidential commissions and the 'contracting out' exercises mentioned earlier.

The enlargement of the executive branch in these ways resulted in something short of coherence. New complexity was accompanied by new fragmentation. While Roosevelt's successors have enjoyed more authority, standing, capacity and scope than their predecessors in the traditional era, they have had great difficulty in realising the potential in the situation:

This fragmentation has profound and pervasive effects upon the role of the President, the one man who is concerned with the whole . . . of the federal executive. Instead of being the head of a hierarchical body of officials who look up to him for authority, the President finds that both law and politics make him the titular head of institutions that lack corporeal unity.[45]

In his chapter Robert Williams characterises the 'giant, heterogeneous executive' as 'increasingly unwieldy and difficult for the President to coordinate or direct' and 'incurably balkanised and inherently unmanageable'.

The reasons for this situation are well known. The President's claim to executive leadership has never been fully conceded by Congress, the courts or the bureaucracy. The President is perceived, unless his name is Franklin Roosevelt, as the short-term occupant of a seat of power. This is the viewpoint of congressmen, judges, bureaucrats, journalists and lobbyists whose involvement in the Washington political community tends to be longer. Also, clientele pressures are rife, and executive resources – legal, programmatic and financial – derive from acts of Congress. Indeed, officials may be authorised by Congress to act independently of political executives. Neustadt considers the position of the 'boss':

Neither as a document nor as accreted precedent does the American Constitution give the President of the United States exclusive warrant to be 'boss' of the executive establishment. It gives him but a warrant to contest for that position, agency by agency, as best he can. Congress and its committees have their warrants too; so do department heads and bureau chiefs.[46]

Turning to the traditional-modern dichotomy, it needs to be said that all American Presidents have held office in a political environment in which a suspicion of strong executive leadership is an entrenched attitude. In this, there is continuity through the 200 years of the republic. Nevertheless, in a comparison of the two eras one

---

45. Richard Rose, *Managing Presidential Objectives*, London, 1977, p. 146.
46. Richard E. Neustadt, 'Approaches to Staffing the Presidency: Notes on FDR and JFK', *American Political Science Review*, Dec. 1963, pp. 862–3.

can discern a difference. If efforts by Presidents to 'control' the executive branch have encountered great difficulties since 1933, it was even more difficult to do so before then, despite the smaller scale of operations in the traditional era.

In accounting for this, several factors can be mentioned. For instance, Cabinet secretaries tended to carry more political weight during the earlier period. They were often leaders of the President's party who had to be consulted. 'The members of the Cabinet are a President's natural enemies,' remarked Charles G. Dawes, who served in the Harding, Coolidge and Hoover administrations.[47] This is less so in the modern era because of the lower political profile which most Cabinet secretaries have and the fact that the President has help in dealing with them and the bureaucracy. This help takes the form of the Executive Office of the President. The modern President, unlike his predecessors, has institutional support resources which are completely loyal to him. The OMB, for example, can liaise with the departments on behalf of the President in clearing legislation and putting a budget together. This kind of coordinating assistance was unavailable to the traditional Presidents. Robert Williams puts the earlier era in perspective: 'During the nineteenth century, a pattern of habits, conventions and expectations became established which made little allowance for an active presidential role in the direction and control of the federal bureaucracy.'

In some ways the post-1933 Presidents found themselves in more difficult circumstances than was normally the case in earlier administrations. They inherited a tradition of weak leadership of a fragmented bureaucracy while their official family was becoming larger and even more disparate. Notwithstanding this, the modern Presidents have endeavoured to function as effective leaders of the executive branch. As Robert Williams points out, they all have tried to ensure that the 'bureaucracy adhered to a common, presidentially-determined line'. Roosevelt showed the way in 1933, according to Williams, when for the first time in American history a vigorous attempt was made to mobilise the entire federal bureaucracy in the exclusive service of the President.

How have the nine modern Presidents tried to accomplish this mobilisation? While the variables of ability, temperament and situation make generalisations difficult, some broad themes can be identified.

First, the Executive Office of the President is the most important instrument of control. Its existence has inspired a new

47. Quoted in Richard E. Neustadt, *Presidential Power: The Politics of Leadership from FDR to Carter*, New York, 1980, p. 31.

terminology – the institutionalised presidency and the presidential branch of government. The EOP will be considered later in this chapter.

Secondly, the modern era has seen unprecedented efforts to examine systematically the ways in which Presidents can achieve effective control. Since the New Deal began, studies have been undertaken by the Brownlow commission, two Hoover commissions, the Ash council, the Heineman task force and various other task forces. The fact that these high-powered investigations were undertaken during the Roosevelt, Truman, Eisenhower, Johnson, Nixon and Carter administrations demonstrates the reality of the new perspective on presidential leadership which Roosevelt instituted and the preoccupation of modern Presidents with achieving a coherent chain of command. While the investigators tended to agree that central direction is too weak, the prescriptions arising from their enquiries have not led, generally speaking, to more effective presidential control. The Heineman task force highlighted one of the chronic problems when it characterised the executive branch as 'a collection of fragmented bureau fiefdoms'.

Thirdly, some modern Presidents have tried to use a traditional instrument – the Cabinet – for coordination and control. Eisenhower made the most elaborate effort in this direction and Ford used the Cabinet more than others. But in general the Cabinet has not been an important instrument through which the modern President has sought to impose a common line on the executive. While it has become a tradition for incoming Presidents to express an intention to use their newly-appointed Cabinet, such vows tend not to be implemented. This is so because (i) there appear to be no adverse political consequences for a President who downgrades the Cabinet; (ii) Presidents since 1940 have devoted more time to foreign than domestic affairs, and therefore the domestic-oriented Cabinet bears limited relevance, in its composition, to the presidential agenda; and (iii) Presidents are more comfortable effecting coordination through staff aides who are completely loyal to them and who are immune from congressional oversight than through heads of departments whose loyalty to them may be less than complete.

Fourthly, Cabinet secretaries as individual heads of departments have been downgraded in favour of the aforementioned staff aides. At the same time, a lag is found here. Roosevelt, Truman and, to a lesser extent, Eisenhower tended to relate to Cabinet secretaries more in the pre-modern way than their successors have. As Robert Williams says, 'Eisenhower was perhaps the last modern President to concede status and grant wide discretion to members of his

Cabinet.' As has been indicated, the more usual modern practice has been for Presidents to appoint somewhat faceless administrators to head the departments in a 'government of strangers'.[48] Political executives who served between 1933 and 1960 such as Jesse Jones, Harold Ickes, Henry Wallace, George Marshall, Dean Acheson and John Foster Dulles are types with few counterparts after 1960, although there are obvious exceptions such as Robert Kennedy.

Fifthly, some Presidents have tried to cope with their leadership problems by adopting a 'formalistic' approach to controlling the executive:

The formal system isolates the top man by situating him at the apex of the pyramid amidst strict controls which regulate the access of people and the flow of information to him . . . The President sees only those issues which have been flagged for his attention. He works alone or in the company of a few select aides.[49]

The best examples of modern Presidents who have employed this classic bureaucratic technique are Eisenhower, Nixon and Reagan. Since they are Republicans, there appears, interestingly enough, to be a division on party lines (if we omit Ford) in this matter. The three are also the only Presidents since Roosevelt to be elected to a second term after serving a full first term.

The advantages of a formalistic approach are that it provides the greatest protection against stressful exposure and the greatest amount of control by the President over the flow of his work. It is orderly and distributes enormous burdens realistically. The disadvantages are that it reduces openness, accessibility and accountability and imposes artificial stability where unstable circumstances exist and flexibility is essential. This approach can distort the President's outlook by deflecting much of 'his' work away from him. Watergate is the kind of thing that can happen when this approach goes wrong. At the same time, the fact that Eisenhower as well as Nixon operated a formal system makes it clear, according to Buchanan, that relying on it 'as a means of coping with stress is not limited to pathological characters'.[50]

Sixthly, some Presidents have used what can be called a competitive or collegial system. This arrangement has a less clear-cut authority structure than the formalistic system, and encourages conflict as a means of stimulating creativity. The advantages are that the leader

48. See Hugh Heclo, *A Government of Strangers*, Washington, DC, 1977.
49. Buchanan, *op. cit.*, p. 44. See also R.T. Johnson, *Managing the White House*, New York, 1974.
50. Buchanan, *op. cit.*, p. 45.

retains a desirable degree of flexibility and increases his access to the information he needs to function effectively. Moreover, he may reduce the likelihood of misjudgment and misinterpretation compared with leaders who may be shielded from reality by a formalistic arrangement. The disadvantages of a competitive system are that the leader risks exposing himself to administrative incoherence, unreasonable pressures and stress, and a consequent loss of physical vitality.

Understandably, a President may be ambivalent about how far to go in one or the other direction. A good indicator is whether a President appoints a powerful chief of staff such as Eisenhower's Sherman Adams or Reagan's Donald Regan. Ford equivocated before making Alexander Haig his chief of staff:

Initially, when I became President, I did not want to have a powerful chief of staff . . . I was determined to be my own chief of staff . . . I would have five or six senior assistants with different areas of responsibility . . . and they would be able to see me at regular intervals during the day . . . But . . . it simply didn't work . . . the demands on my time were hindering my effectiveness.[51]

Franklin Roosevelt is the leading example of a modern President who used a competitive approach:

His favorite technique was to keep grants of authority incomplete, jurisdictions uncertain, charters overlapping. The result of this competitive theory of administration was often confusion and exasperation on the operating level; but no other method could so reliably ensure that . . . the decisions, and the power to make them, would remain with the President.[52]

An element in Roosevelt's strategy was to bypass the traditional administrative structure by creating emergency agencies staffed by people who believed in the New Deal. Roosevelt also appointed expediters to cut through red tape. Harry Hopkins has been called 'Roosevelt's personal liaison with the war overseas'.[53] The end-result of Roosevelt's approach, it is generally agreed, is that by his 'brilliant expedients'[54] he succeeded in fashioning an unusually responsive executive. As Robert Williams says, 'Roosevelt rebuilt the executive branch in his own image.'

The other modern President who is noted for his particularly elaborate efforts to control the executive is Nixon, although in contrast

51. Gerald R. Ford, *A Time to Heal*, New York, 1980, p. 143.
52. Arthur M. Schlesinger, Jr., *The Coming of the New Deal*, Boston, 1958, pp. 527–8.
53. Koenig, *op. cit.*, p. 196.
54. Arthur M. Schlesinger, Jr., *A Thousand Days*, Boston, 1965, p. 624.

to Roosevelt he attempted to do so from a formalistic perspective. Like the other modern Republican Presidents, Nixon suspected, with good reason, that the bureaucracy was laced with liberal Democrats hostile to his conservative policies. 'The White House in those last Nixon years had at least as much difficulty with HEW professionals as it did with Vietcong negotiators. The White House understood neither, and both were its enemies.'[55] Extraordinary measures involving infiltration, impoundment and reorganisation were instituted by the Nixon White House to bring the permanent government into line. Robert Williams discusses these efforts to politicise the bureaucracy and concludes that the exercise was a failure.

President and Staff

Strong evidence that a different kind of presidency emerged from the New Deal years is found in institutional form in the staffing apparatus known as the Executive Office of the President. This is particularly so in relation to the part of the EOP called the White House Office. The creation of the EOP and its subsequent development is self-contained within the post-1933 period. Thus if one is looking for a major element in the present analysis which is distinctive to the modern era and which was non-existent during the traditional era, the EOP provides it.

Nevertheless, as John Hart makes clear in his chapter, the foregoing generalisations should not be seen in categoric terms. The seeds for the evolution of the EOP were sown well before the 1930s. In 1867 the President was authorised by Congress to have a staff of seven. By the turn of the century he had a staff of thirteen; by 1922 it had risen to thirty-one. By the time of the submission of the Brownlow report in 1937, which led to the creation of the EOP two years later, Roosevelt had a White House staff of thirty-seven. Moreover, the Bureau of the Budget, a component of the EOP, in fact predated it.

The difference between the two eras lies in the legitimised and in due course strident institutionalisation of White House staffing in the modern era compared with the low-key, small-scale pragmatism of the earlier period. The statutory legitimacy of the EOP – combined with the immense latitude given to Presidents in using it – facilitated the quantum leap in the scale and influence of the White House staff during the modern era.

The evolution of the White House staff provides interesting evi-

---

55. H.G. Gallagher, 'The President, Congress and Legislation', in Cronin and Tugwell, *op. cit.*, p. 278.

dence of the general nature of presidential development over 200 years. There was gradual, linear development from a modest beginning. Then, under Franklin Roosevelt, something epoch-making occurred which presaged a new era, after which things were never the same. Subsequent developments consolidated the new order, with soul-searching about what had occurred.

The Brownlow intervention in this process is oddly discordant. The creation of the EOP by legislation was an important follow-up to the recommendations made by the Committee on Administrative Management, which Brownlow chaired. In view of this, Brownlow is often credited with launching the powerful staffing apparatus in the White House which we know today. But the irony is that Brownlow specifically disapproved of the kind of apparatus that evolved. He warned against staffers who would make decisions, acquire high visibility and interpose themselves between the President and Cabinet secretaries. As we know, these are characteristics which we have come to identify with senior members of the White House staff. As Hart says, 'The presidential staff quickly broke loose from the tight constraints of Brownlow's framework . . . Today, senior White House staffers regularly do what Brownlow said they should not do.'

Much attention has been devoted to the steady increase in the size of the President's staff since the New Deal. 'The White House staff has grown remorselessly' is a typical comment.[56] While this growth, strictly speaking, has not been linear (there was a decrease in numbers after Ford), the overall increase throughout the period has been dramatic. As Hart notes, the number employed in the White House Office increased from about 58 in 1944 to about 560 in 1974. This growth was accompanied by a parallel increase in numbers in the EOP to more than 5,000 by the early 1970s.

In the matter of size it is interesting to consider the relative position across the federal government. The tenfold increase in the size of the White House Office between 1944 and 1974 can be seen in conjunction with the fivefold increase in the federal civil service since the New Deal began and the fivefold increase in staff in Congress since the Second World War.[57] It seems that the adjustment of the federal government to the new governing situation arising out of the New Deal was felt across the governmental divisions. Indeed, if one compares the growth of the EOP, including its White House and 'institutional' components, with the growth in the

56. Koenig, *op. cit.*, p. 190.
57. The increase in Congress includes the staffs of committees as well as those of individual senators and representatives. See Shaw, *op. cit.*, pp. 280–1.

staffing of Congress, including its various components, these respective developments are similar in scale.

Yet, as Hart points out, too much can be made of the factor of size. As a matter of fact it is very difficult to measure the size of the White House Office. This is so because of imprecision in the matter of turnover and in the divisions between professional and non-professional personnel, full-time and part-time staff, and those who are fully attached to the White House versus the detailees from executive departments. It is more useful to discuss the causes of staff growth than to measure it. It is also more useful to examine the nature of the power exercised by the staff and the growth in their functions within government.

In the discussion of efforts by modern Presidents to mobilise the federal bureaucracy in the exclusive service of the President, it was suggested that the EOP is the most important instrument of control. But using a buffer of staff aides and staff institutions to help the President achieve control is easier said than done, particularly as the executive has become larger and more differentiated. As one authority suggested in 1976, 'The government is now twice the size it was in Roosevelt's day, and it is probably at least twice as difficult for a president to work his will within its confines.'[58] Joseph Califano, who held White House and Cabinet posts in the Johnson and Carter administrations, echoed this sentiment: 'Interest groups and Congress now get into the act very early. They've become more sophisticated.'[59] Similar points are made by Hart, who refers to 'the changed and more complex nature of the constituencies to which a President must relate'. According to Hart, the rapid development of the White House Office is a consequence of 'profound changes in the wider framework of American politics'.

Let us now consider certain aspects of modern staff development in the context of how things differ from corresponding arrangements before 1933. As ever, dichotomous analysis must not be carried too far. Taking the institutionalisation of staffing and the increase in staff size and influence for granted, what other themes can be identified?

First, in the matter of coordinating the activities of the executive branch, this was virtually impossible even to attempt during the traditional era. The 'non-directive' approach of most traditional Presidents, the absence of a unified federal budget before 1921, congressional assertiveness, conflicting loyalties in the departments

58. Mullen, *op. cit.*, p. 191.
59. Joseph Califano, 'The Power Vacuum Outside the Oval Office', *National Journal*, 24 Feb. 1979, pp. 298–9.

and the rudimentary nature of White House staffing all contributed to executive disunity.

In the modern era Presidents have the White House Office and, at present, eight other staffing agencies to help them struggle to achieve the unified direction they hope to provide. While the aforementioned obstacles continue to hamper their efforts, the potential is now there in the 'presidential branch' to shake things up. The EOP, according to Hart, 'constitutes a political force that competes for power in the pluralistic system of American government' whereas the traditional President was only occasionally in a position to compete. At the same time, as Hart points out, the injection of the White House staff into the policy-making process has further fragmented the structure of American government.

Secondly, there is the matter of coordinating institutions. Traditionally the Cabinet was the only avenue open to a President who wanted to achieve a semblance of unity within an institutional framework. But, as has been noted, the Cabinet has largely given way to the EOP in helping the President coordinate the work of the permanent government. For the modern President, numerous institutional scenarios have been used. The traditional Cabinet was given prominence and elaborated by Eisenhower. The National Security Council, created in 1947 to integrate foreign and military policy, was used frequently by Truman and Eisenhower. Nixon created the Domestic Council, and Carter the Domestic Policy Staff, as an *alter ego* to the National Security Council. Nixon experimented with 'overlords' in the form of five senior White House aides. Ford used an Economic Policy Board in addition to the Domestic Council, while Reagan established seven Cabinet Councils, each dealing with a different field of public policy.

However, these coordinating bodies, which tended to include both staff and line executives, have met relatively infrequently. The White House staff aides associated with these bodies have tended to be the real policy supremos. The obvious example is Henry Kissinger in his capacity as National Security Adviser. Not surprisingly, Kissinger objected strongly when President Ford informed him that he could 'only' be Secretary of State and would have to give up his jointly-held National Security Adviser portfolio. In general, individual EOP coordinators, including the budget director, have often been more important than Cabinet secretaries, although some who have served as Secretary of State, Secretary of Defense and Attorney-General have succeeded in maintaining an effective independent influence. In practice there has been much variation because, as Hart says, no two Presidents have organised their White House in exactly the same manner.

Thirdly, there is the matter of public policy. In this, one finds a marked difference between the role of the President's staff before and after the New Deal. While pre-Brownlow staffers were concerned with organising the President's workload and with such political matters as party, patronage and elections, they did not get overtly involved in policy. But when, despite Brownlow's warnings, power moved from line executives to senior members of the President's staff, it was inevitable that control over the substance of the administration's policies would go as part of the package. The focus of staff activity changed from a concern with some of the President's preoccupations to a concern with all of them. Some staff aides began looking at governance from the President's perspective, helping him to do the things he would do himself if he did not 'need help'. 'The staff and president are linked by a shared fate . . . advisors are virtual extensions of the president's personality, extra hands and brains to do his bidding.'[60] As Hart makes clear, the power of members of the modern President's staff has arisen from the joining of their political and policy functions.

Greenstein says that by the time of Kennedy's presidency members of the White House staff were directly formulating policy and implementing it.[61] Thus the boundary between line and staff broke down relatively early in the modern era. Truman was receptive to listening, in a structured setting, to a representative range of policy advocates, and Eisenhower was often willing to do so in foreign policy matters. On the other hand, Eisenhower insisted that his staff subordinates digest lengthy documents into one-page summaries, a task which Sherman Adams, his chief of staff, said 'was sometimes next to impossible to do'.[62] After 1960 Presidents tended to prefer distilled policy options, prepared by the White House staff. The process of filtering policy options and their advocates through staff aides gave the 'gatekeepers' the crucial power of selection and emphasis. Even Carter, who tended to burden himself with too much detail, had a chief of staff, Hamilton Jordan, who is reputed to have rarely returned telephone calls from Cabinet members.

Fourthly, the modern President has 'constituencies' which are larger in number and more demanding than was the case with the traditional Presidents, and his staff helps him deal with them. As was mentioned earlier, ordinary people direct more attention to the

60. Benjamin I. Page and Mark P. Petracca, *The American Presidency*, New York, 1983, p. 172.
61. Greenstein, Berman and Felzenberg, *op. cit.*, p. v.
62. Sherman Adams, *First-Hand Report*, New York, 1961, p. 51. Some felt that Adams, who was chief of staff from 1953 to 1958, had more authority than many of the traditional Presidents. Cunliffe, *op. cit.*, p. 249.

modern President than to his traditional counterpart. Greenstein considers this change sufficiently important to cite it as one of the basic ways in which the post-Hoover presidencies differ from their predecessors:

. . . There appear to have been major changes in the quantity and quality of public attention to incumbent Presidents. For many Americans the complex, uncertain political world of our times seems to be dealt with by personification, in the form of perceptions of the quality of performance and personal virtue of the incumbent President.[63]

This public attention has two aspects, according to Greenstein. 'Presidents are expected to be symbols of reassurance, possessing extraordinary "nonpolitical" personal qualities.' This is the chief of state role. 'At the same time', says Greenstein, 'they are expected to be politically effective, bringing about favorable national and international social conditions.' This is the chief executive role.

These public expectations place a heavy burden on the modern President, and he needs all the help he can get to convey the impression that he is fulfilling them. 'Without such assistance', says Hart, 'the modern presidency would be a perilously weak institution.' In consequence, Presidents have surrounded themselves with an increasingly complex and specialised array of staff aides to deal with constituencies in and out of government. As Hart says, 'A number of functionally specialised units now exist within the White House Office to connect with, service and manipulate important élites.' In addition to facilitating 'outreach' to such obvious targets as Congress, the executive branch and the media, recent Presidents have sought to 'lobby the lobbies' — such as business, ethnic and women's groups — through the White House Office of Public Liaison and to deal with state and local government through the Office of Intergovernmental Relations. All this is a far cry from the days when Hoover's designation of a press secretary constituted the earliest formal use of the White House as a linkage to a key presidential constituency.

The links between the White House staff and their major targets — the bureaucracy, Congress and the media — have been elaborated to such an extent that the current arrangements would be wholly alien to Hoover and his predecessors. While the change is dramatic enough between the traditional and modern eras, it is equally dramatic with respect to each of these relationships within the modern period. The bureaucracy, Congress and the media have themselves undergone major transformations since 1933, and the

63. Greenstein, 'Change and Continuity in the Modern Presidency', p. 46.

changes involving both the White House and its constituencies are obviously interrelated.

Hart identifies two tendencies that have accompanied this evolution: an increase in specialisation and a decrease in institutionalisation across administrations. Staff relations with the bureaucracy illustrate both tendencies. I have already dealt briefly with the Office of Management and Budget, but its development is interesting for present purposes. The Bureau of the Budget, as it then was, acquired a range of specialised duties during the Roosevelt-Truman-Eisenhower years. In addition to its annual budget duties, it began to clear legislative proposals originating in the departments, to draft legislation, to clear and draft executive orders and to make recommendations on whether enactments should be vetoed. In the process the BOB was acquiring a life of its own, enabling it to provide staffing assistance to successive administrations irrespective of party. This institutionalisation was viewed with less than enthusiasm after about 1960. The result was a change in the agency's name and efforts to politicise it in favour of the current President through additional presidential appointments at the top. Greenstein considers that the consequent creation of a more deferential BOB/OMB was achieved at a cost. He suggests that one reason for difficulties in implementing some of Johnson's Great Society programme was that a constricted, de-institutionalised budget bureau did not have the time and resources to anticipate the difficulties. [64]

Fifthly, the modern era has seen more friction between the White House and the bureaucracy than was the case previously. In part this arose from the fact that most traditional Presidents had neither the inclination nor the resources to be the *chief* executive. Now that Presidents are attempting to achieve something resembling real control of their official family, increasingly through the White House Office rather than the OMB, the fact that sparks fly is not surprising. The normal difference of perspective between political executives and bureaucrats contributes to the friction. The inexperience and lack of information of the White House aides who are attempting to achieve control is also dysfunctional. The Nixon years, as ever, provide an extreme example. More than thirty of Nixon's White House aides were under thirty years of age; many had come from jobs in advertising; and many had little or no substantive knowledge of public policies or, it appears, democratic processes. The fact that some of them went to jail for committing criminal acts confirmed the worst fears of the career bureaucrats.

Where Hart deals with the nature of the friction between the

64. *Ibid.*, pp. 78–9.

presidential and permanent governments during the modern era, he refers to a tendency towards arrogance and insensitivity on the part of staffers and to the 'adversarial relationship' that has developed between the amateurs in the White House and the experts at the operational end of the administrative process. The fact that the experts are often prevented from putting their case to the President because the 'palace guard' considers them unimportant has at times created a situation amounting to sheltered ignorance. Jack Valenti identified one aspect of the problem when he described working in the White House as 'the ultimate seduction'.[65]

Sixthly, there is much more of an atmosphere of electoral politics to the operation of the White House than during the pre-modern era. Traditionally, a President serving his first term could assume that his party would nominate him for a second term if he wished to serve again. During the modern era there has been less certainty. This is a consequence of the retreat from traditional party norms and the rise of candidate-centred nominating politics. The new situation was acutely evident to Johnson in 1968, Ford in 1976 and Carter in 1980.

Presidents must therefore give more attention to electoral politics than ever before, and this necessity manifests itself in a number of ways in relation to staffing. At an obvious level there is the Office of Political Affairs in Reagan's White House Office, an overt acknowledgement of the need to maintain a professional campaign organisation during a President's first term. But Presidents are usually less direct about this. Carter, for example, gave his White House campaign specialists titles like Ombudsman and Special Assistant for Special Projects. Most important, the top jobs and numerous others in the White House in recent administrations have tended to be held by persons who lack experience of office-holding in government or even in a political party but who are experienced in the management of election campaigns. Examples are H.R. Haldeman, Hamilton Jordan and James Baker, who were White House chiefs of staff under Nixon, Carter and Reagan respectively and who were sometimes characterised by journalists as the 'number two' men in their administrations. They differed from Eisenhower's chief of staff, Sherman Adams, who had served as Governor of New Hampshire as well as in the management of the President's election campaign before working in the White House.

There has been much criticism of the transfer of campaign aides to positions in the White House. The following is typical of such criticism:

---

65. Jack Valenti, *A Very Human President*, New York, 1975, p. 61.

An unintended consequence . . . is that it enhances the pressures there to run a continuing campaign rather than a government. Campaign staff typically have little or no previous experience in the intricacies of executive branch operations. The skills required to be an advance man, to write campaign speeches, or to organize state primary races are very different from those required to put together a budget or review complex disputes about energy policy.[66]

Seventhly, there is staff-related criticism of the presidency, such as the above-mentioned, that is associated with the modern era, particularly the more recent part of it. As Hart notes, such criticism also surfaced in the traditional era, but the dominance and scale of modern staffing in the White House has resulted in a more persistent and strident critique. The events of the Nixon years fuelled the debate. As Wildavsky has said:

President Nixon has done more to discredit our political institutions than any other person, group or social movement in this century . . . No President before Nixon, so far as we know, has simultaneously been involved in so many scandals or had so many of his advisers indicted and convicted.[67]

But the criticism deals with issues broader than Watergate.

One aspect of the criticism draws on analogies with monarchy. The President is perceived as the centre of the life of a royal court and the object of excessive deference by his staff aides. The presidency has 'an aura of majesty, splendor, and magnificence fully equal to the most resplendent European monarchies of the eighteenth century'.[68] The White House staff is replete with 'sycophants' and 'toadies'. They shield and isolate the President, so it is said, from the real world, with too few of them willing to express disagreement with the President or to employ the candour of a Louis Howe or a Henry Kissinger:

His [the President's] lack of access to social and interpersonal equality, his inability to expose himself to similarly strong egos . . . who do not feel any sense of subordination, is not only a disadvantage for the president, but a subtle and insidious threat to his comprehension of himself and his problems . . . There is a significant risk that deference will distort his ability to produce rational decisions.[69]

While the 'toadies' problem is undoubtedly more severe than in the traditional era, such criticism is not new. Jefferson and Jackson

66. Richard Rose, 'Government Against Sub-Governments', in Richard Rose and Ezra N. Suleiman (eds), *Presidents and Prime Ministers*, Washington, DC, 1980, p. 335.
67. Aaron Wildavsky, 'System is to Politics as Morality is to Man: A Sermon on the Presidency', in Aaron Wildavsky (ed.), *Perspectives on the Presidency*, Boston, 1975, pp. 526–7.
68. Buchanan, *op. cit.*, p. 53.
69. *Ibid.*, p. 60.

attacked presidential royalism with considerable political success. Also, Presidents vary a great deal in their susceptibility to artificially positive feedback. Truman is a good example of a modern President who kept his head and his modest lifestyle despite the trappings. Someone said of Truman in the late 1940s: 'In Roosevelt we had the friend of the common man. Now we have the common man.' Carter is another interesting case; he identified with the common people in his personal behaviour but with less political success than some of his predecessors.

Another staff-related criticism of the presidency is that the White House staff have usurped the authority of the political executives who head the departments and agencies. This usurpation is seen to extend in particular to Cabinet secretaries, and the criticism is often linked to expressions of regret concerning the decline of the collective Cabinet. As has been noted, staff aides who have endeavoured to run the executive branch from the White House during recent presidencies are perceived as unqualified to do so. Such criticism was much less applicable during the traditional era when Presidents did not usually attempt to direct the executive in the modern way, when Cabinet secretaries had more political weight and when the President's staff were muted by present-day standards.

It is easy to see why modern Presidents have increasingly encouraged their staff associates to take charge. Staff aides see governance from the President's perspective and talk his language, often being from his home state, while Cabinet secretaries acquire a different perspective as they become enmeshed in a network of allegiances which result in divided loyalties. Executives and bureaucrats in the departments can exhibit a frustrating unresponsiveness to presidential direction, a tendency about which Presidents from Roosevelt to Reagan have complained. The problem has escalated as executive size and fragmentation has increased, provoking the EOP to evolve into what has been called a miniature White House version of the executive branch. The White House has also felt obliged to provide a haven for endangered species carrying out line functions such as the Peace Corps and the Office of Economic Opportunity.

Despite the advantages in exercising presidential authority through staff aides, there are also disadvantages which have been the subject of criticism. For example, the White House Office is now so large that a staffer, to use Franklin Roosevelt's memorable phrase, can 'go into business for himself'. When turning down a request from an aide for someone to help him with his work, Roosevelt maintained that the aide was not operating properly if he needed an assistant.[70] This outlook contrasts dramatically with the position

70. Rose, *Managing Presidential Objectives*, p. 34.

under Nixon and Carter when their National Security Advisers – Kissinger and Brzezinski – had exceptionally large staffs of their own. When executives who head departments are upstaged so conspicuously, the result can be a serious loss of morale, especially when, as with Carter and Reagan, the President himself has never previously held national office. The experience, expertise and diversity of outlook of the permanent government may be squandered, so it is argued, in the course of formulating policy. Eisenhower was 'available at all times to any Cabinet member for consultation',[71] but such access is no longer encouraged, not least under Reagan, who has been described as the least accessible President in recent American history. Thus, critics are saying such things as: 'In recent administrations staff members have become part of the problem rather than part of the solution'; 'The President is not strong but weak. He has lost control of the departments, of domestic policy, and . . . even of his own house'; '. . . A presidential bureaucracy . . . has expanded to the point where the President is victimized rather than helped by members of a staff whom he himself cannot begin to supervise.'[72]

A final staff-related criticism of the presidency is that as the power of the White House staff has increased, the accountability of the administration has decreased. This arises because the staff are considered to be an extension of the President and therefore entitled to the privileged position that is associated with him. Thus, unlike appointments to the executive departments, staff appointees do not require Senate approval nor are their duties delineated, nor are they obliged to testify before congressional committees. More sweeping executive privilege is claimed for the President's staff than for any other component of the executive branch.

Presidents rely heavily on their staff aides because they are not in the political firing line in the way that executives in the departments are. Therefore, Presidents can have it both ways: they can shift policy-making authority from line to staff while cutting traditional and potentially awkward avenues of accountability and oversight. In this, modern Presidents differ fundamentally from their predecessors. Interestingly Congress, mindful perhaps of the 'privileged' position of its own staffs, has been relatively acquiescent.[73] While

---

71. Ann Whitman (Eisenhower's secretary), quoted in Greenstein, 'Change and Continuity in the Modern Presidency', p. 61.
72. Pious, *The American Presidency*, p. 247; Gallagher, *op. cit.*, pp. 270–1; Greenstein, 'Change and Continuity in the Modern Presidency', pp. 79–80.
73. On the other hand, a statute enacted in 1974 made appointments to the posts of Director and Deputy Director of the OMB subject to Senate confirmation.

Hart points out that in this attitude Congress is being consistent with its past tradition of hands-off-the-President, it needs to be added that past Presidents had far less intrusive and powerful staffs.

The President and Foreign Relations

It is appropriate that the section of this chapter which deals with foreign relations should follow the section which deals with staffing. It is appropriate because the development of a large and differentiated staffing apparatus is intended, among other things, to provide the enhanced capacity that is needed in connection with the President's increased concern with foreign relations. As Phil Williams notes in his chapter, modern Presidents have been devoting one-half to two-thirds of their working time to foreign policy and national security. Significantly, these concerns have not displaced traditional presidential preoccupations with domestic affairs, but are supplementary to them. The consequences for the presidential workload are daunting. Kennedy and Johnson are said to have worked 16-hour days, and Carter at times to have worked 80-hour weeks.

This change in the presidential agenda makes it clear that one of the most significant differences – perhaps the most significant difference – between the traditional and modern presidencies concerns foreign affairs. Specifically, the traditional Presidents were much less concerned with foreign and military affairs, with notable exceptions, than the modern Presidents. In fact few Presidents between John Quincy Adams and Theodore Roosevelt showed much knowledge of foreign affairs or had travelled abroad. While the domestic presidency dominated the period before the New Deal, the modern presidency, according to Phil Williams, 'is perhaps above all else a foreign policy presidency'. Theodore Sorensen, one of Kennedy's closest White House aides, has said that foreign affairs occupied far more of Kennedy's time and energy as President than domestic affairs. Comparing the President's concern with domestic and foreign affairs, Sorensen said that in the case of the latter Kennedy gave far more attention to detail, was more concerned with shaping alternatives and was more inclined to follow a proposal through from origin to execution.[74]

Not only have the modern Presidents spent far more time on foreign affairs than their predecessors, but in doing so they have often been concerned with matters of greater moment. One cannot but be impressed by Kennedy's comment on the difference in his

74. Theodore C. Sorensen, *Kennedy*, New York, London, 1965, p. 562.

approach to foreign and domestic matters. 'The big difference', said Kennedy early in his term, 'is between a bill being defeated and the country being wiped out.'[75] As Phil Williams puts it, American Presidents since 1945 'have been confronted with problems, responsibilities and burdens far in excess of anything known to their predecessors.' Williams examines roles of the modern Presidents which were unknown to their predecessors: cold warrior, peacekeeper on a global scale, and chief decision-maker in matters which could lead to general war. Writing about the Kennedy years, Arthur Schlesinger starkly contrasts the potential inherent in the modern Presidents' military arsenal with the severe restrictions which impinge on their authority in other respects: 'No doubt the mid-century Presidents could blow up the world, but at the same time they were increasingly hemmed in by the growing power of the executive bureaucracy and of Congress.'[76]

While it is clear that a fundamental change in the President's agenda can be associated with the modern era, how categoric is the change? Phil Williams identifies significant strands of continuity between the 'foreign policy' presidency of the modern era and the presidency prior to Franklin Roosevelt. For example, the United States has long been involved in Latin America, with episodes of intervention occurring during both eras. Some of the more forceful statements and actions by modern Presidents concerning Cuba and Nicaragua were presaged by Theodore Roosevelt when he 'took Panama'. When Johnson intervened militarily in the Dominican Republic in 1965, he was the fourth American President to do so.[77] America's interest in the Pacific predates the modern era, as does the commercial involvement of the United States throughout the world.[78] In the latter connection, America's growing industrial ascendancy on the eve of the Second World War, combined with its low profile in world diplomacy, reminds one of the more recent position of Japan.

The timing of the change to the foreign policy presidency cannot be precisely pinpointed. Phil Williams suggests 1947 as the crucial year. This was the year of the Truman Doctrine and the general acceptance of the cold war situation, and it saw the creation of the Defense Department, the National Security Council and the Central

---

75. *Ibid.*
76. Schlesinger, *A Thousand Days*, p. 624.
77. Graham T. Allison, 'Making War: The President and Congress', in Cronin and Tugwell, *op. cit.*, p. 233.
78. For a brief discussion of the promotion by Presidents of American economic interests abroad in the nineteenth century, see Pious, 'The Evolution of the Presidency', pp. 271–2.

Intelligence Agency. Moreover, the decades since 1947 have a cohesion which differentiates them very clearly from the first decade and a half of the modern era. The years of the domestic presidency include the early incumbency of Franklin Roosevelt, who, as Phil Williams suggests, would almost certainly have been astonished by 'the sheer scale, extent and apparent permanence of American involvement overseas' presided over by his successors. As has been indicated before, it is misleading to assume that all aspects of the modern presidency, even the most important ones, were identifiable at its outset.

Up to now there has been a stress on the seminal role of Franklin Roosevelt in the development of the modern presidency. The important role of Harry Truman in this process needs also to be acknowledged. For if Roosevelt launched, among other things, the enlarged domestic presidency, Truman can be said to have instituted patterns of presidential behaviour which added the complementary element of the foreign policy presidency. Roosevelt, of course, provided a vital bridge in his wartime leadership, but there was no certainty that his forceful approach could be sustained under his successor. In the event Truman, too, was forceful in particularly difficult political terrain. He was confronted with a strong reaction against Roosevelt's protracted dominance of national politics, and he also had to suffer opinion poll ratings which dipped to post-war lows. Notwithstanding these handicaps, Truman exercised the expanded powers of the President with impressive vigour in a range of demanding situations, both foreign and domestic. In Greenstein's view, 'like Roosevelt, Truman himself does emphatically seem to have been a major independent influence on the shape of the modern presidency.'[79]

This is all the more impressive in that Truman had very limited experience of foreign affairs before becoming President. Searching for an analogy, Truman remarked that relations with the Soviet Union could be understood 'if you understand Jackson County', the county in Missouri where Truman had served as chief administrator.[80] In fact only one of the eight post-war Presidents – Eisenhower – could be said to have brought direct relevant experience to his global leadership role. It is generally agreed that the Presidents who served immediately after Truman – Eisenhower and Kennedy – also discharged their international responsibilities with skill and restraint and that the United States was fortunate in the

79. Greenstein, 'Change and Continuity in the Modern Presidency', p. 57.
80. Jonathan Daniels, *The Man of Independence*, Philadelphia, 1950, p. 285.

three chief executives who presided over the transition to a world leadership role:

On the whole the Presidents . . . achieved the abrupt transition from isolation to total responsibility with dignity and moderation. In an imperfect world it was unlikely that the leader of any other nation placed in America's shoes would have performed as credibly . . . The Truman policies seemed firm without being unduly truculent, the Eisenhower ones ponderous without being disastrous, the Kennedy initiatives intelligent and mature.[81]

What happened during the subsequent years of the 'imperial presidency' is another matter.

In a number of striking ways the emergence of the President as a global leader was accompanied by fundamental changes in the American outlook. It will be useful to mention a number of these changes and to contrast them with what existed before.

The most obvious change was in the position of the United States in world affairs. Unlike any of their predecessors, the post-war Presidents presided over a nation which was generally considered to be the most powerful in the world in economic and military terms. The status of the United States as a superpower produced exaggerated rhetoric which would have been wholly alien to pre-war America. An example is this statement about the presidency made by Kennedy while a presidential candidate: 'Upon him alone converge all the needs and aspirations of all parts of the country, all departments of the government, all nations of the world.'[82] By the 1980s, while still one of the two superpowers, the United States found itself less dominant within the international system than during the 1940s and 1950s. Also, as decades of crisis passed, Presidents learned to live in a more complex world than that of the early post-war years.

The four post-war decades have been dominated by persistent tension between the United States and the other superpower – the Soviet Union. This conflict between East and West provides a strand of continuity through the eight administrations since the New Deal, and no traditional President faced anything at all resembling this situation. Soviet-American competition has taken various forms, including cold war, *détente*, troop movements, threats, aerial overflights and the building of alliances. Through it all, suggests Phil Williams, 'the presidency has become the prime embodiment of a kind of national *machismo*', with crisis decisions being made and implemented through the sustained personal involvement of the President.

---

81. Cunliffe, *op. cit.*, p. 228.
82. Speech in January 1960 reprinted in Robert S. Hirschfield (ed.), *The Power of the Presidency*, 2nd edn, Chicago, 1973, p. 133.

The President's responsibilities in connection with East-West relations have been heightened by the spectre of nuclear confrontation. Since 1945 the calculations of Presidents have been strongly influenced by the existence of weapons of unprecedented destructiveness. Moreover, beginning with Eisenhower, they have had to live with the knowledge that America's principal adversary also has a nuclear delivery capability. It hardly needs saying that the traditional Presidents had no comparable problem. The modern President's role is further dramatised by the fact that elaborate procedures exist to ensure that he alone can give the order to use nuclear weapons. As an historian of the presidency has said, the fact that an American President 'might, with the best of intentions, commit the world to catastrophe . . . is the supreme nightmare of our time, for which the past provides no parallel.'[83]

The post-war assumption by Americans that an international crisis affecting their country is always possible – and is perhaps imminent – has focused the nation's attention remorselessly on the crisis manager in the White House. This persistent outlook extending over decades is distinctive to the modern era:

Contemporary Presidents face crises of a scale unknown to their predecessors. Since the end of the American nuclear monopoly, the presidency has existed in a state of perpetual crisis in its enforced vigil to prevent some incident or issue from escalating into general war.[84]

The Cuban missile crisis in 1962, consisting of fourteen days of superpower confrontation, is the preeminent example of such a situation. 'The decisions that Kennedy was called upon to make were . . . the most delicate and the most perilous that any President has ever faced.'[85] But the resolution of an international crisis may be less than successful. Crisis-management failed when Carter sent, and then withdrew, an air mission to rescue fifty-four hostages held in Iran in 1980. In general, it is widely agreed that a President who leads a nation geared to a persistent expectation of external threats and who controls an immense military establishment enjoys unprecedented deference to his authority as crisis manager so long as it is exercised effectively.

A consequence of being a superpower is that one's capital city becomes exceptionally important. The modern period has seen Washington become the leading capital in the world in terms of diplomacy and newsgathering. Since New Deal days there has been a steady procession of heads of government and other world leaders to

83. 'Cunliffe, *op. cit.*, p. 275.
84. Koenig, *op cit.*, p. 372.
85. *Ibid.*, p. 380.

the White House, with far more presidential time being devoted to such visits than before Roosevelt. One thing has led to another — a White House Situation Room, a 'hot line' and an extension of the precincts of the White House to adjoining buildings. Gone are the days when President-elect Warren Harding, on being asked what his foreign policy would be, could reply: 'You must ask Mr Hughes [Harding's Secretary of State] about that.'[86] Gone, too, are the days (which included 1932) when it was customary not to talk about foreign policy during presidential election campaigns. Modern aspirants for the presidential nomination must demonstrate a knowledge of international issues, preferably obtained first-hand during trips abroad.

But the traffic is not always to Washington. Since the 1930s Presidents have from time to time participated in summit meetings. These meetings have taken place during war and peace, at home and abroad, with one foreign leader or more, and with allied and Communist leaders. Such meetings were rarely held prior to the Second World War and are therefore a distinctive feature of the modern presidency. In his review of summitry Phil Williams makes a useful distinction between those meetings which dealt with generalities and those which produced agreements on substantive issues, with Nixon and Carter providing examples of the latter approach. In an earlier context there was a reference to difficulties that Presidents may face as a result of their lack of access to social and interpersonal equality and lack of exposure to similarly strong egos. This 'problem' can be overcome in summit meetings — Truman's meeting with Stalin, Kennedy's with Khrushchev and Nixon's with Mao come to mind — but generally the superpower factor means that most world leaders who meet with the President do so in a situation of status inequality.

One of the most dramatic changes between the pre-war and post-war presidencies concerns alliances with other countries. During its first 150 years the United States was profoundly isolationist. Between 1800 when its alliance with France was terminated and 1942 when the United States entered into a full wartime alliance, the United States was uninterested in formally associating itself politically or militarily with other countries.[87] After Woodrow Wilson tried unsuccessfully in 1919 to shift Americans away from this outlook, Republican publicity literature in the presidential campaign of 1920 asserted: 'This country will remain American. Its next President will

---

86. Alexander De Conde, *The American Secretary of State*, New York, 1962, p. 82.
87. During the First World War, the United States fought as an 'associated power'.

remain in our own country.'[88] Notwithstanding such attitudes, superpower status and the cold war situation led post-war Presidents to involve the United States in a worldwide system of aid programmes and multilateral and bilateral alliances, with NATO being the most important. Phil Williams examines the efforts of modern Presidents to cope with their new role as alliance leader. He traces their endeavours to reconcile divergent interests in the 'free world' in the course of learning to live in an increasingly complex world.

It is difficult to generalise about presidential-congressional relations before and after the Second World War in relation to foreign and military policy. Generally, Presidents have taken a firmer line during both eras about foreign and military policy than about domestic policy. At the same time, the domineering outlook of Congress during most of the traditional era is reflected to some degree in foreign and military affairs. For example, Congress rather than the President took the lead in involving the United States in war in 1812 and 1898. It is difficult to imagine anything like that happening after the Second World War. Moreover, traditional peacetime Presidents directed small military establishments, whereas their successors have had enormous ones, whether or not hostilities existed. The latter circumstance has obviously enabled modern Presidents to score points in their international dealings. According to one estimate, between 1945 and 1975 there were 215 presidential deployments abroad of American armed forces, constituting confrontations and shows of force.[89] This is difficult to reconcile with the likelihood that the framers of the Constitution never intended American troops to be used outside the country without congressional consent.[90]

Phil Williams discusses the relations of the post-war Presidents with Congress in the field of foreign affairs, and he finds an oscillatory pattern. From a deferential posture in the 1940s, Congress became assertive about foreign affairs in the early 1950s and then became deferential again. After the subsequent 'imperial' period under Johnson and Nixon, Congress adopted its most assertive posture since the war. Then, after 1980, Congress began giving way again to the President.

This section of the chapter will end as it began with a comment on presidential staffing as it relates to foreign and military affairs. As

88. Andrew Sinclair, *The Available Man: Warren Gamaliel Harding*, New York, 1965, p. 162.
89. Barry M. Blechman and Steven S. Kaplan, *Force Without War*, Washington, DC, 1978.
90. Pritchett, *op. cit.*, p. 11.

these matters have come to occupy more of the President's time, new ways have been found to deal with them. As a consequence, there is a fundamental difference in the methods employed in the traditional and modern eras. Traditional Presidents worked through the relevant executive departments – State, War and Navy. Since Truman, Presidents have had the additional option of working through the national security apparatus in the White House, and all Presidents since 1947 have availed themselves of the opportunity to do so for reasons which have been discussed. This has meant that the Secretaries of State and Defense have often found themselves upstaged by the National Security Adviser, particularly after 1960. Three of the Secretaries of State who served under Truman and Eisenhower – Marshall, Acheson and Dulles – were not upstaged, but this has been the fate to some degree of all their successors except Kissinger, who of course served as National Security Adviser before moving to the State Department.

It is interesting to note that just as the EOP has evolved in a direction fundamentally different from what Brownlow intended, so too has the national security system moved away from what was envisaged by the National Security Act of 1947. The National Security Council was intended to provide a forum in which foreign and defence policy could be looked at in a coordinated way in the presence of the President and the relevant line and staff executives. It would provide a broad basis for policy formulation in a crucial and much enlarged sector of the President's concerns. As it turned out, the NSC has met relatively infrequently. Instead, the National Security Adviser, working closely with the President and supported by his own staff, has enabled the President to acquire personal control of a sector of public policy which previously had been lodged in a bureaucracy which Presidents complained about as being sluggish and unresponsive to their direction. Yet each modern President has had his own distinctive way of working this system, not least because disadvantages as well as advantages have manifested themselves when the formulation of security policy has been centred in a 'house without windows'. One needs only mention the 3,000 bombing raids on Cambodia in 1969 and 1970, undisclosed until 1973, to illustrate what can happen.

Conclusions

Before making some general comments about the development of the presidency, I shall deal with a matter mentioned only briefly up to now – the President's relations with the media. 'Television is reality,' according to Ron Nessen, President Ford's Press Secretary.

Nessen added: 'If it hasn't happened on television, it hasn't happened.'[91] One risks being fatuous in pointing out the distinctiveness of such a statement to the recent history of the presidency. It is in fact difficult to overestimate the impact that the onset of television has had on the White House. The President's media consultants perceive their job as trying to ensure that the President dominates television. They see television as an extension of the presidency and organise his schedule around efforts to get events of their choice on the network news broadcasts in the early evening. These broadcasts reach 40–50 million viewers. As Carter's television adviser, Barry Jagoda, said: 'A presidential appearance on television in the evening dominates our national life for that moment. It is a way of bringing the country together for explanation or elaboration.'[92]

Not surprisingly, the networks' massive coverage of the President's activities is equalled by the large-scale efforts of the White House to influence what television portrays.[93] Hart discusses the increase from a single Press Secretary under Hoover to a staff of forty-six working under Carter's Press Secretary, Jody Powell. Elaboration occurred with the complementary appointment by Nixon of a more broadly-based Director of Communications, a post which has continued under Ford, Carter and Reagan. This expansion fits in with developments already mentioned: the enlarged policy agenda, the atmosphere of continuing crisis in international affairs, and the public perception of the President as spokesman for the people. It follows that the President is 'the single biggest continuing story on television news'.[94]

However, despite the elaborate attention devoted to television by the President's advisers, the potential is negative as well as positive. For example, in the context of candidacy, Patterson and McClure maintain that television does not produce results anywhere near commensurate with the candidate's expenditure. They argue that the electorate seldom evaluates candidates on the basis of looks and other surface phenomena emphasised by the image-makers, but on the basis of political performance.[95] Moreover, when events go wrong, the incumbent President is an obvious scapegoat for moralising television commentators. In addition, Presidents may find it

91. Michael B. Grossman and Martha J. Kumar, *Portraying the President: The White House and the News Media*, Baltimore, 1981, p. 45.
92. *Ibid.*, p. 46.
93. *Ibid.*, pp. 28–9.
94. *Ibid.*, p. 28.
95. Thomas Patterson and Robert McClure, *The Unseeing Eye: The Myth of Television Power in National Elections*, New York, 1976, pp. 21–3.

next to impossible to deal with a complicated issue in the one minute and 15 seconds allocated to it in the evening news where visual drama makes for better programming than reasoned advocacy. Another hazard is that Presidents tend to find that they are unable to meet the inflated expectations of the viewing public and may suffer dramatic losses in support, as happened with Carter. Nixon appeared on prime time television more than any other President,[96] yet he left office in disgrace. Finally, a television-oriented strategy can overlook the potential of other avenues of communication. Radio, for example, reaches an immense daily audience, estimated at over 90 million.[97]

The mention of radio reminds one that, while the situation just described is alien to the traditional presidency, broadcasting is not. Hoover made radio broadcasts more frequently (21 in 4 years) than Roosevelt (27 in 12 years), but the latter's fireside chats were infinitely more memorable. The presidential news conference is another media event that bridges the two eras. Begun under Woodrow Wilson, they were held twice a week, with written questions required, by his Republican successors in the 1920s. But it is agreed that the lively twice-weekly news conferences held around Roosevelt's desk were the quintessential examples of the genre. Since then, the frequency and utility of presidential news conferences have been declining steadily. Johnson held news conferences on weekends at his ranch in Texas so as to make it inconvenient for reporters to attend. The most infrequent news conferences — about one every two months — were those conducted by Nixon and Reagan.[98]

Turning to some general considerations concerning the development of the presidency, the evidence in this book makes it clear that basic and permanent change in the presidency and therefore in the American political system occurred during the incumbency of Franklin Roosevelt. It occurred because of the juxtaposition of a number of factors. The development of the United States had reached a stage where public policies applying to an integrated nation and covering a broad agenda were feasible and acceptable. This phase of modernisation coincided with a severe economic depression requiring strong action by the national government. A man was chosen as President who had the inclination and political skills to preside over the transition to a new order. Roosevelt remained in office for an unprecedented twelve years and thus was in

96. Koenig, *op. cit.*, p. 115.
97. Grossman and Kumar, *op. cit.*, p. 50.
98. *Ibid.*, p. 245; Edwin M. Yoder, Jr., 'Downhill Ever Since Truman', *International Herald Tribune*, June 14–15, 1986, p. 4.

a position to see his innovations to fruition. Popular acquiescence was manifest in the electoral endorsements of 1934, 1936, 1940 and 1944. The changes were effectively consolidated by Roosevelt's early successors in the White House.

What are the fundamental ways in which the modern presidency differs from the traditional presidency? Greenstein identifies four basic changes.[99] Three of them have been dealt with fully in these pages. The fourth has been taken up in part. However, Greenstein unaccountably omits a further basic change from his list.

One of the changes in Greenstein's list is legislative leadership. Another is enlarged staffing through the Executive Office of the President. A third is the increased public attention given to the presidency.

Greenstein's fourth change concerns presidential policy-making. He notes that since 1933 the President has been involved in direct policy-making to an extent that was unknown during the traditional era. Hodder-Williams takes up this point from the perspective of the relationship between the Constitution and presidential development. For present purposes it can be said that the vastly expanded agenda and bureaucracy have been accompanied by the vastly expanded discretionary authority of the President. This means taking actions not formally ratified by Congress. In one of its aspects this has meant a great increase in delegated legislation, with the

Table 7.1. EXECUTIVE AGREEMENTS ENTERED INTO
BY PRESIDENTS WITH FOREIGN COUNTRIES

	No. of Years	No. of Executive Agreements
1789–1889	100	265
1889–1939	50	917
1940–54	15	1,948

Source: Joseph E. Kallenbach, *The American Chief Executive*, New York, 1966, pp. 504–5.

executive filling in the blanks. Likewise, the increased involvement of the modern President in foreign and military affairs has been accompanied by direct presidential policy-making in these fields. This becomes clear when one examines the much increased use of executive agreements, as is shown in Table 7.1. Court decisions and non-decisions have facilitated the process as has the enhanced capacity resulting from the development of the EOP.

---

99. Greenstein, 'Change and Continuity in the Modern Presidency', pp. 45–6.

The change that Greenstein omits from his list is the change from a presidency in which foreign and military affairs normally played a minor role to one in which they occupied most of the President's working time. This change did not occur at the outset of the modern period, but its delayed appearance should not preclude its inclusion in the pantheon of major changes.

The delayed onset of the foreign policy presidency reminds one of the ragged nature of change. It has been noted that some of the traditional Presidents had modern ideas. Likewise, within the modern period presidential behaviour has not always been cut from the same cloth. Although there is frequent mention in this book of the momentous changes that date from 1933, the position is not clearcut. Other significant years can be identified – 1947, 1960, 1974. Very little is truly distinctive to the last half-century. A study by Herbert Kaufman which bridges the traditional and modern periods illustrates how strong the factor of continuity can be. Kaufman examined 175 federal agencies that existed in 1923 and found that 85 per cent of them still existed in 1973 and 62 per cent had the same organisational status.[100]

As far as development within the modern era is concerned, it would seem feasible to divide the half-century into four periods, as in Table 7.2. This table derives from an analysis by Greenstein.[101] The formative period is subdivided by Greenstein into the breakthrough by Roosevelt, the institutionalisation of Roosevelt's innovations under Truman and the ratification of the new order by Eisenhower: 'When the Republicans returned to power in 1953 and the institutional changes and role expectations of the modern presidency were not fundamentally altered, the Great Divide had been crossed.'[102] It is clear that the most striking changes of the modern era occurred during its first three incumbencies. An important factor was the long duration of these presidencies, enabling people to become accustomed to the new situation. Roosevelt, Truman and Eisenhower served the equivalent of seven full terms. This contrasts with the shorter incumbencies of their five successors.

The long formative period over, its accomplishments bore fruit during the brief period of the 'strong' presidency from 1960 to 1966. This period covers the Kennedy years and the early Johnson years, culminating in 1965 and 1966 in the enactment of an extraordinary volume of liberal legislation dating in some cases from Truman's

100. Herbert Kaufman, *Are Government Organizations Immortal?*, Washington, DC, 1976, p. 134.
101. Greenstein, 'Change and Continuity in the Modern Presidency'.
102. *Ibid.*, p. 58.

Table 7.2.   DEVELOPMENT OF THE MODERN PRESIDENCY

President	Stage of Development
Roosevelt Truman Eisenhower	Formative
Kennedy Johnson	Strong
Johnson Nixon	Imperial
Ford Carter Reagan	Post-imperial

Fair Deal. The possibilities arising from a robust working of the modern presidency were seen to be epitomised during these years following earlier episodes of a sometimes impeded and stalemated presidency. Kennedy's handling of the Cuban missile crisis was a highlight of the period. There was of course plenty of strength in the formative period as well, and therefore the division between formative and strong should not be viewed in too categoric a way.

Nevertheless, the strong period can be seen in terms of a realisation of preferences that date from 1933. From the beginning of the New Deal until the White House got bogged down in Vietnam in the mid-1960s, the public pinned its hopes on the presidency as never before. During this period scholarly and popular writing about the presidency, of which there was a great deal, praised and even glorified it. The conventional wisdom was that the President was the good guy while congressmen and other political actors, if not bad guys, at least did not have the President's insights about what was needed and too often stood in the President's way. Praise of the presidency got into the textbooks, resulting in Thomas Cronin's memorable phrase − 'the textbook presidency':

The textbook presidency describes and extols a chief executive who is generally benevolent, omnipotent, omniscient, and highly moral . . . For more than twenty years after the Franklin D. Roosevelt presidency, most textbook treatments of the presidency seriously inflated presidential competence and beneficence.[103]

103. Thomas E. Cronin, *The State of the Presidency*, 2nd edn, Boston, 1980, p. 76. An example of extravagant praise of the early modern presidency can be found in Rossiter's *The American Presidency, op. cit.*, pp. 60−7.

Turning to the imperial period, this extends from about 1965 to 1974 and covers the later part of Johnson's presidency and the whole of Nixon's. This decade marked 'the end, at least temporarily, of American liberalism's fascination with the heroic Presidency and of its view that presidential power was the only effective means of achieving the goals of liberal democracy'.[104] It also saw protracted estrangement between Congress and the President, culminating in Nixon's resignation, and was a time of domestic upheaval. The latter included the campaign against the Vietnam War, the violence at the Democratic national convention of 1968, urban rioting, and the assassinations of Robert Kennedy and Martin Luther King.

The 'imperial' designation for the decade derives from the title of Arthur Schlesinger's influential book *The Imperial Presidency*.[105] According to Schlesinger, rights reserved to Congress by the Constitution and long-standing practice had been taken over by the President. The most important usurpation was the decision whether to go to war. With the possible exception of Mao Tse-tung, the American President, by the early 1970s, had become the most absolute monarch among the great powers in issues of war and peace. Even the Soviet leader Leonid Brezhnev had to consult more people and secure more institutional clearances than the President before sending armies into battle. 'Beyond the boldest dreams of their predecessors', Johnson and Nixon claimed inherent and exclusive authority to go to war, whether or not the life of the nation was threatened, whether or not there was congressional authorisation, whether or not an international organisation had endorsed the action.

Having tasted the fruit of unilateral authority in foreign affairs, Nixon set his sights on the domestic presidency as well. He sensed an opportunity to consolidate all federal power in the White House – as against Congress, the executive branch and the electorate. For Nixon 'the imperial presidency was the perfect shield and refuge.' He had 'an urgent psychological need for exemption from the democratic process'.[106] He also had an electoral mandate, having been endorsed in 1972 by every state except Massachusetts.

What Nixon was moving toward was . . . a plebiscitary Presidency. His model lay . . . in the France of Louis Napoleon and Charles de Gaulle . . . with the President accountable only once every four years, shielded in the years between elections from congressional and public harassment,

104. Norman C. Thomas, 'Reforming the Presidency: Problems and Prospects', in Cronin and Tugwell, *op. cit.*, p. 321.
105. Arthur M. Schlesinger, Jr., *The Imperial Presidency*, Boston, London, 1974.
106. *Ibid.*, p. 216.

empowered by his mandate to make war or to make peace, to spend or to impound, to give out information or to hold it back, superseding congressional legislation by executive order.[107]

Schlesinger sees Nixon as 'a genuine revolutionary' in his desire to have 'the right to nullify the Constitution and the law. No President had ever made such a claim before.' As it turned out, 'Watergate ended the most serious effort in American history to change the nature of the presidency.' The specific Watergate-related events are well-known and need not detain us.[108] However, it is worth quoting Schlesinger's illuminating view of Watergate from the perspective of earlier presidential scandals:

> . . . Scandals . . . came every half century − the Grant scandals of 1873, the Harding scandals of 1923, the Nixon scandals of 1973. But crookedness in the simple days of Grant and Harding was old-fashioned graft . . . stealing money for oneself was in an old American tradition. What distinguished the Nixon crowd was, in a sense, the purity of their motives . . . They were not thieves, except by the way; rather they were moralistic opportunists who had been led to understand that the Presidency was above the law and that the end justified the means.[109]

A final comment on the imperial Nixon: he displayed more monarchical yearnings than any other President. For example, he introduced ceremonial trumpets and attired the White House police in resplendent uniforms rivalling European palace guards until public ridicule stopped it. Nixon also apparently liked to have his presence announced.[110]

As for the post-imperial period, this began with Nixon's resignation in 1974.[111] His early successors − Ford and Carter − laboured

107. *Ibid.*, pp. 254−5.
108. The articles of impeachment, voted by the Judiciary Committee of the House of Representatives, detail Nixon's 'high crimes and misdemeanors'. The text may be found in Theodore H. White, *Breach of Faith: The Fall of Richard Nixon*, New York, London, 1975, pp. 345−8.
109. Schlesinger, *The Imperial Presidency*, p. 268. A study of 'Presidential Lying' attempted to measure the extent of deception employed by Presidents in news conferences. The results showed that Nixon was the most deceiving, followed by Kennedy, Ford, Johnson and Eisenhower, in that order. Henry Alker, 'Presidential Lying', paper presented at the annual conference of the American Psychological Association, Washington, DC, 1976, and cited in Buchanan, *op. cit.*, pp. 77, 82. Buchanan's view is that the severe limitations that are imposed on Presidents put them at an enormous disadvantage unless they engage in 'expedient misrepresentation'.
110. Morris Udall, 'Some Thoughts from the Campaign Trail', *Presidential Studies Quarterly*, vol. 5 (Fall 1975), pp. 36−7.
111. See Vincent Davis (ed.), *The Post-Imperial Presidency*, New York, 1980.

under a depressed national mood. A survey conducted in 1974 showed that, for virtually every subgroup surveyed, trust in the presidency had declined by about 50 per cent compared with a similar survey two years earlier.[112] Subsequently, a poll registered an approval rating for Carter as low as 23 per cent, the same as Nixon's lowest rating. This grim public outlook reflected the heritage of the imperial presidency and its indications of what can happen when the 'strong' presidency goes wrong. Vietnam and Watergate 'seared in the nation's memory the presidency's capacity for wrongdoing and imprudence . . . and misjudgment.'[113]

Adding to the problems of the post-imperial presidency were moves in Congress to curb the chief executive. This was reflected in legislation enacted in the 1970s. Nixon's impoundments provoked Congress into specifying procedures by which the President could be forced to spend appropriated funds. Congress rescinded most of the 470 statutes providing for presidential declarations of emergency and established new procedural accountability in emergency situations. The Case Act required that all executive agreements with foreign countries be reported to Congress. Restrictions on overseas aid were imposed in relation to more than a score of countries. In other instances, opportunities for vetoing executive actions were incorporated in statutes. The best known of the President-curbing actions of the 1970s is the War Powers Resolution of 1973, which seeks to limit the President's right to wage war without congressional approval. While this resolution has been much criticised for its unintended implications, it nevertheless reflects the outrage which greeted some of the events of the imperial interlude.

Congressional assertiveness was also reflected in a series of internal reforms. The best known of the formal reforms was the creation of the Congressional Budget Office and budget committees in both houses in 1974. At the informal level, individual Congressmen, including new members, became more independent of control from the leadership within Congress and the White House. One consequence was a strengthening of subcommittees and their chairmen. Another was that assertiveness extended to foreign affairs in ways that were uncommon before 1974. In general, post-imperial Presidents have had to cope with a Congress that is more diffuse, decentralised and sceptical than before. Writing in 1978, Samuel Patterson said, 'Congress is far more formidable as a political body

112. Arthur Miller *et al.*, 'Presidential Crises and Political Support: The Impact of Watergate on Attitudes Toward Institutions', paper presented at the Midwest Political Science Association convention, Chicago, May 1975, pp. 27–8.
113. Koenig, *op. cit.*, p. 2.

today than it was in the more quiescent days of the 1950s and early 1960s.'[114] Of course the political skills and circumstances of the post-imperial Presidents are important factors. Reagan has had a more satisfactory relationship with Congress than either Ford or Carter. Among Reagan's strengths are that, in line with Neustadt's view of presidential power, he has demonstrated an impressive capacity for persuasion, backed by the vital resource of strong popular support. Reagan also operates at a farther remove from Watergate than his two predecessors.

The President's relations with his party were discussed earlier in terms of changes between the traditional and modern eras. Narrowing the time scale to the past dozen or so years, one finds that some tendencies that were identified are now more pronounced. The President's party, whether Democrat or Republican, is more phantom-like than ever. Ranney asks whether there are two parties or no parties.[115] According to King,

It is open to ask whether the United States any longer possesses such things [as parties] . . . The parties still exist as makers of rules. They still exist as givers of cues to millions of voters. But they would appear no longer to exist as national organizations or even as temporary coalitions of state and local organizations.[116]

Greenstein compares the formative and post-imperial situations:

During the formative period of the modern presidency, the 'decentralized' national party system was widely viewed as a restraint on the mobilization around the President of national policy-making coalitions. By the 1970s state and local party organizations were so fragmented that, by contrast, the 1930s through the 1950s seem to have been high points of party government. At least in the earlier period there *were* party organizations.[117]

The post-imperial President thus operates in the virtual absence of permanently organised parties. This circumstance largely frees him from the constraint of dealing with party barons 'out there'. On the other hand, in pursuing his policy goals in this context, the President lacks the support of an established national movement which identifies broadly with his aspirations and has a stake in whether he succeeds or fails. In place of this traditional and, to a lesser degree, early modern arrangement, the President has his personal

---

114. Samuel C. Patterson, 'The Semi-Sovereign Congress', in Anthony King (ed.), *The New American Political System*, Washington, DC, 1978, p. 177.
115. Austin Ranney, 'The Political Parties: Reform and Decline', in *ibid.*, p. 245.
116. Anthony King, 'The American Polity in the Late 1970s: Building Coalitions in the Sand', in *ibid.*, p. 375.
117. Greenstein, 'Change and Continuity in the Modern Presidency', p. 72.

organisation which includes professional political mercenaries who promote politicians and policies for money. It is by no means clear that these candidate-centred teams are an improvement for the President over traditional party organisations. Many political scientists maintain that they are not.

While American party organisations may have become more or less moribund, broad characteristics which relate to public policy and are linked with the parties persist. The designations 'conservative' and 'liberal' are frequently used as shorthand in academic and journalistic accounts. This is not the place to attempt an analysis of these 'cues'; Burns discusses them at length in *The Power to Lead*.[118] It suffices to say that it is widely assumed that there are conservative and liberal office-holders in both parties and that the latter are thicker on the ground in the Democratic party than in the Republican party. These designations are linked to the modern Presidents in Table 7.3. The table shows that Roosevelt ushered in a period of

Table 7.3. LIBERAL AND CONSERVATIVE PRESIDENTS SINCE 1933

	Liberal Democrat	Liberal Republican	Conservative Democrat	Conservative Republican
Roosevelt	x			
Truman	x			
Eisenhower		x		
Kennedy	x			
Johnson	x			
Nixon				x
Ford				x
Carter			x	
Reagan				x

liberal predominance which lasted until 1968 and which saw one Republican and four Democratic administrations. The subsequent conservative period presaged by the nomination of Goldwater in 1964, saw one Democratic and three Republican administrations. Eisenhower is clearly the most liberal of the modern Republican Presidents, and Carter the most conservative of the modern Democratic Presidents. Burns discusses Carter's position:

Within five months of his [Carter's] inaugural he said he was making a balanced budget by 1981 his top priority, despite the glaring inconsistency of this undertaking with his commitment to reduce unemployment, aid the

118. James M. Burns, *The Power to Lead: The Crisis of the American Presidency*, New York, 1984. See also Thomas Ferguson and Joel Rogers, *Right Turn: The Decline of the Democrats and the Future of American Politics*, New York, 1986.

needy, and fulfill several hundred other campaign promises. By his third year in office his position on many issues was hardly distinguishable from those of liberal Republicans and in some instances from true-blue conservatives.[119]

Congruence between recent presidential and public orientations was shown in a national poll in 1985 in which only 15 per cent of respondents said the term 'liberal' made them think better of someone while 27 per cent of respondents said the term 'conservative' did so.[120]

In addition to congressional assertiveness and party incoherence, various other tendencies in the political environment of the post-imperial Presidents have contributed to the 'diminished presidency'. Nixon's heavy-handed efforts to infiltrate and subordinate the permanent government made officials even more wary than before, and the substantial growth in their activities and expenditure since the formative years have not made attempts by the White House to achieve control any easier. Nor has the tendency of political executives and career bureaucrats to join forces to preserve departmental autonomy from the President and his staff. Issue networks have provided further impediments for the post-imperial Presidents. This form of group life existed earlier, but the incidence and sophistication of such liaisons is on the increase. Heclo sees a spread of 'policy professionals' seeking to hive off a self-contained piece of the policy-making process, with the deconcentration of power in Congress facilitating their endeavours.

The tendencies just described, taken together, have resulted in what King has called an 'atomized' politics.[121] This means that people interested in specialised aspects of public policy are going their own way to such an extent that interest aggregation does not occur or is next to impossible to achieve. Consequently, politics becomes more complex and unpredictable; coalitions become more difficult to construct; and leadership, not least on the part of the President, becomes more difficult to effect. This individuation of political life has meant a decline in predictable groupings and thus a decline in the basis for bargaining. While, as mentioned earlier, 15 and 27 per cent reacted positively to the labels 'liberal' and 'conservative', it is significant that so many respondents were disinclined to acknowledge either label. Two opposing ideological armies of the 1930s and 1940s have given way to large numbers of small detachments, with personnel frequently changing sides.[122]

Neustadt has written approvingly of King's concept of an

---

119. Burns, *The Power to Lead*, p. 37.
120. *International Herald Tribune*, 4 Dec. 1985, p. 4.
121. King, *op. cit.*, pp. 388–95.
122. *Ibid.*, p. 372.

atomized politics. In the context of a discussion of the Carter presidency Neustadt provides supporting evidence.[123] He notes that Congress has become 'more dispersed' than at any time since the early nineteenth century:

No longer ago than Truman's time the Hill had 180 subcommittees; there are almost twice as many now. As recently as Johnson's time a bargain with a standing committee chairman was a deal; now it often is only a hope. The same can be said of party leaders.

As for the 700 Cabinet and sub-Cabinet executives appointed by Carter and constituting the 'Administration', they are, according to Neustadt, more fragmented and less coherent than ever, not least because they have the shortest tours of duty in the Washington community. Neustadt also acknowledges the divisive effects of organised interests:

It is as though the single taxers, the free-silverites, the prohibitionists, the suffragettes were working still in Washington with branches dotting the congressional districts, funded by direct mail drives, managed by full-time professionals, . . . schooled as well as anyone in media events, and able to negotiate at both ends of the Avenue.

Neustadt also discusses the increases in staffs 'all over town' in Carter's Washington. In Congress, for example, 'professional aides to subcommittees number some 3,000 now, up from 400; professionals on personal staffs 10,000, up from 2,000; all in 30 years.'

It is obvious that the post-imperial presidency is more constricted than the strong and imperial presidencies. In fact the post-imperial situation is reminiscent of the formative period of the modern presidency. The old institutional checks and balances are back with a vengeance following the strong/imperial decade. It might indeed be argued that – with Congressmen, bureaucrats, lobbyists and journalists reclaiming lost ground with new vigour – the presidencies of Ford, Carter and Reagan are weaker than the formative presidencies of Roosevelt, Truman and Eisenhower. Dialectically, it could be argued, as Schlesinger does, that the separation of powers has been reinvigorated. The judiciary, Congress, the executive agencies and the press 'all drew new confidence as institutions from the exercise of power they had forgotten they possessed. The result could only be to brace and strengthen the inner balance of American democracy.'[124]

Despite the constraints which have made life difficult for the post-imperial Presidents, there is no doubt that we are still very much in

---

123. Neustadt, *Presidential Power*, pp. 212–4.
124. Schlesinger, *The Imperial Presidency*, p. 277.

the era of the modern presidency. The imperial period was an episode rather than a revolution. After detailing his catalogue of debilitating features of the 'diminished' presidency of Ford and Carter, Koenig sees history permitting the confident prediction that the presidency will rise again.[125] Ron Nessen, Ford's Press Secretary, said in 1976: 'There is an inclination to disbelieve anything the President says or does. That is the damage Nixon did. He made everybody cynics.'[126] Yet only eight years later, we were being advised that 'Reagan has undoubtedly brought about a revival of patriotism, confidence and national purpose', and 'In terms of the institutional presidency, Reagan has unquestionably restored the authority of the office.'[127]

There have been widely differing assessments of the extent of the President's power. Brogan said that 'the President of the United States is the most powerful secular officer in the world.'[128] At the other extreme Gallagher asserts: 'The Presidency is a weak office. It always has been. Only very few men have transcended its weakness.'[129] Neustadt says that the underlying theme of his book *Presidential Power* is presidential weakness.[130] In a cross-national study of chief executives Blondel classifies the American presidency as a 'constitutional presidential system', and he says this system is difficult to work since there are very marked restrictions on the chief executive.[131]

Whatever weaknesses impinge on the exercise of presidential authority as viewed from a global perspective, it is evident that the new order ushered in by Franklin Roosevelt is much stronger than what existed before, and it still prevails today. As Cronin said in 1980, 'the cult of the strong presidency is alive and well . . . The American public . . . has not lost hope in the efficacy of strong purposive leadership.'[132] The President is perceived, in and out of government, as having a mandate broader than the broken-mirror reflection of public opinion provided by Congress. As a consequence, one can be assured that future circumstances will give rise to renewed cries for heroic and assertive Presidents.

125. Koenig, *op. cit.*, p. 7.
126. Shabecoff, *op. cit.*, p. 33.
127. *Newsweek*, 27 Aug. 1984, p. 18; David S. Broder in *International Herald Tribune*, 22 Aug. 1984, p. 4.
128. Introduction to Rossiter, *op. cit.*, p. xi.
129. Gallagher, *op. cit.*, p. 282.
130. Neustadt, *Presidential Power*, p. xi.
131. Jean Blondel, *World Leaders: Heads of Government in the Postwar Period*, London, 1980, pp. 59–60, 52–3, 263–4.
132. Thomas E. Cronin, 'An Imperilled Presidency?', in Davis, *op. cit.*, p. 144.

Postscript

Up to this point, the material in this book was written before the disclosures, beginning in November 1986, that the Reagan administration had been selling arms to Iran and diverting profits from these sales to the rebel forces, or 'Contras', in Nicaragua. The circumstances associated with 'Irangate' are sufficiently significant for it to be instructive to relate them to the analyses in the preceding chapters and the earlier part of this chapter.[133] The scandal usefully illustrates various themes developed therein.

Richard Hodder-Williams pointed out that the President is in a stronger position when directing the nation's foreign policy than when directing its domestic policy. This is particularly true insofar as his relations with Congress are concerned. Moreover, a forceful, even robust, presidential role in foreign affairs seems feasible in the superpower era. Indeed, as Hodder-Williams puts it, 'There is little doubt that the Constitution as it is currently understood grants certain extra-constitutional or inherent powers to a President' in relation to foreign affairs. 'But it is also true', he adds, 'that these powers are limited.'

The 'Iran sale' affair provides insights into where the limitations may be. For example, Presidents are subject to limitations if they serve at a time when Congress has become assertive in response to perceived wrongdoing by other recent Presidents. They are subject to limitations if they fail to comply with the law. They are subject to limitations if they bypass established channels of democratic accountability and rely for their advice on people who lack political skills. Finally, Presidents are subject to limitations if their foreign policy is, in certain of its aspects, seen to be indefensible.

In his discussion of presidential-congressional relations, David Mervin noted that the limitations have a way of surfacing in the later years of incumbencies. He discussed this tendency in the cases of Woodrow Wilson, Franklin Roosevelt and Lyndon Johnson. Indeed it can be argued that every modern President has suffered a loss of standing and influence as his incumbency neared its end. Roosevelt began to experience a downturn in his relations with Congress during his second term. Truman's approval rating dropped to a devastating 23 per cent during his second term. Eisenhower ended on a much higher plateau than Truman in the opinion polls, but nevertheless his second term was downbeat at the end. A week before Kennedy's death, James Reston wrote in the *New York Times* of a feeling of

133. This section was written in June 1987 while the Senate and House select committees were meeting jointly to investigate the Iran-'Contra' events.

'doubt and disappointment' concerning the President. Johnson ended on a note of failure, withdrawing from the primaries in 1968. Nixon resigned rather than face impeachment. Ford nearly lost the Republican nomination to Reagan in 1976 and was then defeated by Carter. Carter left office out of favour as a result of the Iran hostage crisis. As Godfrey Hodgson sees it, Reagan's four predecessors were all driven from office.[134]

Like his predecessors, Reagan has found that as his presidency nears its end things are no longer playing well in Peoria. The Iran-'Contra' débâcle has resulted in a failure to sustain the great popularity he enjoyed during his first six years in the White House. His various explanations of his role in the Iran affair have met with what for him has been unaccustomed scepticism. Polls conducted the month before and the month after the disclosure of the arms sales showed a decline of 17 per cent in his approval rating – a drop from 64 to 47 per cent. After the Tower Commission submitted its critical report in March 1987, the rating dropped to 40 per cent and as many as 32 per cent of respondents said that Reagan should consider resigning. Furthermore, the polls have consistently shown a marked tendency for respondents to disbelieve various aspects of the President's version of events related to the Iran affair. A *Newsweek* poll in June showed that 62 per cent did not believe Reagan's assertion that he had been unaware of the diversion of profits from the arms deal to the 'Contras'.

Freed from earlier inhibitions induced by Reagan's exceptional popularity, journalists adopted a new tone after November 1986 saying, among other things, 'The Teflon is wearing thin' and, adapting the President's famous catch-phrase, 'We ain't seen nothing yet.' It was said of the 'great communicator' shortly after the scandal became known: 'This was a Ronald Reagan never before seen on national television. His jauntiness has turned to strained sarcasm, his easy charm to defensiveness . . . This time the magic didn't work.'[135] Another commentator said that there had been 'an astonishing collapse of Ronald Reagan as an institution'.[136] Similarly: 'The President whose simple charm and simpler views worked magic to make America stand tall is now caught looking muddled and shifty.'[137]

---

134. Godfrey Hodson, 'Pygmies in the Giant's Chair', *The Independent* (London), 27 Feb. 1987, p. 17
135. *Newsweek*, 24 Nov. 1986, p. 27.
136. William Shawcross, 'The Scandal breaks the Beltway', *The Spectator* (London), 20 – 27 Dec. 1986, p. 10.
137. *The Economist* (London), 29 Nov. 1986, p. 13.

The loss of standing with the public has been, not surprisingly, an important factor in the President's loss of standing in Congress:

Such a sharp decline in public standing is particularly significant for President Reagan. Widespread public support has always been an important reservoir for this President in the pursuit of his . . . policy agenda; its decline thus diminishes a crucial political resource that he has come to rely upon in dealing with Congress.[138]

Mervin commented on 'Reagan's lack of command of the detail of policy-making' and suggested that by distancing himself from detail he could also distance himself from criticism in Congress and elsewhere. This advantage was evident when the Tower Commission depicted Reagan as remote from wrongdoing subordinates. In the Commission's words, the President 'was poorly advised and poorly served'. However, reaction since the Tower report has been harsher as Reagan has emerged as less remote in relation to 'Irangate' than was believed earlier.

One of the main reasons why Reagan has been so severely criticised is that there may have been a failure by the administration to comply with various laws. According to one analysis, four statutes may have been violated:[139] the Intelligence Oversight Act, which requires prior congressional notification of covert operations; the Arms Export Control Act, which requires congressional notification of arms sales abroad; the Export Administration Act, which restricts exports to terrorist-supporting countries; and the Boland Amendment, which from October 1984 to October 1986 prohibited the use of American funds to aid the 'Contras' in Nicaragua. It is maintained that the sale of arms to Iran and the diversion of profits from the sales to the 'Contras' occurred while the Boland prohibition was in effect.

'Irangate' represents an important stage in the recent struggle between Presidents and Congress over the control of foreign and intelligence policy. During the first two decades after the Second World War Congress tended to be deferential to the White House in the conduct of such policies. Since then, various major events have led to efforts by Congress to alter the balance. These events include Vietnam, Watergate and revelations of controversial activities by the Central Intelligence Agency. In April 1984, for example, it was revealed that the CIA had been involved in the covert mining of Nicaraguan harbours while failing to keep certain congressional leaders informed as required by the Intelligence Oversight Act. This

138. James McCormick and Steven Smith, 'The Iran Arms Sale and the Intelligence Oversight Act of 1980', *Political Studies*, vol. 20, no. 1 (Winter 1987), p. 35.
139. *Ibid.*, p. 29.

episode led to the passage of the Boland Amendment and to the alleged bypassing of it by Colonel Oliver North and his associates in 1985 and 1986.[140]

The Boland Amendment prohibits the expenditure of funds by 'the Central Intelligence Agency, the Department of Defense or any other agency or entity of the United States involved in intelligence activities' for the purpose of 'supporting, directly or indirectly, military or paramilitary operations in Nicaragua'. In response to allegations of violations of this law, the White House has asserted that it does not apply to the President or his National Security Council. Moreover, the White House maintains that the President has a constitutional right to conduct the nation's foreign policy, and Congress cannot infringe it. Those who disagree with the White House on the application of the Boland Amendment say that it would be difficult to deny that the staff of the National Security Council constitutes an 'entity' concerned with intelligence work. There is, in addition, substantial evidence of liaison between North's NSC group and the then CIA Director, William Casey, in the Iran-'Contra' affair. As far as the constitutional argument is concerned, Hodder-Williams produced evidence in his chapter to support the view that Congress has a legitimate role in foreign affairs.

While the Tower Commission inquiry has not yet run its course, some scholars have reached conclusions about legal aspects of the affair. Two political scientists have argued that 'The administration violated the letter and the spirit of the Intelligence Oversight Act of 1980 . . . A central purpose of the act, to provide a mechanism for consultation with Congress, was deliberately undermined.'[141] Laurence Tribe, a constitutional lawyer at Harvard, has rejected any claim of presidential immunity in the Iran-'Contra' affair, asserting that at the very least the President did not 'take care that the laws be faithfully executed', as the Constitution requires. He added:

If the puppets are subject to the law and violate it, the puppet master cannot escape accountability. And therein lies what appears to be the most serious breach of duty by the President — a breach that may well entail an impeachable abuse of power, however politically unlikely impeachment of this affable officeholder may be.

'Congress's control over the purse strings would be rendered a

---

140. Charles Krauthammer has identified five different 'Boland Amendments' since 1982. These specify policies concerning the use or non-use of government funds in relation to support for the 'Contras'. *International Herald Tribune*, May 23 – 4, 1987, p. 4.
141. McCormick and Smith, *op. cit.*, p.34.

nullity', says Tribe, 'if the President's pocket could conceal a slush fund dedicated to purposes and projects that are prohibited under the laws of the country.'[142]

Senator Daniel Inouye, chairman of the joint select committee looking into 'Irangate', said the affair was worse than Watergate, and a national opinion poll in January showed that nearly 40 per cent of respondents agreed.[143] There are indeed echoes of Watergate – questions about what the President knew and when, defensive presidential speeches on television, allegations concerning cover-ups and the shredding of documents, a televised congressional investigation, the appointment of a special prosecutor, the forcing out of a White House Chief of Staff.

Analogies with Nixonian skulduggery became compelling on 25 November when Edwin Meese, the attorney-general, revealed to an incredulous press that a small team of presidential plumbers had arranged the covert arms sales to Iran, not only to spring American hostages in Lebanon but also to generate money for the Nicaraguan Contras.[144]

The Republicans have a talent for producing great scandals, but whether Reagan will join Grant, Harding and Nixon in the first division of scandal awaits the results of the endeavours of Special Prosecutor Lawrence Walsh and the congressional investigators. After six months of 'Irangate', there are expectations of prosecutions in due course for conspiracy, obstruction of justice, perjury and tax irregularities as well as for violations of statutes already mentioned. As Walsh has said, 'Except perhaps for Watergate, the situation is virtually unprecedented.'

Pertinent points are contained in the chapters by Robert Williams, John Hart and Phil Williams. Robert Williams noted that Truman 'possessed no powerful chief of staff or cabal of aides to insulate or isolate him from the work of his administration'. Neither did Roosevelt. This approach can be contrasted with that of subsequent Presidents whose aides did insulate them from departmental administrators. The point is that this process was carried even farther by Reagan's handlers. According to Reagan, some members of his staff insulated him from other members of his staff in the matter of the diversion of arms-sales profits to the 'Contras'.

Specifically, Williams refers to a tendency by White House staffs 'to prevent agency heads from determining the President's priorities and political agenda', and he quotes Arthur Schlesinger's assess-

142. Laurence Tribe, 'Irangate: A Constitutional Crisis?', *International Herald Tribune*, 23 – 4 May 1987, p. 4.
143. *Newsweek*, 11 May, 1987, p. 15; *Newsweek*, 2 Feb. 1987, p. 18.
144. *The Economist*, 29 Nov. 1986, p. 39.

ment that 'tension between the permanent government and the presidential government was deep in our system' by 1961. Such tension is illustrated by the futile opposition to arms sales to Iran not only by Secretary of State George Shultz but also by Secretary of Defense Caspar Weinberger, with the President rejecting both of them in favour of the advice of White House aides.

Various themes in John Hart's examination of the White House staff have echoes in 'Irangate'. For example, Hart points out in relation to Nixon's staff that 'The worst of the behavioural defects associated with the men around the President was their utter disrespect for the law of the land.' We have noted similarities between Irangate and Watergate, with possible violations of the law among them. Hart also reminds us of Louis Brownlow's famous suggestion that presidential assistants should have 'a passion for anonymity'. Since the EOP was formed, such passion has not been conspicuous. Yet Colonel Oliver North and his associates might be said to represent a belated, if perhaps misplaced, realisation of Brownlow's ideal of anonymity:

[There is] a small group of active military officers operating under the aegis of the National Security Council – a group whose mission, though shrouded in secrecy, seems to have been to direct covert actions too sensitive even for the CIA. This team . . . ran specific covert operations by order of the President.[145]

One is reminded of Roosevelt's concern that a member of the White House staff might 'go into business for himself'. Putting it another way, Senator Inouye called the North operation 'the privatisation of American foreign policy'.

Hart deals with the important issue of the accountability to Congress of the White House staff, noting that in the case of the National Security Adviser the post lacks even a statutory identity. As Hart says, 'the White House Office has remained immune from all but the most perfunctory congressional oversight of its activities.' The claim by Presidents of 'executive privilege' for their staffs and a reluctance by Congress to press the matter has resulted in a degree of leeway for the President's staff which is difficult to reconcile with the idea of responsible government. When this results – as appears to have happened with 'Irangate' – in a privately-funded foreign policy designed to circumvent the will of Congress, a consequence could well be a renewed effort to improve accountability. The congressional hearings on 'Irangate', like the earlier ones on Watergate, constitute an important step in this direction. It is also

145. *Newsweek*, 22 Dec. 1986, p. 12.

significant that in January 1987 Reagan's fifth National Security Adviser – Frank Carlucci – signed a directive prohibiting his staff from participating in covert activities.[146]

Phil Williams points out that the National Security Council has enabled the President to develop his own foreign policy staff separate from the State Department. It would seem that under Reagan the staff became a shadow CIA as well. This arrangement has enabled Presidents to overcome the impediments and delays of the executive bureaucracies and, in the case of intelligence, to circumvent congressional reporting requirements applicable to the CIA. Phil Williams sees flexibility in this arrangement: 'Each President has used the NSC in ways which reflected his own personal preferences and decision-making style.' In other words, it lets Reagan be Reagan.

Finally, it is interesting to see how the political scene can change in a matter of months. A statement from Phil Williams' chapter makes it clear that it was written before 'Irangate'. Williams says that the Reagan administration has 'avoided major fiascos'. While this was a fair assessment at the time it was written, it is discordant with later assessments. 'Call it a scandal, a crisis or merely a mess, the hostage-ransoming, money-laundering arms trade with Iran now ranks among the great presidential follies of modern times.'[147] Another passage in Phil Williams' chapter is also intriguing in the light of what was to come: 'The idea of a six-year term . . . is very attractive.'

146. Of Reagan's five National Security Advisers, Carlucci's experience was the most relevant for the job. He worked in the three agencies the outputs of which he was supposed to co-ordinate for the President – the State Department, the Defense Department and the CIA. Of the other four Advisers, only the first – Richard Allen – could, like Carlucci, be considered a foreign policy professional.
147. *The Economist*, 29 Nov. 1986, p. 39.

INDEX

311